IT'S HERE!

A FRONT-WHEEL-DRIVE CAR
THAT TRULY HANDLES
LIKE A SPORTS CAR!

TOYOTA

THE NEW

REACH FOR A STAR!

Even the most demanding enthusiast will be impressed by this shooting star brought down to earth.

Unlike lesser-minded cars, the new Celica GTS boasts front-wheel-drive with rigid, equal length drive shafts for

Fwd

spectacular controllability and stability to help keep torque steer from ever pushing you around again.

To take corners like a sports car its all-new design 4-wheel independent strut suspension nails down a more than commendable .80 G lateral acceleration.

The 1986 Toyota Celica GTS. Only the name has not been changed.

From its wind-piercing front end to its flush, wind-swept rear glass, Celica's lines are a study in redefined

aerodynamic efficiency. But the changes aren't merely cosmetic.

16 VALVES

Under the shroud of its sleek, sloping hood lies the leading edge of auto-motive technology: an omi-nous 2.0 liter, dual overhead cam, 16-valve, Electronically Fuel-Injected twin-cam engine.

Formerly found only in exotic sports cars, the same technology found in this power plant produces 135 unbridled horses at 6,000 rpm for mind-bending, road-blis-tering performance to snap you from 0-60 in 8.2 seconds.

The performance contin-ues: 4-wheel power disc brakes. Variable assist power rack-and-pinion steering. Stabilizer bars fore and aft. And big, beefy 205/60HR14 steel-belted radials on 14-inch aluminum alloy wheels.

Inside you'll find a cockpit fit for a Rising Star. Tilt and telescopic steering, 8-way adjust-able Sports Seat with optional

leather, full instrumentation that includes large, easy-to-read analog gauges that will take you into tomorrow. With ease and style.

And while the engine is singing at full throttle, you'll be listening to a different tune: on a new "live sound" speaker system that lets you feel like you were at the recording session itself. To produce richer sound through the frequency range, each of the four separately enclosed speakers is coupled with an optional electronic AM stereo/FM/MPX tuner with full logic cassette deck and 5-way acoustic tone equalizer.

The all new Celica GTS. 16 valves, Electronic Fuel Injection, front-wheel drive…all at an affordable price. Climb in. And feel a heavenly body in motion.

GET MORE FROM LIFE—BUCKLE UP!

CELICA!
WHO COULD ASK FOR ANYTHING MORE!
TOYOTA
© 1985 Toyota Motor Sales, U.S.A., Inc.

GOOD NEWS

THE 1986 TOYOTA CELICA GTS.

Did we say fast? Word has spread like wildfire, that the all new 1986 Celica is a car to be reckoned with. And this, from no one less than bonafide experts.

JONATHAN THOMPSON, Associate Editor
ROAD AND TRACK

"What I like best is it's got a nice flowing, rounded line."

"A nice tight easily drivable car, you can rev it and it doesn't fuss."

PETE LYONS, Contributing Editor
CAR AND DRIVER

"The 16-valve engine is a little jewel."

"The aerodynamic shape really rivets *my eyes.*"

"It's an outstanding styling job."

JACK NERAD, Feature Editor
MOTOR TREND

"I think the Toyota engineers have done an amazing job making this front wheel drive car feel like a rear wheel drive car."

"A step forward *in* virtually all areas, it handles better, it's faster from 0-60, it's faster all around the track, it's a big step forward and it's comfortable too."

"It's one of the best interiors in any car; bar none, at any price, I think the seats are the best production seats *available.* I just think they're outstanding."

STAFF

LEE KELLEY *Vice President / Publisher*

FRED M.H. GREGORY *Editor*

ALBERT ESPARZA *Art Director*

ERWIN M. ROSEN *Managing Editor*

MARIANNE GREGORY *Copy Editor*

FERN DITZLER *Administrative Assistant*

CONSULTING STAFF

TONY SWAN *Editor, Motor Trend*

WILLIAM CLAXTON *Art Director, Motor Trend*

DON EVANS *Editorial Director, Specialty Publications*

JANE BARRETT *PPC Research Librarian*

ADVERTISING SALES STAFF

ROBERT E. BROWN *Senior Vice President, Corporate Development*

JOHN MARCINSKI *Director, Sales & Marketing, Corporate Development*

ED MCLAUGHLIN *Account Executive, Corporate Development*

DANIEL T. CORNS *Associate Publisher, Motor Trend*

BETSY HAWKINSON *Ad Service Coordinator*

COVER ILLUSTRATION: DARRELL D. MAYABB

CONTENTS

FOREWORD

The Joy of Cars

Motor Trend has been chronicling the history of the automobile for almost forty years, and what a time it's been. I can remember when we put the first issue of the magazine together in 1949. We had no idea of what the future would bring, but we knew that there were people out there whose passion for cars at least equalled our own. These auto enthusiasts, as they came to be known, may have been as different from one another as night and day, but they had one thing in common, their abiding interest in cars.

What is it about the automobile that can be of appeal to both a doctor and a plumber, a mailman and an executive? Why does the car exert such a hold on so many people? Deep thinkers have been trying to figure it out for years, but I think the answer is a simple one: cars are fun. They can take us away from the day-to-day routine and give us pleasure. People enjoy driving them, owning them, and, yes, reading about them.

That's why I'm especially proud to have the opportunity to publish this book and to share with you the fascinating story of the first hundred years of the automobile. It's a tale I think you'll enjoy, and I hope you have as much fun reading it as we did bringing it to you.

Robert E. Petersen

WHO COULD ASK FOR ANYTHING MORE!

THE 1986 TOYOTA MR2.

What a kick! A car that's more fun to look at than most cars are to drive. More fun to drive than almost anything on the road. Toyota's 1986 MR2.

Get in and you've got both hands full of excitement. A firm, leather-wrapped steering wheel. A unique grip-contoured 5-speed shifter or optional 4-speed automatic and a great big tach with a great big 7500 rpm redline that says this car was born to run.

More heartbeats per second as you discover what this proven

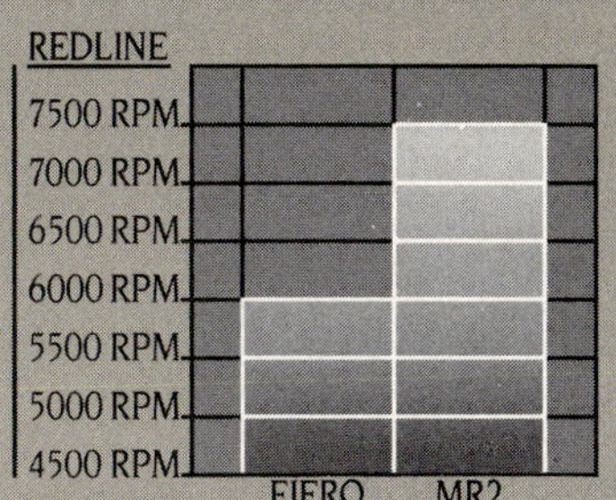

TC-16 mid-engine, two seater with electronic fuel-injection, twin overhead cams and 16 valves can do—0 to 60 in 8 seconds flat.

Curves come and go with a flick of the wrist thanks to the 46%/54% weight distribution, four-wheel independent suspension, front stabilizer bar, gas shocks and rack and pinion steering.

And for those times when rolling easy is more fun than driving hard, MR2 is more than ready. Pop the optional moonroof. Settle back in the 7-way adjustable Sport Seat—glove-soft leather available. Also available, an AM stereo / FM/MPX radio with cassette. Turn it up and discover what cruising in a sports car is all about.

And MR2's sophisticated performance means one more

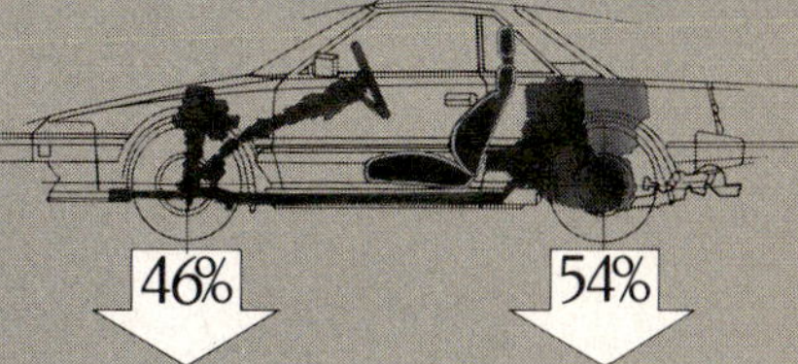

thing. Victory. MR2 won Motor Trend's 1985 Import car of the Year Award.

The 1986 Toyota MR2. More affordable performance, and best of all—more kicks.

GET MORE FROM LIFE—BUCKLE UP!

CONTRIBUTORS

Dean Batchelor is one of America's most respected automotive journalists. He is an advisor to the Harrah's Automobile Collection, a prolific author, and his work has appeared in *Motor Trend, Road & Track* and numerous other publications here and abroad.

T.C. Browne is the former publisher of *Sports Car Graphic* and *Motor Trend* magazines, a Contributing Editor of *Motor Trend* and a noted automotive journalist and historian.

Bruce Caldwell is a frequent contributor to *Hot Rod, Car Craft* and other magazines; the author of many high-performance auto books; and a compulsive collector of fast automobiles.

Dr. David E. Cole is the Director of the Office for the Study of Automotive Transportation (OSAT) of the University of Michigan and an Associate Professor of UM's Mechanical Engineering Department.

Donald Davidson is the color commentator for the annual Indy 500 radio broadcast, frequent contributor to many racing publications, and is regarded as the world's foremost authority on the Indianapolis 500 race.

Jerry Flint is assistant managing editor of *Forbes* magazine. He is a former Detroit Bureau Chief of *The New York Times* and the author of *The Dream Machines*, a book about cars from 1946-65.

Len Frank is the co-host of The Car Show, a popular Los Angeles radio program and a Contributing Editor of *Motor Trend* magazine. He often judges vintage and classic car concours.

Don Fuller is a Contributing Editor of *Motor Trend* and an active road racer. He frequently covers major auto races for a number of publications and writes about motorcycles as well as cars.

Fred M.H. Gregory is a former Senior Editor of *Motor Trend* magazine and a frequent contributor to *The New York Times, Town & Country* magazine, and numerous other publications.

Lawrence T. Harbeck is Director of Management Projects for OSAT and an Associate Research Scientist for the University of Michigan Institute of Science and Technology.

Ray Hutton is the European Editor of *Motor Trend,* former Editor of *Autocar* Magazine, the oldest auto publication in the English language, and one of Europe's and Great Britain's noted automotive journalists.

Mike Knepper is a former editor of *Motor Trend* and *Car and Driver* magazines, and was a staff member of both *AutoWeek* and *Road & Track.* His work has appeared in *Harpers Bazaar, Penthouse* and many other publications.

Ro McGonegal is a former Senior Editor of *Motor Trend.* An erstwhile drag racer and high-performance enthusiast, he was editor of both *Super Stock* and *Car Craft* magazines during the height of the Musclecar era.

William Neely is a columnist for *Motor Trend* and noted author who numbers the biographies of A.J. Foyt and Cale Yarborough among his many books. His work also includes co-authorship of the classic *Stroker Ace.*

Ted Orme is the Washington Editor of *Motor Trend* and a full-time observer of the workings of government. His work has appeared in the *Washington Post, Washingtonian* magazine and many other publications.

Steve Spence is a former Executive Editor of *Motor Trend.* An award-winning reporter, he's been on the staff of the *Honolulu Star-Bulletin* and *Los Angeles Times.*

Paul van Valkenburgh has been Technical Editor of *Sports Car Graphic* and a competitor in the Trans Am racing series. He's an automotive engineer and author who numbers the biography of Mark Donohue among his credits.

Gary Witzenburg is a frequent contributor to *Motor Trend, Playboy* and other magazines. He is an automotive engineer and competes regularly in road racing events.

J. Patrick Wright is the former Detroit bureau chief of *Business Week* magazine and the author of *On a Clear Day You Can See General Motors,* the controversial biography of John Z. DeLorean.

PETERSEN PUBLISHING COMPANY

R. E. Petersen, Chairman of the Board/**F. R. Waingrow,** President/**Robert E. Brown,** Sr. Vice President, Corporate Development/**Peter F. Clancey,** Sr. Vice President, National Advertising Director/**John Dianna,** Vice President, Group Publisher, Automotive Performance Group/**Thomas J. Siatos,** Vice President, Group Publisher/**Paul Tzimoulis,** Vice President, Group Publisher, Photography/Marine Division/**Robert MacLeod,** Vice President, Publisher/**Miles Killoch,** Vice President, Publisher/**Philip E. Trimbach,** Vice President, Financial Administration/**James J. Krenek,** Vice President, Manufacturing/**Nigel P. Heaton,** Vice President, Circulation Marketing Development/**Lee Kelley,** Vice President, Publisher, Automotive Specialty Publications/**Leo D. La Rew,** Treasurer/Assistant Secretary/**Maria Cox,** Director, Data Processing/**Bob D'Olivo,** Director, Photography/**Al Isaacs,** Director, Corporate Art/**Carol Johnson,** Director, Advertising Administration/**Don McGlathery,** Director, Advertising Research/**Vern Ball,** Director, Fulfillment Services/**Henson Lacon,** Director, Subscription Sales

ADVERTISING OFFICES

Los Angeles, Ralph Panico, Western Advertising Director, 8300 Santa Monica Blvd., 3rd Floor, Los Angeles, CA 90069, (213) 656-5425/**New York,** Charles C. Alexander, Eastern Advertising Director; Anthony Coelho, New York Branch Manager, 437 Madison Ave., 28th Floor, New York, NY 10022, (212) 935-9150/**Detroit,** Steve Flemion, Branch Manager, 333 West Fort Street, Suite 1800, Detroit, MI 48226, (313) 964-6680/**Chicago,** Duane R. Placko, Midwestern Advertising Director, John Hancock Center, 875 N. Michigan Ave., Suite 3131, Chicago, IL 60611, (312) 222-1920/**Cleveland,** Dewey F. Patterson, Branch Manager, 3 Commerce Park Square, 23200 Chagrin Blvd., Suite 605, Cleveland, OH 44122, (216) 464-1522/**Atlanta,** Richard E. Holcomb, Branch Manager, 4 Piedmont Center, Suite 601, Atlanta, GA 30305, (404) 231-4004/**Dallas,** Jeff Young, Branch Manager, 800 West Airport Freeway, Suite 201, Irving, TX 75062, (214) 579-0454.

PETERSEN MAGAZINE NETWORK

Ralph Panico, Western Advertising Director, Los Angeles/**Charles C. Alexander,** Eastern Advertising Director, New York/**Duane R. Placko,** Midwestern Advertising Director, Chicago/**Steve Flemion,** Detroit Branch Manager/**Dewey F. Patterson,** Cleveland Branch Manager/**Richard E. Holcomb,** Atlanta Branch Manager/**Jeff Young,** Dallas Branch Manager/**Anthony Coelho,** New York Branch Manager.

100 YEARS OF THE AUTOMOBILE

(ISBN 0-8227-5092-9) Copyright © 1985 Petersen Publishing Company, 8490 Sunset Blvd., Los Angeles, CA 90069. Phone (213) 657-5100. All rights reserved. No part of this book may be reproduced without written permission from the publisher. Printed in U.S.A. This book is purchased with the understanding that the information presented is from many varied sources from which there can be no warranty or responsibility by the Publisher as to accuracy or completeness.

I've helped Dad take care of the old convertible ever since it was new. Always with Quaker State. I learned early about Quaker State's unique formula—it starts with Pennsylvania Grade Crude. About its stable viscosity, and its smooth flowing, steady protection. I had a good teacher. Thanks, Dad.

Quaker State.
The Big Q stands for quality.
Always has. Always will.

INTRODUCTION

If the story of the automobile's first century were a movie, Cecil B. De-Mille would have to direct it. It's an epic tale in every way, with a cast of thousands. It has heroes and villains, life and death, fame and fortune, genius and folly, and you can even work a bit of sex into it.

But where do you begin? If you want, you can trace the story as far back as when man chiseled the wheel out of a block of stone, or tamed the first horse. The same motivation prompted the invention of the automobile: a desire to get from one place to another *faster*.

Only it wasn't until an accumulation of knowledge converged in the 19th century that clever minds had the tools to work with. The man we credit with having built the first *practical* automobile, Carl Benz, wouldn't have gotten very far if others hadn't made breakthroughs in a number of fields—electricity, chemistry, and metallurgy, among them. In a way, then, the automobile was perhaps the culminating event of the Industrial Revolution. It was certainly the agent for a Social Revolution which dramatically changed the way people had been living for thousands of years.

Consider that before the automobile, from pre-history to the reign of Queen Victoria, the primary, indeed the only, means of transportation for the vast majority of people was by putting one foot in front of the other.

The aristocrats and the rich, of course, had their horses and coaches, and trains and bicycles were coming on the scene, but the way most people got around was by foot; they lived, worked and died within walking distance of where they were born.

Today, we can't even imagine living within such limits. The automobile changed all that.

Maybe that's why cars mean so much more to so many people than the other useful artifacts of our times. Maybe that's why we Americans, at any rate, have been accused of having a love affair with the car. We can't bear the notion of confinement; when we want to go, we want to *go*. And it's our cars that let us do it.

But as we sit back with the wheel in our hands, a foot on the throttle, and the lines in the highway flashing by, how often do we wonder about this freedom machine itself? After all, every single one of the thousands of bits and pieces in a modern car had its origin in some person's imagination. Who were these people? How did they think up all this stuff?

There's no way we'll ever know that. There are too many thousands of people over too many years to credit each one. But we do know the names and histories of those who started it all. We know how it grew and what it all means. And that is what follows—the story of the Age of the Automobile, the first hundred years.

—Fred M.H. Gregory

For seven years now, the radar detector experts have had one standard
(But don't take <u>our</u> word for it)

Over the years, one radar detector has been selected as the standard—time after time. But rather than just tell you about it, here are some of the things <u>the experts</u> have said about ESCORT—then and now.

1978
● ESCORT is introduced—the first dual band superheterodyne radar detector.

1979
● ESCORT's first review, *Car and Driver* tests twelve radar detectors.

"Only one model, the Escort, truly stood out from the rest."

"If you can imagine the Turbo Porsche of the radar detectors, this is it..."

"In no test did any of the other detectors even come close."

1980
● *Car and Driver* compares four detectors.

"...the Escort has gone on to become the most coveted piece of high-performance road equipment since the turbocharger."

"ESCORT Overall rating: Still the best; unmatched in either performance or features."
● *BMWCCA Roundel* compares ten detectors.

"Escort—the winner and still champion!! This design consistently outperformed the other products and is the standard to which the other detectors are compared."

"If you want the best, this is it. There is nothing else like it."

1981
● *BMWCCA Roundel* compares seven detectors.

"The Escort works. It's the best there is. In terms of what all it does, nothing else even comes close."

1982
● *Car and Driver* compares ten detectors.

"The ESCORT, a perennial favorite of these black-box comparisons, is still the best radar detector money can buy."

1983
● *Car and Driver* compares six detectors.

"...live with a new Escort for a while and you'll realize that it has advanced new circuitry that should go down as a genuine breakthrough."

"The Escort radar detector is clearly the leader in the field in value, customer service, and performance..."
● *BMWCCA Roundel* compares eleven detectors.

"The Escort has been continually updated over the years through an evolutionary development program."

"The Escort simply keeps getting better."

1984
● *Rotary Rocket* compares seven detectors.

"While there hasn't been a major facelift for some time, and why should there be for such a classic, the circuitry has undergone countless refinements to keep the Escort at the leading edge of technology."

1985
● *Car and Driver* tests twelve remote mounted radar detectors, comparing them to...

"We wanted to know how the low, front mounted detectors would compare with the best conventional radar detector from our previous tests, so we fed (an) Escort into our evaluation as a reference."
The result? The top placing remote unit collected 274 points under the scoring system. And Escort?

"You may be interested to know, however, that the same data-reduction would give the Escort a score of 412 points..."
● *Road & Track* compares ten detectors.

"Externally, the Escort has changed hardly at all over the years; internally, it has undergone several major revisions, each establishing new performance standards in the field... it is highly recommended."

Try ESCORT at no risk
Take the first 30 days with ESCORT as a test. If you're not completely satisfied return it for a full refund. You can't lose.

ESCORT is also backed with a one year warranty on both parts and labor.

ESCORT $245 (Ohio res. add $13.48 tax)

TOLL FREE **800-543-1608**

By mail send to address below. Credit cards, money orders, bank checks, certified checks, wire transfers processed immediately. Personal or company checks require 18 days.

Cincinnati Microwave
Department 100-154-A01
One Microwave Plaza
Cincinnati, Ohio 45296-0100

Tune in "Talktalk," the satellite call-in comedy talk show. Sunday evenings on public radio stations. Check local listings.
©1985 Cincinnati Microwave, Inc.

MILESTONES

1678 Jean d'Hautefeuille uses cylinder and piston to pump water.

Charles Huygens builds first explosion engine using gunpowder.

1688 Denis Papin builds steam engine in Kassel, Germany.

1705 Thomas Newcomen develops steam engine to pump water from mines.

1710 Antoine de la Mothe Cadillac founds Detroit.

1770 Nicholas Cugnot builds steam-powered gun carriage. Runs into wall.

1776 Alexander Volta proves explosive gases can be ignited by electric spark.

Jeremiah Wilkinson invents "fixture," the key to making interchangeable parts, in U.S.

1782 James Watt introduces crank to harness rotary power, in England.

1792 First U.S. toll roads open in Pennsylvania and Connecticut.

1799 Eli Whitney develops interchangeable parts for muskets.

1801 First steam coach built by Richard Trevithick in England.

1805 First U.S. self-propelled vehicle, called *Orukter Amphibolos*, a steam dredge, built by Oliver Evans.

1815 George Stephenson constructs first successful steam locomotive.

John Macadam introduces roads made of broken stone, in England.

1824 Joseph Aspdin introduces Portland cement, in England.

1834 March 17: Gottlieb Daimler born at Schorndorf.

1844 Charles Goodyear patents rubber vulcanization process.

Nov. 24: Carl Benz born at Karlsruhe.

1855 First self-propelled steam fire-engine in U.S. patented by A.B. Latta.

1856 Henry Bessemer discovers how to make steel, in England.

1859 E.L. Drake brings in world's first oil well, in Titusville, Pennsylvania.

1863 Jean-Joseph Etienne Lenoir, a Belgian living in Paris, builds a self-propelled vehicle and drives it on a nine-kilometer round trip.

1864 Nikolaus Otto founds factory to make internal-combustion engines, at Cologne, Germany.

1876 Nicholas Otto patents four-stroke engine in Germany.

1878 First auto race, from Green Bay to Madison, Wisconsin; J. Carhart and A.M. Farrand win, driving Oshkosh steam car, averaging 6 mph.

1879 May 8: George B. Selden files patent application for a vehicle powered by a one-cylinder, Brayton engine.

1883 Benz & Cie., Rheinische Gasmotorenfabrik founded in Mannheim, Germany.

1884 Feb. 12: Patent #16027 issued in France for an internal-combustion engine to be installed in a Delamare-Deboutteville steam car.

1886 Carl Benz patents world's first practical motorcar.

1889 John Dunlop patents first pneumatic tire, in Ireland.

Peugeot builds first car, a steamer.

1893 Sept. 20: Frank Duryea first drives horseless carriage, built by brother Charles.

1894 First organized motorsports event, Paris-Rouen Trial.

First brick surface laid on rural road, Wooster Pike, near Cleveland, Ohio.

1895 Frank Duryea wins first major U.S. auto race, Chicago to Evanston, 50 miles in 9 hours. Duryea brothers form first U.S. auto company in September.

First automobile road race, organized by the Automobile Club de France, Paris-Bordeaux-Paris.

First pneumatic automobile tires by Michelin brothers in Paris-Bordeaux race. They retire after too many flats.

First race accident sidelines Prevost's Panhard after colliding with a dog in Paris-Bordeaux-Paris event.

First U.S. auto advertising appears, Benz ad in *The Motorcycle*.

Nov. 2: *Autocar*, world's longest-running car magazine first published, in England.

Nov. 5: G.B. Selden granted patent No. 549,160 for his Road Engine.

1896 First 4-cylinder engine, Panhard et Levassor 80x120 mm.

Henry Ford builds his first car in Detroit. It fails.

First U.S. auto race track, Narragansett Park, opens in Rhode Island.

1897 Japan imports some steam cars from U.S., its first motor vehicles.

Aug. 21: Olds Motor Vehicle Company organized, builds first Oldsmobile.

Gilbert Loomis takes out first auto insurance, pays $7.50 for $1000 worth of liability, in Westfield, Massachusetts.

Stanley twins form Steam Car Company.

1898 Enzo Ferrari born.

Renault introduces first shaft drive, replaces chains.

First independent auto dealership in U.S. opens, in New York.

H.H. Franklin produces first air-cooled car.

1899 First U.S. factory built specifically to make cars, opened by Ransom E. Olds.

First auto garage opens, in New York.

Renault founded in France.

A.L. Dyke opens first auto parts and supply business, in St. Louis.

April 29: Bullet-shaped *Ne Jamais Contente* (Never Satisfied), driven by Camille Jenatzy, first car to travel over a mile-a-minute—65.79 mph

1900 First National Automobile Show held, in Madison Square Garden.

The Ohio, built by Packard, uses steering wheel in place of tiller.

March 6: Gottlieb Daimler dies in Cannstatt.

William McKinley becomes first President to ride in an automobile.

1901 John and Horace Dodge open machine shop in Detroit.

Curved-dash Oldsmobile runabout, first U.S. car made in quantity.

First car to be named Mercedes built by Daimler Motoren.

Connecticut first state to enact motor vehicle law.

New York first state to license cars, collects $954.

First speedometer, in an Oldsmobile.

David Buick, maker of bathroom appliances, builds first car.

Sept. 10: Spindletop, a gusher, comes in near Beaumont, Texas; price of crude oil drops to less than five cents a barrel.

1902 First 8-cylinder engine: Charron, Girardot and Voight, Paris.

Cadillac Automobile Company organized.

Thomas B. Jeffery Company builds first Rambler auto.

American Automobile Association formed.

J.D. Maxwell and Charles D. King build Silent Northern Car, first with running boards.

First front-mounted engine in U.S. car, Locomobile.

1903 June 16: Ford Motor Company formed, capitalized with $28,000 in cash.

First 6-cylinder engine: Spyker, Amsterdam.

Vauxhall, first all-steel-bodied car.

Buick Motor Company organized.

1904 M. Rigolly drives Gobron-Brillie to world-record 103.55 mph at Ostend, Belgium. First man to exceed 100 mph.

Studebaker sells its first gasoline-powered vehicle.

1905 Spyker produces first front-wheel-drive car, in Holland.

Society of Automotive Engineers founded.

First Glidden Tour held.

First stolen car reported, in St. Louis.

1906 Woodrow Wilson says: "Possession of a motor car is such an ostentatious display of wealth that it would stimulate socialism."

First Grand Prix, near Le Mans, in France, won by Ferenc Szisz, driving 90-hp Renault, averaging 65 mph for 770 miles.

Michelin pioneers first removable tire rim at Grand Prix.

Buick introduces storage battery as standard equipment.

1907 Tokyo's Jidosha Seisakusho Company builds Japan's first gasoline-fueled car.

Oakland Motor Car Company (later Pontiac) organized.

First parkway, Vanderbilt Motor Parkway, a privately owned toll road opens on Long Island, New York.

President Taft orders first official White House car, a White steamer.

1908 Cadillac makes the first car to use interchangeable parts.

Sept. 16: William Crapo Durant organizes General Motors holding company absorbing Buick, Oakland and Oldsmobile.

Cadillac wins Dewar trophy for pioneering parts interchangeability.

Oct.1: First Ford Model T appears, sells for $850.

First family transcontinental trip made, in a Packard.

Thomas Flyer wins New York-Paris race.

First mile of concrete pavement laid, Woodward Ave. in Detroit, at a cost of $13,534.59.

1909 Suzuki Loom Works founded.

June 5: First event at Indianapolis Speedway, a hot-air balloon race.

Hudson Motor Car Company organized.

1910 First V-8 engine: Model CL DeDion Bouton.

1911 Charles "Boss" Kettering, of Dayton Engineering Laboratories Company (Delco), installs first self starter in a Cadillac.

Chevrolet Motor Company organized.

May 30: Ray Harroun wins first Indianapolis 500 in a Marmon Wasp.

First running of Monte Carlo Rally, Turcat Mery wins.

Auto stocks first listed on New York Stock Exchange.

Court rules Selden patent "valid but not infringed," ending disruption of the auto industry.

1912 First standard starter and independent electrical system on a production car, a Cadillac; built by Henry Leland and Charles F. Kettering.

SAE first standardizes screw threads and other parts.

First white lines appear in the middle of streets, in Redlands, California.

First pressed steel body developed by Edward Gowen Budd.

1913 First moving production line installed at Ford's Highland Park plant, it's designed by Clarence W. Avery.

Installment financing first used to sell cars.

First drive-in gas station opened, by Gulf, in Pittsburgh.

Automatic Bendix drive for starters introduced.

Forced-feed lubrication introduced by Packard.

1914 Work begun on Lincoln Highway, first trancontinental road, going from New York to San Francisco.

Kwaishinsha Co. makes first Dat car ("sun" added to name in 1932).

First stop sign goes up, in Detroit.

First traffic lights, in Cleveland.

Packard develops spiral bevel gear.

Pierce incorporates headlights in fenders.

Detroit passes law forbidding gas pumps at curbs.

Renault taxis save Paris, rush troops to the front.

Henry Ford raises minimum daily wage from $2.30 to $5.00.

Nov. 14: First Dodge comes off the assembly line.

First mass-produced V-8 appears, in Cadillac Type 51.

1916 Woodrow Wilson signs Federal Aid Road Act, providing first federal money for road building.

Tokyo Ishikawajima Shipbuilding, later Isuzu, builds first car.

Hand-operated windshield wipers introduced.

Charles W. Nash leaves GM, takes over Thomas B. Jeffery Company and forms Nash.

1917 Ford's River Rouge plant opens, largest industrial complex on Earth.

Mitsubishi Model A introduced.

1918 Chevrolet joins General Motors.

1919 Rene Thomas becomes first driver to break 100 mph at Indy.

First power brakes introduced, by Hispano-Suiza.

First state gasoline tax, in Oregon.

Henry Ford buys out investors, becomes sole owner of Ford Motor Company.

1920 Toyo Cork Kogyo, later Mazda, founded.

1921 First drive-in restaurant opens, Royce Hailey's Pig Stand, in Dallas.

First auto sales recession.

First Lincoln cars introduced.

First adjustable front seat, by Hudson.

1922 National Department Stores open first suburban shopping mall, near St. Louis.

Air cleaners introduced.

1923 Ford's Model T reaches peak annual production of 1,817,891 units.

Morris Garages, Oxford, England, builds first MG.

First 24-hour race for production cars held at Le Mans.

Alfred P. Sloan becomes president of GM.

Exceeds the minimum daily adult requirement
for driving excitement.

PONTIAC GRAND AM SE
WE BUILD EXCITEMENT

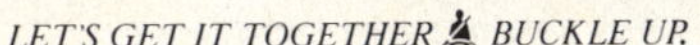

LET'S GET IT TOGETHER. BUCKLE UP.

1924 Walter P. Chrysler produces first car bearing his name.

First high-speed toll road *autostrada* from Milan to Como, Italy.

Dodge produces first all-steel-bodied closed car.

Anti-knock Ethyl gasoline allows development of high-compression engines.

Double-filament headlight bulbs appear.

1925 Lincoln Highway completed.

25-millionth U.S. car built.

1926 Harley Earl forms GM's Art and Colour section, first Detroit auto styling studio.

Pontiac car introduced by Oakland.

First use of shatter-resistant glass, by Cadillac.

Daimler-Benz formed.

Cannonball Baker drives a truck from New York to San Francisco in less than six days.

1927 World War I air ace Eddie Rickenbacker becomes president of Indianapolis Speedway.

May 21: Last Model T built, No. 15,007,033.

Lockheed develops hydraulic brakes.

Sept 14: Dancer Isadora Duncan demonstrates basic flaw of chain drive, is strangled when scarf catches in Amilcar sprocket.

1928 Synchromesh transmission introduced, by Cadillac.

Chrysler takes over Dodge, introduces Plymouth and DeSoto.

Sakichi Toyoda sells loom patent rights to finance car research.

Ettore Bugatti builds six Royale cars, largest built to date; no royalty ever buys one.

Automobile radios appear.

April 4: Carl Benz dies at Ladenburg.

1930 Cadillac introduces first V-16 automobile engine.

1931 Toyo Kogyo begins to sell first Mazda vehicles, 3-wheel trucks.

50-millionth U.S. vehicle produced.

1932 Pontiac Motor Division replaces Oakland.

First fender skirts appear, on a Graham.

1933 First drive-in movie opens, in Camden, New Jersey.

Individual front-wheel suspension, called Knee-Action, introduced by GM.

1934 Toyoda Automatic Loom Works starts car production.

First Dasun exported.

1935 First parking meter installed, in Oklahoma City.

First Jaguar is introduced, SS 2.7 Saloon.

Toyota rolls out A1 prototype, its first car.

1936 First production diesel car offered by Mercedes.

1937 GM's Art and Colour section renamed Styling Section.

Oldsmobile offers first automatic transmission.

Auto plants unionized throughout the U.S. car industry.

Gearshift lever moves to steering column.

Dec. 7: Buckminster Fuller granted patent on futuristic Dymaxion car.

1938 Chrysler offers fluid-drive transmission.

First Mercury cars introduced.

1939 Nash offers first air conditioning as option.

First flashing electric turn signals introduced by Buick.

Lincoln Zephyr appears with no running boards, starts trend.

1940 Sealed beam headlights introduced.

Pennsylvania Turnpike, first modern U.S. long-distance road, opens.

1942 War forces national speed limit, 35 mph.

1945 Henry Ford II becomes president of Ford.

Nov. 14: Anton "Tony" Hulman buys Indianapolis Speedway, reinvigorates the 500-mile race.

1946 First fiberglass-bodied car, the Stout 46.

First automobile radio-telephone appears.

1947 First MG TC arrives in America.

First official Ferrari, the Type 125 Corsa V-12.

Kaiser and Frazer launched.

Henry Ford and William C. Durant die.

1948 Honda Motor Co. established with capital of $3300.

British Daimler introduces first electric windows.

Goodrich introduces first tubeless tires.

Feb. 1: Red Byron's Ford wins first NASCAR race, at Daytona Beach.

First tailfins appear, on a Cadillac.

1949 First keyturn starter introduced by Chrysler.

1950 Ford overtakes Chrysler to become Number Two car maker in U.S.

William Levitt builds Levittown, cars make suburbia possible.

1951 Chrysler offers hemispherical-type combustion chamber engine.

1952 First power steering offered by Cadillac, Olds and Buick.

1953 Michelin markets first radial ply tire.

First practical disc brakes used on Le Mans-winning C-Jaguar.

First 12-volt electrical systems appear on GM cars.

Corvette is first plastic-bodied car to be made in quantity.

Kaiser-Frazer buys Willys-Overland.

1954 First production gasoline fuel injection, on Mercedes-Benz 300SL.

Studebaker and Packard merge.

Nash-Kelvinator and Hudson combine to form American Motors.

1955 Alberto Ascari becomes first driver to crash into Monaco harbor.

Worst racing disaster, at Le Mans, 82 killed.

1956 Ford stock goes on the market, sole family ownership relinquished.

Interstate Highway Act passed.

1958 First CVT (Continuously Variable Transmission) introduced, on the DAF Daffodil.

Production of Packard cars stops.

Datsun exports first cars to U.S.

1959 Earle MacPherson's struts first appear on British Ford.

Feb. 14: Lee Petty wins first 500 at Daytona International Speedway.

1960 Jack Brabham brings mid-engined Cooper to Indianapolis, starts new trend that dooms the Indy roadster.

Chrysler discontinues DeSoto line.

First Toyota exported to U.S.

1961 First U.S. V-6 offered by Buick.

Phil Hill becomes first American World Champion driver.

1962 Shelby begins producing Cobra.

Studebaker offers front disc brakes as option.

1963 Parnelli Jones first driver to break 150 mph at Indy.

Dec. 20: Studebaker halts car production in U.S.

1964 First Wankel rotary-engined car, NSU Sport Prinz.

April 17: Ford unveils the 1965 Mustang.

1965 Motor Vehicle Air Pollution Control Act passed.

Nov. 12: Highest speed ever attained by a wheel-driven car, 418.5 mph, by Bob Summers driving the Goldenrod streamliner at the Bonneville Salt Flats.

1966 Ralph Nader publishes *Unsafe at Any Speed*. National Traffic and Motor Vehicle Safety Act goes into law.

1967 First rotary-engined Mazda, model 110S, introduced.

1969 Datsun introduces 240Z in U.S.

1970 Clean Air Act passes Congress.

1973 Volkswagen Beetle production ends at Wolfsburg, West Germany, after 25 years and 16.2 million cars.

1973 Oct. 19: Arab oil producers impose ban on exports of oil to U.S. First Oil Embargo.

1974 55-mph national speed limit imposed to conserve fuel.

1977 Tom Sneva first driver to break 200 mph at Indy.

A.J. Foyt, first man to win Indy 500 four times.

Renault purchases interest in American Motors.

1978 Volkswagen begins production in U.S.

First plastic monocoque car, Lotus Elite.

1979 Second Gas Crisis forces drivers into gas lines.

1980 Chrysler, facing bankruptcy, gets government bailout loan.

1983 Dec. 22: Federal Trade Commission approves joint venture between General Motors and Toyota to build cars in California.

Chrysler pays back government loan, announces record profits.

1984 July 12: New York becomes first state to require drivers, front-seat passengers, and children under 10 to wear seat belts.

General Motors restructures company into small-car and big-car divisions.

1985 General Motors locates plant for its new car division, Saturn, in Tennessee.

1986 Centennial of the automobile.

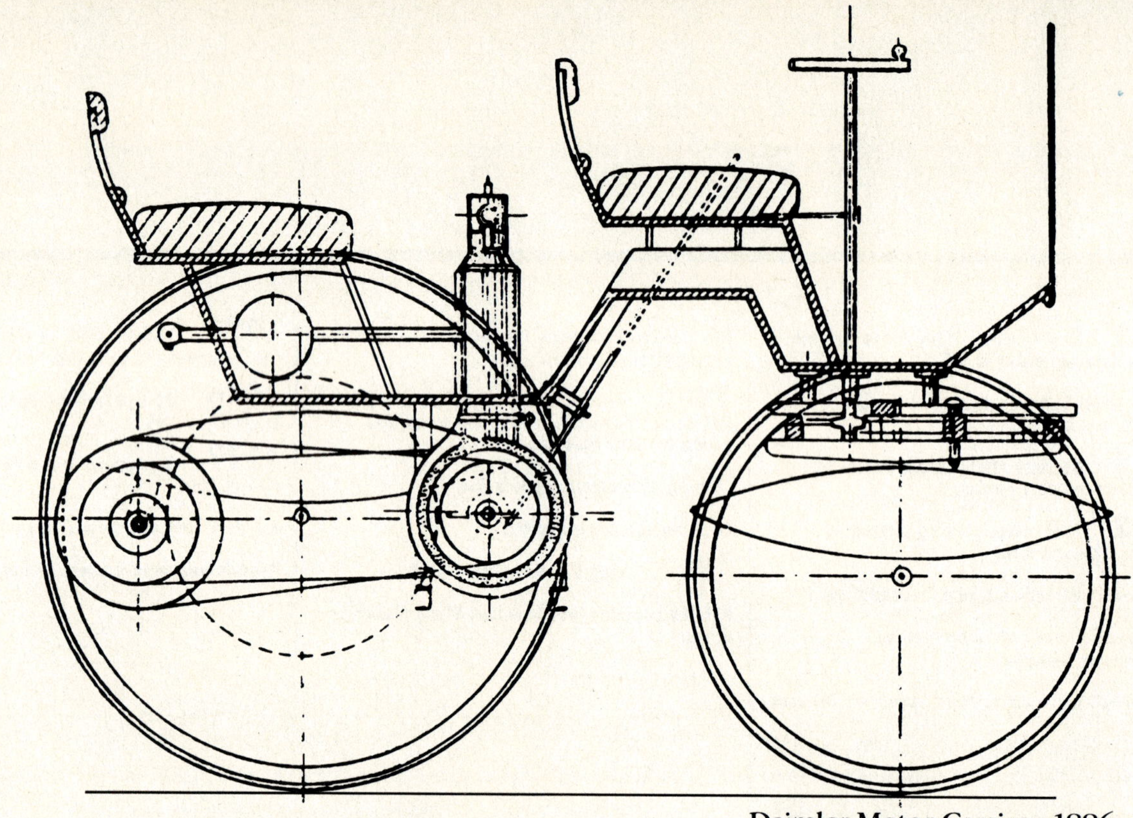

Daimler Motor Carriage 1886

Engineer all other cars

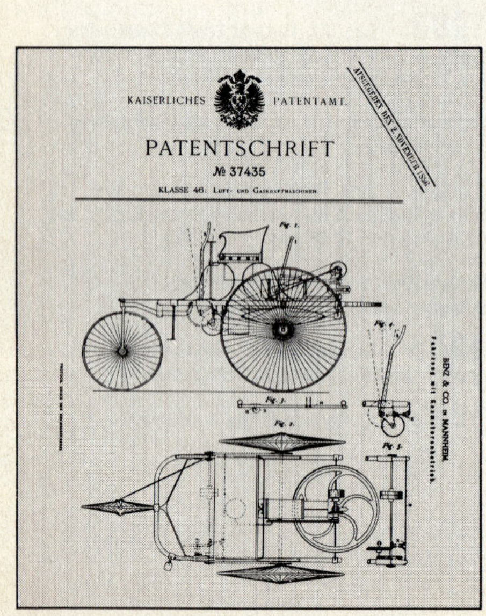

It was on January 29, 1886 that the German Government issued Patent No. 37435 to the engineer Carl Benz for his invention of a self-propelled, gasoline-powered "Motorwagen."

Simultaneously with the achievement of Benz, fellow engineer Gottlieb Daimler built and ran a motorized carriage of his own.

The Benz patent was to become the official birth certificate of the automobile. Joint credit for developing the world's first practical motor vehicles has belonged to Gottlieb Daimler and Carl Benz ever since.

This issue of *Motor Trend* commemorates the one-hundredth year of the automobile. And we are pleased to participate in this significant occasion.

But for us, it is a prelude to another and even more significant occasion.

Next January 29 in Stuttgart, West Germany, in formal ceremonies attended by leading

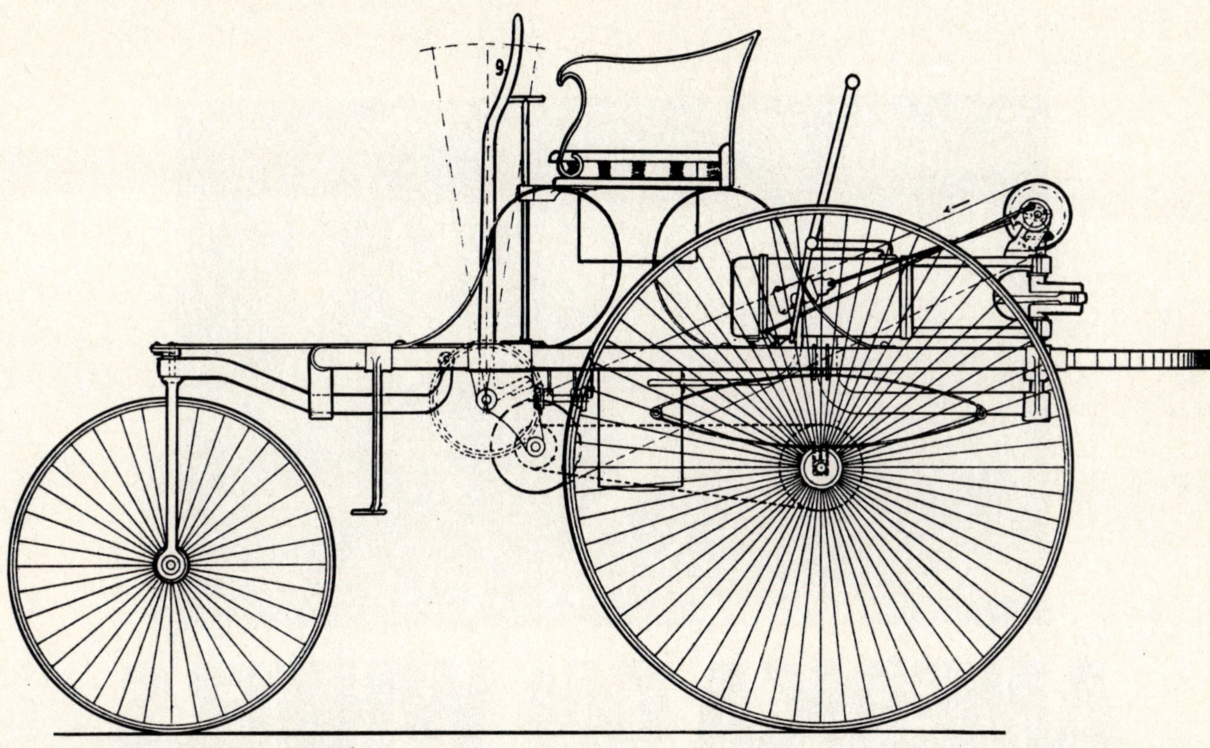
Benz Patent Motor Car 1886

ed before in the world

Carl Benz

Gottlieb Daimler

two men who started it.

We could do no less. For the efforts of Gottlieb Daimler and Carl Benz, after serving to found the age of the automobile, were to ultimately found the company that today bears their name: Daimler-Benz A.G., builders of Mercedes-Benz automobiles.

Daimler-Benz has always been not only conscious of its unique legacy but inspired and nourished by it.

We will be proud to honor the memory and the achievements of Gottlieb Daimler and Carl Benz in that special ceremony next January 29.

But in another sense, Mercedes-Benz honors them every day—by building automobiles worthy of their names.

governmental, scientific and industry leaders, we will officially commemorate the precise day the automobile started. And the

Engineered like no other car in the world

AMERICA ON WHEELS

How geniuses, financiers, and pitchmen turned a four-wheel novelty into the world's biggest industry.

By Len Frank

☐ Years before Daimler and Benz developed their first vehicles, Americans were beginning to lay the foundation for their own auto industry. As early as the late 1700s, Oliver Evans, in Philadelphia, knew about reciprocating power and the technology of his time; Samuel Morey patented, in 1826, a "gas and vapor engine"; and John Ericsson, a cantankerous genius, patented a "caloric engine" that preceded Rudolph Diesel's similar work by about 75 years. Forging, casting, lathe turning and general blacksmithery were widespread. Locomotive technology had become quite sophisticated; sewing machines, weapons, milling and weaving machinery, were either mass-produced (by the standards of the day) or at least products of a machine technology. And, the stationary steam engine had become commonplace by the mid-1800s. So why no automobiles?

The answer seems to have lain in the realm of imagination, or lack of it, and the prevalence of legal and fiscal conservativism. And, the country was in the grip of the Railroad Monopoly and did not have the benefit of a decent road system, like the one Napoleon left France.

The push came, finally, as the 19th century was disappearing, when H.H. Kohlsaat, publisher of the *Chicago Times-Herald*, proposed an automobile race. What he staged was not so much a speed contest as a test of reliability and engineering excellence. If there had been a slogan for his Chicago-Milwaukee-Chicago race, Kohlsaat would have chosen the horsemen's "racing improves the breed." What he got was, "race on Sunday, sell on Monday."

The contest was run in a foot of snow on Thanksgiving weekend, 1895. The Duryea, built by Frank and Charles Duryea of Illinois and Massachusetts, beat a Mueller-Benz, and provided the spur the emerging industry needed. It made the Duryeas famous in *world* automotive circles—they went on to win the London-Brighton run—and gave encouragement to a large number of non-participants, among them Ransom E. Olds, Alexander Winton, and a middle-

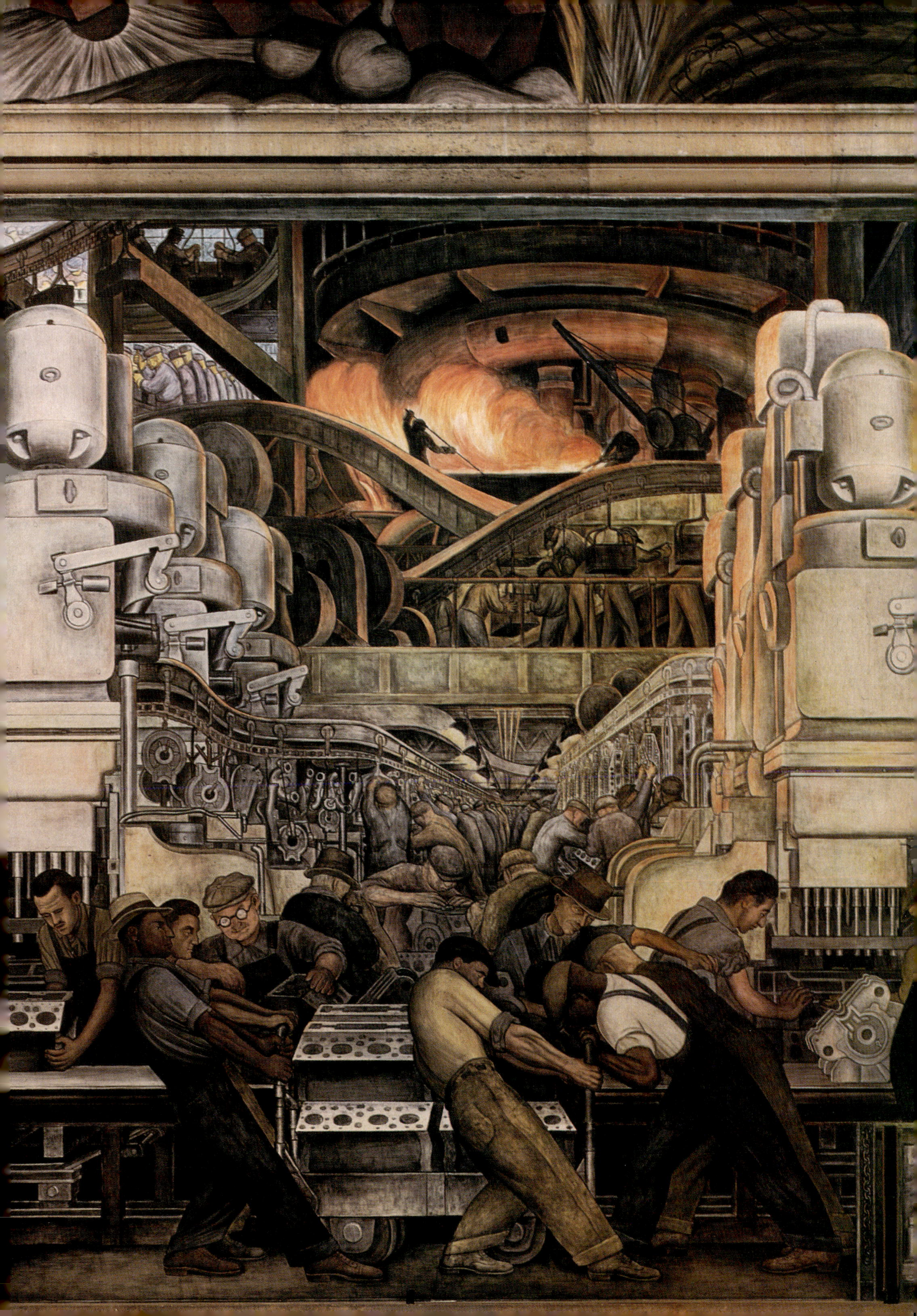

aged refugee from a Michigan farm named Henry Ford.

By then, the United States had all the necessary elements for a car industry—technology, materials, a skilled labor force, affluent buyers, and available capital. Hundreds of individuals and companies were engaged in invention, development and investment and many were on the brink of producing a car. We were ready.

Charles B. King, a college-trained mechanical engineer, began work on a four-cylinder in 1894 and had it powering a wagon by 1896. Elwood P. Haynes, a metallurgist who invented Stellite and was one of those responsible for stainless steel, did the design work and had a car fabricated by the Apperson brothers, who later built cars under their own name.

Alexander Winton built a motorcycle in 1895, a car a year later, and, by 1898, had built and sold 20 four-wheelers. Within a very few years, King, Haynes, Duryea and Winton were joined by Knox, White, Stanley, Stearns, Locomobile, Columbia and Packard. Their cars were series-built, but still artisanal, that is, hand-built by small groups of craftsmen. Repairs, which were frequent, had to be done by men equally skilled. This restricted distribution and ownership.

Still, in 1900, total production of automobiles in the U.S. was an astonishing 4192, and more than 50,000 paid to see the first U.S. auto show at Madison Square Garden.

The first man to seize the opportunity was Michigan's Ransom Eli Olds. An early experimenter, Olds built a three-wheeled steamer in 1891, a few electric cars, and a gas lightweight in 1897. But the car which would immortalize him and make him the first auto mogul was his Curved Dash Runabout. It was light, quiet, easy to drive, affordable and popular. It was even built in Germany under license.

Olds' success helped establish Detroit (or, more accurately, Dearborn, Lansing, Flint and other areas in Michigan) as the

G. B. SELDEN.
ROAD ENGINE.
No. 549,160.
Patented Nov. 5. 1895.
Fig. 1.
Fig. 2.
WITNESSES
INVENTOR
Geo. B. Selden

ABOVE:
Virtually every car maker used racing to promote and prove its car. Harry Stutz (at left in lower photo) built his reputation on the track. And Henry Ford (at tiller in top photo) used his famous 999 race car to set records and get publicity.

LEFT:
The Selden patent put a crimp in the early auto industry by levying a royalty on every car made. Henry Ford finally beat the patent in court and the car business flourished without further hindrance.

24

Karl Benz was first to remove the horse from the carriage. But it took the Michelin Brothers, back in 1895, to replace the carriage wheel with the world's first inflatable automobile tire.

By 1899 things really started to roll. Automobiles equipped with Michelin tires were performing at speeds over 60 miles per hour.

In 1906, Michelin invented the first removable rim and to the relief of drivers everywhere, the first inflatable spare.

Michelin also produced the first low-pressure, high-mileage tire, as well as the world's first tubeless tire.

And not only did Michelin introduce the first radial tire, we did it fifteen years before anyone else could put any type of radial on the market.

When American car companies decided to offer radials as original equipment on their cars, once again, Michelin led the way.

And in 1979, a car equipped with radials (guess whose) won the Formula One World Championship in Grand Prix racing for the first time.

When all is said and done, it's really unimportant to be the first. Unless you can also be the best. Not just occasionally, but consistently. Year in and year out. Which is precisely what being Michelin is all about.

Now, for those who think these developments aren't all that important, we have a suggestion. The next time your Porsche needs a new set of tires, strap on some carriage wheels and see how she handles.

MICHELIN®
BECAUSE SO MUCH IS RIDING ON YOUR TIRES.™

IF IT WASN'T FOR MICHELIN,
THIS IS WHAT TODAY'S CAR MIGHT LOOK LIKE.

center of the automobile industry. Eastern auto entrepreneurs, like Col. Albert Pope, a believer in steam and electricity as power, fell by the wayside. Pope built his cars in New England and relied on the highly skilled labor in the area—trained in the armaments, sewing machine, weaving, and shoe industries. These skills were in short supply in Detroit, so, in a way, the move west also precipitated truly automated production procedures which didn't need so many trained hands.

The first instance of this came two months after a fire destroyed Olds' plant in 1901, where his workers were handbuilding Curved Dash Runabouts at the rate of two or three per week. Olds had projected a car a day before the fire. By August he was hopelessly behind and went to Henry M. Leland, then head of Leland and Faulconer, manufacturers of precision equipment, for help. They struck a deal for 10 to 20 engines a day, 2000 in all. It was a brave move since Olds had, at that time, delivered only about 200 cars. Later, to cope with an unforeseen increase in power due to Leland's meticulous manufacturing, John and Horace Dodge, Canadian brothers who had been bicycle manufacturers, were contracted to build improved transmissions. Olds could now meet demand by relying on suppliers, setting an industry pattern that's prevailed to this day. But, having gathered his production capacity, Olds now had to sell his cars.

Till then, automobiles had been produced for the rich, and even though the Army and Post Office placed orders, and doctors were among the enthusiastic first customers (they still made house calls), the consensus was that the auto was a rich man's toy. This had been the European approach, and had been copied by the East Coast manufacturers.

Ransom Olds, to prove that *his* auto was a practical machine, sent the young Roy Chapin to New York (from Detroit) for the opening of the second auto show, driving an Olds. Chapin and John Maxwell, Olds' chief road tester, picked a car off the line, checked it out, loaded it with spares, and Chapin went off alone. Both men would later go on to the greater things:

Chapin to head Hudson, among other successes, and Maxwell to found his own company which, with Chalmers, became the basis of Chrysler Corporation.

Chapin left late, and since the Olds had no lights, had to stop for the night. The next day he drove 278 miles on dirt roads that had only seen 5-mph wagon traffic. Chapin's Jones speedometer registered 35 mph at times. He covered 820 miles in seven and a half days, at one point having to use the tow-path along the Erie Canal to avoid impassable roads, tantamount to driving up an airport runway today. To Chapin, it pointed out the need for better roads and when he became Secretary of Commerce (under Herbert Hoover) he worked toward that end.

Olds, meanwhile, sold his New York distributor 1000 Runabouts—by far the largest order ever. The news of the Detroit-New York run and the publicity of the 1000-car order had the same effect as the earlier *Times-Herald* race, but now there were automobiles that could be bought and

TOP:
Whether the 1902 Olds Curved Dash Runabout made girls swoon is doubtful, but it certainly established that cars could be built in volume for an affordable price.

ABOVE:
With Frank J. Duryea at the tiller, this car won the Chicago *Times-Herald* race in 1895 and helped start an industry in which the Duryeas, unfortunately, did not prosper.

Olds sold 3300 of them in 1902, many fewer than were ordered. This opened a market for people like Thomas B. Jeffery, who made Rambler bicycles, and switched to building Rambler cars, an effort that would ultimately result in the development of American Motors.

But, like other auto tycoons who would follow, R.E. Olds lost control of the Olds Motor Works to his financiers, in 1904, over the question of producing luxury cars. He wanted to continue with the light, cheap Runabout, while the Smiths, sons of his chief money man, wanted luxury cars. Olds left and went off to found Reo (from his initials).

Henry Leland, having been introduced to cars by Olds, continued to make his mark in the business. A mechanical genius—he was the youngest master mechanic in his native New England at a time when being a master mechanic really meant something—Leland worked in the arms industry and for Brown and Sharpe, the foremost manufacturer of precision tools and measuring devices in the U.S., before coming to Detroit. He learned the habit of thinking of .001 as a sort of crude standard at a time when most measuring was still being done in paces and pieces of string.

In Detroit, which he considered the seat of opportunity, he founded Leland and Faulconer (Faulconer's contribution was capital), a precision machine company and the best gray iron foundry in the nation. It set standards for quality and trained Horace Dodge, among others. Leland's expertise was sought out by fledgling entrepreneurs. He became involved in Ford's first venture in late November, 1901. Ford himself lasted four months in that enterprise, leaving after considerable disagreement and some unpleasantness, and the financial partners asked Leland to appraise the assets so they could liquidate. Leland suggested they stay in the auto business; he wanted to sell them an improved engine that Olds rejected, and had some ideas about how to make better cars than the Curved Dash Runabout. The partners took his advice and the result was Cadillac.

Then, Leland, for the first time in the U.S. at least, assembled a team to design his new car, and hired William Metzger to sell them. Twenty years before Sinclair Lewis made "go-getter" a term of derision, Metzger *was* one. Within a year, the Cadillac was the second largest seller in the U.S., *and* the rest of the world, behind Olds. Metzger learned part of his sales technique from Olds, but went much further. By September of 1903, Metzger had dealers from coast-to-coast, and Cadillac was facing the same production shortfall that Olds had encountered.

Despite the success, there was dissension at the top in Cadillac and growing unhappiness with Leland wearing two hats: as a power in Cadillac and partner in Leland and Faulconer, which was supplying engines at a high price. Fearing he might lose the Cadillac business, Leland found Studenbaker, in South Bend, Indiana. It had been building wagons for more than 50 years—everybody's pappy went West in a Conestoga—and was so anxious to get into automobiles, it agreed to pay L & F $15 more per engine than Cadillac, and to take 3000 the first year.

Leland's fears about Cadillac proved unfounded. Indeed, his son, Wilfred, took over plant management. By 1905, production and quality had increased dramatical-

ly and the Model 30, a four-cylinder luxury car was added. It was the little Cadillac Model B, though, that gained the respect of Europe for the first time. There, American manufactured goods were considered as cheap junk, built for low price and offering little utility.

Frederick Bennett, the Cadillac importer for England, took the first exported Cadillac virtually off the boat and won a local hillclimb/reliability trial, the first of many such victories. Still, there were complaints about parts and service difficulties, so Bennett swore to the Royal Automobile Club that Cadillacs needed no special "fitting,"

Depending on the manner in which you'd like to put things behind you, Ford builds four very different Mustangs that share one common denominator: The Mustang Spirit.

Mustang Convertible.

The only thing between you and blue sky is a matter of seconds. A power top with a glass rear window comes down with ease. But if you're not getting enough air, put your foot down and get a quick reply from either a 3.8 liter fuel-injected V-6 in Mustang LX Convertible, or a 5.0 liter V-8 in GT Convertible. *

Mustang GT.

If you think that 0-55 is the only thing Mustang GT* has going for it, you have another thing coming: Ford's Quadra-shock rear suspension system. Two vertically mounted gas-filled shocks plus two horizontally mounted axle dampers help stick GT to the road. Furthering the process are a 5-speed manual transmission and Goodyear "Gatorback" radials. And for good measure, there's new multi-port fuel injection.

Mustang LX.

There's very little left to the imagination in a Mustang LX. For one very realistic price you get: power rack and pinion steering, styled road wheels, speed control, full instrumentation, a 2.3 liter 4-cylinder engine, interval wipers, an AM/FM stereo with the premium sound package and more. And it's all standard for a price you can get away with in a Mustang.

Buckle up—together we can save lives.

Mustang SVO.

In creating Mustang SVO, we've thereby altered the balance of power on the road.

The idea was to build a very intelligent Mustang, not necessarily a very quick one. But as we found, the two are not mutually exclusive. Through technical triumph, Ford Special Vehicle Operations has developed a 2.3 liter turbocharged four-cylinder engine that produces almost three times more horsepower per cubic inch than the average American built V-8.** Equally as smart are a 5-speed manual overdrive transmission with special Hurst® linkage, Goodyear VR radials and four-wheel power-assisted disc brakes. All of which makes Mustang SVO a very intelligent way of putting everything else behind you.

Best-built American cars.

"Quality is Job 1." A 1985 survey established that Ford makes the best-built American cars. This is based on an average of problems reported by owners in the prior six months on 1981-1984 models designed and built in the U.S.

Lifetime Service Guarantee.

Participating Ford Dealers stand behind their work, in writing, with a free Lifetime Service Guarantee for as long as you own your Ford car or light truck. Ask to see this guarantee when you visit your participating Ford Dealer.

*Late availability. See your Ford Dealer for details.
**Based on SAE standard J-1349.

Have you driven a Ford...lately?

Ford Mustang.

tools or experts to repair. This was *absolutely* not the case with any European or British car (with the possible exception of Lanchester) and Bennett's claim was roundly disbelieved.

The RAC set up an elaborate experiment, running three Caddys around the new Brooklands race track, dismantling them, scrambling the parts, mixing in replacements, reassembling them, and subjecting them to a further 500 miles around the track. The cars passed in a breeze and won the Dewar trophy, the automotive Nobel Prize—the first American car to do so. The world favorably re-evaluated American products and methods of production and soon copied Leland's methods.

The same year, 1908, saw the emergence of "Billy" Durant. He was Flint, Michigan's leading citizen and salesman. What he sold, primarily, was confidence in William Crapo Durant; secondarily, he sold the products of Durant-Dort, the largest carriage manufacturer in the U.S. Both Durant and Dort had become millionaires as a result of his sales ability. He was the World's Foremost Expert in the mass marketing of personal transportation and had, in a relatively short time, surpassed Studebaker and Fisher to take that honor.

Durant got into the car business through Buick, one of many faltering car companies around then. David Dunbar Buick made a fortune in manufacturing bathtubs and spent it, and more, developing a motorcar. In the process, he got a patent for an overhead-valve engine, one of the first, but was still in trouble. Durant quadrupled capitalization by going to the banks, a strategy he would follow from then on. His exploitation of Wall Street is far more important in the story of the American car than, say, hydraulic brakes, or overhead cams. Largely on their confidence in his confidence, investors poured money into Buick each time Durant asked them to, and by 1908, it was the largest producer of cars in the world with 8489 units. Billy Durant was in business.

Henry Ford was the antithesis of Durant. He was a mechanic; Durant didn't care what made things work (though he cared when they didn't). Durant was outgoing and gregarious; Ford was introverted and shy. Durant played on Wall St.; Ford saw bankers as part of a huge, hazy conspiracy against which he was continually at war. Durant saw cars as counters in a game, a means to a further fortune; Ford was passionate about automobiles from the first moment he intuited their existence. Ford had already failed in two auto businesses before Durant allowed himself to be drawn into control of Buick. Ford wanted to change the world; Durant thought it was wonderful just as it was. Both Ford and Durant were relentless, capable of working 16-hour days for months on end, but they had almost nothing else in common, except the use of racing cars to build publicity.

Henry Ford ran from the isolation and grinding physical labor typical of farm life in central Michigan and gravitated to the mechanical jobs around the farm, finally escaping to Detroit to work with machinery full time. Beyond the barest fundamentals, he was self-educated. He eventually became chief engineer of the Detroit Electric Company, which in those days meant that he tended the boilers. He was 37 years old and lacked the price of a subscription to *Cycle Age*, but he built his first car in 1896, with advice from Charles King. It failed, and so did the second, but the American public came to know Ford as an almost mythic character. Durant is largely forgotten today. Not so in the fall of 1908.

While Ford, who had raised the money for his third venture into the car business in 1903, was starting production of the various models that preceded the Model T, Durant was creating an empire. First, with J. P. Morgan, Durant tried to create something called International Motors. When Morgan dropped out, Durant simply crossed out "International" and substituted "General." General Motors, in the person of W.C. Durant, immediately began trading its stock for that of Buick, acquired from, of course, W.C. Durant. He then put on his most persuasive face (Walter P. Chrysler, who got his start from Durant, said Billy "could charm a bird right down out of a tree") and within 90 days, about the end of 1908, Olds, Oakland, and Buick were all part of GM.

Durant sought to swallow other companies, including Ford and Cadillac. Cadillac, with Leland negotiating, wanted cash, no stock, thank you. In a few months the price had gone from $3,500,000 to $4,125,000 to $4,500,000. Cadillac had introduced the four-cylinder Model 30 and won the Dewar Trophy. Durant found the cash. It was a bargain—within a few months, Cadillac showed a profit of $2,000,000. Durant's offer of stock was scorned by Ford, who also wanted cash. After the Cadillac deal, Durant tried Ford

Ransom Eli Olds was the first auto mogul, pioneering volume production and the establishment of a far-flung dealer organization. A promoter, he staged successful publicity stunts and was among the first to use advertising to sell cars.

BBDO
An Advertising Revolution.

Captains of Industry in a rare group shot at an occasion lost to history. From left: Firestone, Rosenwald, Edison, Lipton, Schwab, Ford, Chrysler, Eastman and Wilson. That most of the men owed their fortunes to cars and related products shows the power of the auto business.

again (the price was $8,000,000—business was good) this time offering cash, but over two years. Ford said no thanks and changed the course of history. It is likely that he never really considered Durant's offer seriously.

Durant *was* able to buy (or trade for)—in addition to Cadillac, Olds and Oakland—AC Spark Plug, Weston-Mott, Reliance Truck, Ranier Motors, Michigan Motor Castings, Welsh Motor Cab, McLaughlin Motor Car, Ltd. (later GM of Canada), and a dozen more including Heany Lamp Co. of Columbus, Ohio. Once in his pocket, Durant preferred to leave the actual operation of the plants to others. He spent his time *dealing*. moving money around and rearranging stocks, trading and acquisition, and building growth. His dream was nothing so modest as that of his predecessors: he didn't want to build *a* car, he wanted to build them *all*.

By the summer of 1910, trouble was apparent. By fall it was obvious that GM was out of money. The banks got the scent of blood and began closing in. They had no confidence in the long-term existence of the automobile anyway. Durant triggered his own downfall by trading an enormous block of GM stock, more than had gone into the purchase of Buick and Cadillac combined, for Heany Lamp Co. Heany's chief asset was a piece of paper, a patent on the tungsten filament incandescent lamp. Durant wrapped up the deal, told everyone

not to worry, and went to England. By the time he returned, the banks had taken control of GM.

Many of Durant's companies were liquidated—Cartercar, Marquette, Welsh, Ranier. The Heany patent was challenged by General Electric and eventually overturned. General Motors Truck Company was formed from the bones of two other firms, and later became GMC. In Durant's absence, new names began to emerge. Charles Nash, whom Durant made head of Buick, became president of GM, his place at Buick was taken by Walter P. Chrysler. Intelligent business oversight came to General Motors and Buick in particular.

A snowball effect was taking place. As the industry concentrated around Detroit, rail transport improved to speed shipments of cars, suppliers moved closer to their customers, all sorts of people came, drawn by jobs and opportunity. Progress fed on it-

With 10 million Model Ts behind him, Henry Ford reflects on his first crude creation. There were still five million more Ts to go.

self: Charles Kettering at Delco perfected the self-starter (it was not the first); Bendix developed the starter drive; closed bodies made long-distance travel more practical; Oakland and Hupp began building all-steel (though open) bodies by 1912; and, in 1913, building on the success of his Model T, which he launched in 1908, Henry Ford introduced the moving assembly line in Highland Park, Michigan. Except for a few companies like Studebaker in Indiana, Willys in Toledo, and Pierce-Arrow in Buffalo, 90 percent of all the automobiles then made were built in the Detroit area.

And the whole time, Billy Durant was

When the Dodge brothers started making their own cars in 1914, they did it right, even building their own board track to test each car as it came off the line.

BOSS OF BOSSES

☐ *Executives in most industries tend to be as bland as their three-piece suits, and few emerge as public figures. The car business is an exception. Since the beginning, it's been dominated by forceful men whom history paints larger than life. Henry Ford, of course, is the archetype; independent to a fault, Ford ruled with an iron hand. He was outspoken, bold, decisive, controversial, arrogant, even eccentric at times, but he left no doubt as to who was boss. Billy Durant of General Motors was considerably more charming than Ford, but had the same kind of dominant personality, there was no questioning his authority. Neither hid behind a corporate facade and each spoke out publicly whenever it suited him.*

Of course, these men were the pioneers, the ones whose searing ambition was absolutely necessary to build the business. After they laid the foundations, another kind of leader was required, someone who could bring order to the chaos inevitably caused by exploding growth. Organization was needed more than entrepreneurship. This created a need for a different kind of boss, one who ruled by virtue of intellect, a man like Alfred Sloan, for instance. He too, though, was a public figure whose theories of management and corporate structure became the blueprint for American business.

Sloan's generation was followed by the managers, systems people who saw not cars, but numbers. That generation of executives also produced its public figures, most notably Robert McNamara, who went from the presidency of Ford to become Kennedy's Secretary of Defense.

But over the last couple of decades, it seemed that the car business had run out of people who could successfully step beyond the executive suite and become national figures. Except for one, Lido Anthony Iacocca.

Iacocca, in a fortuitous way, combines the virtues of all three types of auto executives: like Ford, he's a natural salesman who can make a TV pitch as well as any actor; and, like McNamara, he's a numbers type who can quickly find the shortest path to the bottom line.

Impressive as these qualifications may be, what makes Iacocca special is the aura of confidence, enthusiasm and leadership he projects. He's given credit for saving Chrysler, but, really, he didn't do anything that any other savvy businessman wouldn't have done: fire executives, lay off workers, close plants, and wheedle a bail-out loan from the government. That he did all these successfully is what sets him apart. His strength of character and imposing presence must have been the deciding factor when others were sinking into gloom and were ready to give up. It was Iacocca's ability to rally his troops and get them marching together that ensures his place in the long line of powerful individualists who built the American auto industry.

still at it. He may have been out, but he was not down, and certainly not broke. He financed Louis Chevrolet, a demon race driver, in designing a car, something to compete with the growing sales of the small Model T Ford. Chevrolet, however, wanted a big, luxury model and quit the project in anger, selling back the Chevrolet stock he got for his work and name. And he sold cheap. Chevrolet went on with his racing career but he never again had a role with the car that bore his name. He lived until 1941, reminded a million times a year of his poor judgement.

The Chevy went into production in a converted lamp plant in Detroit in 1912 and was an immediate hit. By 1913, Durant was using Chevy profits to buy GM stock, but very quietly. In 1915, Durant began trading five shares of Chevy for one of GM, and by year's end Chevy had so many GM stock certificates that it kept them in bushel baskets. On September 16, 1915, Durant, with the help of the DuPont family, regained control of GM, which was well on its way to becoming the world's largest corporation.

There was no more doubt, no doomsaying, about the future of the automobile. In the next few years Durant led GM into the refrigeration business (Frigidaire—a huge success), bought Delco (and Charles "Boss" Kettering), Hyatt Roller Bearing (and Alfred Sloan, Jr., who was to personify the modern GM), Harrison Radiator, and established United Motors Division. GM was in place.

There were repercussions from Durant's coup. Charles Nash, who rose to GM's

Dodge. The name stands for revolutionary vehicles. Vehicles with *total* performance, over-the-road and under the hood. And, once again for 1986, the Performance Division of Chrysler lives up to its name.

We offer a full line of clean, contemporary performers. Serious sports cars to be reckoned with, like the Daytona Turbo Z. Sedans that balance performance and comfort, like the Lancer ES. Cars that bring back the fun of open-air driving, like the 600 ES Turbo Convertible. And others that are as gutsy as they are affordable, like the Shelby Charger and Omni GLH.

In short, Dodge offers something for just about everyone.

THERE'S A REVOLUTION IN THE STREETS.

5/50 PROTECTION, STANDARD.

From our popular six-passenger Aries K, to our transportation revolution, Caravan. The original front-wheel drive mini-van, *still* unequaled by the competition.

We're also proud to say we offer the largest fleet of turbo models in America. So most Dodge cars you choose can be ordered with a turbocharger to give you impressive V-8 type performance while maintaining impressive fuel economy as well.

But, we don't just talk performance, we back it, with the most revolutionary thing of all. Dodge's standard 5/50 Protection Plan,* the longest warranty on any full line of American cars.

So if you want to get in on the performance revolution, see your Dodge dealer. Then take the streets by storm.

presidency in Durant's absence, left the company and took over the Jeffery plant in Wisconsin. Within eight months, Nash was the world's largest producer of trucks. And Walter P. Chrysler, who wanted to leave Buick, was persuaded to stay by Durant for $500,000 a year. A very few months before he was making $6000. Soon, Chrysler's salary was raised to $600,000, and, four years later, when he left to save Willys-Overland, he was paid a cool million for the year. That in a time when the average worker was making a few dollars a day and there was no income tax.

Lots of people were getting rich. A couple of red-headed brothers, John and Horace Dodge, made enormous fortunes building things for others—primarily Ford. Like Ford, the Dodges literally went barefoot as children in the Michigan winters. John's first job paid 50 cents a week. They worked for less than that in their father's blacksmith shop, learning their trade. Soon they owned a machine shop in Detroit, where, in 1901, they got a contract to build transmissions for the Curved Dash Olds, first on an emergency basis, then because they did the best work. They met Henry Ford about that time, and by 1910, Ford was the only customer Dodge had.

Friction developed, though, when Ford began freezing the design of the Model T, in spite of genuine improvements suggested by the Dodges, and the brothers decided to start their own car company. They had a contract to supply Ford parts through 1914 and built half-a-million Ford engines. Then, they opened their own plant and, in late 1914, the Dodge Brothers drove their first car off the line. It offered a lot more than the Model T for a bit ($100) more; all-steel body, electric lights and more modern springing. Not exactly stylish, it was at least available in a *range* of dowdy colors (Ford, of course, offered, "Any color you want, as long as it's black.") And to prove their cars, the Dodges built the first on-site test track in America and conducted crash tests. They were a resounding success.

Ford hated it and, in reaction, began planning the enormous River Rouge plant, the fruition of his dream, a factory where iron ore and coal came in at one end and finished cars out the other. Ford began planning for 2,000,000 cars a year. He poured capital into the new plant and refused to pay stock dividends.

The Dodges still owned 10 percent of the Ford Motor Co., however, and in 1916, took Ford to court. Ford had been there before, over the Selden Patent, the clever creation of a Buffalo patent attorney that had been used to charge people like Ford a royalty for each car made. Ford, just as cleverly, successfully challenged the patent, and won. This time though, the Dodges were victorious, and in spite of an appeal, forced Ford to pay a dividend of $1.9 million. It was the last straw, Ford saved his money and in 1919 bought out all

Louis Chevrolet (left, with no hat) watches the car bearing his name being driven away by Cliff Durant, whose father, William C. (portrait), financed the deal. Chevrolet never profited from having his name on the world's best-selling car line.

his stockholders, making multimillionaires of people who invested mere thousands, and becoming one of the most powerful men in the world.

World War I marked the beginning of the American Era that still waxes and wanes today. Henry Ford actually thought he could bring the war to an end. He outfitted a "peace ship," loaded with pacifists of every variety, and sailed to Europe to replace belligerence with reason. Reason found no takers and Ford sailed back, eventually gearing his plants to make fighting machines, as did the rest of the industry. The energy that went into making cars was soon put to producing guns, ships and all the other hardware of battle, doing it cheaper, faster, and better than ever before. It was a complete vindication of the American system of mass production, and settled the question of hand artisanship versus precision machine production.

The war also put many of the marginal auto manufacturers—assemblers, really—out of their misery and further concentrated car making in the Detroit area. And, with the resumption of normality, the car business returned to turmoil as usual. The Lelands, father and son, left Cadillac to found Lincoln; in 1920, both Dodge brothers died, and Walter P. Chrysler left GM for retirement. Charlie Nash turned Rambler into Nash, and founded what would (with Hudson) become American Motors.

The Dodges' heirs were their widows, and far more suited to lavish eccentricities than the running of the giant factory. F.J. Haynes became president and continued to build the business, absorbing Graham Brothers Truck Co., and allowing the brothers themselves to build the Graham automobile, which lasted till World War II. Joseph Frazer came to run the Graham organization, and would appear after the war as a partner in another doomed enterprise, Kaiser-Frazer.

In the depressed period after World War I, Walter Chrysler was lured out of retirement, by a consortium of bankers, to save Willys-Overland, which he did. Willys would later go on to fame with the Jeep in 1940, when American Bantam, which built the prototype, turned out to have insufficient production capacity. Though Ford built Jeeps too, the Willys credit stuck.

Durant left GM forever near the end of 1920. He put it together and made it work, producing cars across the entire price spectrum, but went bankrupt trying to support GM stock during the postwar depression. Durant tried a comeback, putting together a few firms—Star, Flint, and Locomobile among them—but his luck had run out. He died penniless in 1947, the same year that Ford died a billionaire.

Pierre DuPont became the unwilling president of GM (he had retired as head of DuPont). Under him, then Alfred P. Sloan, General Motors became what it was until the Arab oil embargo of 1973—the world's largest corporation. It remains the world's largest manufacturer. Sloan restructured GM, instituted the annual model change, and made it possible for a buyer to move up from one GM car to another as he grew older and more affluent. It was the opposite of the Ford idea (also popular in Europe) of a single model with improvements only as needed. Sloan's policy prevailed and despite the occasional VW, continues to this day.

While W.P. Chrysler was whipping Willys, and later Maxwell, into shape for the bankers, he was making plans for his own company. His first car appeared in 1924, a compact, stylish six. Its Zeder-Breer-Skelton-designed engine gave it better performance than many more expensive cars, though Chrysler enhanced it by using "optimistic" speedometers, and within a few years, Chryslers were competing for AAA stock car honors with Stutz, Auburn, and Cole—all higher priced. Chrysler even had a near-successful try at Le Mans against the likes of Bentley, Alfa and Mercedes.

While the rest of the industry was percolating with innovation, Henry Ford took a different view. He really seemed to believe his beloved Model T would go on forever. It must have come as shock when, in 1927, Chevrolet took his sales leadership away. Ford had been done in by city ways—smoothness, sophistication, styling, the annual model change, a sliding gear transmission, good ride, weather protection. He could no longer combat his adversaries by lowering prices (the T got down to $260 for a stripped roadster, FOB Dearborn) and pressuring his dealers.

The last Model T rolled off the line on May 21, 1927. In 19 years Ford had built 15,007,003 of the cars and changed the face of the world. It was a hard act to follow. The car that replaced the T, the Model A, was the victim of incomplete design and tooling. Though Ford's men (and many of the best had left by then) were geniuses at production, they were novices at making annual model changes. The Model A, consequently, was actually less than just another car. Plymouth had "floating power" and four-wheel hydraulic brakes; Chevy had overhead valves; and Ford's cars still had solid axles, transverse leaf springs, and mechanical brakes. Even Ford's 1932 V-8, was too little, too late. It wasn't until a decade after Henry's death in 1947 that Ford was able to consistently challenge Chevrolet, and by then its early leadership was lost forever.

The seeds for what came to be known as The Big Three—Chrysler, Ford and GM—were sown by the beginning of the Depression, but there were still a hundred loose ends. Henry Ford's regime grew more crackpot day by day. Mighty Dodge still floated almost in an automotive limbo. Packard, Cadillac, and Lincoln were still being challenged by the Peerless, Pierce-Arrow, Franklin, and even more marginal makes like McFarlan, Cunningham, Locomobile, Rolls-Royce (built in Springfield, Mass.), and Duesenberg (to say nothing of Kissel, Cole, Gardner, Mercer, Stutz, Doble, and at least a half dozen more, all trying to make a profit in the high-priced arena). Chrysler's Imperial would soon join them. By Pearl Harbor, only Packard, Cadillac, Lincoln and Imperial would remain.

There had been thousands of nameplates on the market between 1900 and December 7, 1941—perhaps two hundred had survived more than a year. Outside of the 12 badges used by the Big Three (DeSoto and Mercury were the last creations to plug market holes), there remained, by the war, only five *real* auto compaines—Studebaker, Hudson, Nash, Packard and Willys. Hupp and Graham were officially in business, but produced only the tiniest trickle of cars from the revamped Cord 810 dies. Down in Cincinnati, Powell Crosley had gone into the minicar business, replacing Austin/Bantam in the lost-cause department. The little guys could not buck the power and

Walter P. Chrysler (left) trotted out his management team for the unveiling of his first car in 1924. Before, Chrysler worked at GM and then saved Willys and Maxwell from bankruptcy. George Mason (third from the right) later went on to head Nash.

organization of the big companies, which just continued to grow stronger.

Dodge was sold in 1925 by the widows to Dillon, Read and Co., for $146,000,000 "and no cents." Less than three years later, Chrysler bought it for $170,000,000, slotting Dodge above the new Plymouth. DeSoto was later inserted between Dodge and Plymouth, and still later, moved above Dodge.

In 1939, Ford brought out the Mercury to combat Dodge, DeSoto, Pontiac and Olds. The "Merc" was just a slightly larger Ford, but did give the affluent Ford buyer a place to stop on the way to the Lincoln Zephyr V-12. The Lelands, it may be recalled, started Lincoln and made it one of the world's finest-made (though conservative-looking) automobiles. Quality, of course, has never been a guarantee of success in the auto business, and by 1922 Lincoln was in receivership. Ford bought it for $8,000,000, promising the Lelands a perpetual role in the company. It wasn't six months before the dictatorial, arbitrary Ford management caused an irrevocable split and the Lelands left, fading forever from the scene. Lincoln, however, at least got Ford into the V-8 business. Still, by the late 1930s, the big K-Series Lincolns had fallen far behind Cadillac and Packard, and the Zephyr became more a competitor to the mid-range Buick and Olds rather than a luxury car. Despite slick styling and its smooth V-12, it was really no match for the competition.

By the end of World War II, the manufacturers who were still around had made fortunes from military contracts and were ready for peace. General Motors was firmly set in the tracks laid by Sloan; Chrysler had established a reputation for engineering excellence which would last long after the reality had expired; and Ford weathered the demise of Henry, and the succession of Henry II, with the help of a new breed of business managers. Still, it was with some trepidation that the Detroit establishment viewed the entry of Kaiser-Frazer into the car wars. Henry Kaiser had made fortunes in construction, cement,

TOP:
Packard established an enviable reputation with cars like this 1930 745 Victoria, but it floundered after WWII and went under.

ABOVE:
Horace Dodge (left) and brother John take the air in the rear of one of their first cars. Their widows inherited vast fortunes.

Back in 1940 when hats were in fashion, GM rolled out its 25-millionth car. Onlookers included future GM president, C.E. "Engine Charlie" Wilson. As Eisenhower's defense secretary, he caught heat for saying: "What's good for GM is good for the country."

LEFT:
In 1942, Alfred P. Sloan (left) and Charles F. Kettering reminisce over Kettering's original 1912 self-starter.

steel, shipbuilding, and aluminum. He had the clout to take on Detroit. With his money (he bought Willys and extensive production facilities), Joseph Frazer's experience, and the talent of people like designer Howard "Dutch" Darrin, Kaiser posed the first really serious threat to the Big Three in many years.

But, by the time Darrin's glamorous prototypes became reality, they were dull and conventional. The compact Henry J was off the mark, and when the stylish, by the standards of day, 1951 Kaisers came out, it was too late and the competition too strong. Kaiser had missed his chance and went under.

The other independents—Studebaker, Packard, Hudson and Nash—were on the abyss. An attempt was made to combine all four into a strong fourth corporation, sharing engineering and production, but making different cars. It never happened. Pack-

ard, with cash and depth in engineering and styling, said no. It would squander these assets, however, and beyond 1956 there would be no more "real" Packards. A merger with Studebaker produced a travesty with the Packard name on it for a few more years, but no one cared.

Studebaker, an archly conservative company, unaccountably spent its last big dollar to develop a small, uncompetitive V-8. Even its brilliantly-styled sporty 1953 coupes were completely misunderstood by management and marketing types who kept waiting for sanity and two-pants suits (with pants held up by belt *and* suspenders) to return. Sales flagged until 1959 when the Lark—a cleverly done compact that required very little new tooling—gave Studebaker the will to live a little longer. The Lark's claim to fame seemed to be that it was the largest compact.

Sherwood Egbert almost pulled Studebaker from the brink. He inspired the Gran Turismo Hawk and Avanti, as well as the use of disc brakes, superchargers, sunroofs, tachometers, racing promotion, reclining seats and a general European influence. Tragically, Egbert, still in his forties, died. Studebaker wrung concessions from the U.S. and Indiana governments, then moved to Canada for more free lunch. The

last Studebakers, now with Chevy engines, trickled out in 1966.

Without Packard and Studebaker, Nash (which had some success with its compact Rambler) and Hudson (whose compact Jet was a failure) entered an alliance of desperation, called American Motors. It survived for a time on the strength of a new, larger Rambler, which was so successful it nearly got George Romney a nomination for the Presidency. Hudson finally disappeared, after its flathead six was used in the grossly swollen ex-Pinin Farina, Nash Ambassador bodies in 1956. The Nash badge was scuttled soon after in favor of AMC-Rambler, then just AMC.

AMC bought Jeep from Kaiser, Excalibur and Avanti went into the specialty car business, and unheard of companies like Volkswagen started to became major factors in domestic sales. Volvo began to show an interest in opening a major factory in the U.S., and both VW and Volvo were making their major profits here. In 1958 Datsun imported a few peculiar little cars. In 1960, America got a look at Toyopets with brocade upholstery and clip-on, battery-powered vacuum cleaners under the seats. Nobody paid much attention, especially in Detroit. The second Pearl Harbor was under way and, like the first, we waited for it to happen.

The next chapter—some say the last—will be played outside of Detroit—by VWs from Pennsylvania, Nissans from Tennessee, hybrids from California. We now buy automobiles with traditional American names that have major components from France, Brazil, Japan, Korea. Things have changed. Billy Durant wouldn't have cared. Henry Ford wouldn't have approved. And Alfred P. Sloan would just have nodded sagely and capitalized on the situation at every turn. **MT**

500 MILES TO GLORY

The Indianapolis 500 was meant to be a test of machines, but men found their limits there as well.

By Donald Davidson

☐ One of the centers of the fledgling American automobile industry right after the turn of the century was Indianapolis. It ranked fourth in 1908 in cars produced, and by 1913 had climbed to second. It was during these years that the great Indianapolis Motor Speedway was born.

Carl Graham Fisher was an astute local businessman and entrepreneur. Brilliant ideas for seeking publicity for his various projects sprang from his fertile mind as frequently as cuds of chewed tobacco landed in his spittoon. With hardly any publicity for himself (usually by design), he was eventually to head up the Highway Association (which planned the first coast-to-coast highway), construct both the Lincoln and Dixie Highways, develop Miami Beach, and build the Indianapolis track.

Downtown lunch companions of his usually included executives from the automobile manufacturing companies, and Carl would often muse that none of them had any kind of a testing facility to try out their products. Certainly the rutty, unpaved streets of the city and the surrounding neighborhoods were hardly conducive to more than a fraction of the speeds these new creations could attain, so Fisher visu-

alized a race track, a speedway. He was a keen amateur racing driver himself and he had been to Europe and seen the importance of motorsports to the industry over there. If a track could be built not too far from the center of town, he reasoned, the manufacturers would have a testing ground they could rent at any time. Better than that, a series of races could occasionally be organized to provide the finest testing of all: head-to-head competition. Spectators could pay a nominal admission, be entertained by the racing, and presumably remember the winners the next time they were in the market for a new automobile.

The race track concept was in Fisher's mind for several years before he finally formed a corporation in the fall of 1908, with three friends (actually four, but Stoughton Fletcher, the banker who arranged the financing, dropped out when he

decided his involvement might be a conflict of interest).

The partners were Frank Wheeler, Arthur Newby and James Allison. Wheeler headed up the Wheeler-Schebler Carburetor Company, Newby was president of the National Motor Vehicle Company (a very prominent early-day make from Indianapolis), and Allison had several businesses which would eventually evolve into the Allison Division of General Motors and the multi-million dollar Detroit Diesel Allison Company of today.

During the spring of 1909, the sheep-grazed acreage of the old Pressley farm on Crawfordsville pike, six miles northwest of town, was transformed into a two-and-a-half-mile speedway. A pair of parallel straights, each five-eighths of a mile long, and two short straights of one-eighth of a mile apiece were joined together by four sweeping turns that measured precisely 440 yards each from entrance to exit. In fact, the designer had started out with a one-mile circle and simply kept extending his straightaways until he felt he had reached the reasonable limits within the space available. Fisher had originally envisioned a three-mile layout (plus a road course extension through the infield!), but the track would have been pushed too close to the boundaries of the property.

The first competition ever held at the Speedway took place on June 5 and it was, of all things, a hot-air balloon race. Considerable publicity was drummed up and the people came out in droves, perhaps 40,000 strong. Unfortunately, the turnstiles didn't click that many times because the cautious locals had figured out that they could witness the greater part of a balloon ascent from *outside* the grounds. Nevertheless, the track was getting the wide attention Fisher sought.

Sadly, motorcycle races and a three-day automobile racing program (comprising dozens of races, mostly brief sprints for different classes all run off in quick succession) were near-disasters. The main problem was that in spite of all the thought and care that had gone into the construction of the facility, the choice of the surface itself was somewhat ill-advised. The combination of crushed rock and tar hardly lent itself to prolonged tire wear, so numerous crashes ensued. A driver and a riding mechanic lost their lives in one spill and—after an out-of-control machine mowed down and killed some spectators at the south end of the track during the final day's 300-mile grind—the race was halted, the rest of the program canceled, and the track closed.

An ambitious resurfacing program was undertaken a month later, first by covering over the crushed rock and tar with a bed of sand and then by laying no less than 3,200,000 "bat" bricks, each weighing about nine and a half pounds. They were placed on their sides, staggered in rows and "bound" by mortar. Skilled workers were enthusiastically laying an average of 140,000 bricks during nine-hour shifts, and

TOP:
Before the 500, a number of races were held at Indy at shorter distances. The first one, a 100-miler, was won, from a standing start, by Strong (history does not recall his first name) in car #33.

ABOVE:
Ray Harroun, winner of the first Indy 500 in 1911, used a mirror instead of a riding mechanic to watch the rear. Though given credit for a first, Harroun said he saw mirrors used on horse buggies in 1904.

the entire job was completed on December 10, 1909, having taken just 63 days!

Once some brick-christening speed runs had been successfully conducted in freezing cold weather just before Christmas, Fisher announced that a trio of two- and three-day meets would take place on the weekends of Memorial Day, July 4, and Labor Day in 1910. The three programs were conducted with great success from an artistic and safety point of view, but the crowds were often far below expectations, as few as 6,000 showing up on one particular day. Perhaps the answer was instead to channel all of the time, effort and resources into a single, grandiose affair for 1911.

Not a little consideration was given to holding a 24-hour race, similar to those being conducted in other parts of the country. The manufacturers themselves certainly favored such a contest. Instead, Fisher and his partners agreed that something starting mid-morning and concluding late afternoon, something, say, in the region of seven hours, would be more appropriate for holding a paying spectator's attention. Having calculated that approximately 500 miles could be covered in that time, the distance itself evidently had a magic ring .

A 500-mile race, "the greatest, most demanding speed contest ever yet devised," was scheduled for May 30, 1911. Entry blanks were made available in October, 1910, and the first ones were filled out within days. By the time the April deadline arrived, 46 had been submitted, and only two of those proved to be "no shows." The track was opened for practice on May 1st and made available daily thereafter.

Qualifications were conducted on May 26 and 29 as contestants were required to average 75 miles per hour through a quarter-mile speed trap down the main straight from a flying start in order to be included in the field. The 40 cars that succeeded were then lined up and numbered, not according to speeds, but the order in which they had been entered, except for the flourishing local Marmon company, which was granted a concession. Marmon was currently marketing a *Model 32* passenger car and they thought it would be great publicity for that number to be carried on Ray Harroun's car in the race. The fact that it would have to start in 28th position was of little concern. It went on to win the first *500*.

Fisher's belief that success by firms at the track would boost their car sales certainly worked for Marmon. In fact, they were now so firmly on the map that they decided to shut down their racing operation for fear that any lesser accomplishment in the future might tarnish their elevated stature. But the idea of testing passenger cars themselves in racing had already become somewhat outmoded. Sure, Harroun's car had been built at the Marmon factory, but it hardly resembled anything one could see in the showrooms.

Harroun, who lived unil 1968, when he was almost 90, had several nicknames, including "The Little Professor." In 1910 he designed a Marmon for racing that had no provisions for a riding mechanic, for with no rule requiring a second person, he reasoned that not only would the elimination save about 160 pounds of unnecessary weight, but a narrow-bodied centrally located single-seater would cut through the air with greater ease than anything else. His creation carried him to the 1910 AAA National Championship, and during the winter, this was the car he readied for the first *500*.

Shortly before race day, Harroun was advised that some of the competitors were complaining of his being a potential hazard with no riding mechanic to look behind and advise him of an impending pass on

ABOVE:
Ralph DePalma was leading by five and a half laps in 1912 when the engine in his Mercedes blew on lap 199. He pushed to no avail. Local boy Joe Dawson kept charging, made up the deficit, and won.

RIGHT:
In 1913, French ace Jules Goux, drank a split of Champagne at every pit stop, six of them. He went on to drive his state-of-the-art Peugeot to the biggest winning margin ever, 13 minutes and eight seconds.

Introducing the Bosch
There hasn't been a break
but you can feel the

Compared to all the changes in cars since their invention, the spark plugs that help power those cars really haven't changed much at all.

That is, until now.

Introducing Bosch Platinum Spark Plugs. They're not just new plugs. They're the *ultimate* plugs.

They'll outperform conventional copper-core plugs by *far*. At 0 mph or flat-out, in high temperatures or cold.

That's because the combination of platinum and our new extended insulator design results in a lower ignition voltage requirement and wider heat range than the copper or nickel that's found in

The 99.9% pure platinum center electrode plus our new extended insulator design gives the Bosch Platinum plug a wider heat range than any copper plug. And the effective gap between its electrode and tip remains virtually unchanged over the life of the plug.

© 1985 Robert Bosch Corporation. Sales Group.

conventional spark plugs. So at lower speeds, where many plugs foul, new Bosch Platinum Spark Plugs burn themselves clean.

And at temperatures where other plugs might miss, the new Bosch Platinum Spark Plugs continue to deliver full power.

You enjoy better starting and miss-free acceleration. Plus a maintenance-free plug. And, because our new design affords the spark better access to the air/fuel mixture, you save more fuel too.

Pick up a set today. There hasn't been a breakthrough like this in 125 years, but you can feel the difference in seconds.

The Ultimate Spark Plug.

BOSCH

This Duesenberg is typical of the Indy cars of the '20s. The Duesenberg brothers used the track to test their street vehicles between races, and also won the race three times (in 1924, '25 and '27).

either side. He silenced critics by bolting some rods to the sides of the cowling and securing a three-by-eight-inch mirror to the tips so that it was just above his sightline. He was often credited thereafter with having "invented" the rear-view mirror, although he was always quick to note that he had seen one used on a horse-drawn taxi in Chicago in 1904 (during his days as a chauffeur for William Thorne, President of Montgomery Ward), and thought it was a good idea. He was, no doubt, the first to use one on an automobile, however.

The success of the first Indianapolis *500* was far-reaching from the outset and the race has been held every year since, with the exception of the war years 1917 and 1918 and 1942 through 1945.

The passenger car concept had taken a bit of a beating during the 1911 race not only because of the special Marmon but more because some excellent performances were turned in by, horror of horrors, *foreign* Grand Prix cars that well-to-do American sportsmen had imported from Europe. In 1912, one of them darn near won. Italian-born Ralph DePalma, who did not become an American citizen until 1920, drove E.J. Schroeder's gigantic chain-driven Mercedes into the lead on the third lap and steadily built a margin of five and a half laps over second place during the next six and a half hours. With the crowd already steadily filing through the exits as DePalma reeled off his final laps, shouts went up as he was seen to be slow-

ing down. A connecting rod had snapped and punched a hole in the crankcase, forcing the oil to be dumped onto the race track. DePalma pressed on, slower and slower, desperately trying to make it to the finish line. He was entering the fourth turn of his 199th lap when his stricken German monster ground to a halt. He and his riding mechanic then jumped down from their seats and began to push the Mercedes through the turn and down the straight.

Local boy Joe Dawson, driving a National (built not six miles from the track at Newby's Indianapolis factory), was frantically unlapping himself every one minute and 50 seconds or so. Finally he made up the deficit and came home to win as DePalma and his mechanic were still struggling many yards from the finish line. To everyone's amazement, the cheers for DePalma's effort were greeted by smiles and waves from the Italian. It transpired that he was under somewhat of a misunderstanding, believing he was in his final lap and that he was so far ahead he would be able to push home and win. The cheering, he thought, was encouraging him to do just that. Having arrived to learn that (a) he needed a another full lap and (b) Dawson had already won, some of the sportsmanship for which he was famous may have temporarily ceased. Nevertheless, he was quick to seek out Dawson for hearty congratulations, something the bashful and astounded Dawson could never get over.

Prize money in the early years was paid

only to the first 12 finishers, with nothing posted for 13th position on down. It was also necessary to complete the full 500 miles, so those hoping to place within the leading dozen might be on the track long after the winner had finished. The attrition rate was quite high in 1912, DePalma's late breakdown reducing the runners to only ten. Finally, only Ralph Mulford's pit stop-plagued chain-driven Knox remained. Mulford, a Sunday school teacher who raced in a white shirt and bow tie, suggested to the officials that he should be flagged in and given tenth position, but they felt compelled to stand by the rules. There is a frequently printed version of this story that has Mulford walking to a hot dog stand with his riding mechanic while "the crowd rolled in the aisles," which is utter nonsense. The hot dog was not introduced for another 20 years, and besides, the crowd at the Speedway had long since departed for home. What happened was one of the mechanics brought in a hamper of food from one of the few remaining passenger cars in the infield, and the famished crew munched on chicken and sandwiches for a few minutes in front of deserted

TOP:
Jack Brabham showed up in 1961 in a tiny, underpowered, rear-engined Cooper. The Indy establishment laughed. He finished ninth. In 1965, Jim Clark won in a rear-engined Lotus and by 1967 there wasn't a single front-engined car in the starting field.

ABOVE AND LEFT:
The Granatelli brothers, Vince (above in helmet) and Andy, came oh-so-close with their radical turbine cars. Parnelli Jones (left) and Joe Leonard (kneeling, above) nearly won in 1967 and 1968; both were leading when their cars broke.

stands and a few agitated officials. Mulford did finish the race, just before sundown, collecting the $1,200 posted for tenth position. His elapsed time was eight hours and 53 minutes and his average speed was 56.29 miles per hour as he crossed the line for the final time two hours and 31 minutes after Dawson had won the race.

There was one final item of business for 1912. With prize money for 11th and 12th positions posted and not contested, Fisher's people decided to divide it among those who had failed to finish, proportionately according to the distance each had covered. DePalma, therefore, was consoled with $380 he had not expected, while Len Ormsby, whose car failed after only five laps, was rewarded with the smallest amount of prize money ever paid by the track, the princely sum of $9.61.

Ever expanding his horizons, Fisher now sought to make the Indianapolis *500* a truly international affair, and through the considerable efforts of the English motoring correspondent, W.F. Bradley, a number of foreign entries arrived in 1913. One of them, a Peugeot driven by Jules Goux, not only won the race but did so by the greatest margin in history. During his first pit stop, officials were horrified to note that Goux, wearing leather riding boots and a checkered cap pulled on backwards, had stepped from the car and was sharing

with his riding mechanic the contents of a pint bottle of champagne that had been chilling in a nearby ice bucket. Hurried consultation took place just after he had left and the officials were told by an interpreter that this was Goux's normal procedure during European races. Not wanting to spark an international incident, the officials somewhat reluctantly agreed to turn a blind eye during all of Goux's six pit stops, and ultimately he won by a margin of 13 minutes and eight seconds. He rolled into Victory Lane, proclaimed, "Sans le bon vin, je ne serais pas été en état de faire la victoire" (Without the good wine, I would not have been able to win), and by the time the second-place Mercer made it home, Goux and his partner had already consumed a seventh bottle.

The Europeans continued to compete at Indianapolis for another decade, and their designs unquestionably influenced the appearance of the American racing cars and engines. Most of the domestic passenger car firms had dropped out after the first couple of *500s*, leaving the race to be dominated by foreign cars, both factory entered and locally owned. The home front honor was pretty much upheld after WWI by the Chevrolet Brothers, through an assortment of firms, and the Duesenberg Brothers, who had relocated from Des Moines, Iowa and had a thriving business going in Indi-

PHOTO: BOB D'OLIVO

anapolis. The Duesenbergs continued to use the Speedway for its original intent, often driving passenger cars and racing cars to and from their West Washington Street plant for testing.

Cars in the *500* had become more and more specialized, and the technical advances of the 1920s have caused many historians to consider this period "The Golden Age" of the American racing car. Harry Miller, for instance, became the dominant race-car builder. He had no passenger vehicles for sale. If one aspired to be the winning car owner at Indianapolis, one went to Harry Miller and placed a special order for a 100 percent, thoroughbred racing car that utilized ideas which might *someday* find a way into the car on the street.

The maximum cubic-inch displacement allowable in 1911 and 1912 had been 600. That had been chopped to 450 in 1913, and was down to 122 by 1924. In spite of the cuts, the speeds kept going up, so in 1926 a further reduction was made to 91½ cubic inches. The supercharger had come into common use and the new cars were front-driven affairs, sleek and low-slung, with the driver sitting only a few inches from the ground. In 1928, the colorful "Flying Frenchman," Leon Duray (who was really a Philadelphian named George Stewart), lapped the Speedway in one, officially at over 124 miles per hour!

The word was that engine sizes were going to be reduced even further to 60 cubic inches in 1930, but a series of circumstances prevented that from ever coming about. Instead, in an effort to encourage the use of American production engines, it was suddenly increased to 366 cubic inches and the use of supercharging was ruled out for the time being. The announcement in January 1929 was most timely. Not many months later, some of the more affluent car owners lost their investments in the Wall Street crash, and the result was that a few converted non-supercharged front- and rear-drive Millers showed up in 1930 to be accompanied by an assortment of inexpensive "backyard" specials, ushering in what was labeled as the "junk" era.

Chet Miller, later to gain considerable notoriety as driver of one of the Novi racing cars, was making his first of sixteen *500* starts in 1930. The car he drove was built almost entirely of Ford Model T parts at an estimated cost of about $2,300. During the race, Miller was prevented from returning to the fray after a pit stop because an eagle-eyed official had noted that his front right spring was broken. Miller argued that his driving was compensating for the problem, but the official remained adamant. Forty-three minutes later, Chet was able to return to the race in spite of the fact that the team possessed no spares. A journal of the day reported that the mechanics had found an unattended Model T in the parking area and had "borrowed" a spring. After finishing the race they were able to reinstall it, apparently without the owner's awareness of the transaction.

Racing at Indianapolis survived the depression of the 1930s, and sophisticated racing cars again began to dominate the fields. Supercharging was permitted once more in 1937, and Jimmy Snyder, a Chicago milkman, promptly turned the first 130-mile-per-hour lap of the track's history

Times change. Short-sleeve shirts and baggy pants offer scant protection for Paul Russo's 1959 pit crew. Today's crews, like 500 winner Tom Sneva's in 1983, dress for safety like the drivers.

Only 49 men have stood in the Indy winners circle. Just a dozen, including Rick Mears here, have done it more than once.

WHEN A LEGEND RETURNS TO THE INTERNATIONAL ARENA, IT'S AN HONOR TO PLAY A SUPPORTING ROLE.

EAGLE. ENGINEERED FOR CARS

GOODYEAR SALUTES THE INTRODUCTION OF THE 1985 FERRARI TESTAROSSA.

*P255/50VR16

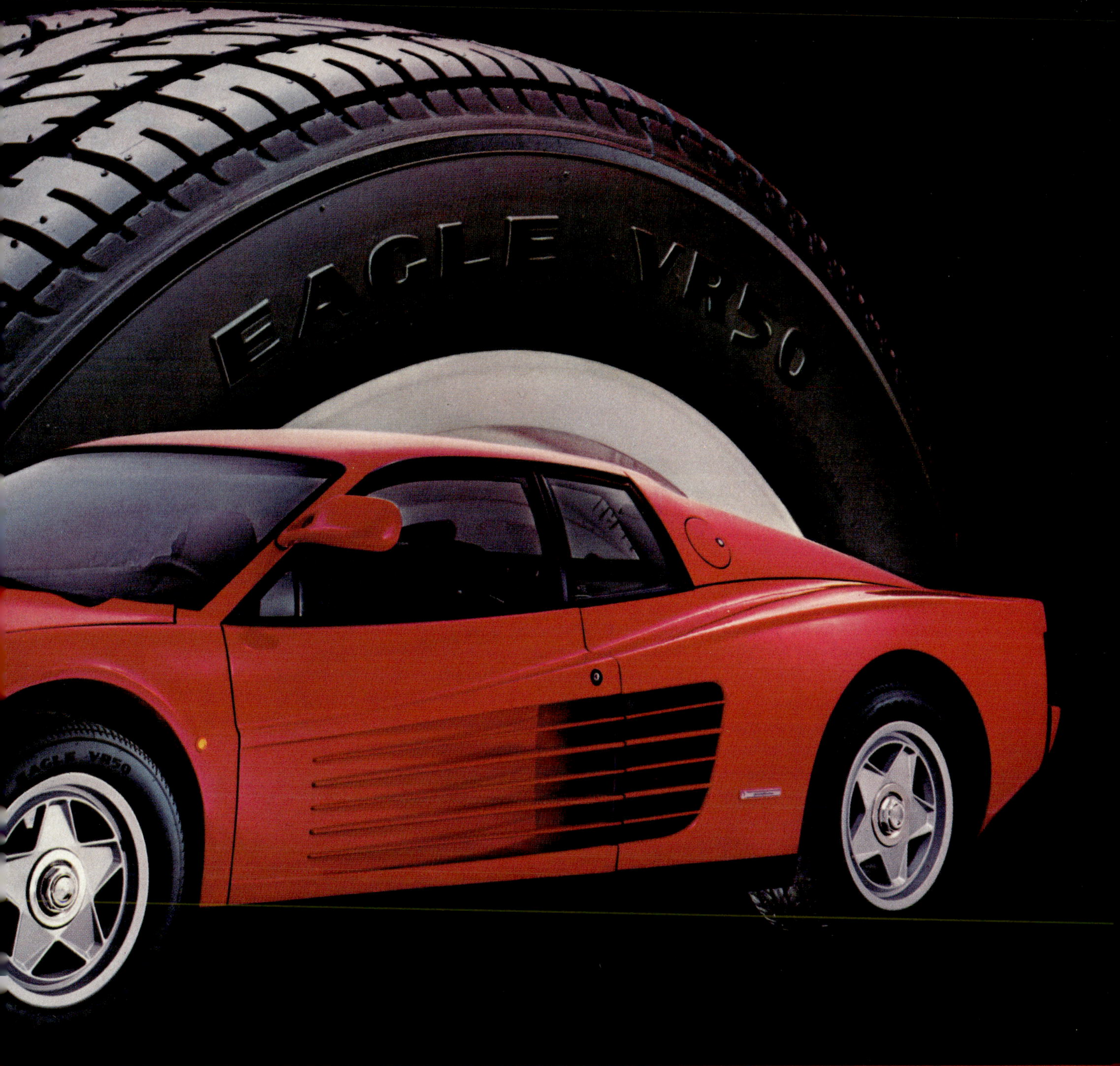

WITH THE PROPER QUALIFICATIONS.

The name alone is enough to quicken the hearts of most automotive enthusiasts.

But the 1985 Testarossa isn't just riding on the reputation of its famous predecessor.

It has already been dubbed the fastest production car in the world. The 12-cylinder, 48-valve engine delivers 380 horsepower—enough to cover the standing quarter-mile in 13.8 seconds at a blistering 108 m.p.h.

Needless to say, when you design a car with these capabilities, you choose your tires carefully. Which is why we are quite proud that Ferrari selected the Goodyear Eagle VR 50.

Of course, the Eagle VR 50, like the Testarossa, is a product of the racing circuit. Its unidirectional tread design is derived from our Formula One racing rain tire. And in special skid pad tests of lateral acceleration in 1982 the VR 50* was the first street tire to record .95g.

So although our selection as the original equipment tire on the 1985 Ferrari Testarossa is indeed an honor, it isn't entirely surprising.

After all, we've been working rather hard at creating a legend of our own.

GOODYEAR

with a six-cylinder supercharged Sparks-engined car.

Carl Fisher had long since disposed of the track, having found more and more of his time occupied by other interests. He turned the presidency of the track over to Allison in 1924, and three years later the group sold the facility. Eddie Rickenbacker, who had driven in five of the first six Indianapolis classics and returned from WWI as America's flying ace to form an automobile firm in Detroit, arranged for the purchase of the track and became its new president.

In 1936 Rickenbacker commenced some much-needed track renovation, most notably by covering over some of the increasingly rough portions of brick surface with asphalt and by altering the angle of the retaining wall. The concrete had originally been installed at a 90-degree angle to the ground rather than to the angle of the banking, which was fine for the early days. As the speeds increased, however, the wall began to take on more the role of a launching ramp, and surviving newsreel footage of the 1930s shows a number of cars vaulting completely over the top, an increasingly chronic problem until Rickenbacker had it solved by revising the wall angle.

In spite of Rickenbacker's input, he too was losing interest in the track. He became president of Eastern Airlines and started getting wrapped up in government affairs as hostilities in Europe intensified once more. He shut the track down right after the bombing of Pearl Harbor and canceled the 1942 race, for which entry blanks had just been mailed.

As the war progressed, Wilbur Shaw, who had won the *500* in 1937, '39 and '40, was sent to the Speedway to test tires for Firestone. He was appalled by the way the track had been allowed to deteriorate and, upon learning that Rickenbacker was ready to sell, went on a virtual one-man campaign to find a purchaser. He discovered that numerous companies were interested in the track, but he feared they sought "product exclusivity" so he strove to find someone who would operate it with no such restrictions.

That someone turned out to be gentle, unassuming Anton "Tony" Hulman of Terre Haute, who stepped in on November 14, 1945, and purchased the delapidated plant for a reported $700,000.

The unpretentious Hulman, who in the early 1920s had starred at Yale in football and track and field, was in the wholesale grocery business, owning, among other products, Clabber Girl baking powder. Other holdings over the years included the gas companies in Terre Haute and Richmond, office buildings in Evansville and Dayton, a brewery, and later, the Coca Cola bottling business in Indianapolis. He had attended his first *500* in 1914, adored automobiles and was easily swayed by Shaw's plea that the track needed rescuing.

The 1946 race was hurriedly arranged. On race day, gigantic traffic jams created havoc for several hours as an astounded

A.J. Foyt

No other driver in Indianapolis history has a record to compare with that of A.J. Foyt. The fiery, tempestuous yet compassionate and privately generous Texan is the only four-time winner of the 500 and also the only driver to have won in both front- and rear-engine cars. He has had more starts than anyone else (an unbelievable 28 consecutive through 1985), more completed race laps (3,996), more different years of race leadership (13), more top-ten finishes (14, which is more than most drivers have had starts), and he remains in striking position (along with Al Unser) to exceed Ralph DePalma's half-century-old record of the greatest number of laps led. The 595 and 555 of Unser and Foyt respectively rank second and third to DePalma's 613. Additionally, Foyt is the only driver other than Rex Mays to have started from the pole position four times.

Bobby Unser

Ever seeking the technical or psychological advantage over his peers, the tirelessly competitive and optimistic Bobby Unser compiled one of the greatest careers in Indianapolis history. He led 440 laps in 10 of his 19 starts and won the race 3 times. He started from the front row 9 times and failed to rank among the 10 fastest qualifiers only twice. Each win came in a different decade ('68, '75 and '81) and he won from the pole in what turned out to be his last start. His 2,611 race laps rank as the fourth highest number ever completed.

Al Unser

Called by Mario Andretti "the most race-savvy driver out there," the steady and phenomenally successful Al Unser ranks either first or second with A.J. Foyt in every major 500 statistical category. He has had ten finishes of fifth or higher, including three firsts and three seconds, is only 19 laps shy of breaking Ralph DePalma's record of 613 laps led between 1911 and 1921, has won more 500 prize money than any other driver ($1,708,097.17 through 1985), and ranks second only to Foyt in race laps completed with 3,155 from 20 starts. He enjoys the distinction of the being the last driver to enter the "old" Victory Lane at the end of the pits (1970) as well as the first into the "new" in front of the tower in 1971. In 1983 he became the first competitor ever to drive against his own son in an Indy 500.

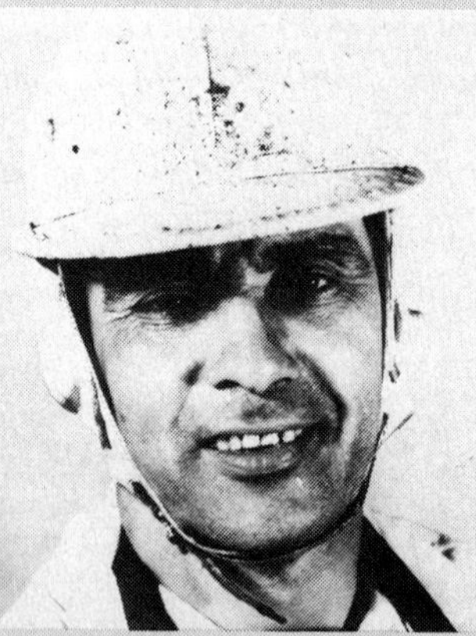

Bill Vukovich

The undisputed champion of the early 1950s was Bill Vukovich, a Fresno farmer of Ukrainian descent who shunned publicity and rarely made public appearances. Vukovich led 150 laps of his second start in 1952 and was leading when the steering mechanism failed with only eight laps to go. He won from the pole in '53 and led all but five laps, the second most dominant victory ever. He had to come all the way from 19th in 1954 but won the 500 for the second straight year. In 1955, driving a brand new car, he quickly leaped from the second row and into the lead. He was out front, apparently on his way to an unprecedented third straight win, when he became tangled up in a multi-car accident with drivers he was lapping, cartwheeled over the backstretch wall and was fatally injured.

Mauri Rose

Straightforward, no-nonsense, pipe-smoking Mauri Rose ranks as a three-time winner of the 500, although he is listed as a co-winner in 1941. After his own pole-winning car dropped out, he took over from teammate Floyd Davis on the 72nd lap and brought the Davis car up from 14th to first at the end. He won outright with one of the famous Blue Crown front-drive cars in 1947 and '48. In 1933 he became the only driver ever to start 42nd, subbing for diabetic Howdy Wilcox II and moving to fourth in 20 laps before falling out! He placed second a year later. After WWII he'd take a long lunch hour from his job at Allison's in order to drive a bare minimum of practice laps on a chosen week day and he'd not appear again until qualifications. Then he'd be gone until race day. Even when he won, he'd be back to work within 24 hours. "You could get jittery hanging around the track," was his reasoning.

Louis Meyer

The first three-time winner of the 500 (1932, '33, '36), Meyer was only 23 years old and in his first start (he'd driven relief in 1927) when he triumphed the first time. He came close to winning in '29 but finished second after losing many minutes due to a stalled engine. He crashed three laps from the end of the 1939 race while running second to Shaw and announced his retirement shortly thereafter. He and Dale Drake purchased the Offenhauser engine business in 1945, but Louis sold out his share in 1963 and became the distributor for Ford's Indianapolis parts and engines until that was taken over by A.J. Foyt in the late 1960s. On the morning of the 1978 500, the ever-genial Meyer took a popular lap of honor around the Speedway to celebrate the golden anniversary of his first win, driving his beautifully restored victorious Miller, and was to attend several Speedway functions as a lively 80-year-old in May, 1985.

Wilbur Shaw

Without question, the driver with the best record during the Speedway's first half century, Shaw won three times and was also runner-up three times. He was the first ever to win twice in succession (1939-40) and placed either first or second in six out of the eight races between 1933 and 1940. He was robbed of a then-unprecedented fourth win when a wheel collapsed, causing him to crash heavily while leading in 1941 at the three-quarter mark. During WWII he visited IMS to test tires for Firestone and was appalled at the deteriorated condition of the facility. Having ascertained that it was for sale, he eventually persuaded Terre Haute businessman Tony Hulman to purchase the Speedway and was subsequently installed as its President and General Manager. The dynamic Shaw perished in a private-plane crash on October 30, 1954, the night before his 52nd birthday.

Rick Mears

The finest record compiled by a driver in recent years is that of two-time winner Rick Mears, who has placed fifth or higher five times in eight starts. He has qualified for the front row five times, including his "rookie" year of 1978, and in 1984 became the first driver ever to lead the 500 at some point in six consecutive years. His average speed of 163.612 mph in winning the 1984 event finally broke the 500-mile-distance record held since 1972 by the late Mark Donohue.

Rodger Ward

Rodger Ward overcame a reputation as a reckless, hard-driving, ill-fated performer (eighth in 1956 was his only finish between '51 and '58) to develop into the dean of the Indianapolis drivers for half a decade. He won in 1959, placed second after backing off to save a badly worn tire in 1960, and then followed that up with consecutive finishes of third, first, fourth and second through 1964. He pulled out of the 1966 event and quit racing, although it turned out that heavy attrition could conceivably have given him his third 500 win had he continued.

Johnny Rutherford

Three times a winner and three times a pole sitter, Johnny Rutherford started the 500 for the 21st time in 1985, second only to A.J. Foyt in that department. He and Foyt remain as the only two active drivers to have competed in the 500 with a front-engine car. A talented artist (in sketching and oils) and a WWII aircraft buff (he once owned not one, but two P-51 Mustangs), Rutherford ranks third in terms of prize money won from the Speedway.

and unprepared management faced the enormous, enthusiastic crowd which turned out. Prize money, crowd sizes, and speeds have continued to increase dramatically every year since then as track conditions and the quality of the entries have just kept getting better and better.

By 1956 only a portion of the mainstraight was still of brick, and that too was covered over after the 1961 *500*. The first 140-mile-per-hour lap was turned in 1954 (by Jack McGrath), and eight years later 150 was achieved for the first time (by Parnelli Jones). The winning front-drive cars of the immediate postwar years found themselves being outpaced by lighter rear-drive cars. Then Frank Kurtis experimented by offsetting an entire body to the left for better handling during the all-left-hand journey. Next Kurtis moved the engine all the way to the left-hand side inside the body and relocated the driver's cockpit to the right for a lower center of gravity, since the driver would now sit down next to the driveshaft rather than astride it. Then George Salih went one better than that by laying the four-cylinder Offenhauser (once Miller) engine on its side for an even lower center of gravity.

In 1961, the Cooper Car Company of Surbiton, England, winner of the World Championship the previous two years with Australian Jack Brabham driving, came to Indianapolis with Brabham and a beefed-up version of their rear-engine Formula One car. In spite of giving up considerable power because of an engine that was only two-thirds the size of its American counterparts, Brabham demonstrated superior handling in the turns and placed 9th, doing much to silence the detractors who had ridiculed the flimsy-looking creation during practice.

Two years later, Scotsman Jim Clark finished second in a tiny English Lotus chassis powered by an American V-8 Ford engine, and in 1965 Clark won with one of 27 rear-engine cars in the lineup. The idea was not new. Rear-engine cars had been at Indianapolis between 1937 and 1951, but none of them had worked like these did. In 1967, not one of the 33 starters had its engine in front of the driver.

Lap speeds in the race exceeded 170 mph as turbine-powered cars made a brief and controversial appearance. Parnelli Jones in 1967 and Joe Leonard in 1968 were both leading with turbines in the closing moments, only to be forced out with minor malfunctions.

Aerodynamic improvements were stepped up in the early 1970s and the long-ineligible rear "wings" were finally allowed in 1972 after the canny McLaren organization had cleverly found its way around a rule. After that, speeds simply skyrocketed from an unofficial 180 in 1971, to 196 in 1972, and 199 in 1973. Restriction of the turbocharger manifold pressure held the pace down for a brief period, but *only* brief-

TOP:
More than just a race, the Indy 500 is a rite of spring, an American institution, and, as for these fans, who say it with beer cans, the first blowout since winter.

ABOVE:
Just a bunch of foreign rookies (from left): Jackie Stewart, Graham Hill and Jim Clark came and conquered. Both Hill and Clark won Indy, Stewart came very close.

ly, as 200 miles per hour was topped for the first time in 1977.

Tremendous safety advancements came with the construction of the cars; they now tended to fly apart upon wall contact, absorbing the shock rather than transferring it to the driver. The result was that the career of the driver lasted much longer.

Twenty-one drivers have lost their lives during practice or qualifying over the three-quarters of a century, but Gordon

54

Smiley (in 1982) has been the only one in the last dozen years. Fourteen more have perished during the race itself, but Swede Savage, who succumbed to injuries sustained during the 1973 *500*, has been the only race fatality of the last 21 years. Whereas Bill Vukovich, Sr. lost his life going for a third Indianapolis win in 1955 and numerous others perished before they could win it once, Al Unser, Johnny Rutherford, and Bobby Unser happily were able to join Louis Meyer, Wilbur Shaw, and Mauri Rose as three-time winners during long careers, while the amazing A.J. Foyt won for a record fourth time in 1977 and qualified in 1985 at the age of 50 for an unbelievable 28th consecutive start.

The investment necessary to field a competitive team had skyrocketed, multiplying several times from the 1960s. Attempting to campaign with a car barely one season old had become a virtual waste of time, as evidenced by Tom Sneva's winning car of 1983 and Teo Fabi's one and four-lap track-record qualifier had both been donated to the Speedway's museum before another *500* was run. A brace of brand new Lola or March chassis (or both) would have to be ordered prior to each season at a cost of about $140,000 each, plus another $50,000 apiece for the turbocharged Cosworth engines to power them. Such necessities as private track testing, wind-tunnel rental, and full-time staffs of up to two dozen people had major teams budgeting three million dollars for a full season, with perhaps one million of that earmarked for Indianapolis alone. Some operations had even sunk up to a quarter of a million into the gigantic, multi-wheeled combination work shop and haulers used for transporting the race cars to the tracks.

But owners have mused in recent years over the fact that having made the colossal investment necessary to get to Indianapolis, fierce competition among the manufacturers now results in products like shock absorbers, spark plugs, and tires being freely given away in return for the considerable commercial value that may be derived from having "been on the winning car."

The pace-car program, which can be traced to 1911, but which really began to develop in the mid-1950s, has soared into a costly but apparently desirable venture for the Detroit manufacturers, who provide up to 150 vehicles (including trucks and vans) in return for the "prestige" of supplying the pace car.

With ABC televising a taped, edited three-hour version of the race during prime-time on the night of the race, and with an estimated one hundred million listeners tuning into the live broadcast over the Indianapolis radio network, the *500*, after three quarters of a century, had rarely ceased spiraling as the basis for expenditure of unfathomable millions of dollars annually through advertising, corporate sponsorship, and year-round tourism.

The late Sid Collins, chief announcer for the radio broadcast for almost 30 years, sought a catchy cue that would signal a station break for commercials, and in 1955 he conceived the phrase, "Stay tuned for the greatest spectacle in racing."

Another 30 years have passed since then, but his description still seems perfectly justified. **MT**

THE ALSO-RANS

For every Henry Ford and W.P. Chrysler there were scores of dreamers who swallowed the bitter pill of defeat.

By Steve Spence

☐ The first manufacturers of gasoline cars in this country were the brothers Duryea, Frank and Charles, of Massachusetts. If their egos hadn't gotten in the way, and if the elder Charles hadn't been so sure the public would never go for a steering wheel when they could have a "tiller" stick, their name might have survived.

As it is, the Duryeas became just another of almost 1,900 "also-rans" in the American automobile industry.

The Duryeas had a good 10-year head-start on Henry Ford and six on Ransom Eli Olds when they built the first Duryea in 1893 in Springfield. A chunk of their Yankee ingenuity was lifted from *Scientific American*, a magazine which had published technical data on Carl Benz's German automobile, the world's first. The Duryeas built a buggy with a four-horse-power motor tucked under the seat, won an endurance race in Chicago and soon produced 13 more, but split up after quarreling over which sibling should get credit. Younger Frank went off to a tool company where he produced a few forgettable runabouts, while Charles got tangled up in four more short-lived adventures—mostly building cyclecars—before history passed him by.

Two more brothers surfaced, Edgar and Elmer Apperson of Kokomo, Indiana, who joined a gas-company engineer named Elwood Haynes to produce the Haynes-Apperson in 1894. This time the brothers united to squabble with Hayes over credit, and the venture was abandoned. Three more experiments followed: one by Charles B. King, who soon drifted off to tinker with aircraft engines; another by Alexander Winton, a Scottish engineer who sold his first car in Cleveland in 1898 for $1,000 (making a $400 profit) and survived for two decades on a small scale; the third was Henry Ford's first car. Winton and Col. Albert Pope, a bicycle maker who produced 40 gasoline cars but made the wrong turn and went with electric cars—and vanished in 1907—became the first true manufacturers.

Another pair of brothers, twins Francis and Freelan Stanley, were turning out

1958 Edsel Pacer.   Harold James Cleworth   July/78

open-air cars in the deep woods of Newton, Maine. They became also-rans for two reasons: first, the engines were steam-powered and therefore expensive to build and tricky to repair and second, the Stanleys were a tad eccentric, refusing to advertise or in any way market the cars; if you wanted a Stanley Steamer, you had to trudge up to Newton for the privilege of buying one of their cars. After Francis was killed in a car accident in 1918, brother Freelan was so bummed out he let the business go under.

Backyard automakers were popping up everywhere, often disappearing as quickly, but the first auto-industry genius was Ransom Olds, who had been building stationary gas engines since 1899 at his Olds Motor Works in Lansing, Michigan. While Henry Ford tinkered with his first car and worked at a Detroit power company, Olds was convincing two businessmen, Samuel Smith and his son, Frederic, to ante up $200,000 to finance his dream of becoming the first major builder of cars. The Smiths put up the money and in return controlled the venture, which would prove Olds' undoing. Olds created the curved-dash "Merry Oldsmobile," the best of the runabouts of the time, and by 1904 was putting out 5,000 of them a year. This made the Smiths rich, but they felt certain the future was in big touring cars, not cute buggies. Olds disagreed, and after telling them so, took his share of the kitty and went off to form, using his initials, REO, a marque that was in the top four by 1908 but hit hard times in the 1930s and eventually abandoned automobiles for truck production.

Olds may have missed the big leagues, but his company spawned many big names in the industry that would follow. One of his engineers was Robert Hupp, who quit in 1908 to form the Hupmobile company (where he was squeezed out three years later). Another Olds man, Jonathan Maxwell, left in 1904 to join the Briscoe brothers, Benjamin and Frank, to form the Maxwell-Briscoe consortium, shortened later to Maxwell and finally becoming Chrysler. Also, Roy Chapin and Howard Coffin left Olds and in 1908, with a $90,000 investment from Detroit department-store owner E.L. Hudson, formed a motor-car company and named it for their patron. (Chapin kept Hudson from sinking in the Depression but lost his good health in the process and died of pneumonia in 1936.)

Olds was just short by an idea or two—principally the one having to do with mass production of a cheap car—and he joined a long list of brilliant engineers and inventors who would be squeezed out of history by the money men who controlled the companies and who were quickly learning the subject of marketing. It was one thing to create cars, another to sell them while maintaining a cash flow.

David Dunbar Buick was an abject example. He had invented a method of affixing porcelain to cast iron—presto, the modern bathtub. He sold a large plumbing company to build gasoline engines and finally cars. Benjamin Briscoe financed the auto venture, but when Buick responded too slowly, Briscoe grew impatient and sold out to a carriage maker in 1903. The prototype arrived with its valve-in-head engine the next year, but having spent all his money, the carriage maker sold out to William Crapo "Billy" Durant, who shoved David Buick aside and later made it the centerpiece of his General Motors Company. David Buick tried making carburetors and two others cars (the Lorraine and the Dunbar) but by 1928 found himself employed at the information desk of the Detroit School of Trades. He died the next year impoverished at 74.

He didn't die a pauper, but a similar obscurity awaited James Ward Packard, who owned a small electric company in Warren, Ohio. Packard managed to buy a lemon Winton—an easy accomplishment in the days before precision assembly—and when he bitched to Winton himself, the automaker told him to go make his own car if he thought he could do better. It was 1900, and Packard did just that. Not long after it hit the rutty roads, Packard's car caught the eye of Henry Joy, son of railroad magnate James Joy, who bought controlling interest and moved to Detroit. Packard's name went on to become revered by royalty and the rich, but he had no voice in the company and remained in smalltown Ohio collecting royalties.

Henry Ford proved to be an also-ran, too. In 1899, Ford made himself superintendent of a new venture called the Detroit Automobile Company, financed by Detroit lumberman William Murphy. But Ford was inexperienced in industrial production, wasn't sure what to build, and a year later the company was dissolved. Still, Murphy backed him again with the Henry Ford Company. Henry built a few cars and went off to establish their credibility by racing them around the country, much to Murphy's chagrin; he thought Henry should have his Scottish nose to the factory grindstone. Looking for Henry in the factory once too often without finding him there, Murphy sacked Ford in 1902. He turned the fledgling company over to Henry Leland, who renamed it for the founder of Detroit, Antoine de la Mothe Cadillac.

Usually, a two-time loser in business is urged to follow another path, but Ford, like Billy Martin 70 years later, kept reappearing. The next year he found yet another sponsor, coal dealer Alexander Malcomson of Detroit, and the Ford Motor Company was created with capitalization of $100,000—although in reality just $28,000 was required in cash since Ford also had as partners two more brothers, John and Horace Dodge, who operated a machine shop and would build engines for Ford (and later their own cars, with the company being sold after their deaths for $170 million in 1928 to Chrysler).

Let us digress here to repeat the greatest investment story of all time. Malcomson's bookkeeper, James Couzens, was invited to manage the Ford beans, and sensing greatness or trying to please the principals, he scraped up $1,000 of his own to invest. As most of Ford's executives did sooner or later, Couzens quit in 1915. A few years later, when Ford angrily bought out all his stockholders for $100 million, Couzens ne-

Powell Crosley made big-bucks from manufacturing "Shelvador" refrigerators, but lost them building icebox-sized cars.

gotiated privately in a deal that got him $1,000 a share more than the others. For his piddling one-grand investment, Ford paid Couzens *$29 million* for his stock!

The supply of brothers seemed inexhaustible. The Studebakers, the world's largest manufacturers of horse-drawn vehicles, out of South Bend, Indiana, began selling cars through their dealers. Soon the Garford Company of Ohio provided engines and chassis, and Studebaker added the bodies. Next it purchased three small auto firms in Detroit, and in 1910 the single corporation was formed. By 1920, it was the No. 3 producer of cars—and then the long-running skid began. President Albert Erskine introduced in the mid-'20s a low-priced car, aptly named The Erskine, which promptly flopped. Then he went 180 degrees in the other direction and bought the sinking Pierce-Arrow luxury car for $9 million, which lost almost a million dollars immediately. Next came a car named for famous football coach Knute Rockne, which also tubed, and in the midst of the Depression, Studebaker slipped into receivership and Erskine shot himself dead. Two men, Harold Vance and Paul Hoffman, rescued the company, but it was touch and go until the end, three decades later.

But it was Ford's Model T that probably did more to clear the industry of small manufacturers. It sold phenomenally well when introduced in 1908, but then it did even better. In 1911, the year 78,000 Tin Lizzies were sold, there were 275 listed car manufacturers in the country. When Henry put his assembly line in motion during fiscal 1913-14, the company incredibly sold 248,000 T's. Worse for the little automaker, Ford's price on the touring car dropped from $600 to $490. The question was: How were you going to stay in business with Ford around? By 1920, half the cars in the world were Model T's.

Along with Ford, the other man who would change the face of the auto industry was Billy Durant. It is safe to say he began buying and selling objects in his crib. Although he was from a wealthy family in Flint, he dropped out of school at 16 and soon made a mint selling carriages. As noted earlier, he took control of David Buick's operation in 1904, and quickly perceived that combinations of car companies were the wave of the future. If one model did poorly one year, other models could offset the loss. In 1908, he and Benjamin Briscoe of Maxwell-Briscoe tried to gobble up Ford and Reo, but Henry and Ransom wanted $3 million each. Durant went off on his own, raised $60 million, bought Cadillac, Oldsmobile and Oakland (later Pontiac) and called it General Motors Company. Then he bought some losers, including Cartercar and Elmore, blew $7 million on a headlight company whose patent turned out to be fraudulent, and purchased any number of parts companies. He tried Ford again, but now Henry upped the price to $8 million. Trying to juggle this crazy empire, Durant got in deep trouble but floated along for a while on sales of Buicks and Cadillacs. But in 1910 the bottom fell out, and Billy Durant became an also-ran, too. A banking syndicate headed by James

Storrow of Boston rescued the company, but Durant was forced out as president. Before he left, he recommended Charles Nash, his man at Buick, be made president. Nash in turn hired self-taught engineer Walter Chrysler to run Buick at a paltry $6,000 salary. But by 1915, Nash had paid off the syndicate; GM was in clear waters.

The imperturbable Durant went off to make a low-priced car built by a Swiss-French engineer named Louis Chevrolet, and the $490 car took off like a rocket. Before long, Durant had an $80-million company. With Pierre DuPont he began a quest to regain GM by offering five Chevy shares for one of theirs. It worked, and in no time he was back at GM, bringing Chevrolet with him. (Nash and Storrow couldn't face this turn of events, and quit, trying to take Walter Chrysler with them, but now Durant offered him a $500,000 salary and he stuck.) But Durant proved as erratic as ever, spending most of his time speculating in the stock market and antagonizing his brilliant staff. He sank a wad on an ill-fated tractor operation. He bought a refrigerator company and sold it to General Motors. "When his fellow directors asked why," historian John Rae writes, "Durant airily replied that both

cars and refrigerators were boxes contan-ing motors." After a brief depression in 1920-21, the DuPonts stepped in and forced Durant out (he left with 2½ *million* shares of GM stock). A vice-president named Alfred P. Sloan Jr. took control and turned GM into the world-beater it re-mains today.

Devastated in the '21 depression were firms with famous names: Locomobile, Moon, Cole, Jordan, Stutz, Marmon, Dort and a host of others. There were 181 manu-facturers in 1922, but five years later, just 44 remained. Walter Chrysler took over the sinking Maxwell Motor Corporation, changed its name to his, and by the end of the Great Depression, the "Big Three" had emerged: GM, Ford and Chrysler, with independents Hudson, Nash, Packard, Studebaker and Willys-Overland getting only 15 percent of the pie.

The Depression of the '30s killed many marques overnight and fatally wounded others. Two typical victims were the finest cars of the time: the Auburn and the Due-senberg. Once again, two brothers—Augie and Fred Duesenberg—had built fabulous cars since 1913 but were never more than employees of the company. In 1924, the dynamic Errett L. Cord acquired Auburn, then Duesenberg two years later, and the brothers continued a small output of spec-tacular cars. In '29, the wrong year, Cord introduced the car bearing his name. If the Depression proved anything, it proved that princely luxury cars could not survive, even in small numbers. Output went stead-ily down, and in 1937 Cord abandoned the auto industry and went uranium mining in the West.

Overlooked by the Big Three was the subject of small cars. In 1939, Powell Cros-ley, the radio king and maker of the "Shel-vador" refrigerator, tried to fill the gap but was a decade or three early. The car was the 924-pound Crosley, powered by a 15-horsepower two-cycle mounted to a ti-ny (for then) 80-inch wheelbase. The coupe sold for $325, the "station wagon" for $425, and 2,000 were sold that first year. The car had an ugly, homemade look, and mechanical problems were common. Can-nonball Baker drove one across the coun-try averaging 50 miles a gallon, but with gas selling for 20 cents a gallon, who cared? Still, the Crosleys sold, and after conversion to a four-cylinder engine in 1945, a remarkable 25,000 were sold in '48. But the novelty wore off; people soon had more money to spend, and in 1952 the company was sold to General Tire, which used the auto plant to build war material for the Korean conflict.

The last successful attempt to start up a car company in modern times was under-taken by industrialist and wartime ship-builder Henry J. Kaiser, who pioneered prefabrication techniques and built the West's first steel plant in Southern Califor-nia. He was no doubt feeling somewhat

bullet-proof when he bought the ailing Graham-Paige auto company in 1945 and joined its chairman, Joseph Frazer, to produce the Kaiser-Frazer. The result was one of the first aerodynamic ultra-modern cars built in this country, and it surprisingly led the independents in 1947-48 by capturing five percent of the market. But the key to success was longevity, and although Kaiser had raised $100 million, he later conceded he should have pooled three times that amount. Kaiser began losing dealerships, and his introduction of the first compact car, the Henry J, didn't help. By 1953, things were looking shaky when Kaiser acquired Willys-Overland and added Jeeps to the ailing lineup. Frazer was soon dropped from the corporate title, and four years later the company became Kaiser Industries, its Jeep rights were sold to the new American Motors, and Kaiser ceased to build cars.

At the same time, the independents in postwar America began a long downward slide. Mergers became the strategy; in April 1953 there were nine major automakers, but 18 months later there were just six. After Kaiser sank, Hudson, which had not kept pace with modern styling, joined another styling hodge-podge, Nash, to form American Motors. The public noticed that Nash's postwar aerodynamic entry, the "Airflyte," looked decidedly like a bathtub, upside-down. Nash seemed to be doing better selling its Kelvinator refrigerators. Soon the names of Hudson and Nash disappeared, replaced by the economy-minded Ramblers. With George Romney at the helm, American Motors concentrated its efforts on the small car.

Packard and Studebaker were married in 1954. The latter's bullet-nosed Starlight of '49 is today seen as art, but in those days people joked that you couldn't tell which direction it was headed. From '48 to '50, Packard's styling appeared to be modern, but the car drove in a stodgy, old-fashioned manner. Studebaker's '53 coupe, may well have been the most beautiful car of the time, but its performance was poor. In 1958, the Packard name was dropped, and Studebaker trudged along with a long line of models that seemed from another planet. In '64, the company

TV pitchman Earl "Madman" Muntz, at the wheel, got race car designer Frank Kurtis, the passenger, to create this semi-handsome car. It too went off the air.

ABOVE:
Try as it might, Studebaker could not totally ruin the design of its classic 1953 Starliner Coupe. But even fins and an egg-crate grille couldn't save the firm.

retreated to Ontario, Canada, where it collapsed two years later.

Newcomers appeared, then disappeared. A company calling itself the Playboy Motor Corporation hoped to build a sports car but couldn't raise more than $6 million. Earl "Madman" Muntz didn't get much further with his Muntz sports car. The most amusing entry was the brainchild of flamboyant promoter Preston Tucker who, in 1948, became a media curiosity when he leased an old Dodge plant in Chicago and tried to produce a weird, futuristic car with

31 CORD

a Cyclops headlight that turned with the wheels. Tucker raised a remarkable $22 million for this space case, which he called (with a straight face) the Tucker Torpedo. He built 50 of them, but under attack from muckraker Drew Pearson and under investigation by the Securities and Exchange Commission, the Torpedo sank to the bottom in a year.

High hopes were held for the Phantom Corsair, and this elegant starship might have made it had not its creator, Rust Heinz, son of food mogul H.J. Heinz, been killed in a car accident just before the war. Heinz hoped to build $12,500 replicas of his $25,000 prototype, a car which you had to see to believe: it was a sword-edged beauty the size of a big Rolls-Royce, soundproofed with cork and rubber, outfitted in red leather, styled with small angular windows and absolutely devoid of chrome. Powered by a 4731-cc Cord 810 V-8 engine, it may have been the most magnificent car ever built, but without Heinz, it was never put into production.

The lesson of the '50s for someone wanting to start a car company was clear: at a minimum, you needed $300 million, but you were best advised to show up with a billion. And that didn't take into consideration the problem of acquiring dealerships. Two more adventurers discovered this rule. In the early '70s, Malcolm Bricklin, heir to a national chain of hardware stores who made a bundle bringing the Subaru to America, built a fiberglass gull-winged "safety vehicle" using existing hardware from American Motors and Ford. He called it the Bricklin and talked the Canadian government into buying a big piece of the action, then began producing the car in remote New Brunswick on a primitive assembly line. There were immediate problems: the gull-wing doors leaked and assembly was erratic, and despite the price ($6500), the venture soon failed.

John DeLorean's odyssey is well-known. In reality, it appears DeLorean hoped only to produce a single stainless-steel-clad sports car in Ireland and had no delusions of becoming the founder of a multi-model automobile corporation. Few doubted De-Lorean's skills, learned at General Motors where he had been a boy wonder, but the required capitalization was staggering, and he too became an also-ran.

Finally, whenever the subject of automotive also-rans and failed dreams arises in conversation, the name Edsel is always the first to be shouted. In 1955, market analysts convinced Ford that there was a sales gap between Ford and Mercury that was crying out to be filled. By the time the new

Edsel model was produced in 1957, it is also agreed that the gap no longer existed.

If the middle '50s was a time of automotive craziness characterized by outrageous tailfins, great grinning grilles and chromium overdoses, then Ford's Edsel should be excused. But it was indeed weird: the "horse collar" grille was vertical, not horizontal. Inside the steering wheel were "Teletouch" transmission punch-buttons. The rear deck had narrow, horizontal taillights.

It wasn't any goofier than some other strange models on the market, but nonetheless it became a symbol of ridicule, a subject of jokes from coast to coast. It sold 29,667 models before Ford buried it forever. (Even DeSoto, another interplanetary form of transportation, outsold Ford's much-ballyhooed new entry in '57. The most popular photograph of the day showed another promising loser, Vice-President Richard Nixon, waving his arms madly from the back seat of a convertible model somewhere in South America on his way to being spat upon.)

But the real lesson of the most famous also-ran is that a huge automobile empire can sustain the utter failure of an expensive new model with no more effect than a mild case of corporate embarrassment. **MT**

THE HARD SELL

Inventing and perfecting the car required genius, but getting people to buy it took a whole lot more.

By J. Patrick Wright

"In 75 years of this business everything has changed but the way we sell cars."—Auto Executive Semon E. "Bunkie" Knudsen to Look *Magazine (1970).*

☐ It may be viewed as an historical absurdity, but for most of the automobile industry's history the way cars are sold has changed very little. The industry's market research has ridden, pretty much, on the instincts, tastes and even the whims of the executives in charge.

Henry Ford's instincts told him to build a car for the masses at a time when everyone else said it was just a toy for the rich. With the introduction of the low-cost "Tin Lizzie" he made his company the runaway leader in the industry, selling 15 million Model Ts over 20 years.

Then, Ford nearly lost everything on a stubborn whim when he refused to admit that the market he discovered had changed, having become more demanding and diversified. By the time he finally introduced the Model A in 1928 to respond to this market, Ford had forever lost the leadership of the domestic auto industry.

John DeLorean, after he left General Motors Corp. in 1973, complained: "The General Motors marketing effort is guided by men whose training in buyer psychology is no deeper than the Dale Carnegie course they all are required to take, and whose idea of sophisticated sales is having a few drinks with the dealers."

Ironically, DeLorean lost his own car company and his reputation as an innovator, in part, because he too lost touch with the marketplace and tried to force an inferior product on the consumer in quantities far exceeding demand.

Still, despite its basic one-dimenisional approach to selling, the auto industry thrived for years because it had a good product, a captive audience, a strong dealer body, and an American public that craved the mobility and independence that a car could give it.

Somewhere West of Laramie

Somewhere west of Laramie there's a broncho-busting, steer-roping girl who knows what I'm talking about. She can tell what a sassy pony, that's a cross between greased lightning and the place where it hits, can do with eleven hundred pounds of steel and action when he's going high, wide and handsome.

The truth is—the Playboy was built for her.

Built for the lass whose face is brown with the sun when the day is done of revel and romp and race.

She loves the cross of the wild and the tame.

There's a savor of links about that car—of laughter and lilt and light—a hint of old loves—and saddle and quirt. It's a brawny thing—yet a graceful thing for the sweep o' the Avenue.

Step into the Playboy when the hour grows dull with things gone dead and stale.

Then start for the land of real living with the spirit of the lass who rides, lean and rangy, into the red horizon of a Wyoming twilight.

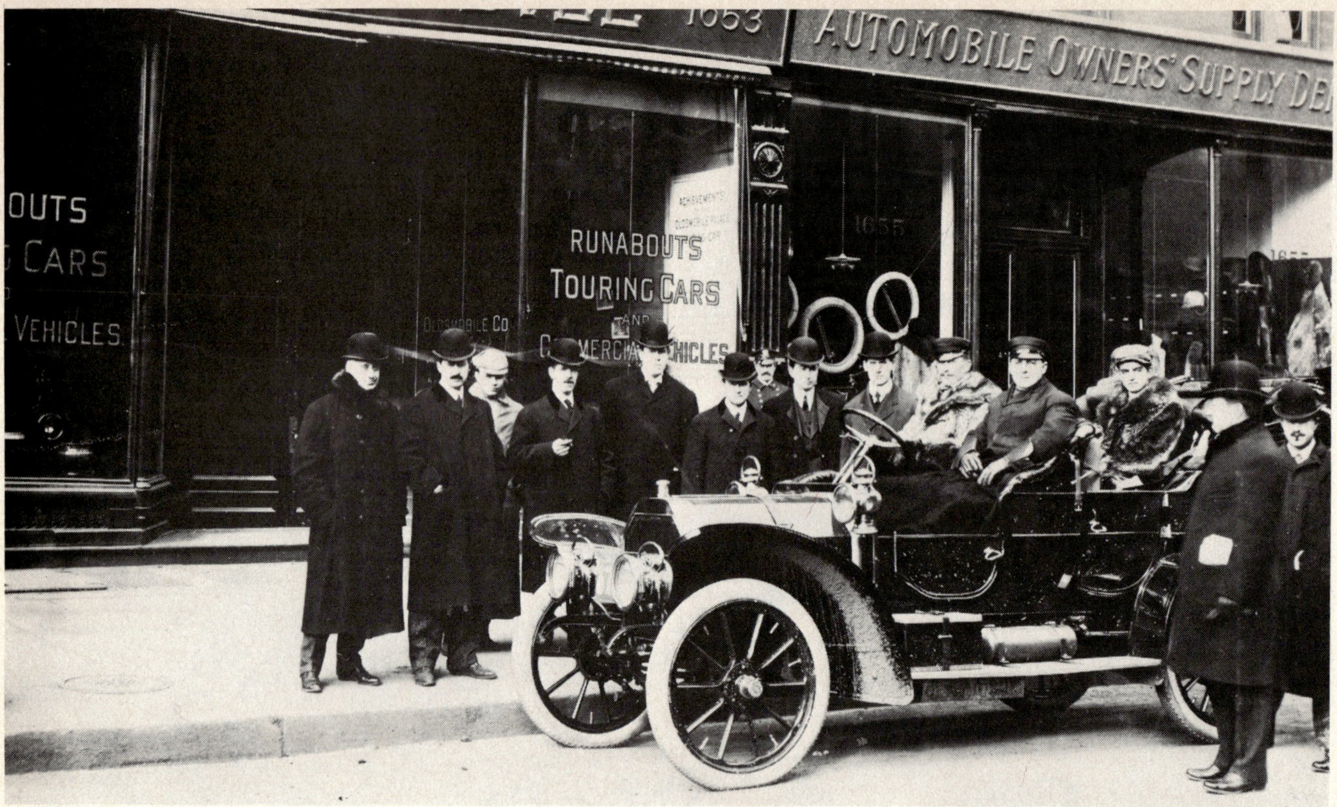

Would you buy a new car from these men? Wearing their respectable bowler hats, some early Oldsmobile salesmen strike a pose.

Advertising for auto accessories was appearing as early as 1905. This pioneering company evidently didn't survive for very long.

But while it thrived, Detroit also grew old and out of touch. It refused to part with its big cars, antiquated sales and marketing programs, and outmoded system of manufacturing and quality control. Eventually a painful change was forced on the industry, just as it had been forced on Henry Ford. And, as then, it came only after a sizeable portion of the market had been lost forever to the competition, in this case imported cars, especially the Japanese. By the mid-1980s, that change was pervasive and deep, and left the industry as well as its markets in disarray and confusion.

To understand this turmoil, one must first understand the history of the auto industry's selling effort. It is a story that has two perspectives: the manufacturer's sales and marketing effort and the operation of the national automotive dealer body.

From Main Street to Madison Avenue

The relationship between Americans and their cars got off to a rocky start, literally: early roads were little more than stone-filled horse paths, sort of a primitive man's version of a Belgian Block durability run.

Though automobiles were very expensive, $3000 or more, a combination of untested manufacturing techniques and poor roads had them breaking down frequently. Jokes abounded about the fragile machines. The popular runabout model, one story had it, got its name because it "runs about a mile." So, most marketing and advertising sought to overcome the industry's bad-quality image by stressing durability and reliability. "When you buy a Cadillac, you buy a round trip," promised a 1903 advertisement.

But more important than the unsubstantiated factory claims, which an early Maxwell ad called "awful braggadocio," were the results of a host of car races and reliability runs staged to establish the viability of motoring. Henry Ford and the Chevrolet Brothers—Louis, Arthur and Gaston—among others, established their reputations and that of their cars through competition. The industry would return to this strategy again and again, most memorably in the 1950s and late 1960s in the belief that "You race 'em on Sunday and sell 'em on Monday." At the turn of the century, even more attention was given to durability runs, the most prestigious of which were the tours started by Bostonian Charles J. Glidden in 1903. Press coverage of these events and word-of-mouth promotion were critical to establishing the reputations of the auto pioneers and their hard iron. Other promotions supplemented the competition events. There were auto exhibitions and parades galore. But the most extravagant was the institution of the auto show.

The first, the New York Auto Show, was staged in 1900 in Madison Square Garden, Later, shows were scheduled in Chicago and soon spread to most major cities. They became a social mainstay of American life. And eventually, when admission was charged, and sales booths, manned by factory or dealer personnel, were set up on the show floors, one of the more improbable marketing concepts of the 20th century was established: customers paying for the privilege of being hustled.

In the industry's first three decades, reliability improved in quantum leaps. There were literally hundreds of car companies, from "mom and pop" operations to full-scale big-name manufacturers. Over the years, 6000 nameplates and 2000 manufacturers would appear and disappear. Competition was fierce, and the best cars were not always the show-room winners. The market often went to the company which did the best job of selling. Consequently, early car builders offered direct, hard-sell pitches which pointed to the many ways their products were different from the

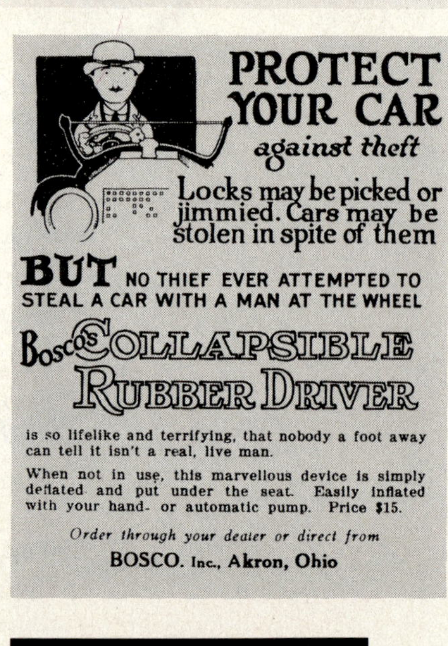

TOP:
The annual new-car frenzy was stimulated by GM's free Motoramas. They were replaced by more commercial events charging admission.

ABOVE:
Americans weren't born with big car fever, it was carefully cultivated over the years with ads like this one for the 1936 Chryslers.

competition's. Packard advertising stressed its flexibility in congested traffic, a new problem, noting that "a striking ability to run around and through traffic is doubly worth thinking about."

As important as the fight for each sale was, by 1920 an even more important battle was brewing over marketing philosophy. This conflict shaped the future of the industry. Henry Ford's hard-headed one model, one style, one color philosophy—

which stressed a price as low as $495—was butting up against a developing theory at General Motors, newly shaped and reorganized, which stressed difference and choice. The concept was explained years later by its prime architect, Alfred P. Sloan: The consumer, he said, wanted to be "served by better and better cars, or what might be thought of as the mass-class market, with increasing diversity."

General Motors, Sloan believed, could offer something for everyone. First-time buyers could start with an inexpensive Chevrolet and then, as they grew more affluent, "trade up" through the Oakland (Pontiac), Buick, Oldsmobile and Cadillac divisions. Along the way, GM would benefit handsomely because the more expensive cars produced bigger profits. The inherent profit in a standard Cadillac by the mid-1960s was four times that of a standard Chevrolet.

Using Sloan's marketing concept, GM

became the richest industrial corporation in the world. Its competitors spent decades and hundreds of millions of dollars imitating GM's profit formula, but they never achieved the same returns.

The broadening demand for cars (there were 3.7 million sold in 1925) spurred new developments which paved the way for the industry's boom over the next four decades. Closed cars made motoring a year-round possibility; the used-car market gave an owner a built-in down payment on his next automobile; installment credit let buyers purchase bigger and more expensive cars; and the annual model change gave people a legitimate reason to buy new cars more often.

Though The Great Depression slowed down the car market and wiped a few companies out, Detroit's major firms were establishing reputations that would last for years: Chrysler for engineering, Ford for proper positioning in the market, General Motors for styling and the industry's strongest sales effort.

The emphasis on styling made the automobile as much an item of fashion as a basic means of transportation. Cars were becoming outward expressions of the way people viewed themselves. People didn't just drive cars, they began to wear them. The auto companies jumped on the fashion aspect. Chrysler, for example, described its "New Airflow Bodies" as "Tailored to taste—individualized interiors, richer fabrics, plastics . . . five-foot cushions . . . added elbow room."

Just as obvious was the appeal being made to the female market. It began in 1923 with an advertisement for the Jordan Motor Car Company that set the industry on its ear. Entitled "Somewhere West of Laramie," the ad copy had blatant sexual overtones that started with the very name of the car—Playboy. It was a watershed in automotive marketing as it inserted sex into a permanent place in auto advertising. The car, psychologists later explained, was a phallic symbol for women and men, just as the horse had been.

What's more, the Jordan ad established women as a tool in automotive marketing. The '50s would feature soft-sell female campaigns such as Chevrolet's long-time affiliation with Dinah Shore and her popular TV show. The '60s would have more explicit use of women as the central themes in advertising, such as the popular Dodge Fever and Rebellion Girl campaigns. And, by the 1970s, bikini-clad California hard bodies were a pro forma requirement for sporty car advertising as the industry reached for the youth market of baby boomers.

The use of sex and women in advertising didn't necessarily sit well among Detroit's hierarchy. In the late 1960s GM Chairman James M. Roche, a devout Roman Catholic, allegedly became so incensed with the Pontiac "Tiger" ads, which featured actress Barbara Feldon extolling Pontiac's virtues while writhing on a tiger skin rug, that he had the campaign pulled after see-

ing the commercial on television.

The war years saw the auto plants converted to military production. When the industry cranked up again, it was greeted by a market which featured a massive fleet of old cars and a pent-up demand that was to explode in the next decade. It responded with a sales fury heretofore unseen. In 1955, the industry sold nearly eight million new cars, a record. And super salesman such as GM's Captain Harlow Curtice were the leading industry figures.

"Everything broke loose in the '50s," explained James Wren, a historian and manager of the Patents Department for The Motor Vehicle Manufacturers' Association. "You had automatic transmission, high-compression engines. The manufacturers stressed the ease of driving. In styling it was the dream car period and a carryover from the classic cars. It was the golden, glory years of cars. The manufacturers truly saw themselves as offering 'all things to all people.'"

Slogans were a big part of advertising themes. Oldsmobile had its "Rocket 88." "See the USA in your Chevrolet" seemed everywhere in print, on the radio and even in the latest medium on the block, television. A young upstart in Ford's Philadelphia district office, Lee Iacocca, made a name for himself with the slogan "56 for 56" which meant a new 1956 Ford could be bought for a payment of $56 a month.

The sales explosion of the '50s was followed by the model explosion of the '60s. New markets for intermediate and compact cars seemed to spring up overnight. Sub-markets developed for musclecars such as the Pontiac GTO, Plymouth Road Runner, and the personal luxury car such as the Chevrolet Monte Carlo. A mind-boggling proliferation of optional equipment left the consumer breathless as well as confused.

And, car buyers were also beginning to sour on high-pressure, domestic dealer sales pitches as well as the deteriorating quality of the products those dealers sold. What is more, the industry was trying to

sell to a vastly diverse market with a sales structure and marketing approach virtually unchanged since the 1920s. Dissatisfied with the domestic manufacturers, consumers began to move toward imported cars which offered lower-priced, stylish and economical small cars of high quality. Detroit executives' response was simplistic. The imports are benefiting from "shallow mystique," they said, adding, "we just have to do a better job of selling."

It was a colossal marketing mistake. Detroit, by the early 1970s, had virtually turned over the small-car market, and one-third of total sales, to importers. It was concentrating on bigger cars and their inherently bigger profits.

It was not as if the domestic manufacturers were bumbling idiots. That was not the case. *Some* impressive, sophisticated selling was being done.

"The Mustang was the first example of classical marketing," said Joseph Campana, who worked for Ford in the late 1960s and became Chrysler's marketing vice-president two decades later. "It was seated so effectively in the eye of the consumer, in terms of the way it was perceived, that the impression was that there was one for everybody."

The problem was that the Mustang was an isolated case. Sound marketing research and strategy was generally unheeded. Chevrolet research indicated that Gemini was the best name for its 1970 mini car. But it was called Vega instead because GM President Edward N. Cole wanted to call it the Vega.

Such authoritarian and arbitrary marketing decisions were commonplace. Importers like BMW, Mercedes, Toyota and Datsun, on the other hand, were catering to the very needs that the domestic manufacturers were ignoring through focused marketing which isolated niches in the marketplace and sold directly to them.

The big fall for the domestic manufacturers came with the advent of the energy crisis in the mid-1970s. Gasoline prices soared, as did the cost of building cars. The

Horsepower and speed have successfully sold cars on a cyclical basis, but it's doubtful that you'd see this kind of pitch today.

Federal government mandated strict fuel-efficiency standards. Big car sales plummeted. Detroit was caught product short. The imports had the only game in town. The industry's marketing response was drastic: redo its entire product lines into smaller packages, while completely revamping its manufacturing techniques to lower costs of car building and raise the product quality to that of imported cars.

It was an eight-year, $43-billion program that threw the industry into massive confusion. The smaller models that were introduced each year through the early 1980s devastated owner loyalties. The industry, which counted on six of every 10 customers coming back next time, found, by 1985, that only three of 10 returned. First-time buyers now had to be fought for. And the industry's most successful tool against imports was not their new products, but rather Federal pressure on the Japanese to voluntarily restrict the number of cars it sent to America.

As the domestic manufacturers scrambled to reclaim old identities or establish new ones, they were forced to evaluate their sales and marketing techniques for the first time in their history. And they embarked on massive new programs.

General Motors, striking at the heart of Sloan's strategy, in 1984 consolidated its automotive operations into two basic divisions—big cars and small cars. The five car divisions, once autonomous entities, now became little more than marketing operations similar to their competitors at Ford and Chrysler. Furthermore, GM questioned the very structure of its auto operations by commissioning a new company, the Saturn Corporation, to search out and implement an entirely new process of building and selling cars to answer the challenges of the future.

And each of the domestic big three, Ford, GM and Chrysler, sought ties with Japanese partners to learn how to build small cars of quality and economy. It was a humble admission for Detroit. After nearly 100 years in the business, the teacher was now the student. The change in attitude from the domestic manufacturers appeared to be permanent and pervasive, encompassing their methods of research and applied marketing strategies.

Ross Roberts, Ford Division general marketing manager explained that his company, at least, had abandoned much of the past: "We can't be all things to all people anymore. We have to concentrate on specific markets. Focused marketing is the only way that we can sell a car, and we're doing it."

Chrysler's Campana sounded a note of déjà vu when he said that attacking the industry's quality problem was the central theme in advertising by the mid-1980s. "We are stressing durability and reliability of our products today in advertising."

Was it 1900 all over again? In terms of auto marketing the answer was a partial "yes" because the industry was in a sense starting out from ground zero with the fortunes of huge companies, local and state economies and the reputation of men hanging in the balance.

Life on Auto Row

In no other industry has discipline been better enforced than in the car business. The manufacturers have sold their products through exclusive, independent-dealer networks over which they exercised enormous control.

Franchises, which were generally one-owner, one-site operations, often could be canceled almost on a moment's notice (30 days was normal). The dealers, who could make fortunes on new-car sales, were beholden to the manufacturers for sufficient allocation of vehicles. By 1909 dealers were lining up outside factory offices and begging for cars to sell.

Finding good dealers in the beginning was a difficult and frustrating task. Anyone with several hundred dollars and an empty lot could open a car dealership. And a number of early manufacturers sank from sight on the strength—actually the lack of strength—of its dealer force.

Henry Ford was the most successful early manufacturer at establishing a dealer network. By March of 1913 he had at least one sales agent in every U.S. town of 1000 or more people. He also set the tone for dealer/manufacturer relations as he dictated stringent terms of operations to his dealers, including a vigorous format for selling cars. With him the "hard sell" became a bona fide industry practice.

But by far the strongest dealer body was built by General Motors in the 1920s and '30s when Richard H. Grant, a legendary sales figure, established the "GM Quality Dealer Program." It was a somewhat sophisticated system for locating dealerships in major markets around the country. The size and strength of GM's dealer network over the years was considered the prime factor in making that company the auto giant that it became.

While dealers were often the business envy of their communities, they did not enjoy a strong ethical reputation. Much of that reputation had to do with the nature of the car sales transaction and the liberties dealers took with it.

For years the manufacturers were able to elicit strict adherence to their price structures. However, as car sales grew more competitive, dealers began to discount. Price competition grew. The manufacturers set up discount structures which encouraged "dealing" by providing a large spread between what became known as the manufacturer's suggested retail price and the dealer's cost—25 percent or more on some models.

The industry further complicated the sales process, in the postwar years, by offering add-on equipment to the basic car. This optional equipment could be purchased for an added price and there was a lot of it: power steering, automatic transmissions, clocks, radios, styling packages. Soon most consumers had no idea what

they were going to pay for a new car and they were in a dither over this.

Furthermore, the very "high pressure" sales process itself was becoming a hassle. Domestic-car salesmen were thought of as pushy cretins who would stop at nothing to sell a car. Deceptive sales practices with odious name such as "bait and switch" and "high-ball, low-ball" became standard fare for an "auto deal."

"To buy a car was to learn to hate," said Milton I. Brand, a Detroit-based marketing consultant, and the car salesman was the object of that emotion.

The importers, however, in the mid-1960s introduced a selling practice that was quite reminiscent of the early American industry. The sticker price *was* the price a customer paid. The new-car packages were complete with little optional equipment to be added. And the sales approach was decidedly low-key.

In the 1970s the numbers of domestic dealerships began to diminish. During the auto sales depression of the early 1980s, nearly 3500 domestic dealers went under. The American manufacturers' dealer body, which was 49,173 strong in 1949, had shrunk to 20,902 by 1985. And many of those dealers who survived did so by lining up an imported dealership to supplement their domestic outlet.

In the past these dealers would have met with severe domestic-manufacturer opposition, but this time they did not. For the first time in their history, the domestic manufacturers needed their dealers as much or more than their dealers needed them.

"The shoe was on the other foot," explained Suburban Chicago Cadillac/Honda dealer, Rob Mancuso.

With the drastic change that had come about in the construction and marketing of cars, so too had come a drastic change in the way dealers were running their businesses. By 1985, the high cost of real estate, overhead and inventory financing had dictated a situation where only the big dealers could survive. And a further consolidation of the existing dealerships into fewer, larger operations with even fewer owners seemed inevitable.

"The small guy is bailing out," said Mancuso. "It is a totally different business now." His capital requirements alone doubled in the first few months of 1985. "With big or multiple dealerships," said Joe Ricci, who has AMC/Renault outlets in Detroit, Chicago and St. Petersburg, "you can cut overhead costs, you are protected from the whims of the economy, and you have clout with the factory."

The dealership of the future, everyone seemed to agree, would have many shapes. One of those shapes was already readily apparent: the multiple outlet with two or more brands operating on one site. Also, large chains began to spring up in the '60s and were flourising two decades later. The most famous is the string of West Coast dealerships owned, at least in part, by legendary TV pitchman, Cal Worthington.

GM reportedly was studying a whole new concept in dealer distribution for its Saturn project cars which could be sold in low-markup, high-volume "discount store" fashion. Saturn dealers might do nothing but sell cars. Customers would have their cars serviced elsewhere, with warranty work, perhaps, being contracted out to any one of a number of budding auto service chains such as Goodyear and Firestone.

In 1983, Martin Swig, a San Francisco multi-outlet dealer, consolidated his six dealerships under one roof in what is believed to be the nation's first auto sales mall. It drew wide attention as perhaps the ideal dealership of the future, offering one-stop shopping.

Following the move, said Swig, "my business jumped 50 percent, to about 5000 new cars a year. We offer everything: a service area with specialists, an auto clothing boutique and an automotive book store. Eventually I would like to increase to as many as 12 dealerships here."

With the change in dealer size and shape, there appeared also to be a change in the time-honored high-pressure sales technique. It was a soft approach that dealers said they now wanted. Explained AMC/Renault dealer Ricci: "We take the approach that it is the customer and dealer working together, not opposing each other. The salesman and the customer are one, trying to find the best deal. We threw out our rectangular tables. No one is taking sides. They are all round tables now."

But have things really changed? Swig, a maverick of sorts, is skeptical: "It's just a nice attempt to disguise a cretin trying to beat you up." **MT**

GM CARS RATED BEST 8TH YEAR IN A ROW.

1982-1984 passenger cars with "Substantially Better than Average" overall injury claim experience.

	Make	Body	Relative Frequency
✔ 1.	Oldsmobile Custom Cruiser	SW	54
2.	Volvo 240	SW	56
3.	Mercedes-Benz 380SL Coupe	SS	57
✔ 4. } Tie	Oldsmobile Delta 88	4D	59
✔ 4. } Tie	Buick Electra	SW	59
6.	Mercedes-Benz 300SD/SE	SS	60
✔ 7. } Tie	Buick LeSabre	4D	62
✔ 7. } Tie	Oldsmobile Ninety-Eight	4D	62
✔ 9. } Tie	Chevrolet Corvette	SS	63
9. } Tie	Jaguar XJ6	SS	63
9. } Tie	Dodge Caravan	SW	63

Source: Highway Loss Data Institute. **Body Styles:** SW=Station Wagon; SS=Specialty. All results are stated in relative frequency of injury claims. A relative injury claim frequency of 100 is average. Relative frequencies of less than 70 are defined by HLDI as "Substantially Better than Average."

The Highway Loss Data Institute (HLDI) is a non-profit public service organization associated with the Insurance Institute for Highway Safety. As it has done for several years, HLDI has summarized and published its findings on the frequency of automotive insurance claims.

This year, HLDI finds that 6 of the top 11 models with overall injury claim experience defined as "substantially better than average," are General Motors cars.

We are pleased that GM cars are rated best again, as they have been ever since HLDI started summarizing its findings eight years ago.

We believe this continued excellence reflects not only our cars—their quality, size, weight, and design—but also how and where they are driven.

The HLDI results show that our cars and our customers go well together. And we trust it will continue that way in the years ahead. Because we are doing our part to see that it does.

That's the GM commitment to excellence.

Chevrolet
Pontiac
Oldsmobile
Buick
Cadillac
GMC Truck

Nobody sweats the details like GM.

THE CLASSIC CARS

The best minds created them, the best hands built them, and only the most wealthy could afford them.

By Dean Batchelor

☐ A classic car transcends the others of its time in aesthetics, engineering, innovation, performance, design, construction and overall appeal. The Classic Car Club of America has its own definition of a classic, and it includes only certain makes and models of cars built between 1925 and 1948. Our view is broader than that.

Many cars have been built since 1900 that seem to fit our criteria, far too many to examine in detail here. But what they all had in common was "an iconoclastic design and identification" which set them apart from other cars of the time. Here are some of the best of the best:

Austro-Daimler

In 1899 an Austrian manufacturing branch was established in Vienna by the Gottlieb Daimler company of Germany. Paul Daimler, Gottlieb's son, was the director for the first six years while the company made Daimler automobiles, but in 1905 he was replaced by Ferdinand Porsche who had just left the Lohner company, also in Vienna. The Austrian concern became a separate company in 1906 and began to manufacture cars to Porsche's designs.

The 1910 Austro-Daimler Prince Henry

model was the first of Porsche's designs to attract wide attention; he had expected the car to win the Prince Henry Tour, and it did—the first time out. The engine was unique in having five valves per cylinder— one inlet and four exhausts—operated by a single overhead camshaft. According to the *Complete Encyclopedia of Motorcars, 1885 to the Present*, "A combination of well-shaped combustion chambers and light, reciprocating parts made for an engine of an efficiency never before seen in a catalogued, non-racing car."

Before leaving Austro-Daimler in 1923 to return to Daimler in Germany, Porsche designed series I, II and III of the ADM model, whose three-liter engine developed 100 horsepower and could move the car at 100 miles per hour.

Karl Rabe replaced Porsche at A-D and

Briggs Cunningham's 1927 Bugatti Type 41 Royale is one of six cars, each different, each spectacular in its own way. Bugatti intended them for crowned heads, but there is no record of a royal personage ever owning one. Today, all are in museums.

PHOTOS: JOHN LAMM

Murphy, Rollston, Walker, and Willoughby. The problem is that bodywork by these craftsmen sometimes appeared on the mediocre and mundane chassis as well as on the Great Ones. Beauty, in those cases, was only skin deep.

When you talk about a Duesenberg J or SJ, beauty goes all the way, inside and out. When E.L. Cord retained Fred Duesenberg to create "The Best Car in the World," Duesenberg did just that. The 1929 Model J was the most costly car on the American market and had more than twice the horsepower of its nearest rival (the Chrysler Imperial), with 265 claimed horses under that long, sleek hood.

The Duesy was also the fastest car on the road then, and for several years to come. At the introduction, the publicity claimed that a stock Duesenberg Model J had been timed on the Indianapolis track at 116 miles per hour, and at 89 mph in second gear. Remember, this was in 1929.

Flashy cars, and particularly those with performance to match, were the darlings of the Hollywood movie crowd, and Hollywood took the Duesenberg to its heart like a long-lost family member; Clark Gable, Gary Cooper, Tyrone Power, Ben Blue, and Marion Davies all had Model Js or SJs, and New York mayor Jimmie Walker, King Alfonso of Spain, and Prince Nicholas of Rumania all had Duesenbergs.

Aside from the size, beauty and performance of the car, or maybe because of them, the Duesenberg was a macho ego trip. The owner could lift the hood and show his friends an engine that was built like an Indianapolis racer's engine—twin overhead camshafts, four valves per cylinder, and, on the SJ, a centifugal supercharger, the first put into production on any car.

The massive crankshaft in the Lycoming-built eight ran in five plain bearings and was balanced by a device unique to Duesenberg. Two cartridges, three and three-quarters inches long and two inches in diameter, were filled with 16 ounces of mercury (to 94 percent of their capacity) and mounted on the crank cheeks between cylinders one and two. When the crank would start into a vibration period (all crankshafts do at some rpm), the friction within the mercury, and between the mercury and the baffles inside the cylinders, would effectively dampen the vibration.

The Duesenberg company built no bodies for its chassis, leaving all that up to selected custom coachbuilders. The customer could choose from Duesenberg designs (by Gordon Beuhrig, chief designer for the company), or he could order from catalogs supplied by the coachbuilders. Mainly, bodies were built by Brunn, Derham, LeBaron, Murphy, and Rollston.

It may be arguable whether the greatest appeal in a Duesenberg was the engine/chassis or the coachwork, but there is no doubt that the combination was superb—creating some of the most classic and elegant cars of the Classic period.

Isotta-Fraschini

Isotta-Fraschini started in Milan, Italy, in 1899 as assemblers of the French Renault, but in 1902 the company built the first of the type for which it was to become famous—an expensive and powerful competitor for the Mercedes. In 1905, during an expansion program, Giustino Cattaneo, a brilliant engineer, came to I-F and his influence would be felt on every car made by the company from then on.

Isotta was heavily involved in racing and won the Florio Cup in 1907 and the Targa

Florio in 1908. By 1909, 75 percent of I-F's production was exported, and most of that to the United States—the overseas success was attributed directly to the company's racing victories.

A new, single-overhead-camshaft engine with rocker arms actuating four valves per cylinder, designed by Cattaneo, was brought out in 1911. It produced 140 horsepower at 1800 rpm which, for those days, was a high-speed engine.

Like Rolls-Royce in England, Isotta-Fraschini made aircraft engines (General Italo Balbo's long-distance flights were made in planes with I-F engines), and, like R-R, the company started producing only one model after World War I. Italy was still a poor country, recovering from the ravages of war, and the money to be made in the automobile market was in exporting, so why not build the biggest and best?

This I-F model, the Tipo 8, had the first production straight-eight engine. It had 366 cubic inches, pushrod overhead valves, and was a long-stroke engine producing only 80 horsepower at 2200 rpm, allowing the car to reach a top speed of about 80 miles per hour.

Replacing the Tipo 8 in 1924 was the first revision, the 8A. Engine size had been increased to 450 cubic inches, and horsepower was up to 120 at 2400 rpm.

Along with the 8A, a shorter, lighter, and more highly-tuned version called the 8ASS (8A Super Sport) was brought out in 1926. This model was guaranteed to achieve 100 miles per hour, yet retain the driving flexibility of the other, more sedate and stately models. The 8ASS was made until 1931 when it was replaced by the 8B.

Unfortunely, with so much of its market in the United States, the depression dealt a death blow to Isotta-Fraschini automobile sales, and the company fell back on its aircraft engines for salvation. By this time, however, the Italian aircraft industry was committed to air-cooled radial engines from Fiat, Alfa Romeo and Piaggio, once again leaving I-F holding the bag.

Isottas were the epitome of Italian design and craftsmanship, particularly during the 1920s and '30s, and again, like Rolls-Royce, Isotta built no bodywork, relying on the European coachbuilders—primarily Castagna, Farina, Figoni & Falaschi, Lotti, Sala, and Touring, with occasional bodies by LeBaron, Fleetwood, J. Gurney Nutting, Lancefield, or Hooper & Co. Ltd.

Isottas were big, elegant, comfortable, dependable and, like most Italian cars, were enjoyable to drive—for the owner or the chauffeur.

The last gasp from Isotta-Fraschini was in 1947, when the company built an attractive four-door sedan (body by Carrozzeria Touring) with a rear-mounted, water-cooled, 3.4-liter V-8 with a single overhead camshaft on each bank of cylinders. The engine was in a unit with a five-speed transmission driving the rear wheels. It is unlikely that more than 20 of this model, the Monterosa, were made, and there is no

Ceremonial use, like this display of Ohio politicians in a 1932 Chrysler LeBaron, helped insure the survival of many classics, some still owned by municipalities.

What will be.

It will be a new design. All that has been will be the beginning. The engine will be larger. Aerodynamic advantages will be taken. The front will be lower for less wind resistance. And for greater driver visibility. The overall height will be reduced. There will be more headroom.

The body will be rigid and solid. The car will be stable. A unique and compact suspension inspired by race cars will help hold the car to the road. The handling will be outstanding. While the ride will be comfortable and quiet. There will be two body styles. Sedan and Hatchback.

The new Honda Accord LXi Sedan. It's the first ever front-wheel drive car with double wishbone suspension on all four wheels. It rides smoothly and comfortably over city streets and highways. It handles like an absolute joy. Every convenience has been considered.

The new Honda Accord LXi Hatchback. Its sleek low look is more than styling. It's a vastly improved aerodynamic shape. Air flows cleanly over the car. Inside, you will find it's quiet and comfortable. There are no comparisons to the new Accord. They haven't been made yet.

© 1985 American Honda Motor Co., Inc.

The New Accord HONDA

CALIFORNIA
A DUZY

Perhaps the best example of an American classic, this Duesenberg Model J Tourster has a Durham body designed by Gordon Buehrig. With 265 horsepower, its engine produced twice the output of other classics of the era: performance matched beauty.

horsepower, but in 1936 the engine was enlarged to 5.4 liters, and the designation was then 540K. In this new guise, the power was rated at 180.

Mercedes-Benz has not actively participated in competition since the mid-1950s, but the company's plan to produce the ultimate in high-speed touring cars has not wavered in 100 years. The postwar 300SL coupes and roadsters, the later 450SL and now the 500 series cars can safely be considered the ultimate in multi-passenger, high-speed-with-safety motoring.

Minerva

Antwerp, Belgium was the home of Minerva Motors from 1900 to 1939, and during that time the company built some of the finest cars of the period. Production ranged from small cars of two, three, and four cylinders in the early 1900s to a 12-liter, six-cylinder model in 1907.

But the Minerva that got the attention of the motoring world was shown at the 1908 Brussels Salon. It was a 1909 model, with a Knight double sleeve-valve engine, which was to become the standard Minerva powerplant from 1910 until the company's demise in 1939.

Sleeve-valve engines were quiet, one of the niceties of a luxury automobile, but not everyone trusted this type of engine. Yet, Minerva won the Winter Cup in Sweden's Winter Trials of 1911, 1913, and 1914, and placed second, fourth and fifth in the 1914 Tourist Trophy. Henry Ford even bought a Minerva for his personal use in 1913.

By 1919 there was a 20-CV *(Cheval Vapeur*, or taxable horsepower) four, and a 30-CV six—the latter being very popular in the U.S.

The most magnificent Minerva of all was the 1930 AL model, with its 402-cubic-inch straight-eight engine and four-speed transmission. The car was big, on a 145-inch wheelbase, fast for its time and size, and sported the most elegant coachwork of the European coachbuilders—usually Van Den Plas, Grummer, Letourneur et Marchand, Hibbard & Darrin (later Fernandez & Darrin), or Weymann.

Hollywood discovered the Minerva, and many of the stars, producers and directors drove them. The legendary Flo Ziegfeld owned several of them, and Rudolf Friml had one with a piano keyboard in the rear compartment.

The big eight, a smaller four-liter eight, and a six were offered through 1934, and in 1933 a short-chassis sports model was available, but this was the end of the line for the big, elegant cars from Belgium.

Owners report that the Minerva was a particularly good road car: smooth, silent, and although big and heavy (around 6000 pounds), it steered easily, and the vacuum-assisted brakes would bring the car to a stop with little driver effort.

In 1935 Minerva took over the Belgian Imperia car company and produced a four-cylinder small car. The most interesting car to come from this amalgamation was in 1937 when an experimental car was built with a transverse, 3.6-liter V-8 engine and front-wheel drive. The car never got into production and hasn't been seen since, but it did precede GM's similar efforts by more than 40 years.

Rolls-Royce

Of all the cars produced in England, three stand out in our search for elegance, luxury, quality and style in the Grand Manner: Lanchester, Daimler and Rolls-Royce.

In 1904 Royce Ltd. was formed, becoming Rolls-Royce in 1906. The last 80 years have seen many great cars from this company which claims to build "The Best Car in the World," but the first Rolls-Royce to become immortal debuted in 1906. It was the 40/50-horsepower six, known to the world as the Silver Ghost.

During the life of the Silver Ghost, 6173 were made, first at Manchester, then at the new plant at Derby, England. In 1920, an American Rolls-Royce factory opened in Springfield, Massachusetts, which produced Silver Ghosts through 1926. The American-built Rolls-Royce had left-hand steering, and some of the best looking of the Ghosts were built at Springfield, with Brewster bodywork.

The 7.7-liter, six-cylinder Phantom I, in production from 1927 to 1931, was also built both at Derby and at Springfield—the latter with Brewster bodywork.

A Phantom II was brought out in 1930, but the big change for Rolls-Royce was seen at the 1935 auto shows when a 7.3-liter V-12-engined Phantom III was shown. This was the first Rolls-Royce to have independent front suspension, and the model was to become one of the most outstanding of an outstanding line of cars.

There are those who would dispute the Rolls-Royce claim of "The Best Car in the World," but there is little dispute that this is the perceived view by most of the public. And there is no dispute that Rolls-Royce builds elegant, superbly crafted automobiles that give their owners a feeling of owning the best.

A Rolls-Royce owner pays dearly for this elevated status, but it would be harder to find an owner who regrets his purchase than it would be to find a non-owner who would like to join the ranks.

To add to the mystique, the company has never advertised horsepower or torque figures since WW II, but the various engines used over the years have always been adequate for any R-R owner's use. And R-R has kept abreast of other technical developments, going to unit body construction in 1965, along with four-wheel independent suspension, four-wheel disc brakes and automatic self-leveling. Later came fuel injection and other state-of-the-art changes.

A Rolls-Royce owner is always pampered, with Connolly leather interiors, burled walnut wood trim, and every known device to make the owner/driver feel important (and as though he's gotten his money's worth). In this, they succeed better than any of the pretenders to the throne—which adds further to owner satisfaction and loyalty to the marque, and it helps continue the R-R reputation.

It is a mystique to match anything else in the automotive world, including Ferrari, Bugatti, Porsche, Mercedes-Benz and Alfa Romeo. **MT**

Even at a weight of over 6000 pounds, Minervas, like this 1931 model, were smooth, silent and responsive road cars with advanced engines and suspensions.
PHOTO: DEAN BATCHELOR

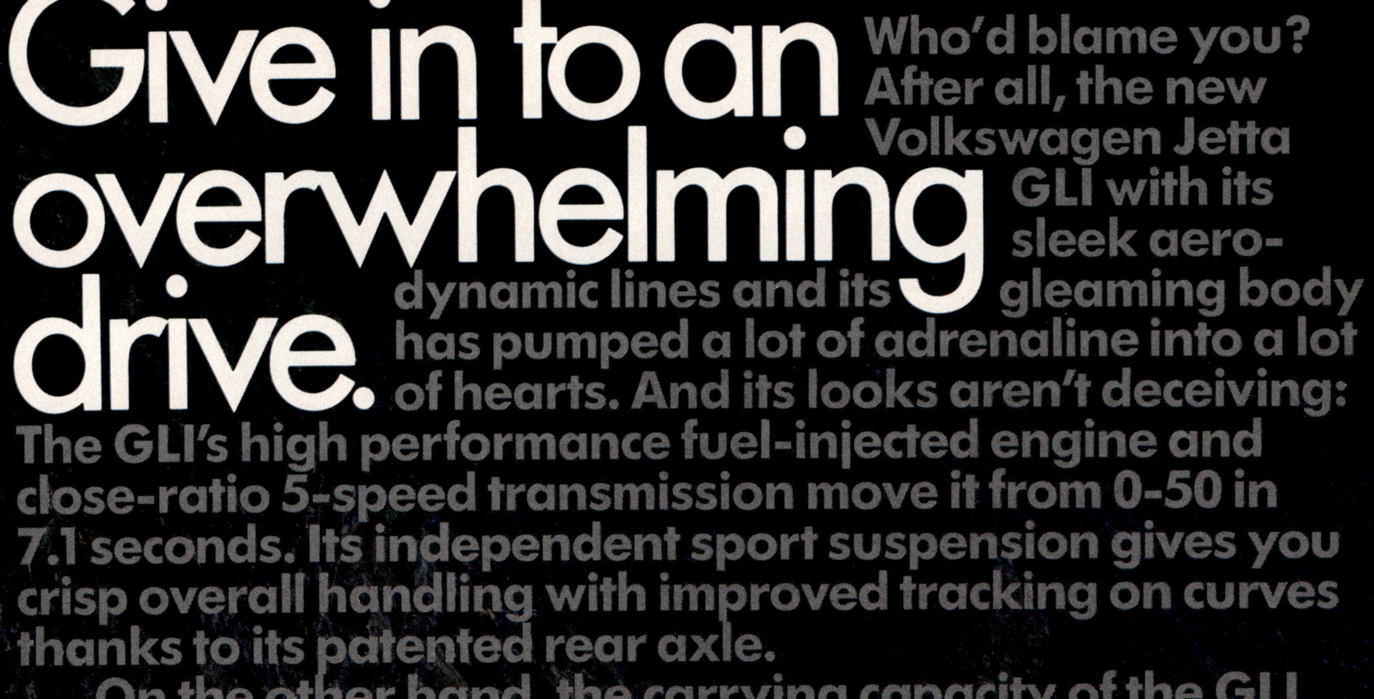

Give in to an overwhelming drive.
Who'd blame you? After all, the new Volkswagen Jetta GLI with its sleek aero-dynamic lines and its gleaming body has pumped a lot of adrenaline into a lot of hearts. And its looks aren't deceiving: The GLI's high performance fuel-injected engine and close-ratio 5-speed transmission move it from 0-50 in 7.1 seconds. Its independent sport suspension gives you crisp overall handling with improved tracking on curves thanks to its patented rear axle.
On the other hand, the carrying capacity of the GLI (5 people and 14 standard size pieces of luggage) makes it unbelievably practical. And its remarkably low price makes it practically unbelievable.
The 1986 Jetta GLI.
It's not a car. It's a Volkswagen.
Seatbelts save lives. All Volkswagens are covered by a 2-year Unlimited-mileage Protection Plan and a 6-year limited warranty on corrosion perforation. See dealer for details about these limited warranties. © 1985 Volkswagen.

FINS AND FANTASY

Was it a Golden Era or The Age of Gorp? The Fabulous Fifties went from one extreme to the other.

By Jerry Flint

☐ Call it the age of excess, if you will. Longer, lower, wider. Tail fins and Buick portholes, Edsel and wrap-around windshields, the hard top, the vinyl roof, four-barrel carburetors, four-tone paint and purple Lincolns, drive-ins and waitresses who chewed gum and said "Hiyuhbub," while the guys stood around looking under each others' hoods.

But there was more to the Fifties than excess. This was the Golden Age: the high-compression engine, automatic transmissions, power steering, and mass production—58 million cars built in the decade—all the parts came together, and they worked. Those cars created a mobile society, an escape from the concrete jungles, and those people who later sneered at the suburbs had never lived in the slums of yesterday's cities. If there were Edsels, some of the most beautiful cars ever created rolled out in the '50s: the 1953 Studebaker, Ford's Thunderbird, the 1955 V-8 Chevrolet, even the Corvair. Independents like Packard and Hudson and Crosley and Willys and Kaiser died, but the survivors had the courage to innovate. Remember Chevy's rear-engined, air-cooled Corvair, and Ford's steel-roofed convertible? Then too.

they created practical cars, like the steel-bodied station wagon, jut right for a generation that was pioneering and needed to haul the fertilizer and sheet rock. If styling was important, why not? This was an age of catch-up for ten million men who had gone to war—catch up on the money, catch up on the family, back to normality, no time for frivolity. Maybe this Organization Man generation needed something wild just for the change. Anyway, everyone forgot how stodgy cars had been before the Fifties. "We thought it was a real breakthrough to match dark mud-colored mohair to mouse-gray mohair," said Gene Bordinat, who became the styling chief of Ford. The leader of the pack was Harley Earl, GM's first stylist.

"My primary purpose for 28 years has been to lengthen and lower the American automobile," Earl said. "Why? Because my sense of proportion tells me that oblongs

How it all started. Though tail fins are not remembered too fondly today, there was a time when being first in fins meant money in the bank. General Motors commissioned this cartoon to keep the story straight and give credit where it was due.

are more attractive than squares."

But when you talk about the Fifties, it's the fins you remember.

Harley Earl got the idea looking at the twin-tailed P-38 fighter of World War II. Airplanes meant excitement; these were the days of *A Yank in the RAF* and *Thirty Seconds Over Tokyo*.

"Today the stylists generally believe it was a mistake to think of automobiles as airplanes, but it was hot stuff then," said Bill Mitchell, who succeeded Earl as top GM stylist. Earl's team developed models with pontoon fenders, cockpits, toggle switches, pointed noses (the 1950 Studebaker had an airplane-like nose), and fins. Only the fins stuck. The first fin popped up on the 1948 Cadillac, just a cute fishtail at the rear, just right for Cadillac, a flip of frivolity and the end of that long serious car. By the middle of the decade, finomania exploded. Chrysler, which had ignored styling for a quarter-century and paid the price, turned the fin into art with the 1957s: high, graceful slanting fins climbing from the middle of the car to the tail. GM was frightened: "We said, by God, we've got to get them," Mitchell of GM recalled. "We tried to outfin Chrysler." The GM fins of 1959 were so outrageous—that finomania died in laughter.

But before the end, even greater fins were on the drawing board. Chrysler planned a big single off-center fin, starting in a ridge on the hood and then running along the roof, rising in a single rib at the tail. "And if you think that was tough," said Bob Anderson, a Chrysler product man who now runs Rockwell International and builds B-1 bombers, "you should have tried to get it on the station wagons."

The industry came out of World War II with plans for small cars—there was even talk of a $500 price—but these were junked since everyone wanted wheels, and it was just easier to produce the old prewar models. In fact, in 1948 the British army tried to convince Henry Ford to take over a car plant in occupied Germany. "Mr. Ford, I don't think what we are being offered here is worth a damn," said young Henry Ford II's aide. Since Ford wouldn't take it, the British told the German manager to go ahead and try to make some jobs by building cars—and Heinz Nordhoff cleaned up the place and started building a tiny beetle-shaped car called the Volkswagen.

The first really new car was the 1947 Studebaker with wrap-around rear windows; Bob Hope joked that he couldn't tell if it was coming or going, but the Studebaker was a success. Next came the step-down Hudson of 1948, and the new models from Kaiser-Frazer, the one success—at least for a while—of the 32 men or companies that tried to enter the car business after the war. (Possibly the most famous was Preston Tucker, whose Tucker Torpedo was the most exciting prospect, even though it never quite made it.)

The first full wave of postwar cars from Ford, GM and Chrysler was the 1949 models. The '49 Ford was only the fourth

The 1949 Buick was the first production "hardtop convertible" and the pillar-less look would soon spread through the industry, reaching its peak with the 4-door hardtops of the late '50s. Buick's portholes and spear became the division's trademarks and the stylists were stuck with them for nearly a generation.

new car in the company's history (after the Model T, the Model A and the Ford V-8 of the 1930s). Ford was number three behind Chrysler then, and the new car being readied for production was big and heavy. The Ford boss, an ex-GM man named Ernie Breech, was worried. "Show us the way to go," he prayed as he drove home one night. The next morning he called his Ford team together and said: "I have a vision. We start from scratch." The '49 Ford was a stunner, clean, with a distinctive spinner nose, with the fenders integrated into the body lines (the slab side), and Ford caught up with the remainder of the industry mechanically with new axles, springs, shocks and frame.

GM made history, too, with the high-compression, short (piston) stroke Cadillac V-8, 221 pounds lighter than the old engine with 7 percent more horsepower and a 14 percent gain in fuel economy. There was nothing particularly revolutionary about the Cadillac (and Oldsmobile) V-8s, but for the first time all the new thinking of what an engine should be was put together, and it worked. These engines killed the straight eights and pushed the sixes to the back burner. And Buick started the hardtop revolution that year. For those who have forgotten, the hardtops had no pillar to the roof behind the front door, giving them a crisp convertible look, and they were originally called "Hardtop Convertibles" although they weren't convertibles.

All the pretty girls and smiles in the world couldn't sell the "bathtub" Nash of 1951. It was followed by a succession of cars that were even worse, and by 1956, when Nash made a desperation try at multi-tone paint, chrome spears, continental kit and vestigial fins, it was too late; only 4000 cars were built. Even the fold-down seats which created a bedroom-on-wheels (left) were insufficient to lure customers.

Chevrolet didn't quite know what to do with its Corvette at first. A coupe and wagon version were shown in Motoramas, never manufactured. The 1953 production roadster (top left) was slow and didn't handle. It wasn't until the V-8 and Zora Arkus-Duntov that the 'Vette clicked.

The 1955 to 1957 Chevrolets are among the classics of the period. Though the '55 is more aesthetically pleasing, the '57 Bel Air convertible (above) is the most desired today, perfect copies bringing as much as $25,000. The '57 Plymouth (left) is not as desirable, but its slim roof line and general coherence make it one of the more balanced designs of the time.

Chrysler came out with the all-steel station wagon, which opened the way for the wagon boom, and the key-operated ignition that was the [...] the starter button. [...]

Big news in 195[...] a small car called t[...] long and a subcor[...] ards. George Mas[...] was a great believ[...] to prove small did[...] Rambler was a co[...] whitewalls and clo[...] bler had a good y[...] and was killed in [...] collapsed in 195[...] brought out and [...] rected. Nash also [...] the rear seat of it [...] joke was that the [...] upholstery more [...]

But the new G[...] cant than chrom[...] king of the stocks[...] it the first car it[...] come from the fac[...] ing and top 90 m[...] race was on. In 1[...] its new V-8, calle[...] of its unique he[...] chamber to challe[...] V-8. The Chrysle[...] Cadillac's 160. Ca[...] 190 horses in 195[...] at 235, and by 1[...] Mercury models [...] but that is test-s[...] means the figures [...] was cheap (25 ce[...]

was a problem, it was that by the middle of the decade, steering and brakes weren't keeping up with straight-ahead power. [...]

was only about $50 under the price of a low-end Chevrolet. Joe Frazer said a Georgia farmer described the Henry J to him "like an unsavory gal ah once knew. She [...]

THE HORSEPOWER WARS

If more was better, then too much was just right.
Or, why you needed 400 ponies to cruise Woodward.

By Ro McGonegal

☐ Youth and money came together in the sixties like never before, and there was plenty of both. Don't trust anyone over 30 was the motto, rock and roll the anthem, and doing your own thing was the style. Some in the establishment saw it as a threat, others as an opportunity. In 1973, Lee Iacocca, then president of Ford, told the *Saturday Evening Post*: "We planned the 1965 Mustang in 1962 as a youthful package . . . . The success of that car is automotive history. The purchasers were mostly in the 18- to 24-year-old bracket, and many single women went for that kind of car. It was a Mustang generation."

Let's slip on the old wide-angle lens and step back for a bigger look. Some argue that the musclecar was atonement for the wanton styling atrocities Detroit had committed during the late '50s and early '60s, but according to popular lore, the idea was hatched in the offices of MacManus, John and Adams, the Detroit advertising agency which handled the Pontiac high-performance account. The ramrod for this project was Jim Wangers, a man whose enthusiasm and energy was matched only by his caginess.

In 1963, he participated in the concep-

tion and the merchandising of the first musclecar, the GTO. Wangers even supplied the lyrics for "Little GTO," a popular ballad that got national play. But none of this would have happened had it not been for an ambitious inside agitator, the young engineer John DeLorean.

Pontiac and the sister divisions had engendered a successful racing program, but in January 1963, General Motors deemed active participation in motor racing (and the horsepower that had slithered from their grip like a hungry anaconda) undesirable from an ethics standpoint.

A mandate prohibited the installation of a standard engine larger than 330 cubic inches in an intermediate-class body; thus the big V-8 was exclusive to the heavy Catalina and Bonneville. Readers of the space between the lines saw this "back-pedaling"

BELVEDERE
GTX
Z/28
BOSS 302
TURBO-JET
427
road runner
GRAN TORINO Sport
SUPER BEE
SS 396
Charger R/T
383 FOUR BARREL
440 MAGNUM
SHELBY G.T. 500
BOSS 429
GTO 400 CID

as a matter of semantics. If the standard engine couldn't be larger, what was wrong with a larger *optional* engine?

Soon, the loophole was big enough to drive a 389-cubic-inch engine through it. Its 335 horsepower was only part of a package which included a heavy-duty suspension, a 4-speed manual transmission, and red-stripe wide-oval tires in a car 800 pounds lighter than the Bonneville.

The GTO made history because it was the first car to offer preposterous pavement-ripping to the average-income buyer, the you-and-me dreamer who couldn't afford a Corvette, or a limited-production quasi-racer, or a Ferrari. With a stroke on the dotted line and a $3400 payment book, the power was his to use at will. The emphasis, of course, was on straight-line acceleration and handling. Uninhibited cornering was left to the notion of the foreign sports car, an odious, 4-cylinder, gas-sipping plot which could eventually water down good red American blood.

Down in Dearborn, Lee Iacocca had seen his vision of a youthful personal car. He sensed the time for small size and high spirits, in short, everything he hoped the Mustang would be. He wanted a simple, stylish car to wedge between the big American automobile and the small foreign sporty jobs he knew made the ultimate sense. The Mustang was born on April 17, 1964 as a 1965 model.

Iacocca's foresight and the guts to make it happen were uncommon in Detroit. In those days, the consumers were taught to think BIG. Iacocca also realized the importance of women buyers and that they would exert a frightening amount of financial clout. Where the GM and Chrysler musclecars were masculine in design, the

Mustang was created for a broader, looser market and destined for a much larger cut of the pie.

Though it wouldn't take long for the 'Stang to develop muscles of its own, it did its best being a very versatile automobile. And in versatility were huge profits. In the Mustang, the lowly six-cylinder made as much sense as the V-8. Those with aberrant genes could call up giddy performance from a special version of the 289-cubic-inch engine. It produced 271 horsepower, and it was only the beginning.

By this time, every soldier in the arch-conservative Detroit hierarchy had gone to the mattresses, supplying a patriotic spawn of power, guts and glory at a price every worker could afford. Whatever the climate, it was most certainly affected by the advent of the overhead-valve V-8. In earlier days, such exotica had been available only to those who could afford the luxury of a Cadillac or Oldsmobile, which had been V-8 powered since 1949.

In 1954, Ford took the first step and introduced the 239-cubic-inch OHV V-8. A year later, Chevrolet counterattacked with a 265-cubic-inch V-8 and lit the fuse to Detroit's most piquant rivalry. For the first time, modern engine technology was affordable to Everyman, and during the next five years, Detroit plunged into an orgy of research and development, the likes of which has not been seen since.

You could have multiple carburetion, fuel-injection or a supercharger just for the asking. These crude, powerful engines rippled the air with unburned hydrocarbons, fumes that were usually accompanied by a cloud of smoke and a woeful moan of bias-ply tires. After five minutes behind the wheel of one of these bombs, migraine

headaches and the ordinary blahs were forgotten. And for the first time, ears rang with esoterica of the J-2 Olds, a car called Bonneville, and a Hurst four-on-the-floor.

Despite a recession or two, America was on a roll that seemed endless. Natural resources were considered infinite, and post-WW II citizens had been ushered unwittingly into the throw-away society. We have plenty here, and if we waste a little, well, what's the difference? With leaded high-test at 30 cents per gallon, a matrix of smooth, wide interstate roads, and as much horsepower as a locomotive under the hood, premium fuel seemed a birthright rather than a privilege.

The hottest Detroit iron averaged 350 cubic inches, although most had a considerably larger engine. Ford had the 352 and Chevrolet the 348-cubic-inch engine, both refugees from light-duty trucks, but pumped up with a larger induction system and a livelier camshaft. In 1961, the Ford grew to 390 cubic inches. Chevrolet flanked it with the single four-barrel 409 and Ford revamped the original to yield 401 cubic inches and topped it off with three two-barrel carburetors.

The competition was fierce and the mood bordered on paranoia. Chrysler hurried the 413 engine into limited production to ward off their bumptious neighbors and to soak up the media limelight.

Detroit had total commitment to motor racing, but was most sympathetic to NASCAR competition and to drag racing. The idea was to race (and win) on Sunday and sell on Monday. To the kindred souls, race cars were the same as the cars they drove every day and said goodnight to every evening. Brand loyalty ran deep. Silent oaths were taken and sealed with a mixture of blood and gasoline, and the bumper sticker of one cabal proclaimed, "On the eighth day, God created the Hemi."

The musclecar was like leaving a V-2 rocket in the charge of a high-school chemistry student. By 1966, you could get 271 horsepower in the Mustang (the Shelby GT-350 Mustang produced 306 horsepower and more), and the Fairlane, Falcon and Comet; the full-size Galaxie got a 427 engine which was conservatively rated at 425 horsepower—with the right option number, you could order one of 50 dual-carburetor 427 Fairlanes that were street-legal but had an induction system and cylinder heads built especially for drag racing. Pontiac had the Goat with three two-barrel carburetors and Olds, the 4-4-2 (four-barrel carb, four-speed and two incorrigible exhaust pipes). The 4-4-2 was also available with the W-30 option, a rare combination of three carburetors, forced cold-air induction, a hot cam and 400 cubic inches.

Chevrolet joined the musclecar race in the middle of 1965 with the introduction of the SS 396 Chevelle (the 396 was a new engine, the keystone of all Chevrolet big-blocks). It produced 325, 350 or 375 horsepower (the last engine came directly from the '65 Corvette where it rated 425 horsepower). The keen L-79 327-cubic-inch,

This was an early, experimental version of one of the ancestors of the Musclecar, the Chrysler 300. Fortunately, some rare executive with taste shot it down.

TOP:
Muscle was everywhere. Richard Petty's Plymouth (43) chases Fireball Roberts' Pontiac. "Stock" cars like these brought people to the showroom to buy copies.

ABOVE CENTER:
Drag strips became marketing tools, selling lots of 409 Chevys and making heroes of speed-shifting drivers like Dave Strickler (left) and "Dyno" Don Nicholson (right).

ABOVE:
Does Butch Leal's Plymouth (right) look unusual? To gain an advantage wheelwells were moved, bodies were acid dipped, and subtle changes made: hence "funny car."

Making cars of the future for almost a century.

José J. Dedeurwaerder President and CEO

The auto industry's hundred-year record of growth and progress is a story of change and challenge. At American Motors we are proud to have been a major contributor to that exciting history.

American Motors became an industry leader in compact car design and innovation in the 1950's and 1960's. That leadership role was expanded in the 1970's by the acquisition of Jeep Corporation with its global reputation for four-wheel-drive quality and durability.

Today, the award-winning Jeep Cherokee and Wagoneer have redefined the boundaries of the four-wheel-drive market with their appeal to comfort-oriented drivers who had never before considered a four-wheel-drive vehicle.

AMC is committed to be even more innovative in both passenger cars and four-wheel-drive vehicles. Our Jeep vehicles continue to set the four-wheel-drive standard worldwide. And our unique partnership with Renault has made European technology affordable in cars like Alliance and Encore.

In 1987, we'll introduce the U.S. version of the Renault Alpine V-6 Turbo sports car, already a proven winner in Europe. That same year, we'll also introduce new compact and intermediate cars that will challenge the market leaders in styling and engineering.

With aggressive product development like this, we will meet the challenges of the next century.

RENAULT | Jeep
American Motors Corporation

1984
1983

seconds and the quarter-mile in 14 or less. Handling was related directly to the throttle. Though most musclecars were abhorrent understeerers, mashing on the throttle summoned a wave of oversteer. Despite their bulk, the four-wheeled water buffalos were usually very good at stopping. According to *Motor Trend*, the whale-like Hemi Cuda, with its giant disc brakes and polyglass wide-ovals, needed only 125 feet to go from 60-to-0 (the modern Corvette, with a vastly better braking system and unimpeachable tires requires the same space).

But these elephantine quaffers gained only 10 miles for every gallon of fuel they burned, and they sent enormous clouds of pollutants into the atmosphere. Environmentalists realized the peril, but the greed of the average consumer, fed by relentless advertising and secured by trust in Detroit and the automobile industry in general, did not wane. At this time, interest in the all-around high-performance car gained momentum with the introduction of the Camaro Z/28, AAR Cuda, Boss Mustang and others. Detroit had seen the chicken scratching on the backyard fence, but continued to offer as much engine as the national conscience and the insurance company would allow.

The first Fuel Crisis came like a cold rain in October 1973, and flotillas of four-cylinder imports were sold in large urban areas like Los Angeles, which had been a haven for the musclecar. Insurance surcharges leaped again. Then the guillotine slammed down. Catalytic converters, low-octane unleaded fuel and five-mile-per-hour bumpers doomed the musclecar to a paper-tiger existence.

Besides worn-out tires and big insurance premiums, what did we get from the factory-built hot rod? The musclecar was supported by a wealth of technical expertise developed through regular production work and from racing experience. A lot of the metallurgy, tire technology and mechanical refinement developed for racing was (and always will be) used to make better cars. The power and the fuel economy produced by small, modern engines is related directly to fuel management systems and the cylinder-head efficiency of high-performance engines. The electronic ignition system we take for granted is another benefit. It has expanded to the microprocessing system without which the modern automobile could not exist.

The appetite for V-8 engines is still a big one, but the '60s generation, which learned propriety, prudence and respect for the environment are big fans of the four cylinder's efficient high performance. They put their faith in the turbocharger, fuel injection, clean air and quiche; in agile handling, maneuverability, recycling centers and in making money. Brand loyalty is feeble and has cobwebs; the modern performance car is usually expensive and not necessarily made in Detroit. The original musclecar is a curiosity now, and not unlike a tattoo discovered the morning after a long night of debauchery. **MT**

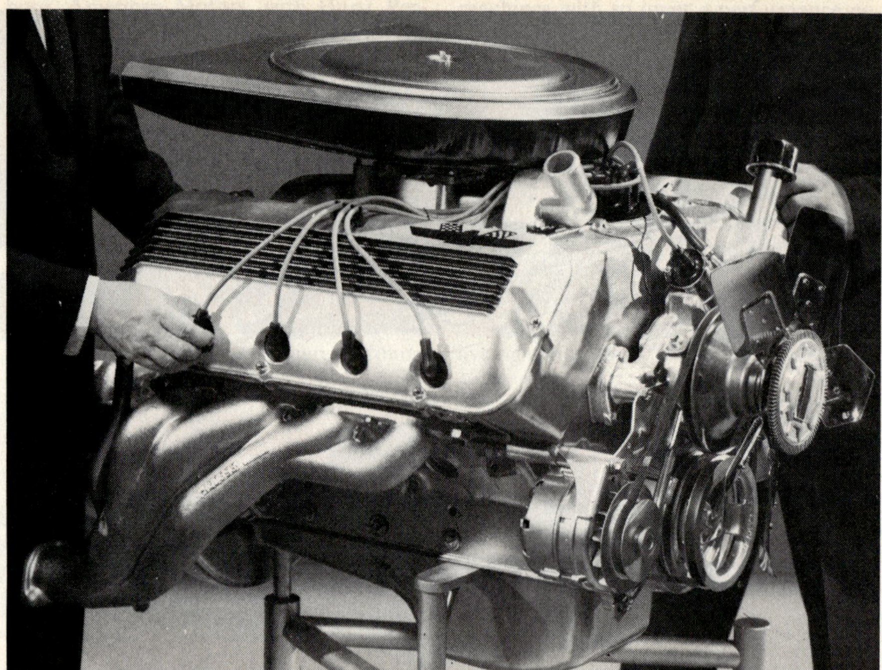

late November, 1898. The winner was a Belgian named Camille Jenatzy. He drove his electric-powered car up the hill at 18 mph. Second was a Bollée piston-engined car, and third was another electric—a Jeantaud, driven by the Compte Gaston de Chasseloup-Laubat.

The pioneer French motoring journal *La France Automobile* announced a week later it was sponsoring a *course de vitesse* (speed event) open to all, on a two-kilometer road in Acheres Park, near St. Germain, France. The event was created to be a speed contest between Jenatzy and Chasseloup-Laubat, but Jenatzy was unable to attend. The result, on December 12, 1898, was the first World Land Speed Record, set by a Jeantaud electric at 39.24 mph.

Hearing this, Jenatzy wrote *La France Automobile* with regrets for missing the event and offered a challenge to Chasseloup-Laubat. On January 17, 1899, the two met at Acheres. The challenger had the first run, and for the first time, the World Speed Record was broken—at 41.42 mph.

Within 10 minutes, the good Gaston took to the course and re-established the record at a speed of 43.69 mph. Two new World Records in one day, a foreign challenger defeated, and the third record within a month's time. *La France Automobile* had front-page news.

The Frenchman's joy was short-lived. Jenatzy returned to Achères on January 27 and raised the record to 49.92 mph. Things were getting serious. On March 4, Chasseloup-Laubat returned with his Jeantaud electric, wearing a new body with a knife-edged nose, a pointed tail, and a full-length underpan—the first LSR special. It worked, and the record once again fell—57.6 mph.

Jenatzy had not taken his defeat with grace, and immediately set his *Compagnie Internationale des Transports Automobiles Electriques Jenatzy* building a new car, the first of the special-built record attempt cars leading up to the Blue Flame.

The chassis rode on semi-elliptic springs, wood-spoke wheels and Michelin tires.

Two electric motors were attached to the rear axle, driving the rear wheels directly with no chains (which had proved a source of trouble on the Jeantaud electric car). Bodywork for this new car provided the most striking feature, with its "cigar shape" resting high on the chassis. Jenatzy dubbed his car "*Ne Jamais Contente*," or the "Never Satisfied." The car weighed 3190 pounds, 675 of it batteries.

On April 29, he made a successful bid to regain the record and established the first over-100-kilometer timed run, and the first at more than a mile a minute—65.79 mph, and 105.94 km/h (kilometers per hour).

Three years later, at the Nice, France *Semaine de Vitesse* (Week of Speed), a competition was held on the Promenade des Anglais to determine the fastest car present—the records, if any, were to be approved by the ACF (Automobile Club de France), the governing body of racing and records.

On April 13, 1902, during the Nice Speed Week, Leon Serpollet brought a four-cylinder, single-acting, steampowered "streamliner"—it actually looked more like an overurned rowboat with a prow at each end—and raised Jenatzy's record by almost 10 mph, to 75.06 mph. Because the Speed Week was near Easter, or because the Serpollet steam car had nicely rounded curves to its body, or maybe both, Serpollet called his car *Oeuf de Pâques,* or Easter Egg.

Several Americans had tried for a World Record by then, most notably William K. Vanderbilt, Jr., whose hobby was racing automobiles—and then, he made his attempts with foreign cars, a Mercedes-Simplex and a Mors.

Henry Ford would do no such thing. Realizing the value of high-speed records (as had the Europeans before him) for selling cars, he prepared the "Arrow," a twin to the "999" raced by Barney Oldfield. Ford's attempt would be made in January, 1904, a week before the New York Automobile Show, on frozen Lake St. Clair, Michigan, near Detroit.

The Arrow was probably one of the most basic machines ever to attempt a World Speed Record. It had a very simple channel frame with the rear axle bolted to it. The driveshaft from the massive four-cylinder, 16.7-liter engine drove exposed bevel gears on the rear axle, with no transmission and no differential. Ford did mount a small metal shield in front of the tiller steering mechanism, but other than that he was exposed to the frigid elements.

The lake and the weather were icy cold that January 12, 1904, and after a long warmup for the engine, Ford accelerated toward the measured mile in leaps and bounds—the lake not being as smooth as hoped for—not knowing if the car would come down straight from its porpoising trajectory or not. Somehow he held it through the mile, which he covered in 39.4 seconds, or 91.37 mph. The speed was accepted by the American Automobile Association, which had timed the run, but not by the A.C.F., and never went into the

TOP:
The bullet-shaped *Ne Jamais Contente*, driven by Camille Jenatzy, was the first car to cover a measured mile in less than a minute.

ABOVE:
W.K. Vanderbilt, Jr. (right), one of the first Americans to go for the record, lines up for a match race with Louis Ross' Stanley steamer.

Wheels and tires don't operate independently. They work together. But until now, you've had to select them the same way they were designed. Separately.

YOU'RE NOT LOOKING AT A WHEEL AND A TIRE.

YOU'RE LOOKING AT A SINGLE DRIVING FORCE.

Introducing the Riken Performance Package. 50, 60 and 70 Series steel-belted radials engineered to synchronize exactly with our state-of-the-art aluminum wheels. Perfectly translating every steering movement. Propelling you forward with a relentless efficiency no randomly matched wheel and tire can duplicate.

The wheel boasts an impressive strength-to-weight ratio through advanced heat-sink technology, to improve your car's suspension system and dissipate brake generated heat. And Riken "V" and "H" speed rated radials have earned high ratings for treadwear, traction and temperature resistance in U.T.Q.G. tests. Confirming our high quality standards.

Of course, you could buy them separately. But if you really want maximum performance from your driving machine, get the Riken Performance Package. At your Independent Tire Dealer.

books as an official record.

Ford accomplished what he had set out to do, however, and Americans universally accepted the speed, giving Ford's fortunes a boost—as planned.

For the first seven years of record setting, the speed had seemed to inch its way upward. But, early in 1906 all hell broke loose in the form of a Stanley Steamer—the most streamlined car to date.

The Stanley "Rocket," as it was called, was a pace-setter: its two-cylinder, double-acting steam engine was mounted at the extreme rear of the body and drove the rear axle via two cranks, spur gears and a differential. The steam boiler was strengthened to hold a pressure of 1000 pounds p.s.i. and was installed ahead of the rear axle; the driver sat low in the body ahead of the boiler. Sound familiar? Springs were full elliptic on all four wheels and enclosed within the wind-cheating body.

To get underway, the driver held his foot on the brake, let the boiler build to maximum pressure, and then released the brake; the 1600-pound (approx.) car, with its 120 horsepower, quickly demonstrated why the name Rocket was appropriate. Fred Marriott, the driver, achieved a top speed of 121.57 mph in the kilometer, and 127.6 in the mile—almost 18 mph over the previous record, set only a month earlier at Arles, France. Unfortunately, and for no reason ever explained, the A.C.F. accepted the kilometer speed but not the mile time, so the record book shows Marriott's record at 121.57 mph.

It was the last time that either steam or electric power would propel a car to the World Land Speed Record.

In the next eight years, the record would fall to Benz cars, driven by Victor Hémery, Barney Oldfield, Bob Burman, and L.G. Hornsted—the latter setting the first two-way record at 124.10 mph at Brooklands, England on June 24, 1914. The other three Benz drivers had all gone faster than Hornsted, the best being Burman's 141.37, but were not considered official. The A.I.A.C.R. (Association International des Automobiles Club Reconnus, which had replaced the A.C.F. in 1909 as the governing body) had decreed that from the beginning of 1911, all records would be the averge of a two-way run. Oldfield and Burman had made only one-way runs so Hornsted was able to gain World Record fame at the slower speed.

It may be a moot point whether the French or the Americans were the most stubborn. The A.A.A. wasn't recognized by the A.I.A.C.R. at that time, so American record attempts were still being made as one-way runs. In 1919 Ralph DePalma drove a Packard V-12 149.875 mph at Daytona, and a year later Tommy Milton's 16-cylinder Duesenberg (two straight-eights mounted side by side) covered a single mile at Daytona at 156.03 mph. Neither speed was recognized overseas.

Kenelm Lee Guinness, founder of the K.L.G. spark plug company, drove his Sunbeam V-12 at Brooklands, England in 1922 and moved the record up to 133.75, the average of two directions.

Six years to the day after Milton's 156-plus run at Daytona in the twin Duesenberg, his speed was surpassed by J.G. Parry Thomas, on Wales' Pendine sands, with a 169.30 two-way average. In that inter-

vening six years, two of the most famous names assocated with the World Land Speed Record made their debuts: Malcolm Campbell and Major Henry Segrave. Each set new records, but their names would appear on the record books many times later at much greater speeds.

Segrave would be the first man to average more than 200 mph, and the first to use a fully-enveloping body on his record car. The twin Sunbeam V-12 engines, one in front and one in back, drove the rear axle via roller chains on each side. On March 29, 1927, Segrave established a two-way average of 203.792 mph at Daytona Beach, after having convinced the A.A.A. to join

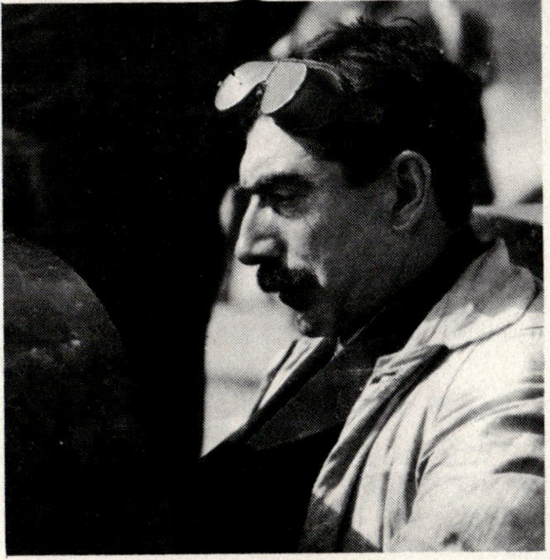

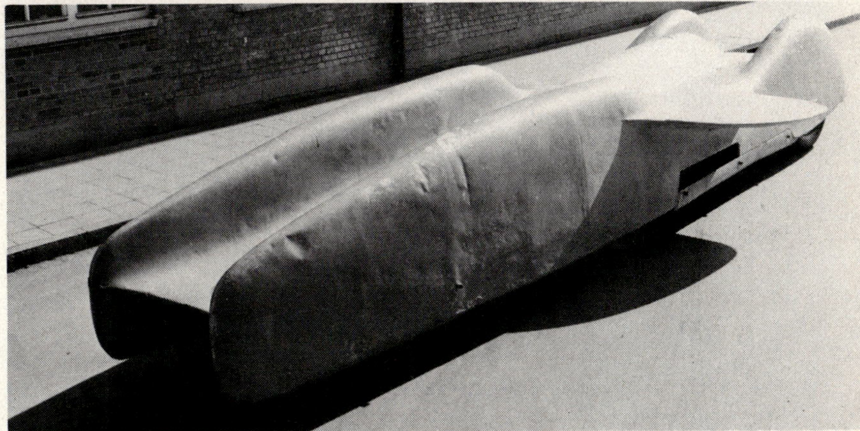

the A.I.A.C.R—a tremendous feat of diplomacy—so his record would have international recognition.

From that date on, with two exceptions, all the new records would be established at Daytona/Ormond Beach, or on the Bonneville Salt Flats. Campbell had set his first two records, in 1924 and 1925, in a Sunbeam, but then switched to the Napier-powered Bluebird and raised the record in 1928 to 206.959 mph.

Cambell's record lasted two months, until Ray Keech, in the White Triplex, which had three V-12 Liberty engines (one in front, and two side by side behind the driver) driving the rear axle, completed a two-way run with an average speed of 207.552 mph. The car was a monstrosity, one of the brute-force-and-bloody-ignorance schools of record car design, but it was the first American car and driver to hold the record after two-way runs became mandatory.

Segrave brought his Irving-Napier "Golden Arrow" back to Daytona Beach in March, 1929 and raised the record to 231.446. It stood for almost two years; then Campbell returned with his "Bluebird" to record a 246.09 average on February 5, 1931.

On his return to England, Campbell found he had been knighted by King George V because of his five successful World Record attempts (the unsuccessful ones were not mentioned). Sir Malcolm would then establish new Land Speed Records four more times, holding the record

from February 5, 1931 until broken by Captain George Eyston at Bonneville, Utah on November 19, 1937.

Before Campbell was through, he set the fastest-ever record at Daytona Beach at 276.82 mph, and then at Bonneville on September 3, 1935, he achieved a life-long ambition by setting the first over-300 record: 301.129 mph—an improvement of 25 mph over his best speed at Daytona, with no change in the car.

True to his pledge, after achieving 300 mph on land, Campbell hung up his helmet and abandoned record attempts (at least on land—he later went into record setting on water).

Campbell's record was broken by another Briton, Captain George Eyston, who arrived at the salt flats in November 1937 with a giant car, the "Thunderbolt." This massive machine had two Rolls-Royce V-12 aircraft engines mounted side by side in the middle of the car, which drove to a rear axle with dual wheels on each side. At the front there were also four wheels, but mounted on two axles with the front track narrower than the track of the second axle (both sets of wheels steered).

A combined displacement of 73 liters (4453 cubic inches) and about 4700 horsepower were sufficient to propel the nearly seven-ton mammoth to a 312-mph average on November 19, 1937. In August, 1938, Eyston once again raised the record, this time to 345.50 mph.

Another Englishman, John Cobb, was

TOP:
Attempting to be the fastest man in the world has proven costly to many drivers. Percy Lambert did not survive this crash of his car, Babs, at Pendine Sands, an early British record venue, in 1927.

ABOVE:
Daimler-Benz built this Ferdinand Porsche-designed, V-12 behemoth in 1939. The war precluded any record attempts with this car. Today it sits, never raced, in the Mercedes-Benz museum near Stuttgart.

ABOVE LEFT:
Fred Marriott wheeled a number of the Stanley brothers' steam cars to unheard-of speeds. In 1906, he drove one of the boat-shaped steamers at 127.56 mph, a record which is still on the books.

TOP:
Mickey Thompson, a famed California hot
rodder, broke 400 mph in his Challenger,
but never set an official two-way mark.

ABOVE:
Dr. Nathan Ostich, a noted surgeon, was
the first to try for the record with a
jet. He failed, but others followed him.

also on the salt with a sleek streamliner designed by Reid Railton, who worked on the Campbell Bluebirds.

It was powered by two supercharged Napier Lion "W-type" engines (three banks of four cylinders each), one in front of the other, and slightly offset, in the center of the chassis. The front engine drove the rear axle and the rear engine drove the front axle, making this car the first with all wheels driven. (Eyston's Thunderbolt had four wheels driving, but all four were on the rear axle.)

The two Napier Lion engines displaced 53.8 liters (3282 cubic inches) and produced 2500 horsepower, and the car weighed about three tons. Two weeks after Eyston had set the record up to 345 mph, Cobb raised it to 350.20.

Eyston wasn't about to let the record slip away from him without a battle, and during the night his crew removed the giant tail fin and covered the radiator opening at the front (both for better aerodynamics). The next day, September 16, 1938, Eyston raised the record to 357.50 mph, and the two competitors packed up to go home to England.

Eyston was through, but Cobb returned to Bonneville in August, 1939 and established the last pre-WW II Land Speed Record. On August 23, Cobb turned in a two-way average of 369.70 mph.

While all this frenzied search for yet more speed was going on at Bonneville, across the Atlantic two German teams, and their ace drivers, were fighting for international records and to be the fastest on the open road.

The Frankfurt-Darmstat autobahn was the scene, and Rudi Caracciola (Mercedes-Benz) and Bernd Rosemeyer (Auto Union) were the protagonists. First Caracciola set the record in International Class B, in 1936, at 366.9 km/h (227.9 mph), to be broken in 1937 by Rosemeyer at 406.3 km/h (252.4 mph). Rudi came back on January 28, 1938 to move the record up to 432.4 km/h (268.6 mph). This is the highest speed ever attained on a public highway, and the highest anywhere in Europe, but it was a sad victory because later that same day Rosemeyer was killed during a record attempt on the same autobahn.

Unknown to the public and probably even to their racing competitors, the engineers at Daimler-Benz were working on a car to gain the absolute Land Speed Record for Germany. This car, code-named the T-80, was designed by Prof. Ferdinand Porsche and built at the Unterturkheim factory under the strictest secrecy.

Power would be supplied by a D-B 603 inverted V-12 aircraft engine, with drive to the four rear wheels (two on each of two axles); the driver sat up front. The car looked more like an Auto Union than a Mercedes-Benz, which isn't too hard to imagine as the AU was also designed by Porsche. Hans Stuck, one of Auto Union's top drivers, was to drive the T-80 at Bonneville. One can only imagine the reaction from M-B drivers Caracciola, Lang, and von Brauchitsch at this bit of news. World War II interrupted this effort, and the car rests, unraced, in the Daimler-Benz museum near Stuttgart.

John Cobb, in his Railton Mobil Special, as it was now called, returned to Bonneville in September of 1947. It would be the last run for the car, and for Cobb on land (he turned to speed records on water), and he desperately wanted to achieve 400 mph.

After fighting rough salt, mechanical problems, and severe tire wear, Cobb took the Railton through two ways of the measured mile, on September 16, 1947, for an average of 394.20 mph. His "down" run had been 385.645 and the return run 403.135—the first-ever over-400-mph run. Cobb lost his life in 1952 during a record attempt on Loch Ness, in Scotland.

Cobb's record would be the last set by a piston-engined car for 18 years, and then it had to be qualified as a "World Record for Piston-Engined Cars," as the jets had taken over.

In 1949 an event occurred that was to later change the Land Speed Record picture; the Southern California Timing Association, tired of holding meets on the dusty and often dangerous El Mirage dry lake, held its first meet at Bonneville.

The 49 cars entered included two streamlined hot rods: the Xydias-Batchelor So-Cal Special, and Howard Johansen's "twin tank," a catamaran-type car.

Dean Batchelor [the author of this story—Ed.], in the So-Cal, set top time of the meet at 193.54 and established a two-way average of 189.74 mph. Within ten years about 20 streamlined hot rods had appeared at Bonneville, capturing dozens of international records and one world record (Dana Fuller's diesel). The fastest of this group, and the one that stood the best chance of getting the Land Speed Record, was Mickey Thompson's four Pontiac V-8-engined car, the "Challenger."

In September, 1959 Thompson made his first serious attempts on the record, turn-

TOP:
The Kenz-Leslie streamliner was among the first, and most famous, postwar American hot rods to chase the land speed record.

ABOVE:
Ohio farmer, Art Arfons, made many epic attempts at the record in a sucession of immensely powerful Green Monster jet cars.

OVERLEAF:
British painter Gordon Crosby captured the drama of one of Sir Malcolm Campbell's many speed record attempts at Bonneville. Pride, courage, and national honor were always at stake when men sought to push the limits of speed further and further.

ing in a disappointing (to him) 367.83 mph one way, but he did set new world records for five kilometers, five miles, ten kilometers and ten miles. Thompson returned in 1960, but he had a lot of company. Donald Campbell was there with his gas turbine-powered car, Bluebird; Athol Graham and Art Arfons both had Allison aircaft-engined cars, and Dr. Nathan Ostich brought the first jet-powered car to Bonneville.

That week was disastrous for all five record seekers. Graham's car crashed with fatal results for the driver. Campbell's Bluebird crashed, giving the driver a severe shaking up. The best Ostich could do was about 250 mph with a car that needed more preparation. Arfons likewise withdrew his Green Monster after several disappointing runs of no more than 250 mph.

Mickey Thompson managed a one-way run of 406.60 mph, the fastest speed at Bonneville at that time, but on the return leg of his two-way run a driveshaft broke and ended his attempt on the record.

Craig Breedlove, a Southern California hot rodder and ex-drag racer, brought the wildest "car" yet seen on the salt flats to Bonneville in 1963. Beedlove's three-wheeled "Spirit of America" was powered by a General Electric J-47 jet engine and the vehicle looked somewhat like a jet fighter with the wings removed and streamlined skirts covering the rear wheels of the tri-cycle gear.

The Spirit was beautiful, and the Spirit was willing. On August 15, 1963 Craig Breedlove set the first World Record with a jet-powered "car" at 407.45 mph. Unfortunately, with only three wheels on the ground it didn't qualify as a car by F.I.A. standards, so the run was timed by the F.I.M—as a motorcycle. Breedlove didn't care; he had his record speed and everyone knew it. And he wasn't through yet.

In July 1964 Donald Campbell, son of the famous Sir Malcolm, with a rebuilt Bluebird, headed an expedition to Lake Eyre, Australia. This lake, also salt, like Bonneville, was inland about 400 miles from Adelaide and the effort to get there with the Bluebird and attendant people, parts and service vehicles, was comparable to a small military operation. It had seemed worth the effort to Campbell, as Lake Eyre was larger than Bonneville (which had also been deteriorating in recent years), and it seldom rained in that part of Australia. The course had the added advantage, to Campbell, of being on British soil.

Nature and human nature being what they are, Campbell fought wet weather, a poor surface, equipment virtually ruined by salt and time, but finally got his record. On July 17, 1964, the gas turbine-powered but wheel-driven Bluebird averaged 403.10 mph for the two-way measured mile. It was Campbell's last attempt in a car, as he turned back to record setting on water. (He was killed in a 1967 record attempt on Lake Coniston in England.)

If World Record attempt followers thought the previous years had been exciting, they were about to receive the greatest thrills they could have expected in their wildest dreams. In Ocober, 1964, the record was broken five times, by three different cars (all jet-powered), and raised from Tom Green's 413.20 (in Walt Arfons' "Wingfoot Express") to brother Art Arfons' 536.71 in his "Green Monster."

Art had first broken his brother's record at 434.02 on October 5; then came Breedlove again on October 13 to move the record up to 468.72, and then to 526.78 on October 15. Art then wrapped up the "speed month" by recording his 536.71.

Breedlove was through for the year, the result of one of the most bizarre finishes in the history of the Land Speed Record. As he came out of the measured mile on the second leg of his record run (526.28 average), Craig pulled the parachute release only to have the chute pull away completely from the car. He was still doing about 500 plus and the only means for stopping the hurtling projectile were two small disc brakes on the rear wheels—designed to be used *under* 150 mph!

No time to wait for that; Breedlove applied the brakes, which promptly burned up and left him looking for an escape. He did his best to turn the car, with the hope of making a large circle at the end of the course until the car would stop, but it was not to be.

He was headed for the line of power poles that cross the lake, and with insufficient steering lock to avoid them, he clipped one off at ground level, which barely slowed the car, and went over a small dike, sailing about 150 feet through the air to land in a lake of brackish salt water—about five miles from the course. As Breedlove climbed out of the car, which had its nose buried with only the tail and rear wheels out of the water, he made his now famous comment, "For my next act I'll set myself on fire." Brave words from a man who was lucky to be alive and knew it.

The Breedlove/Arfons duel wasn't over yet. Breedlove came back to Bonneville on November 2, 1965 with a new car, "Spirit of America Sonic I" (this one with four wheels), and raised the record to 555.483 mph. Art Arfons would successfully raise the record one more time five days later when he made a two-way average of 576.553 mph.

Arfons was through, but Breedlove was not. And the World Record for wheel-driven vehicles would once again be raised. Bob Summers, driving the Summers Brothers "Golden Rod," recorded a two-way average of 409.277 mph. The car was powered by four fuel-injected, Chrysler V-8 engines driving through all four wheels and was incredibly small considering the equipment housed within the body shell.

Bob Summers set his record on November 13, 1965, but it was overshadowed two days later when Breedlove pushed his Sonic I to 600.601 average. It is unfortunate that these two records were so close together in time because it is a far more difficult task to attain these speeds with piston engines driving through the wheels than it is to use a jet which is nothing more than a land-bound aircraft.

Breedlove's record stood for almost five years until Gary Gabelich became the new American Hero on October 23, 1970 when he blasted the LNG-powered "Blue Flame" to new Land Speed Records of 622.407 mph for the measured mile and 630.388 mph for the kilometer (both two-way averages, of course). On the fastest run the car achieved 631.602 mph. The car was designed and built by Reaction Dynamics, of Milwaukee, Wisconsin and backed by the National Gas Industry and Goodyear. The small 8x25-inch tires were inflated to 350 pounds p.s.i.

Since 1970 several attempts have been made on the World Land Speed Record—

Bob Summers studies a model of the Goldenrod, which he drove at 409.277 in 1965: still the wheel-driven vehicle record.

some of them running on short courses, some with only one-way runs, some without F.I.A.-sanctioned timing and one with "timing" by a radar gun similar to those used by police to catch speeders, but these were publicity gimmicks, not serious Land Speed Record Attempts.

Finally, 13 years after Gabelich set his record, Englishman Richard Noble realized his dream of gaining the Land Speed Record for himself, and for England. On October 4, 1983, at Blackrock Desert, Nevada, Noble's Rolls-Royce jet-powered car left a 633.468-mph plume of dust across the dry lake surface. The new record climaxed many years of preparation and frustration for Noble, his crew and his sponsors. Like most record attempts, it brought more personal satisfaction than publicity or financial rewards.

And that's one of the sad facts of international and world record setting—few people care that much. And Noble has an added distinction: his is the first Land Speed Record car to achieve its performance without rubber tires! Because the driving force is from the jet engine, and making tires to withstand the rotational forces at this kind of speed is either physically or financially impossible, Noble built special aluminum disc wheels. Quite obviously they worked.

So the Land Speed Record is back in England, and the America's Cup is in Australia, leaving only the air speed record to America's Lockheed SR-71 (2193 mph). But maybe not for long. Craig Breedlove is coming back in 1986 to regain the LSR and we wouldn't bet against him.

Why do these men spend so much of their life and so much money pursuing a goal that is at best an ego trip? They are a special breed, testing themselves, wanting to be number one at something. You'll find the same fanatical desire among those who climb mountains, sky dive, hang glide or swim channels. I wouldn't compare them to racing drivers or toreadors, although there is as much danger in those occupations, but there are also financial rewards there to go along with the notoriety. With rare exceptions there have been few financial gains in World Land Speed Records, and the record holder's notoriety lasts as long as he holds the record.

As Gary Gabelich said in his introduction to the book *Land Speed Record*, "...those who have actually attempted the record have a deeper feeling—very difficult to express—of what it means to try to go faster than any man on earth. As a driver you develop one of those very special man and machine relationships. I still think of the Blue Flame as a beautiful woman who shared with me a truly rare and wonderful experience." **MT**

Craig Breedlove brought this fighter-without-wings to Bonneville in 1963 and set the first jet-powered land speed record at 407.45. In 1964, after a 500-mph run, the car met a spectacular end in a briny drainage ditch. Breedlove survived to raise the record, in another car, to 600.601 mph. After Craig's run, his wife, Lee, drove the car to a speed of 308.56, still the fastest for a woman.

THE CAR IN EUROPE

Germans created it, Frenchmen popularized it, Italians beautified it, and Britons made it fun.

By Ray Hutton

☐ Amid the claims and counterclaims as to who invented the automobile, it is at least undisputed that the birthplace was Europe. When and where depends on what we mean by an automobile.

There were mechanically propelled vehicles a long time before there were cars as we know them. Railroad engineering crossed over to stagecoaches and traction engines for haulage and agricultural tasks. In 1815 one Josef Bozek demonstrated a four-seater steam car in Prague.

Today, in a museum at Compiègne not far from Paris one can examine *La Mancelle*, a steam carriage built by Amédée Bollée in 1878. It could carry four people and, apart from the boiler and smokestack above the rear wheels, is remarkably prophetic: a front-mounted engine drives the rear wheels and it has independent front suspension and a steering wheel. Just like a car of 20 or 30 years later. But the Bollée was a steamer. The automobile came to life with the development of the *internal*-combustion engine.

An early patent for one of those, powered by coal gas, is credited to Etienne Lenoir who, it is said, installed a half-horsepower engine in a cart and drove from his Paris home to his workshop in 1863. Had he pursued the idea—which he didn't—Lenoir might have been hailed as the inventor of the automobile. As it is, he doesn't even get much acknowledgement for his pioneer engine work.

The principle of the four-stroke engine was developed and defined in Germany by Nikolaus Otto, who started from Lenoir's idea but with the crucial inclusion of a compression stroke. That was in 1876. The compact four-stroke engine combined with the availability of gasoline, a by-product of petroleum refining, set the scene for the development of the automobile.

Who did it first? The Austrians have claimed that Siegfried Marcus preceded Otto's invention by driving a gasoline-powered car around the streets of Vienna in 1875. Historians now think that date is

GRAND-PRIX A·C·F 1906 Sarthe
SZISZ sur RENAULT
PARIS-BORDEAUX 1895
1ère VOITURE sur PNEUS MICHELIN
CIRCUIT des ARDENNES 1906
DURAY sur LORRAINE DIETRICH
PARIS-VIENNE 1902
FARMAN sur PANHARD
ARDENNES BELGES 1904
HEATH sur PANHARD
PARIS-MADRID 1903
GABRIEL sur MORS
NICE 1903 COUPE ROTHSCHILD
SERPOLET
GRAND-PRIX de l'A·C·F 1908 Dieppe
LAUTENSCHLAGER sur MERCEDES

wrong. The French put forward Edouard Delamare-Deboutteville, who was granted a patent for a vehicle powered by a four-stroke engine in 1884. This was another converted horse-cart, but after a number of short journeys, the inventor decided that it was unsuitable for carrying materials to his textile factory and it was dismantled. A convenient rediscovery of the Delamare-Deboutteville patents justified the French celebration of the Centenary of the automobile in 1984.

Whether it actually ran or not is less important than where it led. Delamare-Deboutteville had no ambition to make cars; like so many of the pioneers he was more interested in applications for his engine. The same could be said for Gottlieb Daimler, who had worked as technical director at Otto's gas-engine company but in 1882 left to set up an engine-research organization of his own in Cannstatt, Germany.

Daimler built his first motor vehicle in 1885, but it wasn't a car—it was a motorcycle! Less than 50 miles away, in Mannheim, Carl Benz was working independently on a four-stroke Otto-type engine which he tested in 1885 in a car of his own design. Though this is now regarded as the first automobile, it does not conform to the standard pattern in one major respect as it had only three wheels. The first four-wheeled car at this dawn of the motor age was Daimler's 1886 follow-up to his two-wheeler. It was, literally, a "horseless carriage," having been converted from a conveniently sized vehicle from his coach house.

These two Germans forced the pace of automobile engineering. Whereas Daimler concentrated on the development of the high-speed engine—he didn't produce cars commercially until 1893—Benz wanted to make cars. His "Patent Motor Car" of 1886 led to the four-wheeled "Victoria" with modern type kingpin steering and the little single-cylinder Velo, which was the world's first series-production car. It was first offered for sale in 1894, and in the next three years, 381 cars were made.

The people who took most enthusiastically to this new personal mobility were not the Germans but the French. Carl Benz reflected in later life that "If Germany was the father of the motor car, then France was the mother." As early as 1887 Edouard Sazarin had secured the French manufacturing rights to Daimler's engine which was to be made at the engineering firm of Panhard et Levassor.

Panhard was to become the leading car maker of the last decade of the 19th century. It established, with its 1892 model, the conventional layout for cars of the next 75 years: engine at the front under a hood, mounted longitudinally driving the rear wheels via a pedal-operated friction clutch and a change-speed system consisting of sliding pinion gears. At first this kind of transmission (described by Emile Levassor as "*Brutal, mais ça marche*": crude, but it works) left the gears in the open air, but in 1896 they were enclosed in a gearbox which remains, in principle, the stick shift of today.

Panhard won the first organized town-to-town auto competitions—the 1894 Paris-Rouen Reliability Trial and the epic Paris-Bordeaux-Paris race in 1895, when Levassor himself drove the whole 732 miles. There is a monument celebrating his achievement at Porte Maillot in Paris.

This early open-road racing, gentle enough to start with when the cars were slow (Levassor averaged 15 mph in the Paris-Bordeaux) but soon to become dangerously fast, was very important in demonstrating the worth of the automobile. The World Land Speed Record at the turn of the century stood at 65.79 mph and was held by an electrically driven single-seater *Ne Jamais Contente* (Never Satisfied). Electric, like steam, cars enjoyed a brief period of success (the difficulties with the battery vehicles then, as now, were limited speed and range), but it was the gasoline engine that showed the way for the future.

Appropriately, the next big development has its origins in France and Germany. Emile Jellinek was actually a Czech, a diplomat based in Nice, France, who loved cars and acted as an agent for Daimler. He suggested to Wilhelm Maybach, Daimler's associate, that the German company should build a car that would beat the French products in the 1901 Nice Speed Week. If successful, an order for 36 cars would follow.

The new car, lighter, lower and faster than Daimlers that had gone before, featured a steel chassis and a honeycomb radi-ator. The engine had timed valves and the gear-change had a "gate." Known as the 35 Horsepower, it was christened *Mercedes* after Jellinek's 11-year-old daughter. It set a style and standard for the 1900s.

France continued as the world's largest car producer until the burgeoning U.S. industry moved ahead in 1906. By then the basic pattern on the car was fixed, but most of the refinements that we take for granted today were unheard of. Solid, metal-shod wheels had given way to pneumatic tires—the Michelin brothers advertised their wares by racing a Peugeot—but it was some time before the detachable rim arrived so that the task of replacing a punctured tire was eased. With more horses than cars on the roads, shoe-nails were a constant hazard for those fragile early tires.

Some famous names appeared during this period. DeDion Bouton was the world's largest motor firm for a time and sold engines to scores of other manufacturers, among them Renault, which had started in 1899. Peugeot was also a manufacturing pioneer, with a steam car going back to 1889 and Daimler engines in its first Quadricycles. *Fabbrica Italiana di Automobili Torino* (F.I.A.T.) produced its first car in 1899, while in Britain, motoring had a poor start because of the "Red Flag Act" that had restricted cars to a walking pace until repealed in 1896. Early experimenter Lanchester was joined by Wolseley, Sunbeam, Humber and others.

By 1906 a British review shows no less than 434 different models for sale. A perfectionist engineer, Henry Royce, dissatis-

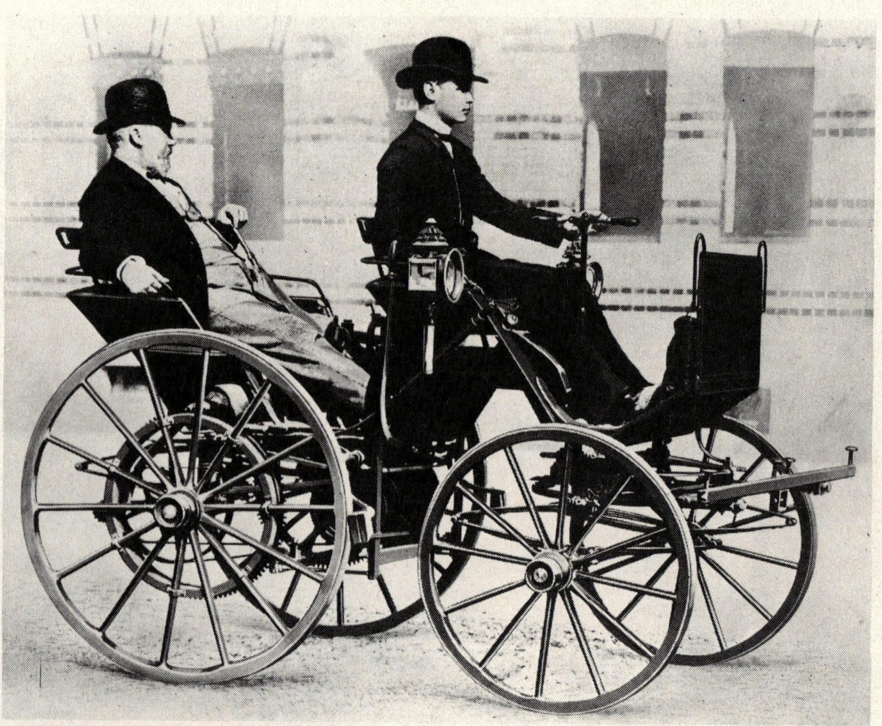

Gottlieb Daimler, no doubt tired after a hard day of automotive pioneering, relaxes in the back of his 1886 horseless carriage while an aide mans the tiller.

ABOVE:
Charles Rolls and Henry Royce joined to produce the 1907 Silver Ghost. They claimed, "Bristish cars were best and Rolls-Royce was the best British car."

LEFT:
At first, cars in Europe were just for the rich and powerful. Here, Kaiser Wilhelm rises in his Mercedes Triple-Phaeton 6 to inspect his troops on maneuvers in 1911.

to be made in high volume—independent front suspension and a tough overhead-valve engine. It was to have had an automatic transmission, but that was abandoned just before production started. Though a trend-setter, the *Traction's* development and the factory expansion that accompanied it, in expectation of great sales success, put too much strain on the company and its founder. In December 1934 they fell into the hands of the largest creditor, Michelin. Seven months later André Citroën died.

Not long after, the new management instructed Citroën's engineers to design a French people's car, with the predominantly agricultural working class in mind. "Four wheels under an umbrella," with suspension supple enough for it to be "driven across a field loaded with eggs without breaking them"— those were part of the design brief for the ugly duckling 2CV, *Deux Chevaux*, the prototype of which was built in 1936. It went into production after the War and remains on sale to this day.

Not to be outdone in this new push to provide cheap, economical cars for the masses, Italy, the smallest of Europe's Big Four car makers (in 1939 they produced 55,500 cars to Britain's 305,000—and nearly three million in the U.S.A.) came up with the *Topolino*. Mickey Mouse was just the right nickname for the lovable Fiat 500, a tiny two-seater coupe, a rear-engined successor to which also remains available, made for Fiat in Poland.

Though car production continued in the U.S. for a couple of years, the onset of World War II in Europe saw the auto industries transferred to making weapons and military equipment. In Britain after 1942 private driving ceased, and cars were laid up or sold—there are many stories of valuable cars, priceless today, being disposed of for just a few Pounds.

When peace came, much of the automobile industry was shattered—France, Germany and Italy combined produced only 5,000 cars in 1945. Britain's car makers pulled out their stillborn 1940 models, and because of extreme austerity measures applied by the government, had to concentrate on export sales. With a few notable exceptions, they were not sparkling new products. While the Germans had to start from scratch and would eventually benefit from it, Britain was tired and didn't have the foresight or the money to invest for the long-term future.

Several established manufacturers, including Ford, examined the Volkswagen and didn't give it much chance of success; its history is written elsewhere in this book, but the Beetle's rejection by the nabobs of the auto world must go down as one of the bigger misjudgments in the story of the car.

William Morris, now Lord Nuffield, had ideas for an economical "World Car" of his own. He had Alec Issigonis design a new Morris Minor, not unlike the VW in its rounded profile but with a conventional front-engine and rear-drive layout. Ironically, Issigonis also proposed a flat-four engine, but finance dictated the use of a prewar side-valve straight four, later replaced with an overhead-valve unit shared with the baby Austin. Morris and Austin came together as the grand-sounding British Motor Corporation in 1952. The Minor had a long life and is today prized as a slightly dotty "classic" but its 1½ million in 22 years was a far cry from the 21 million for the still-continuing Volkswagen.

Outside the captive market of its Empire, Britain was best known for its sports cars. Returning GIs took to the clearly prewar style of the MG TC and its successors, but there were more modern equivalents from Triumph (the TR2) and Austin-Healey (the 100) as well as a number of small-volume specialist sports-car makers.

Jaguar was in a different league—its XK120 offered good looks and tremendous performance at a realistic price. It led, very directly, to the Le Mans-winning C-type sports-racer.

In European racing Italy was dominant and though its run-of-the-mill sedans were no more inspiring than other nations' in the early postwar years, there were shapes and styles emerging from Italy's great coachbuilders that were to have a big influence. Pininfarina's Cisitalia and the Lancia Aurelia B20 set the pattern for a new GT *(Gran Turismo)* class while the race-derived offerings of Ferrari and Maserati became the new exotica: the supercars.

It is a measure of the indifference to the

André Citroën wanted to build cars in volume and adapted U.S. manufacturing techniques to do it. He was also an ace at promotion, even using the Eiffel Tower to hawk his wares. In 1936, after André's death, Citroën began production of the 2CV, *Deux Chevaux* (top). Updated over the years, the car is still being sold.

Beetle that few followed its rugged, simple layout. Renault did, with the rear-engined 4CV, Dauphine and its successors, but no one else in the big league used air-cooled engines. Dr. Porsche's son Ferry kept faith with his father's principles and used VW engines in the back of the first aerodynamic sports coupes built in Austria after the War. The old man died in 1951 after a period in prison for his contribution to the German war effort. The new cars were the first to carry the name *Porsche*.

Gradually, austerity gave way to optimism. Spurred by jet aircraft and nuclear power, automotive engineers started to look for new solutions. Fiat and Renault built gas-turbine prototypes, but Europe's most serious advocate of jet engines for cars was the normally-conservative Rover company. It went so far as to build Le Mans racing gas turbines in conjunction with BRM, and although Rover learned a lot, like fellow American turbine enthusiasts, it was defeated by high fuel consumption and costly manufacturing.

Racing had proved the disc brake, which over the next 20 years would become a universal fitting on the front wheels of ordinary cars as well as on all four for those of higher performance. Michelin produced the *X*, the world's first radial-ply car tire, initially to meet the specific requirements of Citroën but soon to start a revolution in the tire business.

It was Citroën, once again, that produced the most significant car of the mid-1950s. This was the DS, a technical *tour de force* with a low aerodynamic body of radical appearance, self-leveling pneumatic all-independent suspension and a high-pressure hydraulic system to power brakes, steering, suspension, clutch and gearchange. A curious thing to drive—love it or hate it—it was too *different* to be a smash hit with the public and too complex for others to follow its technical lead.

One who did admire Citroën's ideas was Alec Issigonis. After the Morris Minor, he went to the Alvis company to design a new V-8 sedan which never saw production, so he returned to BMC in 1956 with a brief to design a new kind of small car. It was the time of the Suez emergency when oil supplies to Europe were threatened, it seemed, indefinitely, and various unsatisfactory economy "bubble cars" had come on the market. Issigonis was to find a better way of making a low-mpg family car.

The result was the Mini: brave and unorthodox, it was eventually to change our idea of a conventional car. Just 10 feet long but able to accommodate four adults, its secret was in the packaging, the way that the mechanical units were arranged to take the minimum space and leave the maximum for the people.

So the hood had to be short. For cornering stability and good traction, the engine should be at the front and drive the front wheels. The wheels themselves should be small, only 10-inch diameter—and the tire manufacturers, unhappy about the wear rate of such tiny tires, would have to meet the challenge. Issigonis mounted the engine transversely and accommodated the gearbox underneath it, in the engine's sump, sharing the same oil. For suspension he used rubber cones instead of steel springs.

The Mini was every bit as radical as the Citroën DS. Perhaps for that reason it was not an instant sales success (by 1959 the fuel shortage threat had gone away), but those who drove the first ones marveled at the roadholding compared with the rather sloppy rear-drive small sedans they had been used to. Racing and rallying and an acceptance by the rich and famous as a fun runabout did gain the Mini the sales it deserved, but it is one of the tragedies of the British auto industry that it has never really made any money for its makers.

BMC pressed on with the Issigonis idea which was next used by the Austin/Morris 1100, which went further towards Citroën principles by having interconnected fluid suspension devised by Alex Moulton, which brought big-car ride comfort to cheaper, smaller cars.

It wasn't long before other manufacturers adopted the transverse-engine front-wheel-drive layout. Fiat tested the water with its Autobianchi subsidiary and a car called the Primula; the 128 arrived in 1969, the 127, first of the "superminis" (a size up on the Mini), a year later. Then the flood-

gates opened, and every major manufacturer in the world eventually appreciated the space-saving sense of Issigonis' idea, even if they did not adopt other aspects of the Mini's design.

The only constraint upon Issigonis was that he use BMC's existing engines. For a while, in the heady 1960s, the work of another individualist engineer, Dr. Felix Wankel, looked likely to supplant the old Otto-cycle piston engine. Wankel had devised an elegantly simple rotary engine that was eagerly adopted by the then independent NSU company and first offered in one of their cars in 1964. Manufacturers all over the world signed licensing agreements, but only NSU, Citroën, and Mazda in Japan offered Wankel-powered cars for sale. The NSU Ro80 of 1967 was Citroënesque in its unusual and advanced features but only Mazda persevered. The Wankel proved the adage that it is not good enough for radical alternatives to work as well as the established order, they have to be much *better* to justify the expense and upheaval of changed production.

Transmissions are a further example. The old dog-box has changed little since M. Levassor pardoned its crudeness, and the automatic option—slow to gain acceptance in Europe—still derives from the first GM Hydra-Matic. The Dutch company DAF showed a different way when it entered the car market in 1958 with a little car that had a continuously variable transmission using belts and conical pulleys. A development of that idea is being heralded 27 years later as a breakthrough in automatic transmission for small cars.

During the 1960s and 1970s there was a shift of power within the European industry. Germany's vital postwar revival had made it the Continent's biggest car producer by 1956, and ten years later it was

If the art of engineering stands for Audi, state of the art of engineering represents the Audi 5000S. What makes the 5000S look sleek must first make it perform to its maximum capacity.

It's the law of Audi: Form follows function. Each and every inch of this spacious 5-passenger luxury sedan has been designed to achieve a low drag coefficient that aids efficiency and reduces interior noise levels.

The most demonstrable indication of this advanced engineering prowess is to simply experience the car on the road with the windows up at highway speeds.

Wrapped in aerodynamic design, nestled in anatomically designed seats, you are surrounded by a unique sound in this day and age. The sound of silence.

This remarkable combination of power on the outside and peace and quiet on the inside

didn't happen overnight. Audi engineers have spent years honing advancements in aerodynamics, front-wheel drive technology and 5-cylinder engine performance.

This infusion of Audi innovation has also resulted in a refined suspension system that delivers an incredibly precise steering response.

What has emerged is a vehicle so ahead of its time, a vehicle that so thoroughly elevates the driving experience, it prompted Car and Driver magazine to state that, "at Audi, the future of the automobile is being decided."

To test-drive this tribute to advanced German engineering, call toll-free: 1-(800)-FOR-AUDI for the dealer nearest you.

Once you drive the Audi 5000S, chances are you'll venture no further. We designed it that way.

Audi

The art of engineering.

We design cars."

making 2.8 million a year compared with 1.2 million in Italy, 1.6 million in Britain and 1.8 million in France. The American multi-nationals had a firm hold, or at least Ford and General Motors did, for Chrysler's Rootes Group in Britain (Hillman, Humber, Singer and Sunbeam) and Simca in France were less secure. Chrysler was to sell out to the privately owned Peugeot group which became at that time (1978) Europe's biggest, having already absorbed Citroën.

Volkswagen went through a difficult time. It dithered about replacing the Beetle, which continued to sell well and overtook the Model T's all-time production record in 1972. Eventually decisive new management instituted a crash program to develop water-cooled front-wheel-drive models. The first was the Passat in 1973. The transverse-engined Golf, destined to be a trend-setter for its size with its boxy looks, came a year later. It became Europe's best seller.

In Britain, British Leyland grew out of a series of mergers between companies, first BMC and Jaguar (plus Daimler), then with Leyland-owned Standard-Triumph and Rover. It was, ultimately, to be more trouble than it was worth. Successive managements tried to rationalize British Leyland's complex and conflicting model range, but financial difficulties came to a head in 1975 and Britain's car maker was nationalized. Depending on where you looked, this might or might not work: Renault, state-owned in France, made money (then); Alfa Romeo, nationalized in Italy, lost lots of it.

Throughout British Leyland's many changes, Jaguar had tried hard to remain as independent as possible. Its kind of quality, high-performance cars did not sit comfortably alongside the high-volume side of the business; Jaguar would revert to private ownership in 1984. Jaguar's reputation, like that of Mercedes, was based on auto racing, from which it had withdrawn many years before. But the E-type, which amazed the world with its streamlined looks and its racing-type 150-mph speeds when it appeared in 1961, did much to sustain the Jaguar image, as did the world's only quantity-produced V-12 engine which powered it from 1971.

Auto racing was, though, moving a world apart from everyday cars. Single-seaters had become more specialized and were universally mid-engined (thanks, initially, to John Cooper's little firm). Fast road cars had in the past mirrored racing car design; now only the most impractical exotics could afford to follow.

Speed suffered a setback. Late 1973 troubles in the Middle East precipitated the first Oil Crisis. Fuel supplies became erratic, and as part of a continent-wide program to conserve gas, many countries applied speed limits which would never be removed. The freedom of the *Routes Nationales* disappeared; only Germany emerged without a speed limit on its impressive *autobahn* network. In Britain, where motorways were still a novelty, a 70-mph overall limit had been in force—for dubious safety reasons—since 1967. Under the Oil Crisis measures, this was reduced to 50 mph, eventually reverting, under pressure from the motoring organizations, to 60 and 70 mph.

The emphasis in car design moved towards fuel economy, but there was little that could be done immediately; indeed, the first results of the industry's re-think were becoming available only as the second oil shock loomed in 1979. It is a trend that has continued since, and achieved considerable improvements in efficiency without the spur of CAFE (Corporate Average Fuel Economy) and, it should be said, without the strangulation of severe exhaust-emissions controls.

Overall, there has been a shift in the market towards smaller but more space-efficient cars, thanks to the adoption of front-wheel drive and the widespread use of the adaptable hatchback configuration.

Interestingly, despite speed restrictions everywhere other than Germany, car performance continues to improve. Aerodynamics, the result of serious wind-tunnel testing, and more sophisticated engine design can bring better performance or lower fuel consumption—or a little of both. "Aero" is a way of life now for all car makers, but a surprising and increasing number continue to offer multi-valve engines and turbocharging primarily to enhance acceleration and maximum speed.

Appropriately, in view of the automobile's origins, the leaders in this high technology are the Germans. In recent years their car makers have adopted turbocharging (Porsche, following racing experience and BMW), permanent four-wheel-drive for regular cars (Audi), anti-lock braking (Mercedes, BMW and now others) and four-valves-per-cylinder, twin-cam engines (BMW, Mercedes and Volkswagen).

Others are following the German lead. Ford, for example, has fitted Audi Quattro-like four-wheel drive to its sporting XR Sierra, and has anti-lock braking as standard on the latest Scorpio sedan. Audi predicts that by 1990, 30 percent of all cars will be four-wheel drive and that rear-driven cars will be all but dead. The *Système*

George Rochegrosse's poster for the 1901 auto show in Paris gives some indication of how awestruck Europeans were by cars.
COLLECTION OF POSTERS PLEASE, 37 RIVERSIDE DR., NEW YORK, NY 10023

Panhard has had a good run. As electronics plays an ever-more important part in the modern car, Mercedes foresees combining automatic transmission, four-wheel drive, anti-lock braking and anti-wheelspin controls in one computer-controlled package that makes decisions for the driver, presenting the car at its optimum capability for any condition.

But not all of today's challenges are technical. The European auto industry has a serious problem of over-capacity. Robot machinery can make cars faster than before, but the demand hasn't kept pace. There is, for the first time since the Model T, a serious threat from another continent: Japan. Like Ford all those years ago, the Japanese have recognized that if they are to succeed—and be welcomed—in Europe in the longer term, they must make cars where they're sold. Links have been forged between Alfa Romeo and Nissan, and British Leyland (now Austin Rover) and Honda. Nissan is setting up a factory in the North of England. This will give it access to the European Economic Community (Common Market). Some of the long-established car makers are very unhappy about it—Fiat and Renault in particular. Ford and General Motors have grasped at Spain as one of the few European countries with a developing industry and relatively cheap labor.

These are complicated issues. Car making is now a very international business that crosses not only countries but continents. For the first time it is important to consider Europe as a whole and compare it to the United States and Japan. Looked at that way, the continent where it all started completes the first century of the automobile as its major producer and user—and greatest fan. **MT**

There's never been such a thing as "European Style." Each country, each manufacturer has its own distinct look and philosophy. That's been true from the beginning and is still so today. No two designs could be more different from each other than the jellybean-shaped Merkur (called Sierra in its home country), and the spare, angular Swedish Volvo.

STYLE BY DESIGN

*At first, all that mattered was how the car ran.
What it looked like soon became nearly as important.*

By Len Frank

☐ No one can be sure, but it's safe to assume, that the original wagons—two-wheeled carts, probably—were as unlovely as the road apples their motive power left behind them. We can also assume that it probably wasn't long before some primitive man somehow decorated, or individualized, his cart.

History bears this out; long before the time of Christ, chariots had become highly styled with developed shapes, applied decoration and even the elements of *idiomatic* design. Pure design—say, a nail or a woodscrew—is the reverse of idiomatic. There is little that can be done with it outside of its intended use; it is as functional as possible. Very little design is so pure, and the dictum that form follows function is nonsense, for the most part. A screwdriver, for example, is as handy for prying open crates or punching holes in oil cans as for driving woodscrews. The automobile is similar; there's much more to it than mere function and the design possibilities it offers are near infinite.

Automobiles, horse*less* carriages, first emulated horse*drawn* carriages even down to the buggywhip sockets. No real notice was given at first to the gas buggy's much

higher speed (even in the very early days, about twice that of a horse-drawn conveyance). But it still had a *look*, an aesthetic. Carriage makers who did the "body work" for the new self-propelled contraptions were comfortable with the style, and so were their patrons who, after all, footed the bills. But the new form of transportation soon began to take on its own look.

By the turn of the 20th century, streamlining was already known; *Ne Jamais Contente,* an electric record breaker, and the *Mixte*-powered Lohner-Porsche had both appeared with rudimentary aerodynamic bodies and began the evolution of what we think of today as an automobile.

Another important early departure from the horse-carriage look was the *Systeme Panhard,* which had the engine in front, the drive in the rear, and the driver and passengers in between. When racing became important, and power was raised by increasing displacement (over 20 liters in

knockoff of the mid-'20s Hispano-Suiza and was intended for high-volume production on a La Salle chassis. It was a huge success. Next, Earl put his pencil to work on a Buick, but Fisher's engineers, to make the body easier to manufacture, took liberties with Earl's curves and contours and managed to make the car as gawky as the La Salle was elegant.

Undeterred, Earl chalked it up to experience, realizing that his creations had to be tempered by the realities of production-line assembly. General Motors, following Alfred Sloan's theories of capturing customers early and keeping them forever by offering new cars every year, across the entire price spectrum, realized Earl's worth and set him up as chief of its new Art and Colour Section. It would be responsible for all of GM's body designs, with the exception of a few custom Cadillacs. Earl quickly became a design *executive*, learning the ability to pass ideas to his staff of designers to flesh out, and then win approval for these designs from higher management. Earl became the author of GM's style and took credit for it. But over the 30-plus years he headed the studio (which went through several name changes from Art and Colour, to Styling, to Design), he relied on the talents of hundreds of men who remained anonymous to most of the public.

Cars that Earl is credited with designing run the gamut from the European-inspired 1927 La Salle, to the 1933 Cadillac V-16

some cases), long hoods (long, *high* hoods, sometimes) became emblematic of power.

There were, by the '20s, attempts to combine idioms that seemed less than appropriate to automobile design—these were primarily architectural and nautical. They resulted in formal cars with absolutely vertical lines and impressed architectural details like bronze gargoyles, drapery, and cut glass: rolling villas. Others autos had ship-board ventilators, planked "decks," and skiff, or boat, tails. Aircraft influences began to creep in about that time as well: fins, fenders shaped like wheel pants, and rounded cockpit openings.

As the early carriage makers became auto-body builders they had to learn to work with metal and how to use new construction and tooling techniques. Concerns like Studebaker, Durant-Dort, and the Fisher Brothers, all of whom successfully made the transition to auto production, as distinct from custom building, eventually had to seek design help if they were to prosper by making hundreds of thousands of customers happy, rather than pleasing just a few well-heeled patrons.

So began the era of the professional designer, and the rise of Harley Earl. He was the son of a California body repair shop owner who had become a custom body builder, catering to the Hollywood types who were beginning to populate Los Angeles. Young Earl began to do flamboyant designs for his father to execute. Some caught the attention of one of the Fisher brothers, who invited Earl to Detroit to show his stuff. Earl's first design was a shown at the Chicago World's Fair, the revolutionary Art Deco 1934 La Salle, and the Continental-styled 1938-41 Cadillac 60 Special. Perhaps the most famous was the first experimental show car, the Buick Y-Job, which established styling themes that can be seen in GM cars as late as 1948. The 1933 V-16 Cadillac had much the same influence on GM's prewar cars.

Earl's successor was an artist named William Mitchell. He was as flamboyant as Earl, perhaps even more so. Mitchell hop-scotched all over the design world. It must be remembered that at times GM was building half, or more, of all the world's

Gordon Buehrig's classic Auburns, Duesenbergs and Cords have established him as one of the great designers of all time.

cars and had a decided influence on the other half. If a style worked for GM, it was likely to be copied. Consequently, Mitchell's influence cannot be underestimated. He authored such diverse autos as the stunning Corvair Monza SS showcar and the 1980 "Bentley" Cadillac Seville. In between were clumsy designs like the original Stingray (which Zora Arkus-Duntov said "had just enough lift to be a bad airplane"), and the very handsome production Corvairs, Camaros and, a car Mitchell was particularly proud of, the 1963 Buick Riviera.

He must also be credited with the mid-'70s Chevrolet Monza, with its Egyptian-Eye side windows. And, if truth be told, the Pininfarina-bodied Ferrari 365 GTC4 as well. The prototype for the Monza had been built by Pininfarina for GM, but designed in Detroit. The Pininfarina designers had a long, long time to look at it, and the Ferrari was the result.

Actually, this sort of "influence" flows throughout auto design, back and forth across the Atlantic (and now the Pacific). Sometimes it takes the form of a near-copy, at other times various themes are lifted. Perhaps the best example of this kind of emulation is the Chrysler Airflow. Unloved here, it was copied by Simca in France, Fiat in Italy, and managed to influence Volvo and Toyota. Then there's the odd case of the *Traction Avant* Citroën of 1934, which is often described as an unsanforized '34 Ford. The prototype for this car was built by Budd in America, its designers no doubt inspired by the Ford. But Budd couldn't peddle the car here and found a willing buyer in France.

Then there's the 1970 Camaro, the sec-

ond series of the car, which looks suspiciously like a Pininfarina/Scaglietti Ferrari 250GT (short wheelbase) Berlinetta of the mid-'60s. Of course, the Italians are also capable of "borrowing" from one another; the lines of the current Alfa-Romeo GTV6, credited to Ital Design (Giorgetto Giugiaro), are identical to those of the Alfa Zagato Jr. of 1970-'71, which, as the name implies, is a Zagato creation.

We're accustomed today to this rapid dissemination of inspiration and influence, but it was not always so. Perhaps the first American designer who had an international impact was Gordon Buehrig. His career spanned more than 40 years, but his most productive period was spent with Auburn-Cord-Duesenberg, and, without question, his best design from the time was the "baby" Duesenberg that became the Cord 810-812. There were direct copies of it built in Europe; the Museum of Modern Art, in 1950, chose it as one of the outstanding designs of all time; and, as late as the mid '60s, the Oldsmobile Toronado, and the later Dodge Magnum, showed its influence. More replicas of the Cord, and Buehrig's 1935 Auburn Speedster, have been done in fiberglass in recent years than were ever produced originally. Proving once again that imitation is the sincerest form of flattery.

Pinin Farina (whose name was later combined into the corporate Pininfarina) was the first of the Italian designers to cooperate fully with Detroit. One of his first designs appeared on the Cadillac V-16 chassis in 1931. It preceded his work for the 1952 Nash (which one critic called "more Wheatena than Farina") by nearly 20 years, during which time he produced

Fifty years have not dated Buehrig's 1936 Cord Model 810 in the least. Elements of its design can be seen in the Olds Toronado and Dodge Magnum, among other cars.

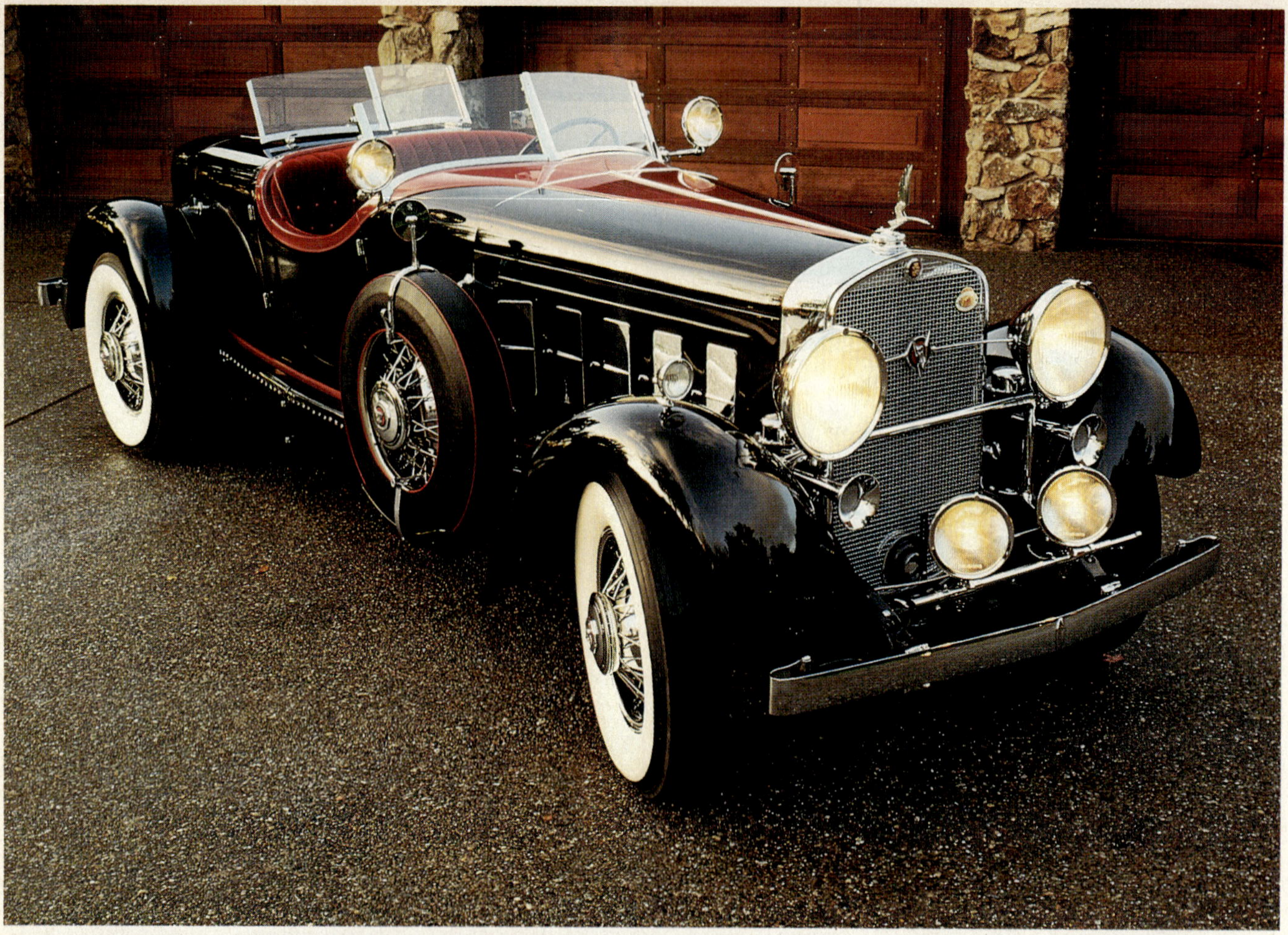

Though famous for the sensual and organic shapes of his later Ferraris, Pininfarina started out by designing cars such as this classic 1931 V-16 powered Cadillac.

Howard "Dutch" Darrin's customized Packard 160 convertibles led him to design the production Packard Clippers of 1941-48.

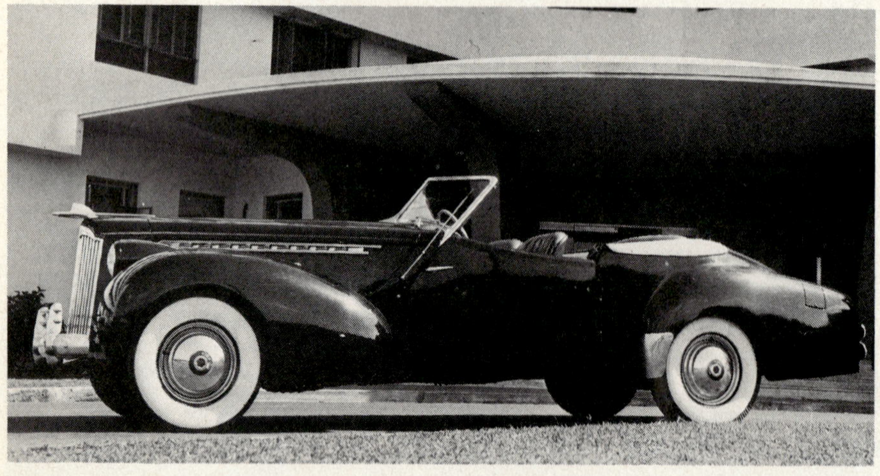

a number of fastback, aerodynamic studies on Lancia and Fiat chassis. They were early attempts to combine classic proportions—a longer, lower, wider, long-hood look—with aerodynamic efficiency. Erwin Komenda's Volkswagen K10 was a sincere copy; the K10 was a Porsche special intended for the Berlin-Rome race just before World War II, and gave its shape to the later Porsche 956. The Farina cars, in turn, owe much of what they were to experiments by Koenig-Fachsenfeld, a German aerodynamicist and designer, whose work was based on that of another aerodynamicist, Paul Jaray. Influence upon influence.

The single car which made Pinin Farina's reputation was the Cisitalia 202 coupe of 1947 (see *Ten That Mattered*). Again, though it was based on prewar aero forms, it had more styling and less pure aerodynamic shape than Farina's prewar Lancias. The biggest difference, though, is that the 202 is beautiful. It resembles some of the prewar work by Touring, another Italian body design/construction firm. But the Touring designs were on Alfa and BMW chassis, both were high, long six-cylinder-powered racing cars, while the Cisitalia had an 1100 cc Fiat engine, allowing the designer to lower the hood between the front fenders, reduce the grille size, and use smaller wheels and tires. The perfectly proportioned result is part of the permanent collection of New York's Museum of Modern Art, the only car so honored.

While Pinin Farina was not the primary designer of his firm (and, indeed, his son and heir, Sergio, is not a designer at all), dozens of outstanding shapes, many of them on Ferraris, came from Farina's stu-
had an 1100 cc Fiat engine, allowing the
dio and carry the PF crest. The firm's long-standing association with GM continues; the new Cadillac Allante will be PF's third low-volume production Caddy. And Peugeot has used PF exclusively since the mid-'50s. Impressive credentials certainly, but perhaps the greatest testimonial to the permanent appeal of Farina's best designs are the prices paid recently for a pair of Ferraris, a 1958 Testarossa and a first-series GTO. Each sold for around three quarters of a million dollars.

Almost of equal value are the designs of Howard Darrin, who died a few years ago in Santa Monica, California. During the Scott and Zelda era he was known as Darrin of Paris and designed spectacular car-

What car was
voted Germany's
most prestigious
motoring award?

Mitsubishi Ga

Das Goldene Lenkrad.
The Golden Steering Wheel. The German equivalent of Car of the Year. How could Mitsubishi Galant, a newcomer to this competition, take highest honors in the country famous for brilliant engineering?

Brilliant engineering.

Quite simply, the Galant is one of the most technologically advanced automobiles ever produced.

The powerful MCA-Jet™ engine is precisely managed by ECI™ electronic multi-point fuel injection for increased acceleration power and improved responsiveness.

Galant's sleek lines, the result of exhaustive wind tunnel testing, yield exceptional aerodynamic efficiency.

Then there's the available, micro-computerized ECS™ suspension system. It automatically adjusts the

1986 Mitsubishi Galant take

lant. Natürlich.

suspension firmness to suit road conditions. It keeps the car level regardless of load. And lowers the ride height at highway speeds for more handling stability as well as reduced wind resistance.

Innovative ergonomic design provides sumptuous comfort. Even the rear seat reclines. And one of the 11 functions of the ETACS IV™ electronic control system prevents you

from locking your keys in the ignition.

An optional stereo even offers you steering wheel-mounted switches.

The list of its wondrous features goes on. And on. So test drive a new Mitsubishi Galant. You'll quickly understand why this automobile is recognized as perhaps the world's most ingeniously engineered luxury sedan.

In any language.

MITSUBISHI
MOTORS

you where you want to be.™

riages for the few who could afford them. Darrin bodies graced Rolls-Royces and Hispano-Suizas and any number of cars which were the height of fashion at the time. Darrin was a master of impractical shapes, cars that were hard to see out of or get into, and folding tops that wouldn't fold. They didn't always work just so, but they were always beautiful to look at.

Darrin's real work, though, started when the depression killed the carriage trade. He returned to Hollywood and began to customize Packard 160 convertibles. Darrin lowered them by cutting a horizontal swathe out of the middle, cast a new cowl, cut the doors down, fitted a V-windshield and achieved spectacular results.

Just seeing one made the viewer realize how wrong the standard car was.

Thus began Darrin's association with Packard. He designed the 1941-48 Clipper, easily the best-looking production car of its day and went on to do the Kaisers, both early and late, although he remained bitter over the production compromises which ruined his original Kaiser designs. He also did the KF161, later simply The Darrin, an interesting, if not entirely pleasing, sports car. Throughout his long career, Darrin was involved in hundreds of other projects, but if all he's remembered for is the Clipper, his place is secure.

The design houses (Pininfarina, Raymond Loewy and Associates, Bertone,

Ghia, and others) are like the in-house studios which mask the work of individuals behind a corporate name. Consequently, it's difficult to credit the person responsible for a given design. Two men, though, emerged from anonymity and made their personal mark—Giorgetto Giugiaro and Franco Scaglione. They performed visual miracles that transcend the design house badge. Scaglione did the Alfa-Romeo B.A.T. series for Bertone, the most radical of which is the B.A.T. 7, a complex of harmonious curves and sweeping, curling fins—pure shapes that cannot be appreciated in photographs. Though it was too complex to ever be a production car, it contributed themes to spectacular cars like the Alfa Sprint Speciale and Ferrari 275 GTB years later. Only a master designer could have handled such shapes and swoops without creating a parody.

Giugiaro also did some of his best work for Bertone, and later Ghia, before starting his own Ital Design. He can be considered the "author" of the Alfa Canguro, Lamborghini Miura, De Tomaso Mangusta, and production cars as diverse as the Maserati Quattroporte and Hyundai Pony (and, although one is a luxury sedan and the other an economobile, there are striking similarities), and the Fiat Panda and Isuzu Impulse.

Raymond Loewy may have actually been personally responsible for one car, a custom Hupmobile in the early '30s, that he used as a demonstration piece to get the Hupp account. But he is credited with many more including the 1939 Studebaker Champion and the larger President series.

Both were extremely handsome and, had they been on Ford chassis, would be greatly sought after today.

The immediate postwar Studebakers credited to Loewy were actually the work of Virgil Exner, who later earned his own reputation at Chrysler. And the 1953 Studebaker Starlight Coupe, which has proven to be one of the rare designs that seem timeless, was designed by Bourke and Koto, who were loewy Associates. It was both understated and spectacular, an almost impossible combination that underscores its genius, and influenced the Europeans more than the Americans. The last Loewy car (by Tom Kellog) was the Avanti which remains in production more than 20 years after its introduction.

Some of the Ford designs of the '30s—notably the 1932, '34, '39 and '40 Ford, the Lincoln Zephyr, and Lincoln Continental—are as good as any from the design houses. In fact, though, some of them started as prototypes built by body companies like Murray, Budd and Hayes. Other details, however, came from within Ford and were overseen by Ben Gregory and Edsel Ford himself. These cars were corporate designs, yet they were cohesive, not of the "horse designed by a committee" variety. Which is doubly remarkable considering the low esteem in which Henry Ford held most designers.

As we've seen, there's been a great deal of intermingling over the years of trends, styles and influences. But there were a few people whose work was so personal, unique and strongly flavored that they had little effect on the designs of others, yet remain important for their singular contributions. Two such were "Butzi" Porsche and Jean Bugatti.

Porsche, who now heads Porsche Design and does very well with watches and sunglasses, left the auto company headed by his father, Ferry, after a disagreement with his cousin Ferdinand Piëch. In the short time he was with Porsche, Butzi did the Carrera GTS (904) to replace the Abarth-Porsche GTL. He was able to combine

good aerodynamics, space (German drivers didn't fit in the GTL, its roof had to be raised), and handsome looks, in the first Porsche fiberglass car. It was also the last Porsche competition car which could double as a more-or-less practical road car. Butzi's other design was the Type 395 which, with minor changes, became the 911. It's hard to look at the latest 911 Carrera and realize that its basic design dates from 1960, and still seems to have plenty of life left.

Jean Bugatti was the eldest son of Ettore. He took over many of the operations of the famous Alsatian firm when his father, resentful of labor troubles, moved to Paris forever. Grandfather Carlo, uncle Rembrandt, and Ettore himself, were all creative geniuses, a talent Jean inherited. Had he created only the spectacular magnesium Elektron Atlantique, Jean's reputation as a designer would be assured, but there was the even more startling Surbaisse, which, with its skirted, front pontoon fenders, narrowly avoided a caricature, and a fine selection of coupes, cabriolets and sedans that kept excitement for

The 1938 Bugatti Type 57 Atlantique Elektron is perhaps Jean Bugatti's finest effort. Its magnesium body is riveted together and the seams become a striking element of the car's voluptuous shape. The famed Bugatti firm never recovered from Jean's untimely death.
PHOTOS: CINDY LEWIS

Bugatti high, even though competitors like Alfa were technically and mechanically better. Jean was not yet 30 when he died at the wheel of a test car. His demise sealed the fate of Bugatti as much as World War II and Ettore's subsequent death.

There are other designers, of course, who made significant contributions to automotive history. Some are known, some remain anonymous, and not all can be acknowledged here. They all contributed something to making automobiles more than mere appliances. They often failed, of course, but when they succeeded they created art, monuments to their talent that will long endure. **MT**

I didn't buy my car stereo backwards.

Why should you?

My car stereo dealer told me if you want clean, clear accurate sound—choose your speakers first. Because if the speakers can't handle it, you won't hear it. No matter what kind of sound your receiver pulls in.

Then he told me: Jensen.®

If you want to hear it the way they played it, choose Jensen speakers first. Jensen invented car speakers in the first place. And they're a leader today. Simply because they know how to deliver the goods.

Naturally I got a Jensen receiver to go with my Jensen speakers. Great team, designed to play best together. Makes sense. Makes great sound, too. I want to hear it all. With Jensen, I do.

JENSEN®

When you want it all.

©1984 International Jensen, Inc.

THE GRAND PRIX

For 80 years the world's best drivers have put national honor, pride and their lives on the line.

By Gary Witzenburg

☐ It's more than likely that the first time two pioneer motorists met on the road, they raced. Speed was what automobiles offered and, from the beginning, it showed in wheel-to-wheel competition. Whether for glory or publicity, the early days of the car were filled with races of one sort or another: city to city contests like the Paris-Rouen run in 1894, speed trials like those in Nice, and all sorts of hillclimbs, sprints and impromptu bashes on the barely existent roads of Europe and America. It wasn't long before the cars exceeded the limits of these dusty paths, often with fatal results. The solution seemed to lie in confining racing to shorter, closed circuits where it was safer, and where you could charge people to watch.

The first Grand Prix (rhymes with "on see" and means "Big Prize") was contested June 26–27, 1906, on a 64-mile circuit near Le Mans. It ran six laps on the first day and six more on the second, under a blistering sun, at speeds approaching 100 miles per hour on the longest straight. A Hungarian Renault test driver named Ferenc Szisz won it in a 13-liter, 90-horsepower Renault over Italian Felice Nazzaro's 16.3-liter, 100-horsepower Fiat, averaging near-ly 63 miles per hour.

More important to driving, however, were the new Michelin detachable wheel rims used by the Renault, Fiat and Itala teams, which allowed tires and wheels to be changed as units. Those without them had to slash away worn tires with knives and laboriously mount and inflate new ones right on their cars.

With a new fuel-consumption rule in place, Nazzaro's Fiat turned the tables in 1907. A piston-displacement limitation took effect for 1908, but the French were humbled by the Germans: Christian Lautenschlager's Mercedes won, and Benz cars finished second and third. (That same year the Automobile Club of America staged the first non-French GP, won by Louis Wagner in a Fiat, at Savannah, GA.)

The major French makers, upset and humiliated, signed an agreement killing GP competition for 1909. Their racing cars,

Marlboro
Matras
Matras

TOP:
De la Touloubre, driving a Bayard-Clement, barrels through a sweeping turn in the first Grand Prix race, held near Le Mans. A Hungarian, Ferenc Szisz, won in a Renault.

ABOVE:
Jimmy Murphy brought a Duesenberg (number 12) to the 1921 French Grand Prix and beat the likes of H.O.D. Segrave (number 10) to become the first American to win on the GP circuit.

RIGHT:
In the '30s, Grand Prix racing became a battleground for national prestige. Nazi Germany spared no expense to win and cars like this Auto Union were the most advanced.

were expensive to build and run, and money was scarce due to a worldwide trade depression. Nothing was said about light car *(voiturette)* competition, however, so attention then focused on a new generation of smaller, lighter, more agile racing cars from the likes of Delage, Sizaire-Naudin and Peugeot.

A minor "Grand Prix" held in 1911 on a part of the 1906 Le Mans circuit was modestly successful and significant for a couple of reasons. First, it prompted the Automobile Club of France (ACF) to revive its major GP the following year. Second, behind the winning Fiat was the only other finisher—a tiny 1.3-liter car called Bugatti.

Boillot and Peugeot

The 1912 "run-what-you-brung" GP featured a David-vs.-Goliath battle between France's revolutionary 7.6-liter, double-overhead-cam, four-valve-per-cylinder, shaft-drive Peugeots and Italy's giant 14-liter, chain-drive Fiats. George Boillot's Peugeot ultimately triumphed over Wagner's Fiat. Also significant was the third-place finish of Victor Rigal's long-tailed British Sunbeam—marking the first use of an "aerodynamic" body on a racing car. The ACF re-introduced a maximum fuel consumption formula for 1913, and Peugeot won the GP again and went on to dominate the season.

Under new rules specifying a 4.5-liter displacement limit and 2,426 pounds maximum weight, no fewer than 41 cars from 14 manufacturers turned up for the 1914 GP. George Boillot, proud, vain, intensely nationalistic and probably the most gifted driver of his time, found himself confronted by a German juggernaut of five Mercedes and three Opels. The 115-horsepower Mercedes were faster and accelerated better than the 112-horsepower Peugeots, but they had only rear-wheel brakes. The Peugeots were equipped with a new four-wheel braking system, which was expected to give them a slight advantage on the hilly 23.4-mile Lyons-Givors course.

For the first three laps, Boillot ran a heroic second to Max Sailer's flying Mercedes, then pitted for tires. According to Charles Fox in his book *The Great Racing Cars and Drivers*, he called for studded "rain" tires instead of the standard grooved type, indicating a handling problem. Never having raced with four-wheel brakes before, he was learning new techniques as he drove.

Sailer's engine broke on the fifth lap, putting Boillot into the lead. Lautenschlager's Mercedes was just a minute behind and closing, but the gallant Frenchman, overextending himself and his car, managed to increase his lead to 70 seconds by the halfway mark. Lautenschlager pitted for fuel, tires and minor repairs, but Boillot would stop a total of five more times to try different tire combinations.

With four laps (94 miles) to go, the Peugeots were fading. Lautenschlager gained two minutes on Boillot, then closed to within 14 seconds when the Frenchman pitted for tires for the sixth time. By lap 18, Boillot was a half-minute down, his car running on three of its four cylinders. He never completed lap 19.

Lautenschlager won, followed by Wagner and Salzer for a Mercedes 1–2–3 sweep. The best-finishing Peugeot was Goux's, in fourth. Among other things, this race showed the importance of team management and strategy and marked the first used signals to the drivers from their pit team.

Within a month, France and Germany were plunged into war. One of the Mercedes had been sent to London (for display) where its overhead-cam four-cylinder engine would serve as inspiration for Royce's Bristol aircraft engine. Another was brought to the U.S. by American driver Ralph DePalma, and it would supply the basic design for the famous Liberty aircraft engine. As for the brave Boillot, he became a combat pilot and was shot down and killed in 1916.

Between the Wars

A new organization, the *Association Internationale des Automobile Clubs Reconnus* (AIACR), devised a two-liter, 1,433-pound formula for 1922, and six-cylinder Fiats dominated the season. The French GP at Strasbourg, won by Felice Nazzaro, saw the first rolling mass start, replacing the traditional interval start. It was also the last Grand Prix in which spare tires were carried on the cars, thanks to shorter lap lengths and improving tire technology.

Sunbeam's six-cylinder Fiat "replicas" won the 1923 French GP, but Fiat's convincing win at Monza with its new blown eight-cylinder 805 demonstrated that supercharging would be necessary for future success. Arch-rival Alfa Romeo promptly stole Fiat's top engineers and appeared with its own supercharged straight-eight P2 to win the '24 French GP. Fiat, sick of being copied, withdrew from racing.

For 1925, a Belgian GP was added to the calendar, a manufacturers' championship was instituted, and the riding mechanic finally was replaced by an American invention called the rear view mirror. V-12 engines were fielded by some manufacturers, streamlined bodywork appeared on French Bugattis and Voisins, and the latter even tried a crude form of frameless monocoque construction. The season champ was Alfa Romeo, narrowly beating the formidable V-12 Delages.

The AIACR came up with a new 1.5-liter formula for 1926, but almost no one bothered to build cars to it; Bugatti's resulting championship was virtually uncontested. England and Germany staged their firsts GPs that year, but only three cars (all Bugattis) started the French GP, and only one completed the full distance. Delage returned to dominate in '27, but the makers' title was dropped and engines became "free" (with minimum weight-keyed engine size) for '28.

GP racing survived with "free formula" rules during the depression years, and organizers ran their races for whatever cars they felt would draw the largest fields and crowds. The new Italian marque Maserati emerged to win five GPs in 1930 with a potent 2.5-liter supercharged straight-eight engine. Bugatti countered with its twin-cam Type 51 the following year, then Alfa Romeo (strongly encouraged by the Italian dictator Mussolini) returned to dominance in '32 and '33.

Another dictator watched a great battle between two 4.9-liter Bugattis, eventually won by the Italian Achille Varzi over the Polish Count Czaykowski, at the banked Avus track in Germany in 1933. He was not pleased. It was time, Adolf Hitler de-

Tazio Nuvolari prepares for the start of the 1937 German Grand Prix. Perhaps the best driver of his time, Nuvolari outlived most of his competitors and raced until 1950. He died in bed at age 61 of a lingering illness.

cided, for a massive state-supported effort from Germany.

Nuvolari vs. the Germans

Powerful teams from Mercedes-Benz and a consortium of smaller makers called Auto Union (the ancestor of Audi) joined the circus in 1934. Their cars were the finest German engineering could devise and would eventually develop more than 600 horsepower and hit 200-mile-per-hour straightaway speeds.

Mercedes' W25 racer started the '34 season with 354 horsepower from its 3.3-liter twin-cam, roller-bearing, supercharged straight-eight engine. Auto Union's "P-wagon" (named for its designer, Dr. Ferdinand Porsche) had 375 horsepower from its 4.9-liter overhead-cam, supercharged, *midship-mounted* V-16. The season began with an Alfa sweep at the French GP, but the Germans quickly became dominant and made the solid-axle Alfas, Maseratis and Bugattis obsolete almost overnight.

Still, the 200,000 spectators lining the 14.2-mile Nurburgring course for the German Grand Prix of 1935 saw something very special: the great Italian Tazio Nuvolari in an underpowered Alfa Romeo P3 vs. the might of the Third Reich. The Alfa had independent front suspension and hydraulic brakes, but its 3.8-liter blown straight-eight developed only 300 horsepower compared to Mercedes' 462 (from a new 4.3-liter) and Auto Union's 400 or so. Nuvolari's only hope was the weather, which dawned rainy and foggy. He and team leader Enzo Ferrari hoped it would stay that way, for the powerful German cars were difficult to control in the wet.

Nuvolari started from the fourth row and jumped to second with a daring outside pass in the first turn, then stayed with Caracciola's Mercedes for most of the first slippery lap before falling seconds behind. His Alfa's 150-mile-per-hour top speed was simply no match for Mercedes' 170 mph.

By lap four (of 22) he slipped to fourth, and the other two Italian cars were already out. Things were looking bleak. But the 43-year-old Italian, who had virtually invented the four-wheel drift, started making up ground at an astonishing rate, using beautifully controlled powerslides through the corners of the still-damp track. By the tenth lap, amazingly, he was in the lead.

"There was panic in the German pits," writes Charles Fox, "and Korspfuhrer Huhnlein came over to [team manager] Neubauer to ask what had gone wrong with the master plan. Neubauer refused to be flustered. 'Give that little Italian a couple of laps,' he said, 'and he'll be lying in some remote corner of the track with either his head or his gearbox broken.'"

The German cars were in and out quickly when the leaders stopped for fuel and tires at the end of lap 12, but Nuvolari's crewmen managed to break their pump and had to refuel by hand. It took two minutes and 14 seconds, and Nuvolari was livid with rage when he finally rejoined in sixth place.

The next time past the pits, incredibly, he was back in second, 70 seconds behind von Brauchitsch's leading Mercedes. Neubauer signaled his driver to go faster, and the Prussian responded with a new lap record. With two laps to go, Nuvolari had pulled to within 32 seconds, and the Mercedes' right front tire was beginning to fail. It blew just six miles from the finish, and as von Brauchitsch slid sideways, fighting for control, Nuvolari sailed past him for the win.

The Germans had somehow forgotten to bring a record of the Italian national anthem, but Nuvolari supplied his own. All of Europe celebrated his victory, which would be his last that year and one of very few before he reluctantly joined Auto Union in 1938. A new formula that year limited engine size to three liters supercharged and 4.5 unsupercharged, but the Germans responded with new cars that were little slower than their 200-mile-per-hour monsters of the year before. Nuvolari would win his last GP at Belgrade in September, 1939, two days after the German invasion of Poland.

Postwar Resurgence

Free-formula GP racing resumed on a ragtag basis in 1947, and by '48 a new French governing body called *Federation Internationale de l'Automobile* (FIA) had gained control. It specified a 4.5-liter unsupercharged, 1.5-liter blown formula, mostly because there were plenty of prewar cars around that met those specifications. Alfa Romeo, Maserati, the new Ferrari team and some old British ERAs contested the supercharged class, with Alfa usually winning except when the fast and reliable 4.5-liter French Talbot Lagos showed up.

Having lost its best drivers to accidents and (in one case) cancer, Alfa decided to skip the 1949 season, leaving the brilliant Alberto Ascari to dominate with Ferrari's new V-12-powered cars. Then, for 1950, the FIA instituted the World Driver's Championship that's still with us today. (Interestingly, America's Indianapolis *500* race was part of the Championship for its first ten years, but few major teams bothered to cross the ocean to compete.)

The first year's title was taken by Dr. "Nino" Farina (brother of the famous designer "Pinin" Farina), driving for a resurgent Alfa Romeo, after a season-long battle with another Alfa driver, 39-year-old Argentine Juan Manuel Fangio. Fangio beat Farina and Ascari for the '51 crown; then Alfa pulled out for good. With no serious competition for Ferrari, Formula One (as it was now known) disappeared for two years. The driver's title moved to the 2-liter Formula Two class, dominated by Ascari and Ferrari in 1952 and '53.

But new Formula One rules for 1954 (2.5 liter unsupercharged, 750 cubic centimeters supercharged) attracted Mercedes-Benz, Lancia and a host of new British constructors as well as Ferrari and Maserati. It was the dawn of a new and exciting era that would move GP racing well along toward today's high-tech age.

Fangio and Moss

Fangio took the first two GPs of 1954 for Maserati, then switched to Mercedes and won four more to win his second World Championship going away. He was the acknowledged master of his day, smooth, calm, always in control and all but unbeatable in the twin-cam, twin-plug, fuel-injected 310-horsepower W196 (the F1 version of Mercedes' 300SLR sports car). But a 22-year-old Englishman named Stirling Moss, driving his own Maserati 250F, almost beat him at Monza, and *would* have had he not run out of gas with but just ten laps to go.

Moss joined Fangio on the Mercedes team for '55 and chased the Argentine to his third world title, winning one race and finishing second in the championship. Then Mercedes pulled out at the end of the season which had produced racing's most terrible accident. A Mercedes had collided with another car during the Le Mans 24 Hour and pinwheeled into the crowd, killing its driver and 82 spectators. Fangio went to Ferrari and Moss to Maserati.

The 1956 season came down to the last race at Monza, and the title could have gone to Fangio, to Englishman Peter Collins (his Ferrari teammate) or to Moss. Fangio needed at least a second-place finish to win it, but he soon pitted with steering problems. Collins was signaled to come in and hand his car to the number one Ferrari driver, which he did, without complaint, even though it meant sacrificing his own chance. Fangio then brought it home second to Moss' Maser.

The next year Fangio clinched his fifth World Championship with what may have been his finest drive. It was the German GP at the dangerous and difficult Nurburgring, and he started on the pole with a record qualifying time. He knew that his Maserati would have to pit once for gas, and that the more fuel-efficient Ferraris wouldn't. At the halfway mark, he was leading by 28 seconds.

Following his fuel stop, Fangio was down by 40 seconds to Collins and Mike Hawthorn in the lead Ferraris. He knew he couldn't catch them at the rate they were going, so he held back for two laps to fool the Ferrari team manager into signaling them to relax their pace. Then he stood on it, setting new track records lap after lap and eventually beating Hawthorn by just four seconds.

Fangio and Moss were the first of a new breed of completely professional drivers who knew their worth and expected to be paid accordingly. The day of the dashing, hard-partying amateur who risked his neck for the thrill of it would soon be over. The late '50s also marked the emergence of a new breed of lightweight, mid-engined Formula One racing car and the beginning of the age of the small British constructor.

Moss had won three of the last four '57 races in a front-engined British Vanwall. In '58, he started the season with a win in Argentina in a tiny mid-engined Cooper, and Maurice Trintignant took Monaco in a similar car. Moss and another talented Englishman, Tony Brooks, then won six of the eight remaining contests for Vanwall. Hawthorn (Ferrari) won the title by a single point over Moss, but Vanwall took the new constructor's championship home to England. (Hawthorn, demoralized by the death of his best friend and teammate Collins that year, retired and was himself tragically killed in a road accident during the winter.)

Australian Jack Brabham was World Champion in '59 and '60, bringing the contructor's crown to Cooper. Under a new 1.5-liter formula, American Phil Hill won for Ferrari in '61 and Englishman Graham Hill for England's BRM the following year. Halfway through the season, Stirling Moss was nearly killed in the crash of his privately-entered Lotus. He recovered, but the brilliant career that had somehow never quite won him the world title was over.

Clark, Stewart and GP Safety

While Bruce McLaren (Cooper) and Dan Gurney (Porsche) took one GP each in '62, the mantle of "Master" passed to Scotland's Jim Clark, who won three that year in Colin Chapman's revolutionary Lotus 25. Once accustomed to the Lotus, which was first to use a semi-reclining driving position to reduce frontal area and first with a full monocoque chassis, Clark won seven of ten races in '63 for his first world championship, and six of ten in '65 for his second. The only times he didn't win were when the fragile Lotus broke, which it did often enough in 1964 to see Ferrari's John Surtees take the title by two points over BRM's Graham Hill.

A new 3.0-liter engine formula took everyone by surprise in '66, and Australian Jack Brabham was champion in a car of his own construction, with power from an Australian Repco V-8. Then came the Lotus 49, powered by a Ford-financed Cosworth V-8 DFV (dual four-valve) engine that would be Formula One's premier powerplant for 15 years to come. Unreliable at first, it soon proved its potential, and Clark won four times with it in 1967. The championship went to Dennis Hulme and Brabham, but the following season's only non-Cosworth-Ford victory fell to Jacky Ickx's Ferrari.

Clark was killed (in a Formula Two race he had agreed to drive for a friend), Graham Hill was champion in a Lotus-Ford,

and a young Scot named Jackie Stewart won his first three GPs in a French Matra-Ford in 1968. And then the highly professional Stewart, shocked by the needless carnage in his sport, a sport that had regularly killed a third to a half of its best drivers, began almost single-handedly to bring about the modern era of safety consciousness in motorsports.

While most drivers still preferred being tossed out in a crash to staying in the car and risking a fire, Stewart was first to use safety belts. He wore fire-resistant underwear and overalls, bought a state-of-the-art (American) helmet, and was instrumental (through a new Grand Prix Drivers Association) in getting foam-filled fuel cells and other safety improvements into GP cars. "These were my first steps toward looking

ABOVE:
This W165 was built by Mercedes-Benz especially for the 1939 Tripoli Grand Prix, the premier race of the day. Developed in less than nine months, the W165s finished first and second (Lang over Caraciolla) and were never raced again.

OPPOSITE PAGE:
The W196 racers of the '50s restored Mercedes-Benz' pre-war glory. The streamlined cars were used on long courses, the open-wheel cars on tight tracks. The W196s won 10 of 13 races they entered and two driving championships.
PHOTOS: JOHN LAMM

after myself," he later explained.

Stewart won six of 11 races to take the title (for Matra-Ford) in 1969. That was the first season the GP cars were not required to wear national colors (British racing green, French blue, Italian red), and, as F1 began evolving from a sport of national pride to one of commercial entertainment, with high-dollar sponsorships paying most of the mushrooming bills, it was also Stewart who led the trend toward lucrative salaries and endorsements for its drivers.

As reigning champion the next year—after his friend and rival Jochen Rindt died in an ambulance, stuck in traffic, on the way to a hospital following a practice at Monza—Stewart turned his considerable energy toward improving the safety of racing circuits and the level of emergency medical attention. Incredibly, the highly-talented Rindt had accumulated enough points in his Lotus-Ford prior to his death to win the 1970 world title posthumously.

A hard-charging Italian/American named Mario Andretti won the first 1971 GP in a Ferrari, but Stewart repeated as champion in a Tyrrell-Ford. The next year saw the first world championship for Emerson Fittipaldi of Brazil (the fifth for Lotus), then Stewart (still with Tyrrell) came back to win his third world title in '73. After that, wealthy and still healthy, he retired from driving, setting still another precedent. Thanks to Fittipaldi's three wins and Swede Ronnie Peterson's four, Lotus repeated as constructor's champion. Cosworth Ford engines scored a clean sweep of all 15 of the 1973 events (as did

Goodyear tires) and American Peter Revson won two GPs in a McLaren.

Niki Lauda and the Turbo Age

Revson was killed in a practice session early in '74, and Ferrari's Niki Lauda, a cool and methodical Austrian, won his first two GPs as Fittipaldi took the championship for McLaren. The next season saw Lauda claim his first championship (Ferrari's first since 1964), while a bold and brash young Englishman named James Hunt won his first GP in a privately-entered Hesketh. The use of strut-mounted aerodynamic wings to produce downforce at speed came into serious question after one car's wing strut broke at the Spanish GP and four people were killed in the resulting accident. In still another tragic incident, Mark

Donohue, the talented and popular American engineer/driver who had come out of retirement to head Roger Penske's GP effort, died three days after a high-speed practice accident in Austria.

Then came probably the strangest F1 season ever. Lauda won the first two races and Clay Regazonni the third for Ferrari; then Hunt took the fourth but was later disqualified (and still later reinstated) after his McLaren was found to be a fraction of an inch too wide. Lauda won two more to Hunt's one, accumulating a considerable points lead. The odd-looking six-wheel Tyrrell cars, with four tiny wheels in front instead of the usual two larger ones for better aerodynamics, silenced the snickerers by finishing one-two in Sweden, led by South African Jody Scheckter. Then Hunt won the British GP in a car that had been repaired and restarted after a first-lap wreck had halted the race. This was a no-no, so those points were protested and later awarded to Lauda. Then, after warning that Germany's Nurburgring track was too dangerous for modern F1 cars, Lauda proved his point by nearly dying in a flaming wreck during the German GP.

Ferrari promptly withdrew from GP racing, but Lauda miraculously recovered and was racing again just three events later. Hunt won the next two and went to the season-ending Japanese GP trailing Lauda by three points. It was rainy and foggy that day; visibility was terrible, and Lauda—hailed as the bravest man on wheels for getting back into a car at all after his terrible, disfiguring accident—climbed out of his Ferrari after two laps and declared the conditions far too dangerous. "For me," he said, "there is something more important than the championship." Hunt proceeded to lead most of the race before pitting for new tires, then drove brilliantly to work his way back up to third to win the '76 title by a single point. Ferrari retained its constructor's championship. The winner of that rainswept race? Mario Andretti in a Lotus-Ford.

Lotus invented the "wing" car for '77, with downforce-producing tunnels under its body and sliding "skirts" along its sides to channel air through them, and Andretti proved its worth by winning four of the season's 17 races. The venerable Cosworth-Ford won its 100th GP in Scheckter's Wolf at Monaco, while Lauda completed his comeback by taking three races and the championship for himself and Ferrari. On a new street course at Long Beach, California, Andretti became the first American to win a U.S. GP; Jacques Laffite won the Swedish GP in a Matra-powered Ligier, the first win for a French car and driver in 25 years. And more significantly, giant French car maker Renault introduced its new (non-turbo) engines at the British GP.

Andretti became America's second World Champion in '78 after his closest challenger—his Lotus-Ford teammate Ronnie Peterson—was killed in a first-lap accident at Monza. Ferrari scored five wins to Lotus' eight, four by Carlos Reutemann of Argentina, and one by a brilliant young French Canadian named Gilles Villeneuve. Lauda won the Swedish GP for Brabham, now run by feisty Englishman Bernie Eccelstone, with a new "sucker" car (a gearbox-driven fan created downforce by sucking air out from under the body), and the car was promptly banned.

ABOVE:
Fangio gets the jump on Moss at the start of the 1955 British GP. Moss went on to win, but Fangio went on the take the World Championship, the third of his record five driving titles.

LEFT:
Short-sleeved shirt, no seat belt, and an eggshell helmet gave precious little protection to Alberto Ascari, here on his way to winning the 1953 British GP. Safety didn't get proper attention until the late '60s.

Ferrari

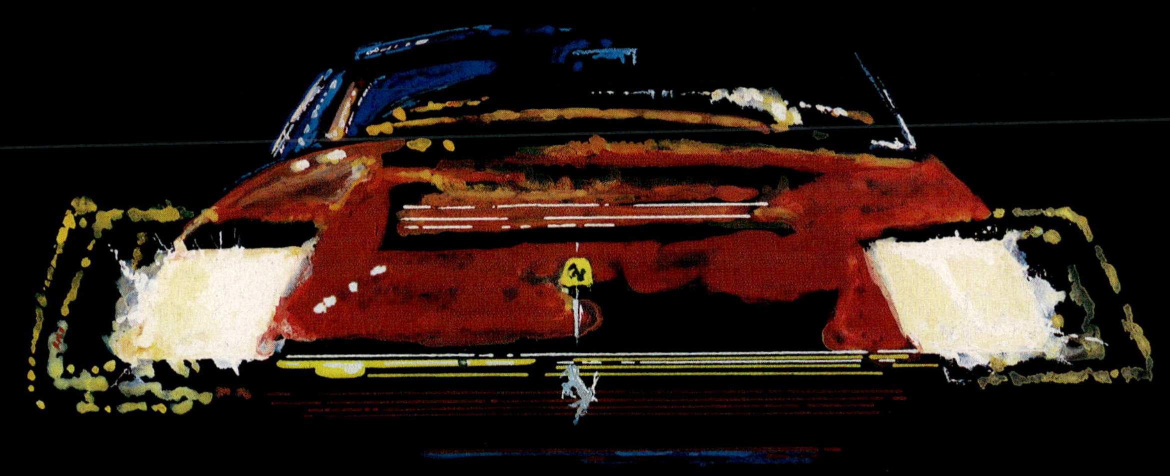

The year 1979 marked the beginning of a long slump for Lotus as others adopted tunnel-car technology and made it more reliable. Renault scored its first F1 win with the steadily-improving turbocar, while Scheckter won the championship for himself and Ferrari. Hunt quit the Wolf team at mid-season and was replaced by Finland's Keke Rosberg, and twice-champion Lauda lost interest halfway through the first practice at the fall Canadian GP and simply walked away from his Brabham racer. The next year saw Renault take three more GPs and rising star Nelson Piquet win three for Brabham, but Austra-lian Alan Jones ascended to the championship in a Ford-powered Williams car.

The ground-rubbing side skirts, which were prone to sudden failures (causing a loss of downforce and, usually, a big crash), were banned for 1981, but the ever-clever Brabham team developed a "cheater" hydraulic suspension that lowered the car for added downforce at speed but raised it in the pits to meet FISA's new ground clearance requirement. The rule-makers declared it legal, which obligated everyone to come up with similar systems to remain competitive. The result was a breed of near-suspensionless F1 "go-carts" that brutalized the drivers' bodies on rough surfaces. Rapid Frenchman Alain Prost scored three wins for Renault but was aced out of the championship by Brabham's Piquet, while Williams took the constructor's title with two wins each from Jones and Reutemann. One of Jones' victories came at the season's last race on a new temporary course laid out in the Caesar's Palace (Las Vegas) parking lot. He dominated the event (which replaced the one at the bankrupt Watkins Glen, N.Y., course), then he retired.

An unprecedented third U.S. GP, run through the concrete canyons of downtown Detroit, was added for '82 and won by McLaren's John Watson. Three more teams—Ferrari, Brabham and Toleman—had joined the turbo brigade, but Rosberg stole the driver's title from McLaren's Watson and Renault's Prost with a Ford-powered Williams. The 1.5-liter turbos were faster, but the 3.0-liter non-turbo Fords were more reliable. The season was marred by two fatal accidents, one claiming the spectacularly talented Villeneuve. And it was significant for the return of Ni-ki Lauda, who signed with Brabham for a huge (undisclosed) sum of money and announced that he expected to be back in winning form by his third race. The season's third event was at Long Beach; Lauda, as he had predicted, won it.

The super-stiff ground-effects suspensions were gone for '83, and it seemed to be Renault's year at last as Prost won four races and led the points chase all season. But the Ferraris and BMW-powered Brabhams improved substantially during the year, and Prost lost the championship to Brabham's Piquet at the very last race. For the second straight year, Ferrari won the hotly contested constructor's title. The Cosworth-Ford engine won its final three GPs—Watson (McLaren) at Long Beach, Rosberg (Williams) at Monaco, Italian Michele Alboreto (Tyrrell) at Detroit, all tight street courses—for a total of 155 wins in 16 years of competition. By season's end, Williams had Honda turbo engines, McLaren had Porsche-developed TAG turbos, Lotus had Renault turbos; Alfa Romeo's turbo and Toleman's Hart turbo were steadily improving, and only Tyrrell of the major teams remained boostless.

The 1984 season put a new twist on the high-tech era as fuel-consumption limits were imposed. Now the engineers had to make their cars not only fast and reliable but fuel-efficient as well, and the drivers had to practice unusual restraint with their cockpit boost controls if they wanted to finish, let alone win. Most races saw more

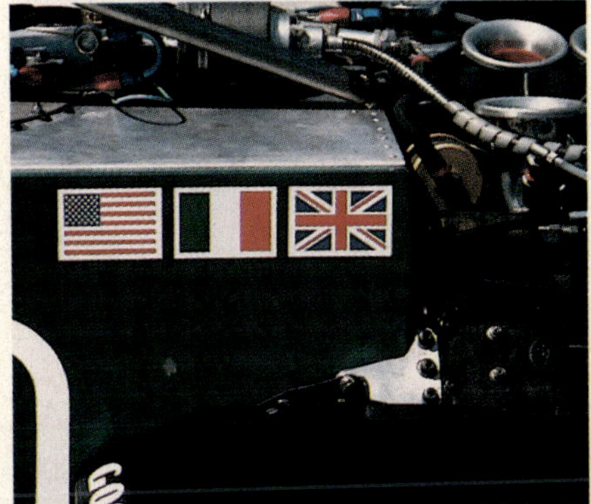

The greatest racing driver ever? Juan Manuel Fangio won one of every two races he contested, 24 in all, and five World Championships.

OPPOSITE PAGE:
Nelson Piquet's Brabham is typical of today's GP cars. Its carbon fiber tub, turbocharged BMW engine and electronic engine-management system are state of the art, and costly.
PHOTO: ROBERT HARMEYER JR.

LEFT:
Jim Clark, the driver, and Colin Chapman, the builder and designer, celebrate victory in the 1963 British GP, one of 25 for Clark, and 73 for Lotus. Ferrari, however, has the most Grand Prix victories, 91 through mid-1985.

THE SPORTS CARS

Any car can get you from here to there, but the sports car makes the trip an end in itself.

By Mike Knepper

☐ In the beginning they were all sports cars of a sort.

Self propelling a buggy or carriage produced a vehicle that was light, had very quick steering, offered minimal comforts, generally seated only two, had very little luggage room and was enormously fun to drive. A sports car.

But they were called, simply, cars. "Sports" came along a bit later when there was a need to differentiate between more sophisticated models and those that retained most of the original traits and were, by and large, being driven by the wealthy young men of the time, the "sports" of country club, horse track and boulevard.

And since all cars started with sports car characteristics, it's a bit difficult to determine when the first "sports car" was built. There are those who hold it was the 1910 27/80 Austro-Daimler designed by none other than Prof. Ferdinand Porsche, a theory no doubt furiously supported by Porsche Club of America members.

In 1906 the Brothers Stanley built a little number called the Stanley Gentleman's Speedy Roadster that had all the attributes of a purpose-built sports car, including a new wrinkle: On the sands at Ormond Beach in Florida the Speedy ran the flying one-half mile at 75 mph, and forever more "performance" would be an integral part of the definition of *sports car*.

Easily the most famous of the early sports cars was the Stutz Bearcat of 1914. And the Thomas company built automobiles in the genre: The winner of the famous New York to Paris race was a Thomas Flyer. But the quintessential early sports car, the one the experts point to as the best of the early breed, the definition in metal, is the Mercer Raceabout, built from 1911 to 1915. It was lean and mean like the Bearcat, but more so, having little more than sweeping fenders, a pair of form-fitting bucket seats, a box covering the engine and a monocle windshield. It offered its occupants the essence of motoring. It wasn't very powerful, just 50 horsepower from a giant, slow-turning five liters, but with lit-

TF 9579

PORSCHE
STUTTGART
PORSCHE

PORSCHE

☐ *The Nissan Z-car is the biggest-selling sports car in history. The market-research people tell us the Corvette is the most-desired car in America. Ferrari is a synonym for sleek, fast and sexy.*

And then there's Porsche. Not the biggest seller, not the car of aspirations of millions of Americans, and certainly never applauded for styling leadership. But there's something about the machines from Zuffenhausen that sets them apart—and a bit above—all the rest. Something Prof. Ferdinand Porsche created and his son perpetuates that transcends easy definition.

For more than 30 years Ferdinand Porsche applied his design genius to developing the products of others. In 1900 there was the Lohner-Porsche. After Lohner, Daimler of Austria, then Daimler-Benz, Auto Union and Steyr.

In 1930, after a year with Steyr, Porsche realized he was going to spend his life working for one manufacturer after another, making them millions with his designs while he existed on a salary, unless he made a definite break. So with son Ferry (Ferdinand Anton Ernst), Porsche opened an independent design office in Stuttgart. The company grew from 19 employees at the end of the first year to 176 in 1938 when new facilities were opened in Zuffenhausen, a suburb northwest of Stuttgart.

Before becoming successful on his own, Porsche had established a formidable reputation in Germany, so it was logical that Hitler turn to Porsche to design the car the Führer called the "people's car," or volkswagen.

The car that was intended to put Germany behind the wheel was radically styled with a strange, bug-like nose that drooped to the ground. But even more strange was the horizontally-opposed air-cooled four-cylinder engine that was mounted behind the rear wheels.

Perhaps it was that strangeness, perhaps the political uncertainties, but established manufacturers balked at producing the Volkswagen, so Hitler had a manufacturing facility built and in 1939 assigned Porsche the job of running the Volkswagen operation. Ferry took over the family business.

But the brilliance of the design wouldn't be proved until years later, after the war that soon curtailed the VW operation, when the car would become the most successful single model ever built.

Porsche turned his talents to the war effort and began designing armaments, one of which was the famous Tiger tank. He was also named president of the Armor Commission of the Ministry of Arms and Munitions, but after an altercation with Reich armaments minister Albert Speer, Porsche was given a mostly symbolic position as Reich armaments councilor. His insistence on exotic designs for tank engines and drive systems when Germany needed simple designs for mass production took him out of direct involvement with the war effort.

However, in the early years of the war when he was very active, dashing from Berlin to Paris to Zuffenhausen to wherever, some of the dashing was done in a streamlined two-seat coupe that had been built in 1939 for a Berlin-to-Rome race that never took place. The car was based on the original Volkswagen, the Type 60, and was called the Type 60K10. Horsepower had been doubled to 50, and the coupe was capable of a sustained 90 mhp on the Autobahn. This strange-looking machine was the first Porsche, and the legacy of its odd shape is apparent in today's 911.

At the end of the war, Prof. Porsche was detained by the Allies for a short time; then, like the rest of the family, he was released to pick up the pieces of the prewar life. However, late in 1945 he was lured to Baden-Baden in the French-occupied zone of Germany and arrested on trumped-up charges of mistreatment of prisoners of war and workers at a Peugeot plant in France that had come under his direction during the war. His health was broken during 20 months of imprisonment in terrible conditions. Shortly after his 75th birthday, he suffered a stroke and died.

But during the ordeal, the family interests were looked after by Porsche's daughter, Louise Piëch—Ferry was also in prison for six months—who, in 1946, established Porsche Konstruktionen GmbH.

Ferry took over when he was released from prison and has been the creative force behind the company since. Although it's his genius that we see manifested in the Porsches of today, the groundwork was laid, the path charted by Ferdinand Porsche and the people's car—both truly automotive originals.

tle more than the weight of its chassis to move, it moved.

The unpleasantness with the Kaiser and company diverted attention from the delights of motoring for a few years in the early part of this century, but when WWI was over, war-weary populations were anxious to renew their acquaintance with the internal-combustion engine, and that enthusiasm made the next two decades-plus the golden years of the sports car. Small builders and giant manufacturers turned out a succession of wonderful creations to meet the ever-increasing demand for fast, challenging, exciting cars.

Vauxhall, Bentley, Lagonda, Aston Martin from England. In France, Bugatti. Alfa Romeo in Italy. Mercedes-Benz from Germany. Then throw in lesser-knowns such as Alvis, Riley, Adler, Amilcar, Squire, and add the sporting tourers, the *voitures de grand luxe*, from Delage, Talbot-Lago, Hispano-Suiza, Pierce-Arrow, Rolls-Royce. And here at home, Packard, Auburn, Cord, Duesenberg, Jordan.

(Between 1916 and 1931 when the marque disappeared, Jordan built good, if unremarkable, automobiles. But Ned Jordan's legacy to the world was not automobiles; it was their advertising which is credited with fostering modern copy writing. The ad for his 1923 Playboy model, titled "Somewhere West of Laramie," is the classic example of the Jordan approach. See page 65.)

It was one of those never-before, never-again eras: giant 8 and 12-cylinder engines, some with superchargers, throbbing beneath long, long hoods that nestled between flowing fenders and finished in proud, upright grilles. There was, is, a rightness about the way those cars looked, the statement they made, that makes the sports cars of the '30s the very definition of the word "automobile." That's what it is still all about.

Motor racing was part and parcel of that *Belle Epoque* and to many it, too, was the best it has ever been. The competition was fierce and nationalistic: the brute strength of Germany's Mercedes-Benz and Auto Union against the light and lithe Alfa Romeos and Maseratis. Nothing, it is said, advances technology like a war, and it was war on the Grand Prix circuits in the late '30s. Tire, engine, brake and suspension technology advanced at a furious pace as each manufacturer looked for an advantage, and much technology developed on the track found its way onto the street.

But then that other kind of war, the bullet-and-bomb type, brought the '30s to a close. When the war began, an era ended. When the war was finally over, a new era began . . . .

M.G. automobiles have been around a long time. The record indicates the first car to carry the M.G. designation, which stood for Morris Garages in Oxford, appeared in 1923 (or 1924, depending on whose book you read). Six special two-seat bodies from Raworth were aimed at "motorists of sporting proclivities and cultivated tastes."

Mass production will give you a Porsche or a Corvette.

It will not give you a Lotus Turbo Esprit.

In an industry that worships at the altar of mass production, it is hardly surprising that 99.99% of its output is produced that way.

However, what *is* surprising is the fact that eleven of those huge automated companies (churning out some 40,000 cars a day) were, at last count, getting engineering and design help from Lotus.

Lotus, on a good day, "churns" out an Esprit and a half.

It is, essentially, a hand-crafted car.

So, the question: Why do some of the true industrial geniuses of this age wend their way to our unconventional plant tucked away in a far corner of the English countryside?

Perhaps because we offer genius of another kind.

Shockwaves at Indy.

That Lotus is made of the stuff of legends first became evident at the Indianapolis 500 in 1963 when a knee-high mini-rocket came blazing out of nowhere to change the face of racing forever.

Up against the behemoth thunder machines of that day, Lotus with its revolutionary chassis design, aerodynamic profile and extreme power-to-weight ratio came in a strong second, its first time out.

In '64 Lotus took both first and second in the qualifying heats.

Then got it all together in '65. Qualifying first, second and third. Winning first, second and fourth.

And the mad scramble was on.

Lotus look-alikes began appearing on Grand Prix courses as fast as they could be hammered out.

Being mere copies, they performed like it.

And Lotus went on to burn itself into the record books at a pace unparalleled in the history of racing.

But enough perspective. Now, what is Lotus today?

It is one of the very few race cars ever to make the complete transition to pure sports car.

In a World of Mass Produced Sports Cars, Stubborn Individualism.

While we at Lotus wholeheartedly embrace today's technology, we employ it to augment the hand, not replace it.

For example: Computer-guided milling machines give us critically precise engine tolerances. Computer-controlled optical scanners eliminate components not up to our standards.

Still, the engine is unhurriedly assembled by hand, with all parts (right down to the valve springs) so carefully matched and balanced that it takes two full weeks to complete a single engine.

Because the same care is taken in building the entire car, six weeks are required from ground zero to its first test run.

The chassis is hand-assembled and hand-welded. The entire unit is then galvanized to lock out corrosion.

The body is of a special carbon-fiberglass composite developed by Lotus. It *can't* rust.

The upholstery is glove-soft Connolly leather, which our friends at Rolls Royce also use. Every seam is stitched by hand and every piece so carefully matched that five hides are required to do one car.

The Lotus body is given nine coats of paint. Each coat is rubbed down by hand. The final coat is a clear coat, hand polished to give Lotus the most envied finish in the business.

Lotus tires are not your usual stock item. Our engineers worked long hours with Goodyear in developing a tire specifically for the Turbo Esprit. One that works in total harmony with the car's weight, power and suspension system.

And now the big one. Can such a precision instrument take a beating?

Consider the unfortunate film director who, not so long ago, sent a Lotus flying off a cliff in expectation of shooting a spectacular fall, followed by a crashing breakup.

He got the fall and the crash. But no breakup. Not even on the second try. Or the third.

Sledge hammers finally were brought to bear and the director got his breakup.

So What Could We Improve?

This 16-valve, 4-cylinder mid-engine dynamo will take you from 0 to 150 faster than a prudent man would care to do it.

Still, we boosted the horsepower a bit to 215. And the new '86s are equipped with fuel injection.

Not for speed. For quickness. Which is what real driving is all about.

A computerized fuel metering system is now also part of the power plant. It virtually *anticipates* split-second power needs. And improves gas mileage, giving the car a touring range of over 500 miles.

And to give you more of the open road while you're out there, a totally integrated, removable roof panel is now standard on every Turbo Esprit.

We also made refinements in the turbocharger, suspension, brakes and tires to keep the car in tune with its new power.

The Esprit is now as close to perfect pitch—power, precision, predictability working in unison—as a car is likely to get.

"It puts me at one with the road as no car ever has," is how one enthusiast summed it up.

He also commented on feeling secure because the car is very forgiving and always has something in reserve.

But that's another whole story....

Lotus If you're ready for it, drop us a line and we'll put you in touch with your nearest dealer. Lotus Performance Cars, L.P. 530 Walnut Street, Norwood, New Jersey 07648

ILLUSTRATION: JOE GOEBLE

FERRARI

☐ *In Italy it's said, only half kiddingly, that Enzo Ferrari is not only as popular as the Pope, he's harder to get in to see.*

The Italians are fervently passionate about cars and racing. They have been an important part of Italian life since the very earliest days of the automobile. Nuvolari, Campari, Varzi and Taruffi are venerated heroes—Italy's Dimaggio, Gherig and Ruth. And then there's Ferrari. Il Commendatore, the builder of those beautiful red automobiles, the provider of racing victories and at 87, the tie between the past he helped shape and the present of which he is so much a part.

Ferrari was born in 1898 when automobiles were something less than common. Nonetheless his father owned one of the first ones in Modena, and it is said young Enzo was immediately fascinated by it and spent as much time in it as he could. He saw his first race when he was ten, decided to become a race driver soon after and had learned to drive by 13.

His drove his first race in 1919—fourth behind winner Ascari—but his racing career really began when he became an Alfa Romeo team driver. Time and Ferrari's apparent enjoyment of the confusion that surrounds the subject have created a legend

about his racing exploits that may be a bit exaggerated. But he did win races. He won so convincingly at Ravenna in 1923 that in honor of the performance the parents of Italian WWI flying ace Francesco Barraca gave Ferrari a piece of canvas from their son's plane bearing Barraca's prancing horse symbol, the *cavallino rampante that has been the Ferrari logo ever since.*

In 1929, Alfa withdrew from racing, but maintained a relationship with newly formed Scuderia (literally, stable) Ferrari, which campaigned Alfas for many years.

The first "Ferraris" were customer cars built for the 1940 Mille Miglia, but were called simply Vettura 815. During the next few years the scuderia's expertise was devoted to the war effort, so it wasn't until 1946 that engineer Colombo could work on the first Ferrari V-12. In 1947 the new motor went into the first automobiles to officially carry the Ferrari name: three Type 125 Corsas, and a legend was officially born.

The 125 almost immediately gave way to the 166, and a Farina-bodied version, the 166 Inter, was the first street Ferrari. The body, built by "Stabilimenti Farina" was almost unbelievably ugly, but where does it say a new-born legend has to be handsome?

For years, Ferraris were essentially race cars that could be driven on the street. A few road versions were built to satisfy special customers. Inevitably the demand for street cars exceeded the demand for race cars, and in 1953 Scuderia Ferrari built the 250 Europa which started the long line of production cars that continues today.

Ten M.G.s were sold the first year of the now-famous marque, and by 1928 the number was up to 300. That was also the year the M-type Midget was introduced. With a light two-seat body, tweaked engine for unusually good performance and a surprisingly low price, the M-type is considered the first "real" M.G. sports car. It was built until 1932. Then came a stream of overlapping models—L, Q, R, Magnettes and such—moving toward the TA Midget in 1936, the beginning of the lineage familiar to Americans. Next in order, the TB Midget, had one year of production in 1939 before the war interfered.

So yes, as the traditional story has it, there were M.G.s scuttling about England to charm the car-loving Yanks on duty there, and just as certainly the occasional TA or TB was packed up and sent to the States where it was a curiosity for most, but of great fascination to a few out-of-step free thinkers. Romantics, most likely. Whoever they were, they were around in sufficient numbers when the fabled TC came to the U.S. in 1947 to make it a small but significant sales success. The second era of the sports car in the U.S. began.

With only 54 horsepower from 1250 cubic centimeters, the TC was underpowered, had skinny tires and semi-elliptic spring suspension for rather tentative handling (it would actually drift through a 25-mph corner) and was not particularly well suited to the wide open spaces (or the cold winters) of the New World. But it found a market. More than 10,000 were built, and most came to the U.S. The TC was replaced by the more sophisticated TD in 1950. (All these dates are U.S. on-sale dates, by the way.) The TF came in 1954 and then, in 1956, the stunning MGA.

Before the war, sports cars were generally the domain of the privileged class. The average driver dreamed of a Packard or Auburn or Cord while he bumped around in his Chevy or Ford. After the war, our wealthy citizenry picked up pretty much where it left off. Packard and Auburn roadsters were gone but were happily replaced by Ferraris, Maseratis, Astons and other expensive European marques. But suddenly the privileged weren't alone out there. Their preserve was invaded. The arrival of the M.G. was the automotive equivalent of the storming of the Winter Palace, the fall of the Bastille. Let them eat cake? Give them the heady aroma of castor bean oil. All that was wonderful about sports cars was available to the average driver. Vive la Revolution, and score one for the class struggle.

The M.G. was first, but it soon wasn't alone. Never quite as exalted, or successful, Triumph also became a key player in the postwar era.

Triumph has actually been around longer than M.G. First, in 1895, as a bicycle, then as a motorcyle, and then, since just after the close of WWI, as a car. In the '30s and '40s, Triumph roadsters looked much like M.G.s and other British sports cars: separate fenders/running boards over ex-

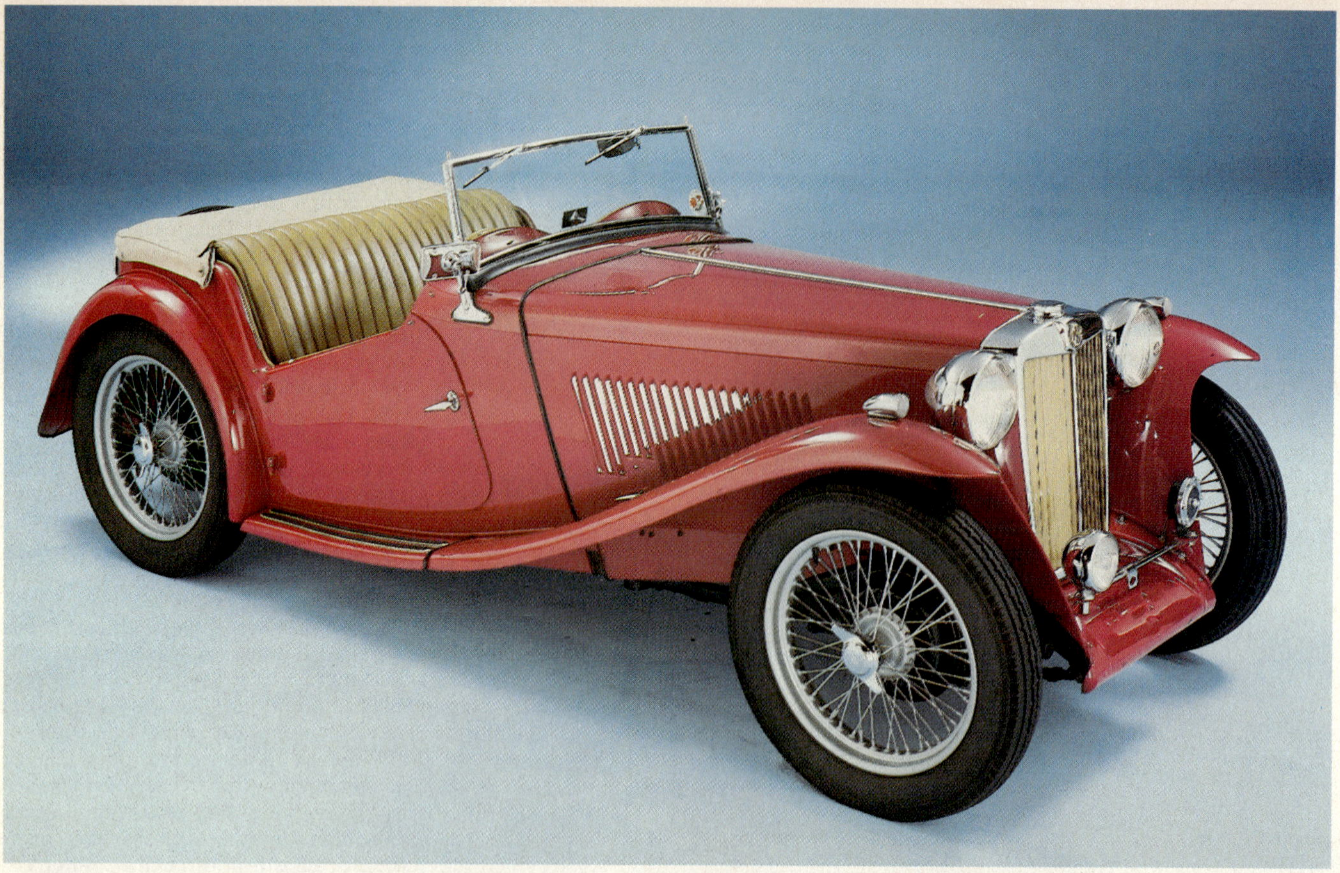

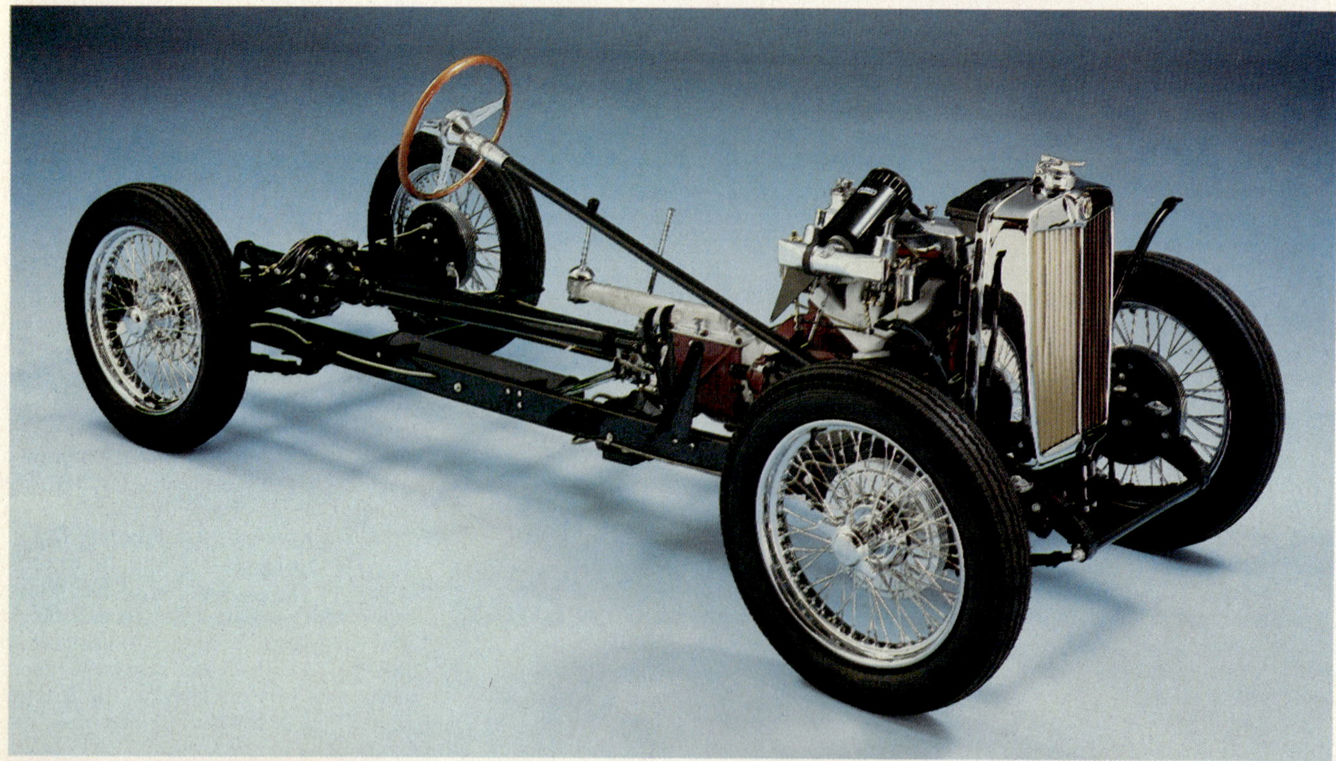

A pair of classic sports cars, the MG TC and Mercedez-Benz 300SL "Gullwing," illustrate sports car evolution. The MG's prewar roots are obvious—frame rails, basic suspension and engine. The 300SL with its triangulated, tubular chassis and fuel-injected engine is the height of automotive development for its time.
PHOTO: BOB D'OLIVO

posed wheels, upright grille, small windshield, spare tire stuck in or strapped to the slanting rear deck and so forth. But at the 1952 Earl's Court motor show, Triumph showed the TR-1 which, with smoothly rounded lines, filled-in fenders and sloping nose, diverged dramatically from the classic British style.

The production version, the TR-2, went on sale in 1953. The TR-3 arrived as a running change in 1956, the 3A in the fall of '58, and the 3B, an interim model using up 3-series parts, in 1962, prior to the TR-4's intro later that year. The M.G. and the TR fanned out to spread the gospel of the sports-car revolution across the country.

There's one thing about people with a common, slightly out-of-step interest: the flocking instinct. The Sports Car Club of America was formed one winter evening in 1948 in the Boston home of one of the aforementioned privileged to formalize the flocking instinct. To characterize the SCCA in those early days as a bit, uh, elitist is probably to not exaggerate. But as the gospel spread, the newly converted in their TDs and TR-3s inevitably developed their own urge to flock, and there was the SCCA, ready-made. Tweed cap and stringback driving gloves, meet Eastern-Establishment money. They had a common cause, and their common meeting ground, the SCCA, despite some monumental bad management and its Machiavellian internal politics, is an integral part of the history of the sports car in this country. It not only provided a locus for the movement, it or-

ganized racing and rallying and made sports-car ownership a classless social activity. An aimless enthusiasm was given a focus.

Inexpensive M.G.s and Triumphs were the entry-level sports cars in those early days, and the step above them was the handsome product of the Donald Healey, Austin Motor Co. partnership.

In many circles, Donald Healey is as revered as Enzo Ferrari and Ferdinand Porsche. Healey, like Ferrari and Porsche, was significant in the postwar sports car story. He was a name and a face, not a corporate identity, and enthusiasts liked the personal involvement.

The first Healey, the Westland, was introduced in January, 1946, and despite an egregiously ugly grille, was, overall, an attractive design. There followed an eclectic succession of Healey models that established Donald Healey as one of the successful small-car builders in Great Britain during the late forties.

But the car that got it going for Healey in the U.S. was introduced at the London Motor Show in October, 1952. The Healey 100, which promised true 100-mph performance for approximately $2500, was the hit of the show; such a hit, in fact, that during the run of the show, salesmen took more than 3,000 orders, most from American dealers, which was far too many for the small Healey works to handle.

The 100 used an Austin 2.6-liter, 90-horsepower four-cylinder and other Austin bits and pieces, so Austin boss Sir Leonard

Born in the U.S.A. The first and latest Corvettes bracket a line of cars that put America on the sports car map. Always fast, always striking, the Corvettes were made respectable by Zora Arkus-Duntov (below), a brilliant engineer who gave the cars handling to match their speed and acceleration. His legacy lives on.

MAZDA FOR 1986.

NOW MORE THAN EVER, THE MORE YOU LOOK, THE MORE YOU LIKE.

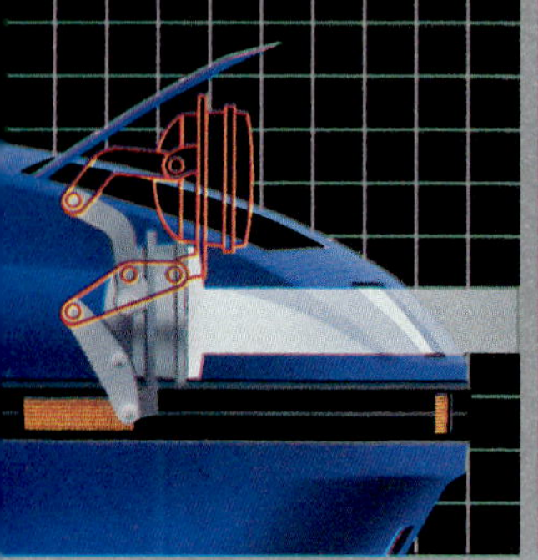
The retractable quartz halogen headlamps always face forward. This unique design lets you "flash-to-pass" without raising the RX-7's headlamps.

A more potent fuel-injected rotary engine now powers the RX-7. And it delivers power more smoothly than any other engine in the world.

Here's where the fine art of ergonomics reaches a new plateau: The RX-7 cockpit. Dual reclining bucket seats are orthopedically sculpted to provide the superb support performance driving demands. Controls are clustered for quick access. The close-ratio 5-speed falls naturally to hand.

The RX-7's bold new form is also highly functional. Its slippery 0.31 drag coefficient is even lower than that of a Porsche 944.

INTRODUCING A NEW LEVEL OF SPORTS CAR PERFORMANCE, SOPHISTICATION AND, SURPRISINGLY, VALUE.

THE 1986 MAZDA RX-7.

$11,995*

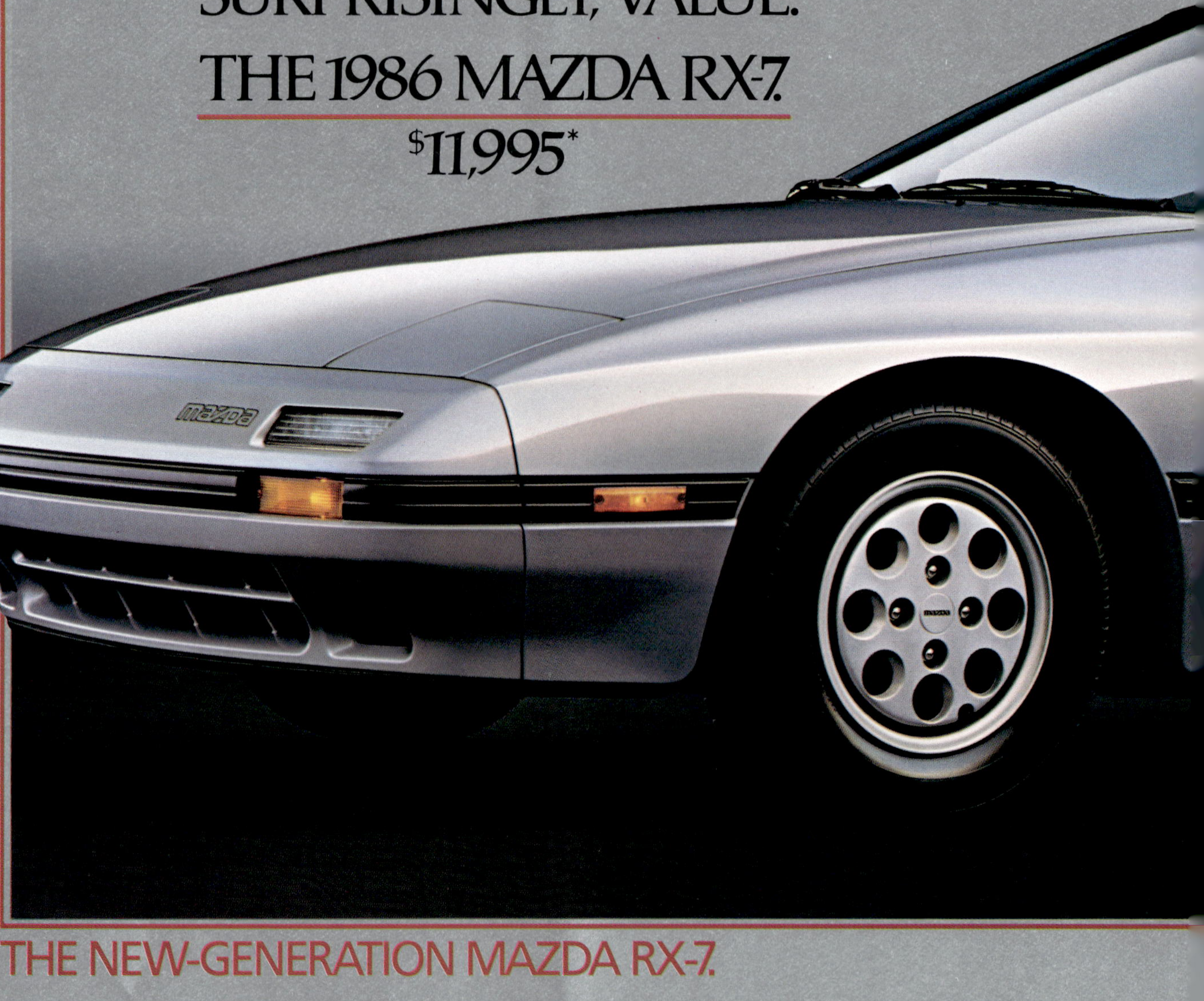

THE NEW-GENERATION MAZDA RX-7.

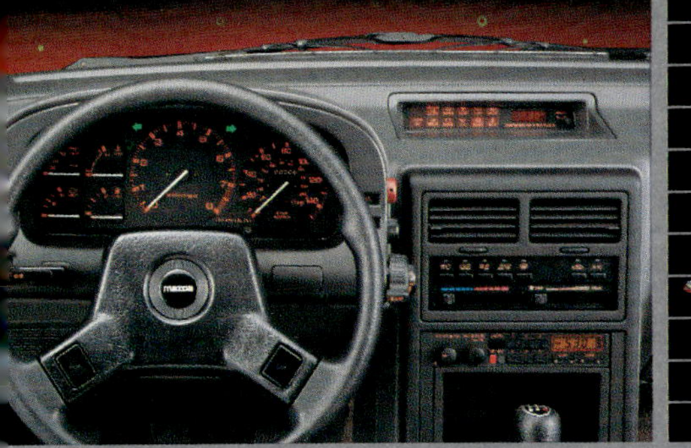

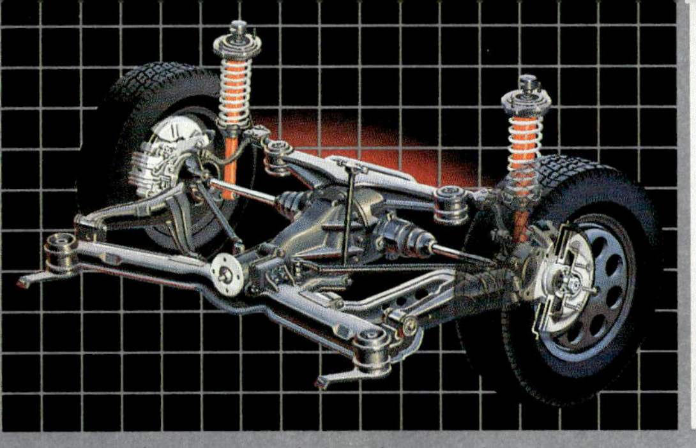

High-performance driving spoken here: Instrumentation is complete—yet completely legible. A special panel houses monitor lights and a digital quartz clock. The thickly-wrapped wheel has integral thumb rests. And a 40-watt AM/FM stereo radio and power antenna are standard.

No one has a more advanced suspension system than Mazda's Dynamic Tracking Suspension System. Under cornering loads, the rear wheels are utilized to actually help steer you through turns. The result is more agile, more precise handling.

Please send me a free, full-color Mazda RX-7 catalog.

NAME

ADDRESS APT. NO.

CITY STATE/ZIP

Return this coupon to: Mazda RX-7 Catalog Offer, Box 5960, MT-I, Orange, CA 92668.

For a free, 26-page Mazda RX-7 catalog, complete the coupon above or call this toll-free number: 800-521-1055.

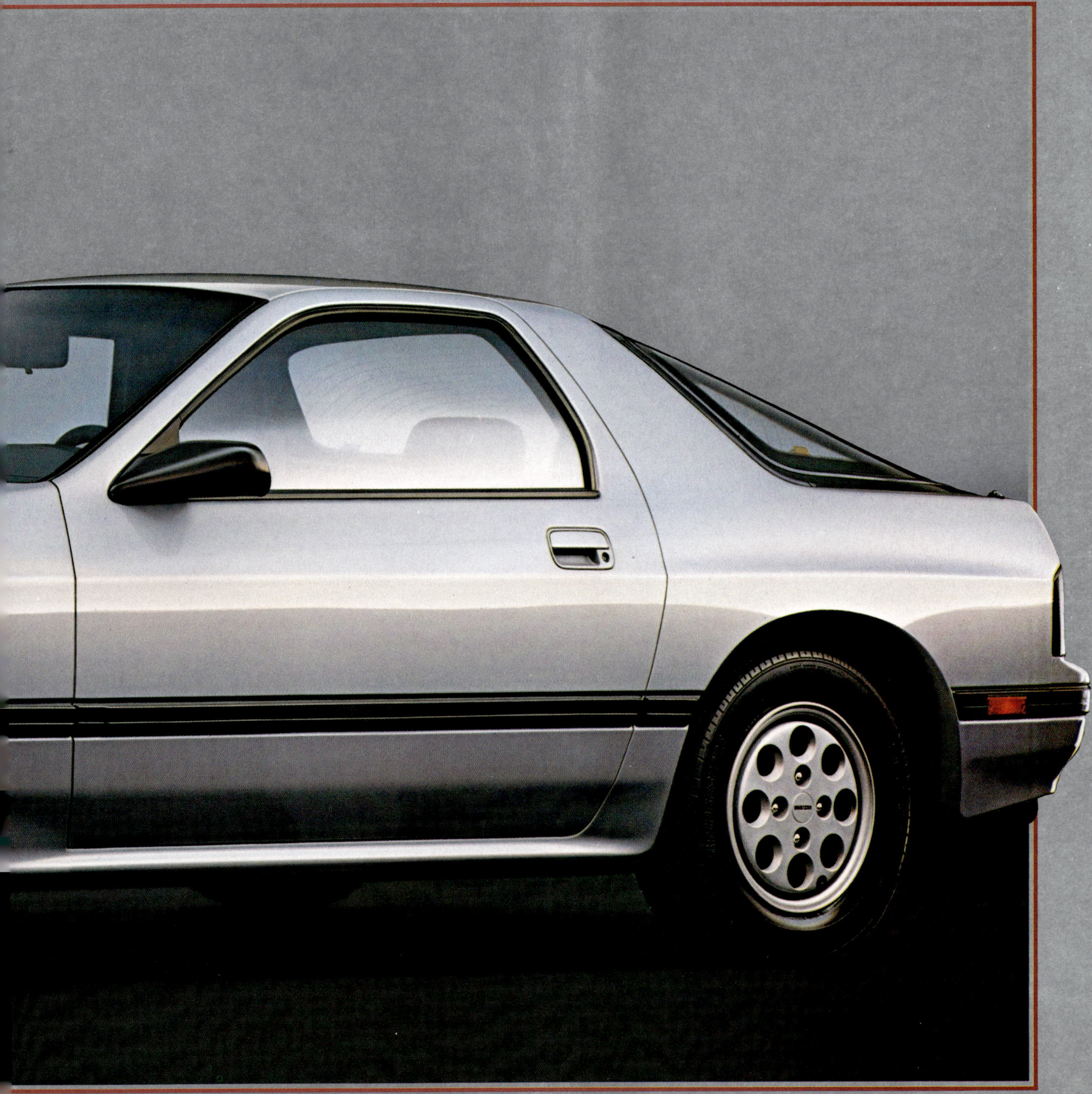

*Manufacturer's suggested retail price. Actual price set by dealer. Taxes, license, freight, options (Alloy wheels on standard RX-7. Automatic transmission on GXL.) and other dealer charges extra. Price may change without notice. Availability of vehicles with specific features may vary. Mazda's rotary engine licensed by NSU-WANKEL. Comparisons with other makes based upon consumer evaluations and/or available competitive data.

Standard features include: Factory-installed aerodynamic body parts. Sport-tuned suspension. 15" alloy wheels. 205/60VR15 radials. Plus 4-wheel ventilated disc brakes.

RX-7 Luxury Package $12,795* (not shown). Standard features include: 14" alloy wheels. Special sunshield. Power door mirrors. 100-watt ETR AM/FM stereo cassette deck with 4 speakers.

The GXL treats you to all of the following: Air conditioning. Electric sunroof. 100-watt ETR AM/FM stereo cassette deck with equalizer and 4 speakers. A 6-way adjustable driver's seat with lumbar support. Tilt wheel. Cruise control. Power steering. Power windows. Power door mirrors.

Tinted glass. Full console with built-in armrest/storage bin. Twin lighted and lockable stowaway lockers. Special insulation package. Plus Auto Adjusting Suspension. 15" alloy wheels. 205/60VR15 radials. 4-wheel ventilated disc brakes. Limited-slip differential. And a rear hatch wiper/washer.

A FAST
INTRODUCTION
TO THE
NEW
MAZDA 626.

A FASTER
INTRODUCTION
TO THE
NEW
MAZDA 626.

626 DELUXE
SPORT COUPE.

626 GT TURBO
SPORT COUPE.

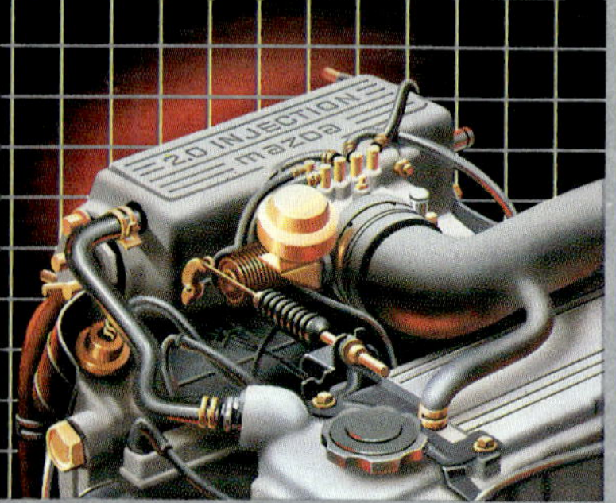

This year, the front-wheel drive 626 benefits from a more responsive 2.0-litre OHC engine equipped with multi-point fuel-injection. The turbo-equipped 626 GT offers a big 43% boost in horsepower.

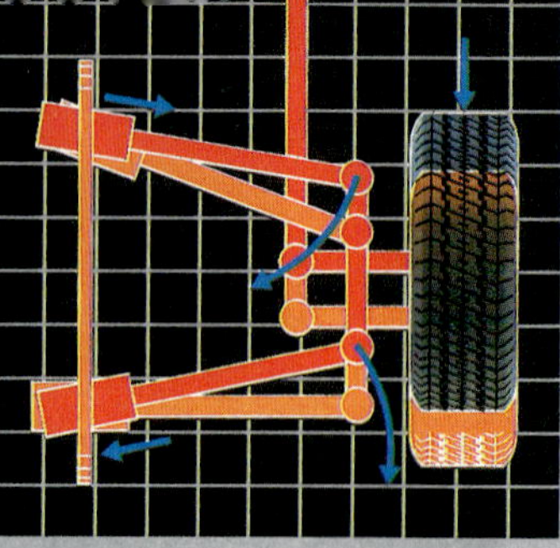

The independent rear suspension uses Mazda's patented Twin Trapezoidal Linkage to neutralize toe-out forces, promote flat tracking and enhance directional stability.

True to its world-class road car heritage, the new 626 is equipped with Euro-style, flush-lens halogen headlamps.

Few cars support a driver in the exemplary style of a 626. Deluxe models feature a 6-way adjustable seat with controls for both lumbar support and

626 Deluxe
Sport Coupe.
$8895*

THE NEW FUEL-INJECTED 626: A WORLD-CLASS ROAD CAR WITHOUT THE WORLD-CLASS PRICE.

This year, the big news is the 626's new multi-point fuel-injection system. And its effects are unmistakable. With a 0 to 60 time of just 10.3 seconds, the new 626 puts you in some pretty fast company. But the new 626 isn't merely faster. It's also substantially more refined. With a new front-end treatment and grille. Euro-style halogen headlamps. A beautifully redesigned interior. And a myriad of other upgrades.

THE 1986 MAZDA 626.

Please send me a free, full-color Mazda 626 catalog.

NAME

ADDRESS APT. NO.

CITY STATE/ZIP

Return this coupon to: Mazda 626 Catalog Offer, Box 5960, MT-I, Orange, CA 92668.

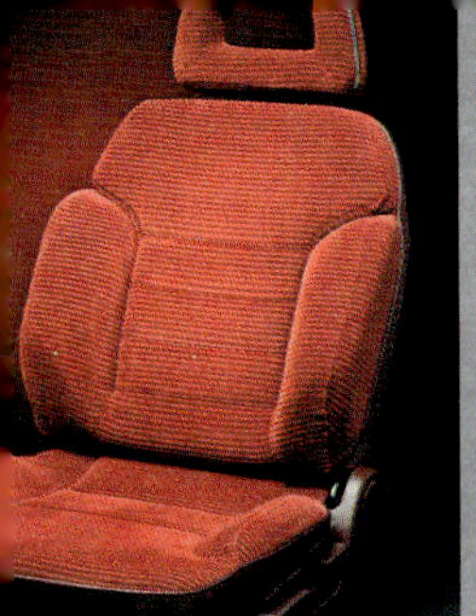

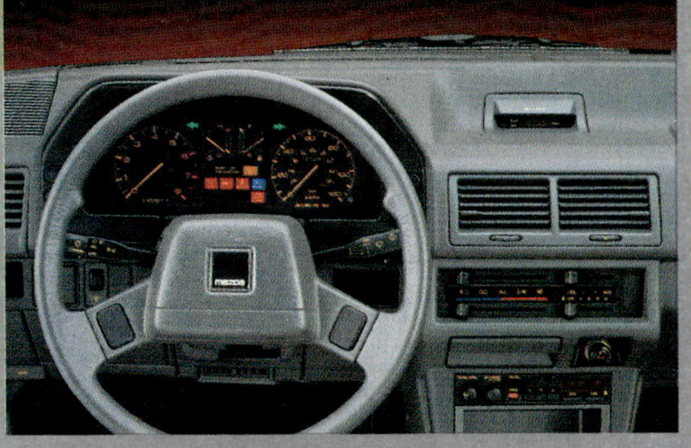

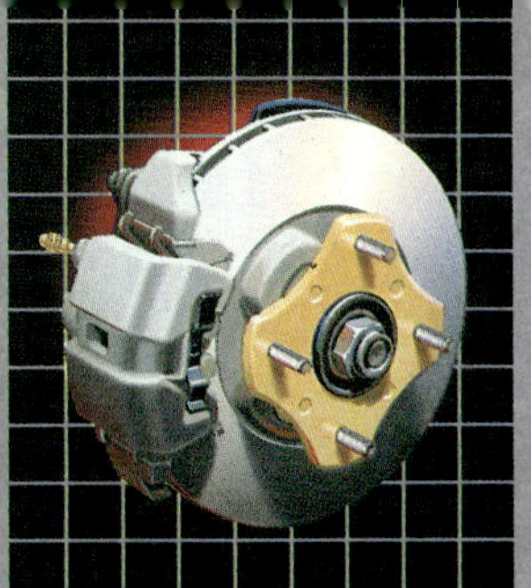

t cushion angle. LX
GT Series cars share
orthopedically con-
red, 9-way adjustable
t with wraparound
er bolsters.

Presenting the ideal environment for man to meet machine: The 626 command center. There's a soft-grip wheel with a built-in tilt feature. Clustered controls for easy access. Tachometer. Temperature gauge. Trip odometer. Tinted glass. Even intermittent-action wipers. All standard.

Ventilated front disc brakes are aboard all 626 models. GT Series cars, in addition, have rear disc brakes.

For a free, 26-page Mazda 626 catalog, complete the coupon above or call this toll-free number: 800-521-1055.

THE NEW 626 GT TURBO: A PHENOMENAL 43% BOOST IN HORSEPOWER IS JUST FOR STARTERS.

Just imagine . . . A car endowed with both the impeccable road manners of a 626 and an ingeniously engineered, water-cooled turbocharger that virtually eliminates "turbo-lag." Imagine, too, being launched from 0 to 60 in a scant 8.1 seconds. With 15" alloy wheels. P195/60R15 radials. 4-wheel disc brakes. Auto Adjusting Suspension system. And more. The Mazda 626 GT is everything you want in a turbo. Plus everything you need.

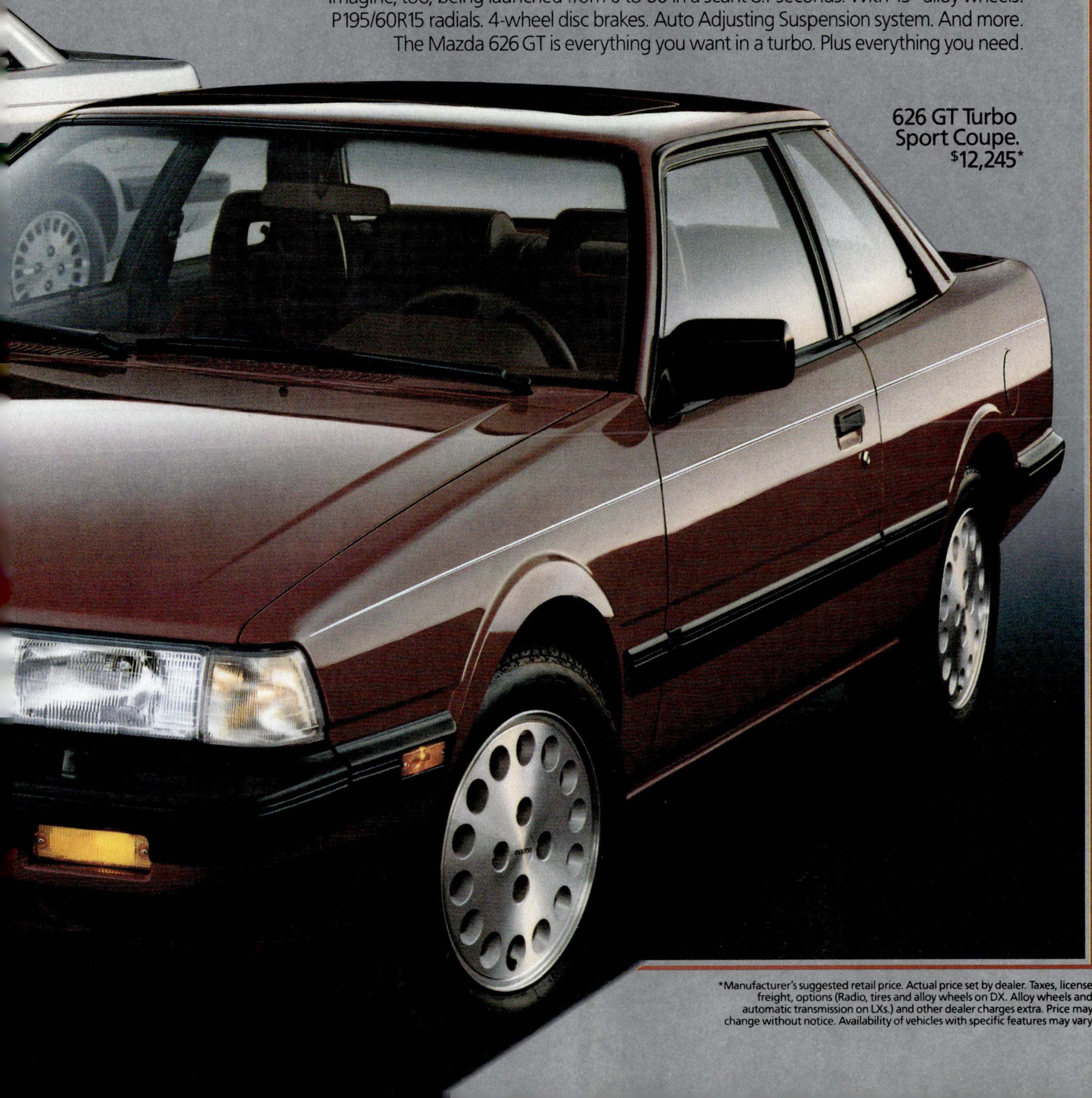

626 GT Turbo Sport Coupe. $12,245*

*Manufacturer's suggested retail price. Actual price set by dealer. Taxes, license, freight, options (Radio, tires and alloy wheels on DX. Alloy wheels and automatic transmission on LXs.) and other dealer charges extra. Price may change without notice. Availability of vehicles with specific features may vary.

Standard features include: 185/70SR14 steel-belted radials. Front window sunshield. Rear window wiper/washer. Dual electric door mirrors. 100-watt ETR AM/FM stereo cassette deck with 4 speakers. Power antenna. 50/50 split fold-down rear seatbacks. Cruise control. Power steering. Power windows and door locks. Dual map lights. And much more.

The LX treats you to all of the following: A 100-watt ETR AM/FM stereo cassette deck. Power antenna. 60/40 split fold-down rear seatbacks. Cruise control. Power steering. Power windows and door locks. 9-way adjustable driver's seat. Full console with built-in armrest/storage bin. Elegant striped velour upholstery. Full cut-pile carpeting. Oscillating center air vents. Door courtesy lights. Remote releases for trunk and fuel door. Plus 185/70SR14 steel-belted radials. Front window sunshield. And dual electric door mirrors. Not shown: The 626 Deluxe Sport Sedan. $8695.*

INTRODUCING
THE ROAD CAR OF
SMALL CARS.

A 1.6-litre fuel-injected overhead cam engine propels the 323 from 0 to 60 in just 10.8 seconds.

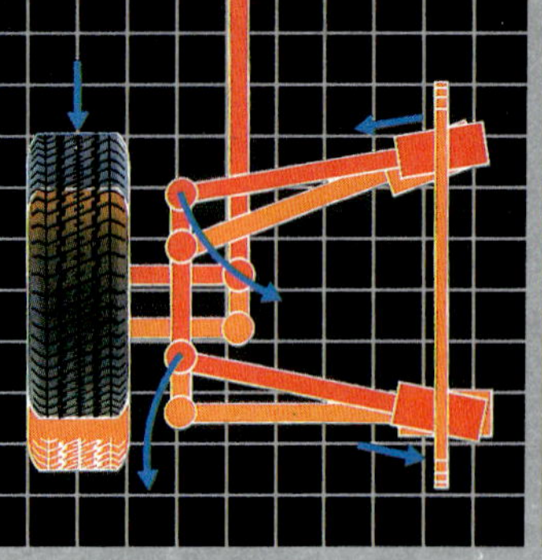

The 323's independent rear suspension uses Mazda's patented Twin Trapezoidal Linkage for enhanced directional stability and flat tracking in turns.

A 5-speed overdrive transaxle is standard on the front-wheel drive 323. A 3-speed automatic is optional.

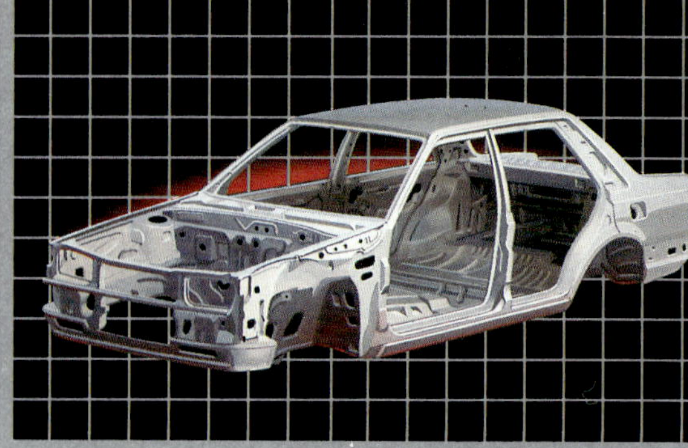

Here's where that solid, road car feeling begins: With the 323's unusually solid monocoque platform. Typically found on larger, more expensive cars, it's a major contributor to the 323's smooth, quiet ride and excellent handling.

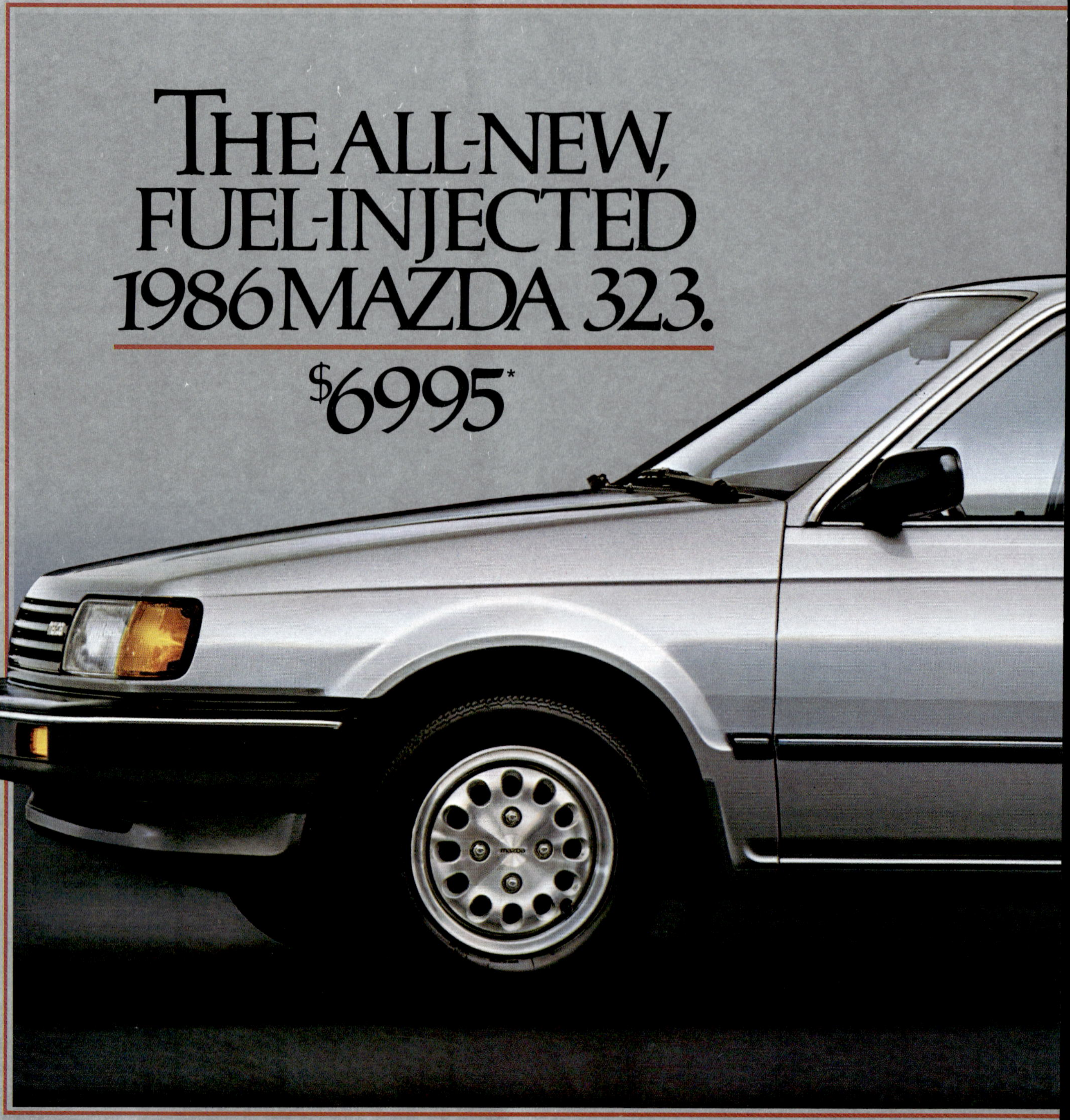

THE ALL-NEW, FUEL-INJECTED 1986 MAZDA 323.

$6995*

Please send me a free,
full-color Mazda 323 catalog.

NAME

ADDRESS APT. NO.

CITY STATE/ZIP

Return this coupon to: Mazda 323 Catalog Offer, Box 5960, MT-I, Orange, CA 92668.

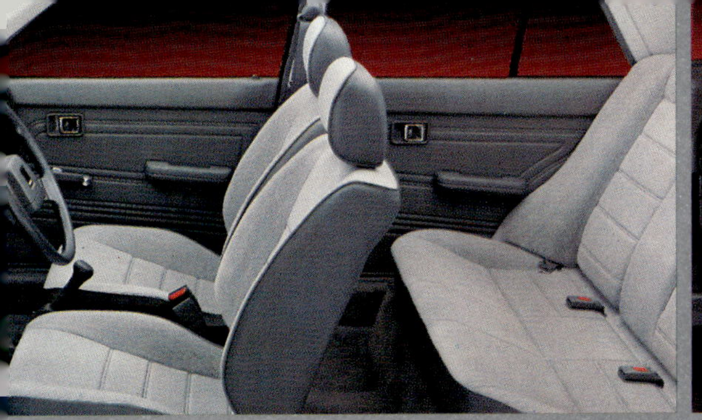

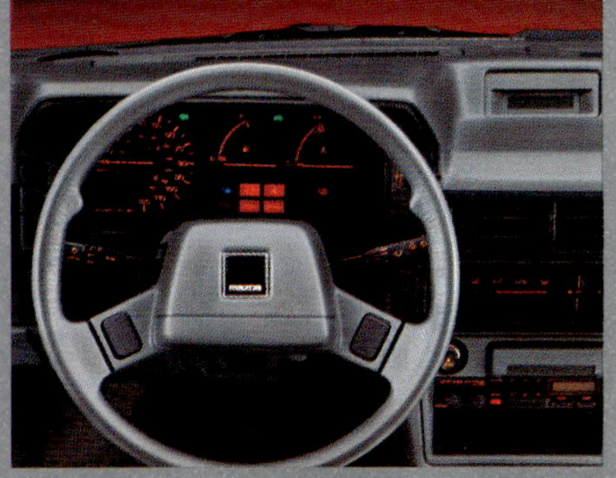

The 323's remarkable interior is actually roomier than a Mercedes-Benz 190E's or a BMW 535i's. With seating for four adults. Plush velour upholstery. Full cut-pile carpeting. 60/40 split fold-down rear seatbacks. Plus something not usually heard in a small car—quietness.

The command center features clustered controls for quick access. Easy-to-read instrumentation. Soft-grip wheel with integral thumb rests. And, of course, tinted glass.

For a free, 26-page Mazda 323 catalog, complete the coupon above or call this toll-free number: 800-521-1055.

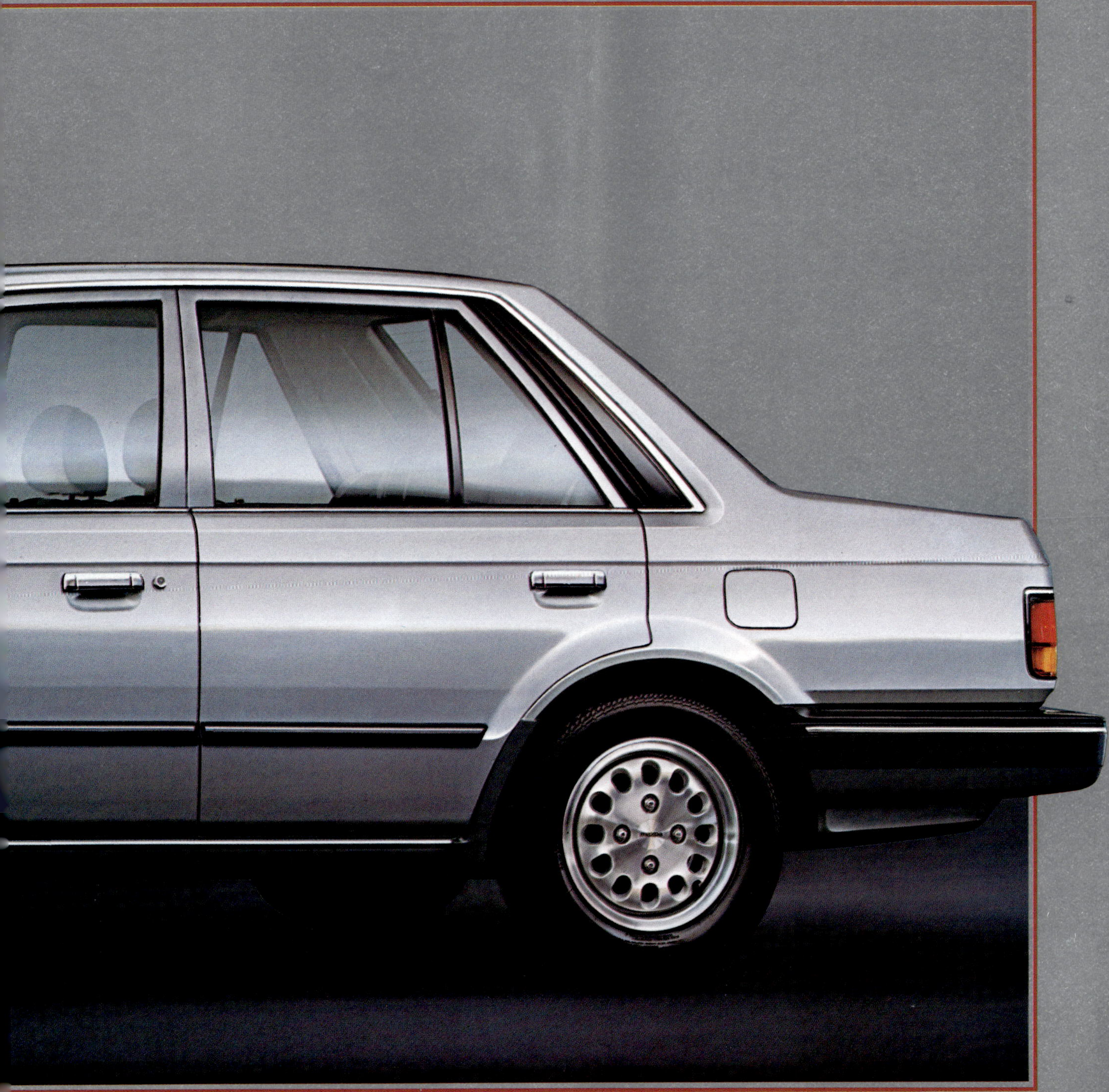

*Manufacturer's suggested retail price. Actual price set by dealer. Taxes, license, freight, options (radio, tires and/or alloy wheels shown) and other dealer charges extra. Price may change without notice. Availability of vehicles with special features may vary. Comparisons with other makes based upon consumer evaluations and/or available competitive data.

Standard features include: Steel-belted radials. Ventilated front disc brakes. Euro-style halogen headlamps. Front mud flaps. 50/50 split fold-down rear seatbacks. Cargo area cover. Rear window defroster. Tinted glass. Trip odometer. Lockable glove box. Remote releases for hatch and fuel door. Swing-out rear quarter windows. And much more.

The LX treats you to all of the following: A 5-way adjustable driver's seat with lumbar support. 60/40 split fold-down rear seatbacks. Fold-down rear armrest. Full center console. Tinted glass. Rear window defroster. Tilt wheel. Tachometer. Digital quartz clock. Trip odometer. Child-proof rear door locks. Front map pockets. Remote releases for trunk and fuel door. Plus 175/70SR13 steel-belted radials. Wheel trim rings. Dual electric door mirrors. Illuminated entry system. Wide body side mouldings. And special pinstriping.

MAZDA

Lord was very familiar with the car, and, recognizing a potential profit when he saw it, he provided the solution to Healey's delightful problem. The partnership lasted until the last Austin-Healey was built 15 years later.

There were two special versions of the A-H 100: the 100S in 1955 and 100M in 1956. Both were lightweight versions with engine modifications built for Sebring and Le Mans, respectively, and later sold as limited production models, very rare today. The six-cylinder 100-Six came in 1956. The elegant Austin-Healey 3000, introduced in 1959 and discontinued in 1976, is the Healey creation that represents the marque in most enthusiasts' eyes. In final form it pumped 148 horsepower out of a 2.9-liter in-line six. Factory specs say 0-60 in 9.8 seconds and a top speed of 122 mph.

In the last years of the production run, the 3000 was generally maligned by auto writers for its antiquated suspension—coil-spring front, semi-elliptic rear and lever shock absorbers—and engine, but never mind. A recent check of *Hemmings Motor News* shows good-condition 3000 MkIIIs with asking prices in the $10,000 range and completely restored examples going for 20 large. They were loved then, coveted now.

The popularity of the M.G. and Austin-Healey in the late fifties inevitably led to sibling spin-offs that were smaller, less powerful, and less expensive. In 1958 Austin-Healey introduced the Sprite which was based on the Austin A35 baby saloon. The unusual headlight treatment immediately earned it the sobriquet "Frogeye" in Britain which became "Bugeye" in the states. A kissing-guppie grille, funny headlights, no trunk and a 998-cubic-centimeter engine. Few automobiles of such limited esthetic and mechanical appeal have come even close to capturing the hearts and minds of so many enthusiasts. By 1961, Austin-Healey had become a part of then-giant BMC, so it came as no surprise, if something of a disappointment, when the old M.G. Midget name was revived that year not on an all-new front-wheel-drive sports car as rumored but on a thinly disguised Sprite. Over the next decade the two cars, known by the collective Spridget, put thousands of low-budget enthusiasts into their first sports car and hundreds of low-budget racers on the track.

The bigger, faster, more expensive TR-4 had replaced the TR-3B in 1962, so Triumph also needed an entry-level sports car, and that was the Spitfire, in 1963. With more size and power, the Spit fit in between the Spridget and TR/M.G.

As mentioned, the Austin-Healey marque disappeared completely in 1967—although the Healey name reappeared briefly on the Jensen-Healey in 1972—but Triumph and M.G. soldiered on for several more years.

Highlights on the Triumph side: TR-250—1968; TR-6—1969; TR-7—1975 (coupe), 1977 (convertible); TR-8—1980; last U.S. TR—1981.

On the M.G. side: MGB—1962; MGB GT—1965; MGB with the ugly front bumper—1974; last U.S. MG—1980.

A latter-day sport would begin with an M.G. or Triumph, step up to an Austin-Healey, and then hope for a Jaguar.

In 1927, the year before the M-Type Midget was introduced, William Lyons, a partner in the Swallow Sidecar Co., put a body of his own design on the little Austin Seven. He drove the car from his Blackpool shops to London in search of an outlet for his effort and soon found not only a willing dealer, the story goes, but a dealer so willing he ordered 500 units. Jaguar was born. Actually, the Swallow Side Car & Coach Building Co. was born. The Jaguar name didn't appear on one of Lyons' cars until the 1935 SS Jaguar 2.7 saloon. (The SS designation disappeared when production restarted after the war.)

Although there have been Jaguars of just about every size and description in the 50 years since, the American market had, until recently, little patience for Sir William's—he was knighted somewhere along the way—idea of a saloon, er, sedan. The XK series of sports cars were the Jags of choice among U.S. enthusiasts.

The XK120 was introduced at the 1948 London Motor Show and went into production as a '49. Six cylinders, 3.4-liter, double-overhead-cam, in-line six, 160 horsepower. For the next several years, only the power rating changed as the jewel of an engine appeared in the XK140 in 1955 and the XK150 in 1957. The very successful C- and D-type racing derivatives appeared in '51 and '55, respectively.

What's perfection? Unobtainable, of course, but in 1961 Sir William and the lads at Coventry came close with the E-

The outer limits. Lamborghini's Countach defines the extremes, both stylistic and financial, of the modern sports car.

type, a svelte beauty that redefined what a sports car should look like. In 1971 a 5.3-liter V-12 was wedged into the low nose, and although the car could reach escape velocity, the attendant sheetmetal changes lost the sleekness of the original.

In 1975, with the 2+2 XJ-S on the near horizon, Jaguar stopped E-type production. That ended a line of sports cars 48 years long if you go back to the Swallow-bodied Austin Seven. The E-type 2+2 had been outselling the coupe, and Sir William reckoned the E-type, which had been developed as far as possible, would require major re-engineering to keep it viable. And, there was some concern in those days about the future of a convertible in a government-regulated business. So the decision was made to scrap the E and go with the XJ-S. Bad move. The XJ-S took a dump in the market and is only now, ten years later, enjoying sales in any significant numbers.

Endings. That's what we're talking about here. Sad endings. For whatever reasons and they were many and varied, one by one the British sports cars went away: M.G., Austin-Healey, Triumph, Jaguar. By 1981, it was all over. R.I.P.

But while those British marques had come to be the definition of "sports car" for most Americans, and are responsible for the movement happening in this country, there were and still are others.

We've had our own home-grown sports

car since 1953, and what enthusiast isn't familiar with the many permutations, good and bad, of the Corvette in the past 32 years. It's gone from its beginnings as a U.S. definition of a British sports car— small, light, fast—to a grotesque, over-styled, over-horsepowered American street racer to today's example of handsome, hi-tech sophistication. Despite fitting the definition of a sports car, a Corvette is a Corvette, a genre of its own, a car that defies categorizing.

More in the traditional sports-car vein we had Fiat's 124 and X1/9, still alive here as the Pininfarina and Bertone. And a long line of spyders (roadsters) from Alfa Romeo continues. And since right after WWII, Porsche and Ferrari have been adding their own very special definitions of the sports car to the scene. Much more expensive than the British and by that virtue enjoyed by relatively few, Porsches and Ferraris have always played their own special role in this sports-car business.

Porsche: Product of no-nonsense Teutonic engineering and its passion for precision and efficiency. But, we'll allow ourselves a flicker of a smile. After all, there is a bit of mad-scientist whimsy about an air-cooled engine mounted out back. They put that bit of multi-cammed exotica out behind the rear wheels and still made the car handle like it was possessed. But only a flicker of a smile, please. Building automobiles is most serious, and the ownership of one must be approached with the same serious mind set.

Ferrari: Red. No other color will do. Red is the color of blood, of wine, of passion. Describe how a Ferrari looks, and try not to think of a woman, try to not use words such as rounded, flowing, lithe, sensual. Describe how a Ferrari performs, and try to not say screams, moans, sighs. Twelve cylinders, carburetors from here to

there, two distributors, enough valves for a half-dozen lesser machines. And soul enough for us all.

There simply can't be two more dissimilar means of moving toward a basically similar end than Porsche and Ferrari. And ain't it grand . . . ?

As the sports-car tradition as defined by M.G. and Triumph was sadly but perhaps inevitably coming to an end, a new era was beginning. We can pinpoint its genesis: the fall of 1969. That's when Datsun introduced the 240Z, and here's what that meant. Two-seats, lively performance, light and quick handling, great looks. All those good sports-car things, but more. An up-to-date mechanical package—engine, transmission, suspension—with all the creature comforts of a sedan and tons of luggage room under a convenient hatch. Big deal. Except for the rear hatch, Corvette did all that in 1963, and that bit of pioneering was so successful Chevrolet discontinued it when the redesigned '69 Corvette came out. Not exactly an era-starting experience.

But a Corvette wasn't for everybody with a desire for a sports car. Many drivers simply couldn't be comfortable with the

TOP:
The 1957 Ferrari Testarossa was one of the last of the racing sports cars which were distinctly similar to street-driven models.

ABOVE:
The Mazda RX-7 is the quintessential modern sports car: affordable, good looking, comfortable and quick.

'Vette's macho, slightly bad, slightly naughty, a touch uncouth image; women in particular were uneasy with the moral connotations attached to all that speed and power. The Z, on the other hand, arrived as virginal as a race queen, with no standard-equipment psychological baggage for a new owner. Nothing threatening, nothing presupposed. And, it cost only $3500. An era was born.

Suddenly, the definition had to be rewritten. A sports car had a roof, creature comforts and all the rest. Awkward side curtains and tops, Dzus fasteners and lift-the-dot snaps, anemic heaters and dreaded British and Italian electrics were part of

the prehistoric past. And good riddance.

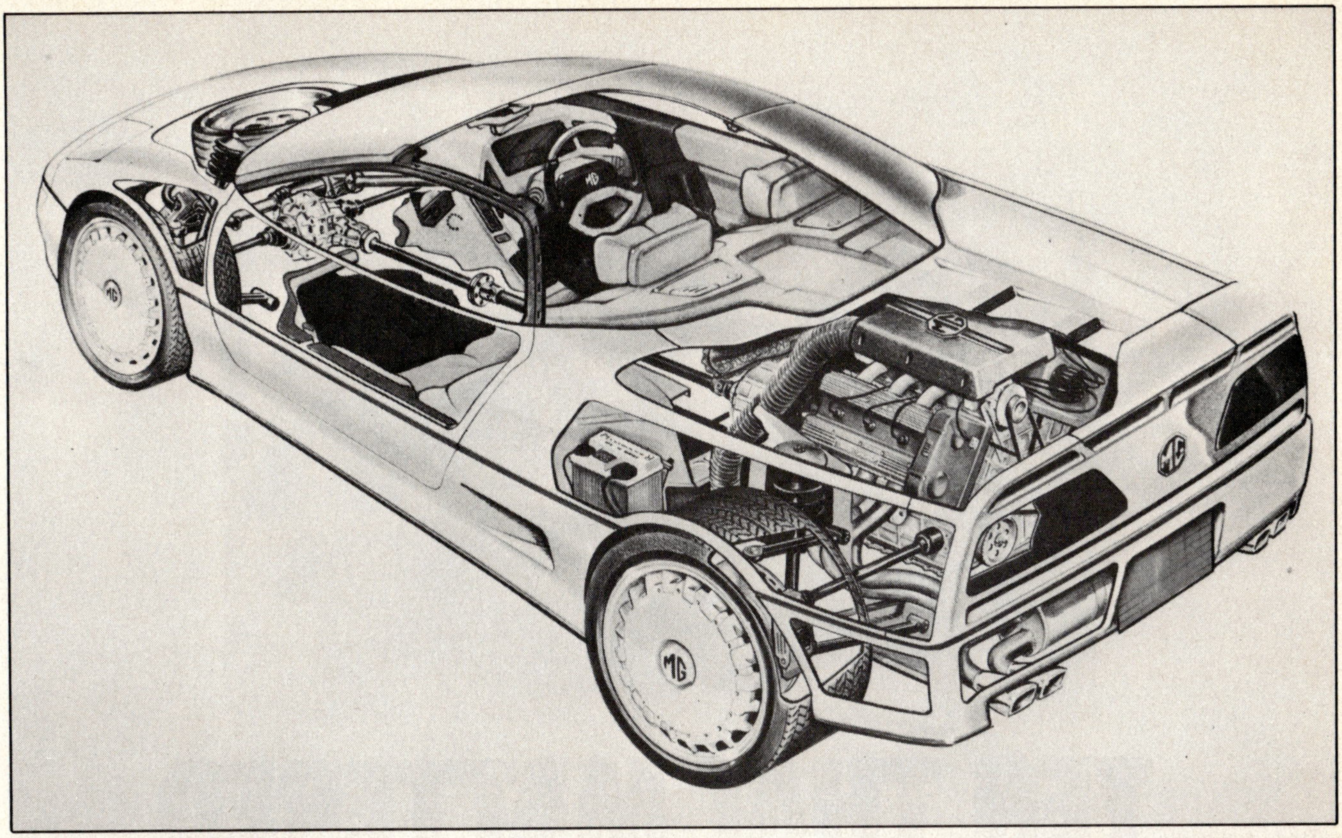

Or was it? It no longer took a certain crazy enthusiasm, a stoicism bordering on masochism to endure sports-car ownership. Those were the things that separated us from them. The lines had become blurred, and now were gone.

But that's okay. Eras are made to be fondly remembered, not go on forever. And what has followed the 240Z has been aces. We are now in the early years of the third sports-car era. It took Mazda almost ten years to follow Datsun's lead and come out with the RX-7, but worth the wait. Porsche started slowly, to be kind, with the 924, but the 944 is a wonder, and the 928 is All-Universe. Pontiac's Fiero and Toyota's MR2 may be pioneering yet another era, even as we watch. Stir in the Starion/Conquest, the Laser/Daytona, the Impulse, and even the Honda CRX and you've got a heady brew.

Obviously, a lot of names, some familiar, many not, have not been mentioned in this necessarily brief look at the history of the sports car. Maserati, Lamborghini, Aston-Martin, A.C., Cobra, Alpine, Osca, Turner, Courier, TVR, Lotus and on and on. They were there, they played a part, and any part is important if the whole is. But the idea here was to zero in on the cars and a few of the people who were key, and the key players just happen to be British.

What's coming? Predicting is always a chancy thing. An author writing a book on sports cars in the early seventies predicted that within a decade "all sports cars worthy of the name will probably be mid-engine coupes." But that's still the most obvious direction the lineage will go. Alfa and Bertone seem determined to keep the faith with traditional roadsters, and front en-

The MG EX-E, a "concept" car built by Austin Rover revives the Morris Garages hexagon and may be the first sign of life from Britain's comatose sports car industry. The EX-E uses a DOHC, 24-valve, mid-engine V-6, and four-wheel drive.

gine/rear drive is still a pretty good set-up for a performance car. But the Fiero and MR2 are on the point right now. Others are sure to follow.

High-tech projectiles with digital readouts, on-board computers, electronically adjustable suspension systems, power seats (with memory) that fit like a pair of Calvins, Dolby stereo, 0.90 g on the skidpad, 0-60 in seven, anti-lock braking. It'll be fun and you'll love it.

If it isn't, and you don't, it isn't really a sports car. **MT**

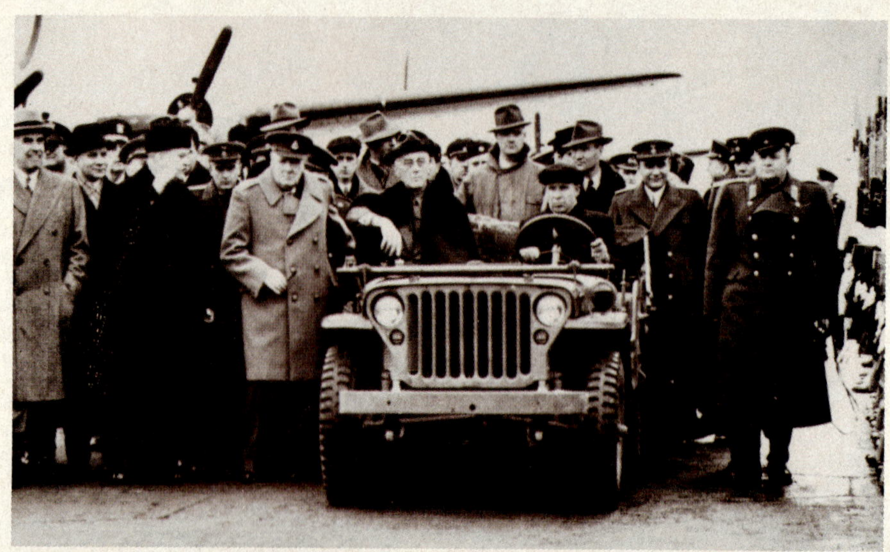

TEN THAT MATTERED

Of all the thousands of different cars the past century has seen, these ten changed the world.

By T.C. Browne

□ There was no beginning. No revolution. (That would come later; and it was social, not mechanical). Only evolution, and roots. But even they are concealed in the mists of time. Perhaps The True Beginning was the first time Man multiplied his own strength with aid from a non-animal partner. Could it have been the engine recalled in *Deus ex Machina*? Some say that ancient Athenians had harnessed steam to power the device that lowered actors playing gods onto the stage in classical plays.

Western man is impatient with such speculations. As the coming of the Industrial Revolution freed him from endless drudgery, it alienated him forever from the infinite. Dates, names, places, and things—particularly useful mechanical things—became his totems, and he seeks to credit those responsible for creating his favorite tools and toys with fame and glory proportional to the reward he enjoys in their use.

It is to this end, therefore, that we have gathered to honor the Founders and Followers of the Automobile on the Centenary of its genesis, and to pay tribute to ten examples of this most coveted of modern possessions which has so endeared itself to us as both tool and toy.

OPPOSITE PAGE:
Of all the car makers who have come and gone, these have left their mark permanently on automotive history. They were responsible for cars that set standards and established trends, and made history.
ILLUSTRATION: STEVE AMOS

pininfarina
HONDA
PEUGEOT
Cisitalia
Ford
CHRYSLER
WILLYS
STEVE AMOS

Benz 1886-1895

☐ California and assorted other jurisdictions insist that your three-wheeled motor vehicle be registered as a motorcycle, and the *Federation Internationale de l'Auto* declares an automobile to have a minimum of four wheels. In spite of the regulation of all two- and three-wheeled international motorsports events by the *Federation Internationale Motocycliste*, this rudimentary, tiller-steered, single-cylinder, water-cooled, spark-ignited, petrol-burner earns the title: "World's First Practical *Motorcar*." Compare this light and delicate trike with Daimler's graceless "motorcycle," built in the same year or with his first four-wheeler, converted from a horse-drawn carriage by grafting on an early engine. Beyond his dedication and perseverance, Carl Benz made a unique contribution to the creation of the motorcar. Unlike Daimler—whose gas-engine efforts ran from marine to aviation to automotive applications—Carl's driving ambition was to create an integrated motorcar. The neat result is this charming three-wheeled conveyance that wasn't adapted from anything.

The first Benz *Patent-Motorenwagen* owed nothing to the horse. It had one front wheel and steered with a tiller, simply because its creator felt too pressured to design some tidy dual-wheel steering geometry. He did get around to that refinement once his basic design had proved itself, but if you don't plan to go faster than a bicycle, one steered wheel would seem enough.

There is some dispute as to when this three-wheeler had its debut. But the patent was granted on January 16, 1886 and the readers of the *Neue Badische Landeszeitung* on July 3 of that year were informed that, "A velocipede driven by Ligroin gas, built by the Rheinische Gasmotorenfabrik of Benz & Cie., was tested this morning early on the Ringstrasse, during which it operated satisfactorily."

Historians also disagree on engine specs. Estimates run all the way from 0.8 to "about two or three" horsepower, and from 250 to 450 rpm. Some details they do agree on are the tubular chassis, single-speed belt drive, horizontal flywheel (Benz feared the gyroscopic effect of a vertical flywheel might upset the single-wheel steering), evaporative carburetor, battery-and-coil ignition, and a homemade spark plug of his own design.

After a lackluster introduction of the Benz Viktoria (so named to commemorate a victory over the problem of dual front-wheel steering geometry), Carl Benz brought to market the Velo model, for only 2000 Marks, a conspicuous success. It was, in fact, the only automotive success up to that time. In 1895, 135 cars were sold, the French market had begun to flourish.

Carl Benz' great rival, Gottlieb Daimler, died in 1900, while Carl got muscled outside by the Directors of his firm. He formed C. Benz, Söhne, with his two sons in 1906. In 1926, *Daimler Motoren-Gesellschaft* merged with *Benz & Cie., Rheinische Automobil und Motorenfabrik AG,* becoming Daimler Benz AG. Carl served on the board until he died in 1929.

We are told that the two automotive titans never met.

German Patent #37435, The World's First Practical Motorcar, may be seen today at the Deutsches Museum, in Munich.

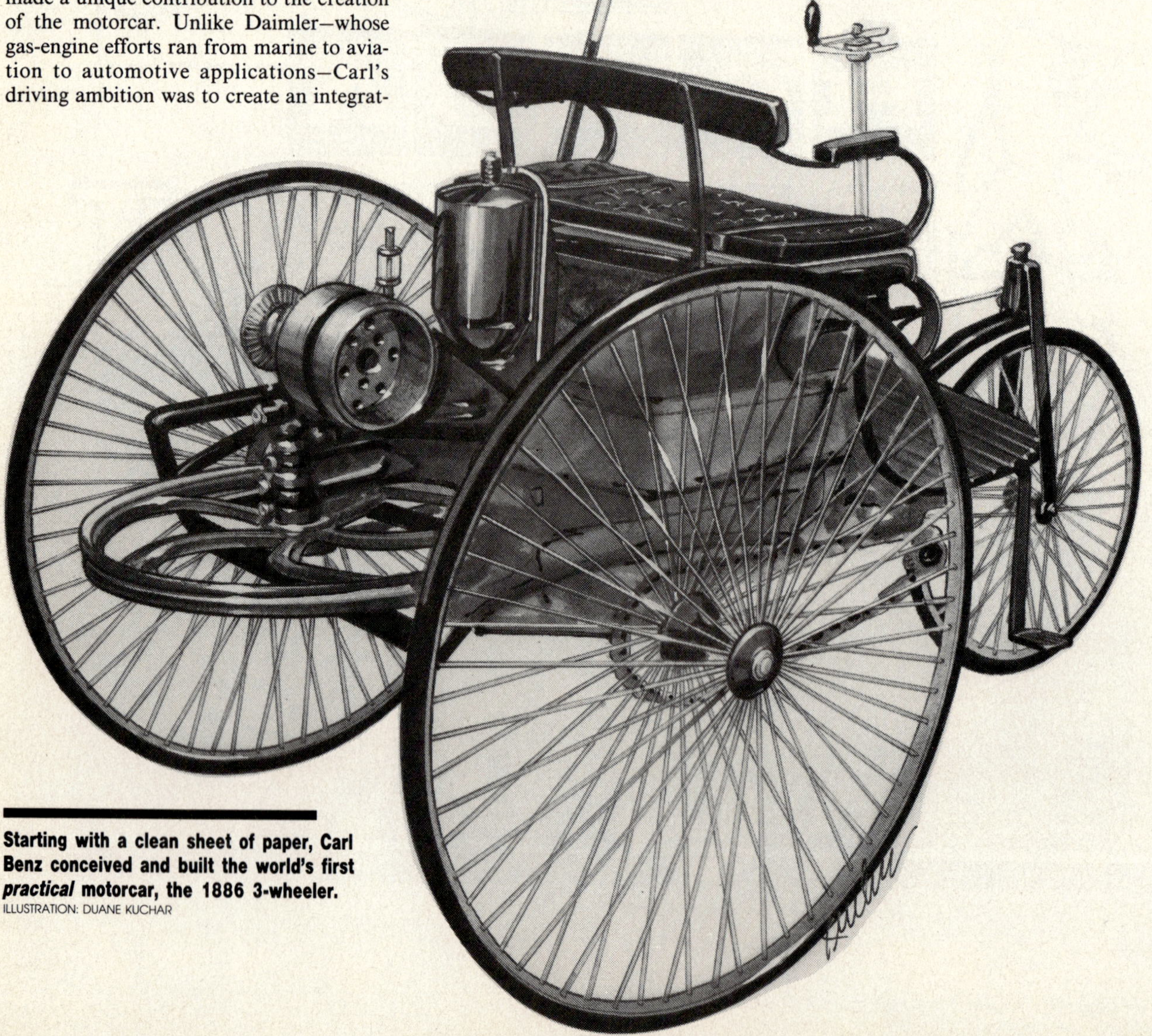

Starting with a clean sheet of paper, Carl Benz conceived and built the world's first *practical* motorcar, the 1886 3-wheeler.
ILLUSTRATION: DUANE KUCHAR

Delco Music Systems drive people to unusual lengths.

Once you start listening to a Delco Music System, you'll find you never want to stop.

For an extremely sound reason.

Delco is the music system specifically designed to match the acoustics of your very own GM car. While the car is still on the drawing board.

You can actually hear why other systems take a back seat to Delco. Stop by your GM dealer and listen for yourself.

But be forewarned. You might be wise to pack an overnight bag.

Delco Electronics
GENERAL MOTORS CORPORATION

You'll love it too much to leave it.

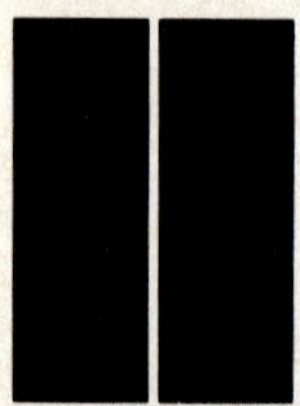

Cadillac 1896–1905

☐ The first Cadillac was an open two-seater. Introduced in 1903, it had a single-cylinder engine of 1610 cubic centimeters producing seven horsepower, and it was no great shakes alongside the leading European cars of the day except for one feature: its engine. It was designed and dominated by the personality and skill of Henry M. Leland.

Before the modern automobile could develop, an absolutely indispensable technical advance had to come into widespread use. While taken for granted today, parts interchangeability was more novelty than custom at the turn of the century. In America, it was in small-arms production that the precision machining essential to its employment first became popular.

Samuel Colt established a factory at Hartford, Connecticut, the most technically sophisticated in the world, capable of precision finishing previously only dreamed of. It was to this plant that Henry M. Leland came seeking work, and here it was that he refined his mechanic's skills and acquired his lifelong respect for precise machining. He soon moved to Providence, Rhode Island, and the shops of Brown & Sharpe, where the devotion to accuracy was at least as religious. It was as if Henry M. Leland was being trained for his coming role in automotive engineering, a discipline that did not yet exist.

In 1885, as Papa Benz was trying out his first velocipede, Henry M. Leland, age 42, was asked by B & S to become their sales agent. He accepted, and was soon known around Deroit, where, in 1890, he and two partners founded Leland, Faulconer & Norton. By 1896, the company was producing gasoline boat engines, when Ransom E. Olds delivered his first curved-dash marvel into this world.

Demonstrating the superiority of precision machining over traditional hand-lapping, Leland earned a contract for 2000 Olds engines, soon embarrassing the only other supplier—the Dodge Brothers—by producing more power from the same basic design.

OPPOSITE PAGE:
At Brooklands, three Cadillacs were taken apart, the parts mixed up in this room, and reassembled. The cars ran perfectly, proving the value of interchangeable parts.

BELOW:
Henry M. Leland's experience in precision machining and casting led to the manufacture of the 1908 Cadillac, the first car to successfully use standard components.

In 1902, William Murphy and Lemuel Bowen—after two years of failing to do it with the Detroit Automobile Company, after missing again when reorganized as the Henry Ford (their chief engineer) Company—were about to give up trying to make their fortunes in the car business. All they really wanted from Henry M. Leland was an appraisal of plant assets, but when he saw what they had, he made them an offer they couldn't refuse: "Here are your appraisals," he cried, "but don't liquidate the company." Then, pointing to what may have been the world's first hot-rod engine, he said, "This produces three times the power of the one now used in the Olds-mobile, the parts are interchangeable, and I can produce it for you at lower cost."

Work on the first Cadillac began in September and was completed on October 12. It weighed 1100 pounds, drove the rear wheels through a two-speed transmission, and cost $750.

In five years, 16,126 single-cylinder cars were sold, but it wasn't until March of 1908 that this landmark car entered the Pantheon of Mechanical Heroes by winning the Dewar trophy.

Observers from the Royal Automobile Club picked three cars right off the floor of the London showrooms, drove them to Brooklands racecourse, compared their performance on the circuit, and had them completely disassembled. The observers then mixed all the pieces, tossed in some bits from the London spares inventory, and everyone went off to the pub for a pint. That night, from a typical English downpour, the place where the stuff was stored got flooded. Next morning, the British mechanics not only had to assemble three cars from that mass of scattered pieces—which was the intended test—but they had to remove the fresh rust first. When the three cars were re-assembled, they lapped the course for 500 trouble-free miles each; and one went on to win its class in the 2000-mile Reliability Run of June 1908.

"Chrysler technology is making
Made in America
mean something again.

It figures. It was Chrysler
engineering that helped make
the American auto industry
the best in the world."

Lee A. Iacocca

60 years of Chrysler automotive leadership.

1924 • Advanced design, high compression engine with replaceable-element oil filter is introduced.

1928 • First full range crankshaft impulse neutralizer.

1929 • Downdraft carburetor.

1931 • Fully automatic spark control, centrifugal and vacuum.
- "Floating Power" engine mountings invented.

1932 • Tungsten alloy exhaust valve seat inserts first produced.

1933 • All-helical-geared transmission.

1934 • Scientific weight distribution and synchronized front and rear springs for anti-pitch ride.

1938 • Rubber insulated steering gear is developed.

1939 • Fluid Coupling is perfected.

1941 • Safety-Rim wheels and Rotor type oil pump are introduced.

1946 • Full flow oil filter.

1949 • Key-operated combination ignition and starter switch.
- "Cyclebond" bonded brake linings are patented.
- Safety cushion dash.

1950 • Chrysler introduces four-wheel, self-energizing hydraulic disc brakes.
- Roll down window in tailgate of station wagon.

1951 • Hemispherical combustion chamber V-8 engine.
- Oriflow shock absorber.
- Power steering.

1955 • Industry's first all-transistor car radio.

1956 • First automatic transmission with push-button control.

1958 • Automatic car speed warning and control.
- Electronic fuel injection introduced.

1959 • First automatic dimming electronic rear-view mirror.

1960 • First practical alternating current generator.

1963 • First 5-year/50,000-mile limited warranty on all engine and powertrain parts.

1966 • Chrysler Cleaner Air Package for exhaust emission control by engine modifications.
- Safety front shoulder harness.
- Separate, self-contained rear heater-defroster system.

1969 • Auxiliary driving light with quartz-halogen bulb.

1971 • Chrysler introduces its four-wheel Sure Brake System.
- Automatic tailgate-door locking system.

1973 • Electronic Ignition System (standard equipment).
- Electronic Digital Chronometer is patented.

1976 • Electronic spark advance control is introduced.

1978 • First American-built production car with front-wheel drive and transverse engine.
- Microprocessor controlled AM/FM Stereo search tune radio with direct frequency entry.

1979 • Radial tires standard on all cars.

1980 • First automatic speed control on FWD car with transverse engine and manual transmission.

1981 • First six-passenger front-wheel drive station wagon.
- First full line of six-passenger FWD cars.
- Continuous flow fully electronically-controlled fuel injection engine.
- First bumper system with ultra high-strength titanium steel alloy.
- First "Silent Shaft" engine in a domestic car.
- First instrument cluster with electronic transmission range display.

1982 • First domestic FWD transverse-engine convertible.

1983 • Industry's first FWD limousine.
- First 5-year/50,000-mile outer body rust-through protection and limited warranty on passenger cars.
- First copper-core spark plugs in domestic car production.

1984 • First domestic turbocharged FWD sports car.
- Widest range of turbo engine models in industry.
- T-115—first van/wagon with FWD.
- T-115—van/wagon, first vehicles to receive Zinc Institute Award of Excellence for corrosion protection.
- First 5-year/100,000-mile outer body rust-through protection and limited warranty on pickups.
- First American turbocharger with integral liquid cooling (has liquid cooled turbocharger bearing housing).

1985 • First computer controlled engine cooling fans on all domestic FWD engines (2.2L).
- First 5-year/50,000-mile powertrain limited warranty on trucks.

The Grand Prix Peugeot
1906-1915

☐ Now and then, a sudden flash of brilliance and wonder cascades across the firmament—an unexpected marvel that dazzles lay and expert witness alike. All too soon it fades and disappears, leaving magic in its wake. Soon, new wizards put the sorcery into play, and everyone forgets the real creators. The Grand Prix Peugeot, known as 76L (for 7.6 liters of swept volume) was such a flash, and the magicians responsible have been lost in the automobile's headlong metamorphosis from the rich man's butterfly it was, into the balance-sheet caterpillar it became.

Prior to 1912, the Peugeot works raced only in light-car events. Their *Voiturette Lion* dominated the class, in spite of an engine with but one enormous cylinder. At least it did until the 1910 GP of Voiturettes at Boulogne, the first such event won by a multi-cylinder car, a Hispano-Suiza 4, driven by Paul Zuccarelli. The two beaten Peugeot drivers, Georges Boillot and Jules Goux, persuaded him to join them in a mad scheme to design and build race cars and to establish their own racing team.

Jules Goux, the driver best situated with the Peugeot family, was selected to present their plan to Robert Peugeot. After protracted negotiation, he finally agreed, to the glee of the three partners and to the profound disgust of the factory professionals who soon dubbed the youthful upstarts *Les Charlatans.*

The final character in our little mystery is Ernest Henry, a Swiss national, about whom so little is known, but who may be the real hero of our tale. He joined the team as a draftsman after the deal had been struck with Peugeot.

French manufacturers had shunned GP competition from 1909 to 1911, but by 1912, all was forgiven, and Peugeot was ready.

The Charlatans—and to this date it is uncertain which one was most responsible—astonished the automotive world at the GP de l'ACF at Dieppe in 1912 with the first engine to combine dual overhead camshafts, hemispherical combustion chambers, and monobloc casting, achieving better breathing and more rapid rotation than anything which had preceded it. As if this weren't sufficiently startling, the valves (of which there were four per cylinder) were closed desmodromically by a stirrup tappet. All this radical change in the auto engine—and there is a body of opinion which insists that no further improvement in basic design has been made since—was brought into the world by four young men of no engineering background to speak of. Perhaps the fact that they were all born in 1885, that momentous year in which Daimler first got his lunger to run, may have had some mysterious influence on their remarkable success.

The race, an event of 956 miles, was won by Georges Boillot. That same year, the French GP, at LeMans was won by Zuccarelli. In 1913, Peugeot won the Indianapolis 500 and the French GP at Amiens. Peugeot took second at Indy in 1914. There were numerous victories in the United States from 1915 to 1919, including the Vanderbilt Cup at Santa Monica and Chicago, a second at the Indy 500 of 1915, a first at Indy (it ran 300 miles) in 1916, and the Indy 500 and Targa Florio of 1919.

This engine design eventually competed in various events on both sides of the Atlantic, with displacements of 7600, 7400, 5654, 4400, 2980, and 2400 cubic centimeters, always with four cylinders and 16 valves. In 1913, the L76, with a narrow, single-seat body, streamlining of obvious protrusions, driven by Goux averaged 109.987 miles per hour for the flying half-mile at Brooklands. At the time, the absolute one-hour speed record, for anything, was 104.270, held by an airplane. Goux also broke that record by a run of 150 miles at 106.003.

Zuccarelli died in practice for the 1913 French GP. Boillot entered the French air force and was shot down over No Man's Land by a German fighter. Ernest Henry tried to get along with the factory engineers at Peugeot long enough to get a V-8 aero engine into production, but it didn't work. After the war, he went to work for Ballot where he designed an inline eight with all his magical potions included that became another fantastic racing success. He died in 1950. Jules Goux soldiered on in GP racing, enjoying modest success, and lived until he was 80.

The old French saying, "The more things change, the more they stay the same," can apply to this car. Three-quarters of a century ago it had such "high tech" features as dual overhead cams, hemispherical combustion chambers, four valves per cylinder, monoblock casting, and even a desmodromic valve *closing* mechanism. Considering the progress in material and manufacturing, have today's engineers really created anything more advanced?

OPPOSITE PAGE:
Following his 1912 victory at the Grand Prix of Dieppe, French driver George Boillot (seen here brooding behind the wheel) won the 1913 French GP at Amiens in this car. His teammate, Jules Goux, won the Indianapolis 500 in a similar model, and versions of this GP Peugeot dominated racing on both sides of the Atlantic.

IV

Ford Model T 1916–1925

☐ The previous decade played host to a pair of major events involving the newly arrived motorcar: The assassination of Archduke Franz Ferdinand and his wife Sophie, at Sarajevo, in a 1910 Gräf & Stift, widely viewed as the spark that ignited The Great War and the rushing of French troops from *Les Invalides* to the front (then perilously close to Paris), in 600 Renault taxis, thus barring the *Boche* from the City of Light, at least until 1941. Meanwhile, the world was really being turned upside down across the Atlantic by a guy nobody ever heard of.

Henry Ford understood the motorcar and grasped its potential better than anyone alive. He said, just before launching the most commercially successful motorcar of all time: "The automobile of the past attained success in spite of its price because there were more than enough purchasers to take the limited output of the then-new industry. The automobile of the present is making good because the price has been reduced just enough to add sufficient new customers to take care of the increased output. The car of the future, the car for the people, the car any man can own, is coming sooner than most people expect. The market for a low-priced car is unlimited."

Henry Ford launched the $850 Model T in 1908. The English doubted anything so cheap could be worth owning. The Americans had no such reservations. By 1909, two thousand each month were flowing out of the Detroit plant, and it became necessary to commence shipping cars knocked-down, to be assembled eventually in plants at Kansas City, St. Louis, Long Island City, Los Angeles, San Francisco, Portland, and Seattle, as well as the first overseas factory at Manchester, England. By 1915, the millionth Model T had been built. By 1924, ten million had hit the road, and the all-time low price of $290 was posted that December. Before being replaced by the Model A in 1928, more than 15,000,000 would be produced.

The Model T wasn't just cheap, it was good. The buyer got what he paid for and no ugly surprises. The idea that, whenever it broke, anyone could fix it was very nearly the case.

To drive it is an experience. There is no shift lever or foot throttle to worry about; the brakes are on the rear wheels only. The right pedal works a transmission brake; the left selects low or high speed; the central

Henry Ford's manufacturing genius created a social revolution by providing reliable, low-cost transportation for the common man in the form of 15 million Model Ts.

pedal engages reverse, while the handbrake slows the rear wheels when pulled back, but acts as neutral selector, holding the left pedal between low and high, when positioned at half-cock.

Here we go: For cold starting, walk to the front of the car, yank the choke wire below the radiator, and prime the carburetor by swinging the starting handle. Return to the dashboard and turn on the trembler coils. Retard the ignition with the control lever on the left side of the steering column, go to the front one more time, give the crank a lusty swing, and when the 2.9-liter, four-cylinder flat-head lights up, run to the steering column, advance the ignition, and switch off the coils, placing responsibility for firing the plugs on the flywheel magneto. As the engine speeds up, push in the choke.

Now we are ready to move off. Release the handbrake. Depress the left pedal, pulling down on the throttle (right) lever. Any speed on level ground is adequate to release the left pedal, engaging high. Adjust your speed with the throttle lever, and don't expect more than 50 miles per hour.

ABOVE:
This 1909 Model T is among the first of Ford's Ts. Though they appeared in a number of different body styles, they stayed relatively unchanged for 19 years.
PHOTO: JOHN LAMM

LEFT:
The proliferation of Model Ts helped stimulate a national road network and all the services needed for a mobile public. Dirt roads like this one disappeared.

Chrysler Airflow 1926–1935

☐ It seemed like a good idea at the time. By 1934, all America was singing "Happy Days Are Here Again"; legal booze was back at last. Prosperity was "just around the corner," and the Depression seemed long ago and far away. The Chrysler Corporation was to celebrate its tenth anniversary by launching a car that would wallow in the trough and finally be recognized as

Walter P. Chrysler's First Big Mistake. Not until the Edsel would a new model enjoy so much careful planning before public exposure and receive such enthusiastic yawns following the introduction.

What went wrong? A lot of things. To begin, Walter P. Chrysler was a skilled engineer. In its first ten years, his company had earned a reputation for superior automobiles, superior because of the technical skill of the founder and the talented engineers he had attracted. So when the time came to do something spectacular for the birthday, an engineering *tour-de-force* leapt to mind. And the mind it leapt to was that of Carl Breer, member of the troika responsible for important engineering decisions, now that Walter was CEO.

Car of tomorrow? Not in sales for Chrysler, but certainly in the influence it exerted on the shape of future cars.

The Airflow's design was radical for a car, but in keeping with the day's design trends. The streamlined look was apparent in everything from trains to architecture.

One autumn day in 1927, enroute to Port Huron, Breer spotted a flock of Canadian geese flying south for the winter. As they neared, he also noticed that they were really a squadron of fighters from a nearby Army Air Corps base. You can guess the rest: "Why can't automobiles move through the air with equal harmony?" he asked himself. Why not indeed?

In Highland Park, he called in Owen Skelton and Fred Zeder and asked them the question. Then they all went to see the boss who approved a plan to create a new aerodynamic model, code-named Trifon Special, and it was off to the wind tunnel at Dayton.

Before the Airflow emerged, six years of research and at least one weird test vehicle would—to coin a phrase—come and go. The wind tunnel revealed that the cars then in production were aerodynamically more efficient backing up than going forward. These three grown-up engineers had a car built with the body reversed and drove it around Detroit as well as up Fifth. Avenue in New York. People did notice, but no one asked to buy.

As the testing progressed, the engine was moved forward over the axle, legroom increased, the rear seat moved ahead of the rear axle, weight distribution changed from classic 45/55 to 55/45, front springs were strengthened and their rate reduced. To no one's amazement, the ride improved. Unit-body construction was considered but rejected in favor of a new, cage-like chassis, with the occupants cradled inside. It was a good car, and while the experts liked it, the man in the street wasn't sure. After the round of auto shows, considerable paid promotion and lots of favorable comment from *Harper's Bazaar* as well as *Autocar* and *MoToR*, the public became convinced and began to order Airflows in record numbers. And the corporation kept up the pressure: one car was sent over a 110-foot cliff, tumbling end-over-end to certain doom, landing on its wheels, and driven off under its own power. Another went to Utah to do the flying mile at 95.7 miles per hour, a record for the class. All for naught. Production delays, caused by the substantial retooling required by the new car, undermined public confidence. Failure to make prompt delivery to those buyers who had ordered early generated rumors that Chrysler had finally made a lemon. The bottom fell out of the Airflow market. Finally, in 1937, production of the DeSoto and Chrysler Airflows ceased.

The Airflow really was the car of the future, as the success of the next attempt at aerodynamic styling—Lincoln Zephyr—helped demonstrate, but the familiar remark that it was "20 years ahead of its time" was of course refuted when no such car showed up in the line in 1957.

To demonstrate the safety and structural integrity of the Airflow, it was chucked off a cliff, preceding similar demonstrations by Volvo and others by 50 years.

VI

The Jeep 1936-1945

☐ It's not that the Jeep was such an engineering *tour de force*. Or that it went so fast, or handled so well, or carried so much. It wasn't particularly distinguished for any of these qualities. It's just that it's . . . you know . . . *sacred*. And for a person introduced to the Jeep 45 years ago in the line of duty to be writing about this *idol*, is something like a Muslim writing about Mohammed. It's actually sacrilegious. And to explode some of the popular myths about the vehicle that won the war single-handedly is risky. I hope the lightning doesn't come down while you are reading.

In the first place, the "Truck, quarter-ton, 4 X 4 Command Reconnaissance" wasn't even called "Jeep" in the beginning. Oh, all those pot-bellied Legionnaires in your neighborhood will affirm that "Jeep" was derived from G.P. (for General Purpose) and so on, *ad nauseam*. Nonsense! To begin with, American Bantam (not Willys-Overland) was the first to offer a vehicle to meet War Department requirements for a truck, quarter-ton, 4 X 4 Command Reconnaissance, a device for which the search had been on since just after the Kaiser War. The Army had been fooling around with various adaptations of production cars and trucks (mostly Model T Fords) for 20 years when a specification was finally written, and 135 manufacturers were invited to bid. Only American Bantam met the deadline, and they missed the absurd 1300-pound weight limit by a wide margin. When the time restraint was lifted to allow Willys-Overland into the competition, Ford was talked into entering. All three submitted prototypes in the same order and an odd cooperation ensued: First, Willys and Ford cooperated to muscle American Bantam away from the trough. Then, moved either by patriotism or profits, Ford used its vast R&D facilities to improve the basically superior Willys version in exchange for a piece of the action. The result was the first occasion of one car company manufacturing another company's car. Willys' edge was a more powerful engine and the low bid. After the shouting died down and the boys were back home, the final tally revealed that Bantam had produced 2576 of the quarter-ton, 4 X 4 Model 40 BRC (1940 Bantam Reconnaissance Car), the first to be shot at by Erwin Rommel's Afrika Korps. Ford had earned cost plus six percent on 277,896, while Willys had collected on 357,114.

Could we have won the war without it? It wasn't as decisive as the A-Bomb, but the Jeep played a major role in World War II.

American Motors is in dire straits today. But without a Jeep, there wouldn't even be an American Motors. And for lack of one, American Bantam is no more. Here's what happened: "Jeep," a character from E.C. Segar's comic strip, "Popeye," knew everything and could do anything. In 1940-'41, the Dodge-built half-ton Command Reconnaissance was known as the "Jeep." When the smaller ¼-ton CR came along, it was dubbed "Peep." If, as the legend goes, the name resulted from the Ford Designation GP (for General Purpose), it would have been spelled "Geep," right? And nobody would have called the American Bantam or Willys-Overland versions by that name since they were the Quad and the MA (later MB). As is often the case, some eager correspondent got confused and misapplied the name of the ½-ton to the ¼-ton, and the rest—as they say—is history. Except for this sordid footnote: As the Jeep's wartime fame began to spread, Willys-Overland registered the name as a trademark, and began to run advertisements to the effect that their guys and the U.S. Army had " . . . created and perfected the jubilant Jeep." American Bantam cried foul, and in 1943, the FTC lodged a complaint against Willys, resulting in a cease-and-desist order five years later. Unfortunately a tad tardy to revive American Bantam. Whom should we credit for this wonder wagon? The Army got the idea; American Bantam hired automotive consultant Karl K. Probst (who took five days to block out the basics in July, 1940 and then built the prototype in the 49 days allowed). A contract for 70 pre-production cars came next; these cars entered service in the winter of 1940/41, with field testing in muddy Louisiana under command of Col. Dwight D. Eisenhower. Production Jeeps got Ford's front end and Willys' engine.

Willys Motors, as it became, built the civilian Jeep—licensing Hotchkiss in France and Mitsubishi in Japan to do the same—until bought up by Henry J. Kaiser, in 1953, with a 1963 name change to Kaiser-Jeep Corporation. This amalgam was subsequently swallowed by American Motors, a firm created by wedding Nash to Hudson, the issue of which is a course of *Ancien Cuisine,* even now being found a little hard to digest by Régie Renault.

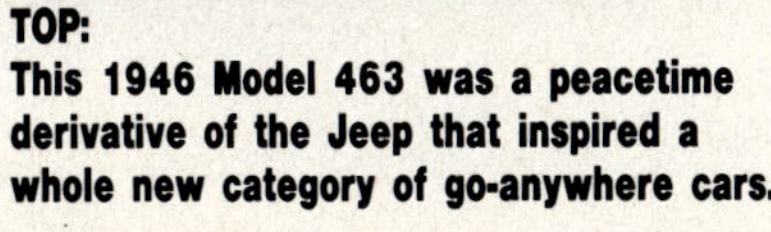

TOP:
This 1946 Model 463 was a peacetime derivative of the Jeep that inspired a whole new category of go-anywhere cars.

ABOVE:
The basic principles of the Jeep haven't changed in 40 years. This 1961 version doesn't look much different from today's.

Rugged and dependable, the Jeep helped mobile commanders like George Patton to move quickly and decisively into battle.

VII

Cisitalia 202   1946–1955

☐ If cars are indeed rolling sculptures, this 1947 Cisitalia 202 Coupe must be the automotive Venus de Milo on roller skates.

While there is a moving tale of Piero Dusio (founder of Cisitalia SpA) and his violent excursions into the world of sports, racing, and Grand Prix cars, with Tazio Nuvolari, Dr. F. Porsche, and others of lesser fame, it will have to be sought elsewhere. We must focus our attention on this one example of artistic brilliance that re-arranged the traditions of automobile design much the way Vesuvius rearranged Pompeii. While there are those who claim Giovanbattista "Pinin" Farina copied the work of others in creating this beguiling monument to his virtuosity, Nino Balestra and Cesare de Agostini, on page 57 of *Cisitalia,* explain the unique talent of Pinin Farina in a novel way. "He had thus transformed himself into a slow but relentless bulldozer: the hills of tradition were flattened, the halls of fossilized tastes caved in gratifyingly. In the end, his horizon was clear. He began with the first elements which had been in his mind for years: he began with a sloping windscreen. It seemed a contradiction because—they said—all window panes have always been straight. He carried on by progressively eliminating the woodwork. He persisted in removing edges and projecting parts which in a collision could become extremely dangerous. All this went on while the idea of placing the radiator horizontally and no longer vertically began to creep into his mind."

After war damage to his own house in 1944, Dante Giacosa—the great Fiat designer—moved into the Dusio home. There he drew up plans for an open-wheel racecar, using tiny Topolino chassis bits, but adapting an 1100-cubic-centimeter Fiat engine. He tied it all together with the first automotive tubular space-frame chassis, welded up from a supply of chrome-moly tubes left over from his host's prewar bicycle manufacturing enterprise.

Giacosa showed the work to Dusio. The man nearly wept with desire. As the war wound down, he got his workers cracking on a prototype of what would one day become the car you see here.

We will now, however reluctantly, abandon the racing and move on to the touring cars. In 1931, after leaving big brother's firm—Stabilimente Farina—Pinin Farina opened his own shop, enjoying an immediate success. After expanding his premises before and during the war, he had the misfortune to lose it all to fire in 1946. By the time the new Cisitalia car was ready to don its street apparel, he was operating out of a wooden shed. It was this humble shack at which a rolling chassis eventually appeared, and from it that this tiny GT coupe was finally delivered, to be greeted by astonished delight everywhere it went. And it went everywhere, winning trophies, medals, and best of all, orders.

Arthur Drexler, Curator of Design at the New York Museum of Modern Art, preparing a display of cars in 1951, wrote in the catalog, "The Cisitalia's body is slipped over its chassis like a dust jacket over a book. The back of the car, particularly the fender, is lifted at an angle rising

Whether as a roadster or coupe, the Cisitalia created a new aesthetic which has permanently influenced the design of sports cars and our perception of them.

'86 OLDS

No one can predict with absolute certainty where the creative engineering genius of man will take us. But one thing we know for certain is that Oldsmobile will always be in the forefront of the "new technology." Just as we were from our start in 1896. Like we were with the first Toronado in 1966. And like we are today with our new 1986 Toronado.

Oldsmobile products will speak directly to the needs of today and tomorrow with style, quality, comfort and value. You see, with Oldsmobile, if you wish to get an inkling of the future…just take a long, hard look at our present new Toronado…again, a category of one.

TORO

The category of personal luxury cars is again a category of one. The car that has defined personal luxury for a generation now redefines the category.

The Toronado offers an outstanding ride, with a choice of three suspensions. A revolutionary "body" computer regulates 88 vital functions, from digital instruments to diagnostic checks.

Toronado has been riding the leading edge of automotive technology for 20 years. Inspired aesthetics and engineering is what you have come to expect. This car obeys but one basic rule: never, never be conventional.

NADO

The luxury of a complete electronic car.

Under Toronado's surface courses bloodlines of engineering excellence spanning more than eight decades. Now, chassis, suspension, drivetrain and control systems which have evolved to advanced levels of excellence are yours to command. And to assist you in your command, Oldsmobile has invested Toronado with an amazing new aspect to technology.

The first body computer on an Oldsmobile. It is "The Brains" of the electronics system. Sensors located throughout the car provide complete control for the heating, ventilation and air conditioning system; the instrument cluster; the gages; the message center; and the ECM (Electronic Control Module), which monitors, controls and virtually fine tunes the engine, even as you drive. The body computer also controls a driver warning system to inform of conditions requiring attention. A "Lamp/Out" and voice warning system are also available.

Smart? You bet! But that's only a glimpse at the world of the new Toronado. The true test of Toronado is to test-drive one yourself. Do it soon at your Oldsmobile dealer.

There is a special feel in an *Oldsmobile*

from the strict horizontal base line which gives stability to the design. Thus both ends of the car gain an extraordinary tension, as though its metal skin did not quite fit over the framework and had to be stretched into place. This accounts, in part, for that quality of animation which makes the Cisitalia seem larger than it is." It may also explain the absence of any other cars on display at MOMA.

The mechanical details of this 40-year-old are ordinary and could stand a lot of modernizing. But, if you asked your favorite designer to improve its shape, what do you suppose he'd change?

The proportion and balance of the Cisitalia were achieved with an economy and grace that's seldom been equaled in automotive design.

VIII

Der KdF-Wagen 1956–1965

☐ What remains to be said about the Volkswagen Beetle? Nothing really. But there are a handful of facts that have received less emphasis than others. While it is tempting to complain that the idea originated with Hans Ledwinka, why would we want to blame such a nice man for such a terrible car? Should we ruminate about whether Adolf Hitler was really serious? Of course he was. But about something quite different from what Dr. Porsche was after. And can you really fool all of the people, all of the time? Sure you can. Witness the world's most popular automobiles: The Model T was perfectly awful. It would run you over, given half a chance. And break your arm at lesser odds. But it had an excuse: being early and primitive. Those other two favorites *Kraft durch Freude*, or People's Car, as we have come to know and love it, and the Citroën Deux Chevaux, which we never learned to call "Two Horses," are sobering reminders that bad taste *is* timeless and that 50 million Frenchmen *can* be wrong. But it is the most popular car of all time with which we are concerned. What of flattery by imitation? If the VW was all that marvelous, why not more copies? A decent question that deserves a serious answer. There are two reasons. Here is the obvious one: It *was* widely imitated, in a sort of self-mimicry. All those Beetles made in Mexico and South America are clones, sponsored by parents back in the Fatherland. You know—the Boys from Brazil. Put otherwise (Henry's Scheme), there is no way your simple, basic design is going to be cribbed with any commercial success if you flood

A triumph of packaging, the Beetle's versatility, capacity, economy, and utility assured its worldwide success.

By 1976, the Beetle could boast fuel injection, metallic paint, and "sports-style" wheels—some even considered it sexy.

the market with the real thing. Rolex Oyster and Cartier Tank watches have been copied for decades, but who ever heard of Timex being ripped off?

The other protection against counterfeiting is to make your design so clumsy no one will take it seriously. While Hitler may have been shucking and jiving when he sold savings stamps to his Pure Aryans so they could save up the $256 for a VW to be delivered after the Twilight of the Gods, Henry Ford II was quite sincere when he went to Germany, just after the war, to receive the VW plant as a gift, if he would just get it producing. Unable to locate anything worth reviving, he gave it a pass. Lord Nuffield thought it might be droll to build Morris Minors in the Weissach Works, but got distracted by a dinner invitation or something. The distinguished management of Rootes Group (Humber, Hillman, Singer, Sunbeam . . . you remember) reported the VW wasn't suited to the modern world. So the occupation forces, in need of cheap and dirty transport, got the smokestack belching. When production at Wolfsburg ceased in 1978, 16.2 million—the all-time record—had been disgorged. And you can still buy a new one in Brazil.

All of which proves something most of us already know: Rich people don't think like poor people; dumb people don't act like smart people. The Germans collecting ruble in wicker baskets in 1948 were mighty poor and very dumb (witness their recent adventure with *Festung Europa*). But they were smart enough to grasp the notion that the worst ride is better than the best walk. And that's how the Volk for whom the wagen was originally intended, after a surfeit of Strength, finally got some of the Joy.

Inside, the Beetle was cramped, spartan, noisy and dull, but anybody could drive it and it got you where you wanted to go.

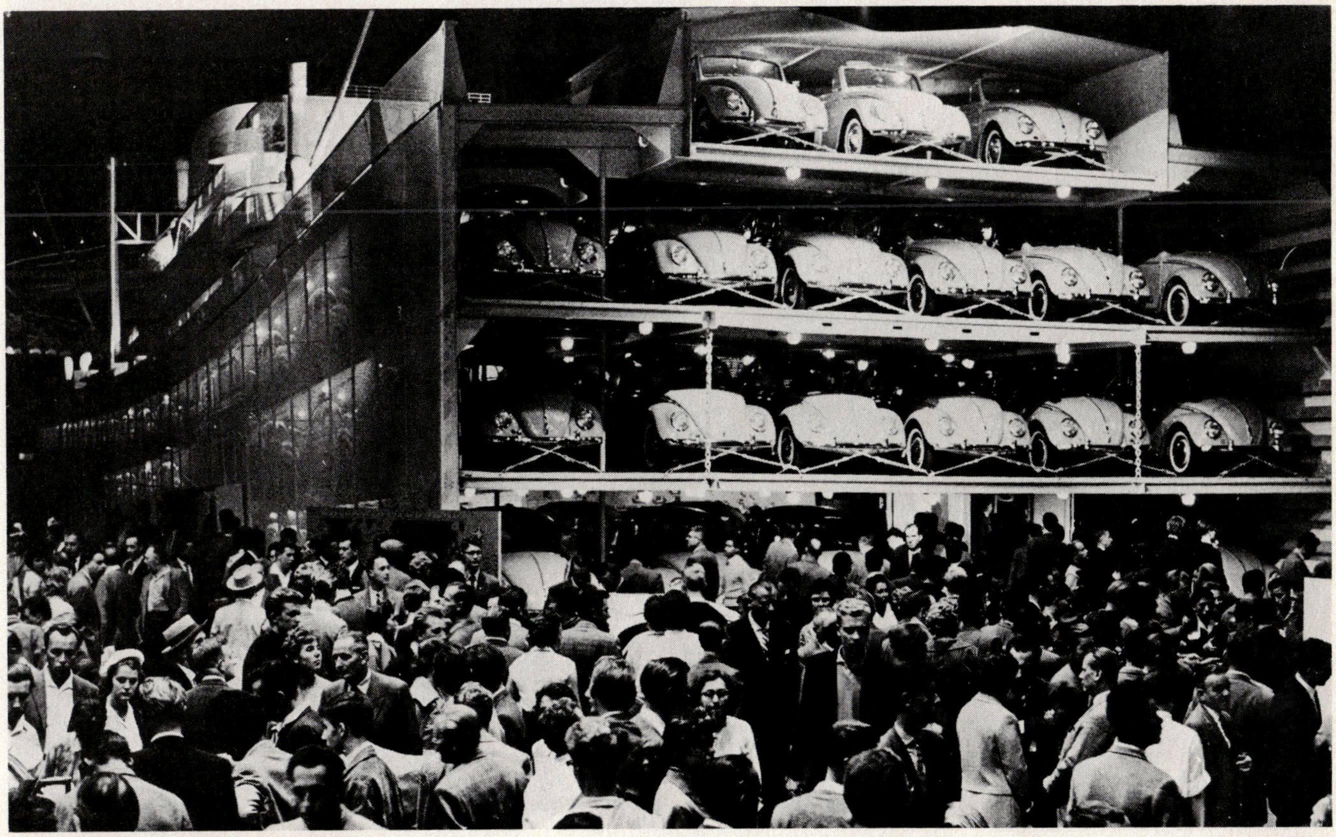

A VW auto show display emphasized the world-conquering ubiquity of the car that surpassed the Model T's production record.

IX

Ford Mustang 1966–1975

□ Against a backdrop of recent domestic automobile strife: declining sales, massive lay-offs, and previously loyal American buyers lining up at the Japanese car store to pay over-sticker for whatever's available, it's hard to accept' the remarkable success of a Detroit car whose debut took place only 20 years ago.

Not so hard to believe is that this modest little klunk stimulated a whole industry to mimic it with copycat models. After all—that's the way Detroit works, right?

Finally, it shouldn't overstress our credibility mechanisms to recall that it was the Hero of the Chrysler Rescue who played midwife at the birth of this uniquely American wonder car.

Anthony Lido Iacocca had a plan. As an obscure sales executive (although he had a Master's in Engineering) for Ford, he was acutely aware of a pent-up and apparently rising demand for a new car to replace the widely lamented two-seat Thunderbird. Everybody admired his idea for a youthful "personal car." It was fresh, agile, and looked sporting. Best of all—because of his engineer's ability to recognize which of Ford's parts inventory would fit into his dream car—*it wouldn't cost much.* That, of course, is what puts you on the High Road to fame and fortune in Motor City. The car would sell for under $2500, and 100,000 a year looked believable.

On that fateful April day in 1964, when the breathlessly awaited Mustang appeared for public viewing, it seemed to the Ford dealers that all America was in their showrooms. And they weren't all lookers, either. Annual volume of 100,000 began to look more like the sales of just the convert-

Its size and demeanor have made the Mustang a perfect platform for hopping up. It's had an important role in high-performance motoring from the Shelby to the SVO.

ible. And that's the way it turned out. By the end of the first model year (the fall of 1965), Ford factories had punched out 681,000 of the cute little buggers—a record for first-year sales of any new model.

Lee Iacocca had taken a bunch of off-the-shelf Falcon parts, dressed them up in horsey clothes and started the whole pony-car revolt.

How did he do it? By spreading models and options across a wide band of the market. Here was the first car a newly militant secretary could identify with—and afford. That would be the base coupe: 6-cylinder, 170-cubic-inch Falcon engine, three-speed manual transmission, and no radio—about $2385.

The hotshoes who bought the 260-inch V-8 were sorry right after, as it grew to 289 after six months, and annoyed when the Hi-Performance 289 appeared in the GT 2+2—not all that far off the powerplant in the legendary Shelby GT350.

You could have three-speed, automatic, four-speed, special handling package, power steering, disc brakes, and air conditioning (if you *didn't* choose the Hi-Per 289). There were eight-track Lear tape decks, interior groups, GT packages, and "accent" stripes. Cunningly manipulated, the extensive options list would yield up almost any econo-box, street-racer, or boulevard bird-catcher anyone could dream up.

The whole effort reached its apogee in 1970 with the Boss Mustang, and then gradually tapered off, as Ford backed away from Trans-Am, USAC and NASCAR involvements, to die with a whimper, when the exalted name was applied to the sorry Mustang II.

There is, however, a sort of happy epilogue: If Iacocca's dream hadn't become such a successful reality, he probably would not have ascended to the presidency of the Ford Motor Company. In which case he might not have attracted so much attention from Ford's *real* boss, Henry the Deuce. Which means he most likely wouldn't have been fired. Now, that suggests he might have continued at Ford. Whereupon Chrysler could very well now occupy the same warm corner of all our hearts as Studebaker, Packard, Willys, Hudson, and Chadwick.

From the relatively tame original car (top) the Mustang soon metamorphosed into the spoilered, striped and ground-pounding Boss 302 Musclecar of 1970 (below).

Four useful Japanese expressions

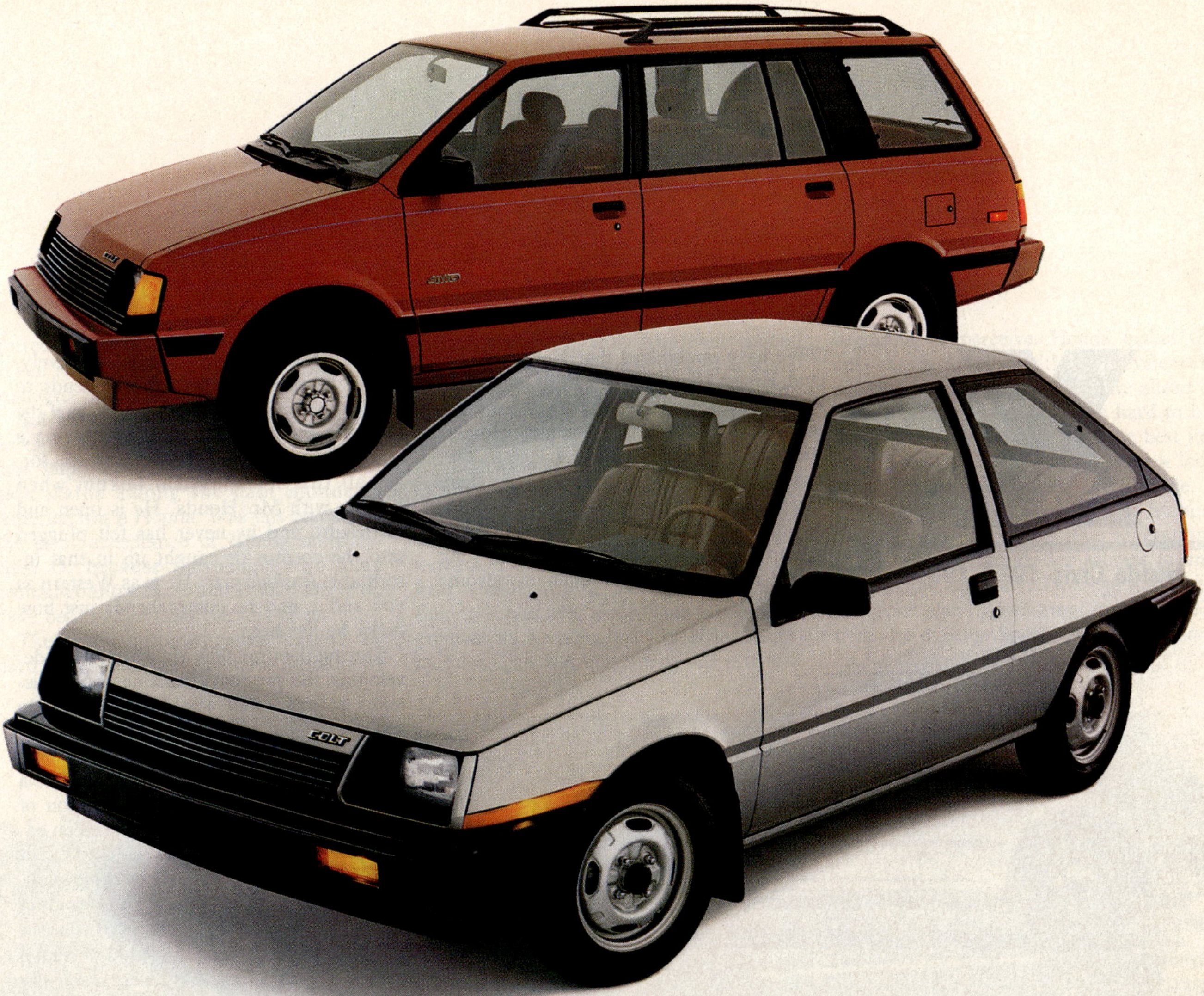

Say you're shopping for that special Japanese import. And the price is *definitely* an object. Easy. Repeat after us, "1986 Colt." This neat phrase also means quality, economy and value.

$5431

3-door base sticker price excluding title, taxes and destination charges at publication close. Dealer has full information.

Or you want some stylish, classy words for a handsome four-door sedan. Write this down. "1986 Colt Premier." The more formal usage promises true elegance inside and out.

What about a 7-passenger wagon with middle and rear seats that fold backwards *and* forwards? Pronounce that one "1986 Colt Vista." This most versatile expression contains all the handy variations—even "4-wheel drive."

Finally, you're certain to have some questions about performance. There's a very quick way to answer them. Try "1986 Turbo Colt." This is guaranteed to give people a big kick.

These unforgettable expressions are imported for Dodge and Plymouth, built by Mitsubishi Motors Corporation. They'll translate easily into usage. So make them a part of your vocabulary today.

Colt. It's all the Japanese you need to know.

THE CAR AND CULTURE

The car—artists and writers have glorified, vilified, romanticized, satirized and immortalized it.

By Steve Spence

☐ Signs of the automobile's effect on culture and the arts are everywhere, even along a bleak stretch of flat, monotonous land just off Interstate 40 near Amarillo, Texas.

Picture an unsuspecting interstate traveler tooling along this epic stretch of Panhandle boredom for the first time. He fidgets, shifts about in his seat, keeps changing the radio station—when suddenly, off to his left out the window, out there in the middle of a chewed-up field of parched wheat, he sees what appears to be—whatzat?—a row of ten Cadillacs. Except they're half-buried, nose down, all neatly in a row, as if someone has dropped them from the bay of an airplane into soft mud.

Our motorist brakes, looks again, then stops. He gets out and approaches this modern Stonehenge. After a while, he leaves, but he will drive for hours considering what he will tell everyone back home in Seattle. And even though he has no idea how these Cadillacs got there, or why their swoopy tail fins point mysteriously toward the stars, or what it means, this experience has made his day. He has just had an "earth art" experience.

He can thank Stanley Marsh 3 (yes: 3, not III), an unconventional Texas millionaire who is famous for owning about 90 percent of the world's helium supply and for making Richard Nixon's "enemies list" after writing Pat Nixon and informing her he was opening a "museum of decadent art" and could he have some samples of her wardrobe, which he promised would occupy an entire floor.

After Marsh saw an exhibit in 1969 of pop art by Claes Oldenburg—particularly a giant rendering of a cheeseburger—Marsh invited various artists down to create some earth art on his 20,000-acre spread. The ten Cadillacs were the work of an avantegarde consortium of artists and architects from San Francisco who called themselves the Ant Farm. They recommended planting the Cadillacs into the earth at the same precise angle as the slope of the Great Pyramid (the same angle, someone noted,

---

OPPOSITE PAGE:

The first monument to motorized man is this Paris sculpture by Dalou and Lefebvre immortalizing Henri Levassor's gallant victory in the classic 1895 Paris-Bordeaux road race.

PHOTO: FRED M.H. GREGORY

duplicated in the downward plunge of the Titanic), and titled the work, *Cadillac Ranch*. (They departed soon after for the Great Barrier Reef near Australia where they dressed up in porpoise costumes and went beneath the sea in some kind of impenetrable bubble-thing in hopes of making friendly contact with dolphins.)

The Ant Farm crowd didn't stick around to explain their work, but Marsh did in a magazine some years ago. "The Cadillac symbolizes your fantasy, whatever your fantasy—sex, money, freedom. This was especially true in all those tail-fin years after the war. *Cadillac*. The word was a standard by itself then. To have a Cadillac was to be living. It was a total dream: a genteel middle-class Hugh Hefner bed. The *Cadillac Ranch* is a celebration of the American Dream," Marsh instructed.

Now, Marsh is obviously a tad eccentric: he owns a pig named "Minnesota Little" which has wings tattooed on his flanks; he commissioned a second artist to create a football-field-sized pool table using giant soft balls and a 100-foot cuestick that he moves from one location to another; he once dyed a Clydesdale horse pink and painted his hooves red, and so forth—but who's to say his understanding of the automobile's place in modern culture is off base? And consider this: In a nation where the car is as common and necessary as the toilet, Marsh's *Cadillac Ranch* may be the only monument to the car on United States' soil.

Some time after the Caddys were imbedded nose down in a grave of concrete—the cars are '48 to '64, the tail-fin years—a reporter asked Marsh the big question on everyone's mind: "Why'd you do this?" Stanley the 3rd replied, "Why'd they build the pyramids."

A continent away, in the French town of Jouy-en-Josas, one imagines another motorist coming around a bend in the road and being confronted with another bizarre work of automobile art, *Long Term Parking*. Rising 60 feet in a glen of delicate leafy trees of the sort found in French Impressionist paintings is a 20-feet-square block of concrete binding together 60 real cars, all painted in bright party colors. It took the artist, who is known by the single name of Arman, seven years to complete what he describes as "a visual accumulation of the most typical object of the 20th Century. We are being invaded by cars." This was not Arman's first piece of car art. Earlier, he put a bomb in an MGA sports car, closed the doors and triggered the firing switch. The result of this, which looks pretty much like some unfortunate cars found in Beirut these days, was titled *White Orchid* and now resides in someone's private collection in West Germany.

There is another homage to the automobile in America, located appropriately enough in a shopping center in Hamden, Connecticut. The artist, Jim Wines, created a life-sized sculpture he calls *Ghost Parking Lot*. Using old cars, bloc bond and asphalt, Wines lined up the cars in painted parking stalls, but chopped three of them so they appear to be slowly disappearing into the asphalt, literally being absorbed back into Mother Earth. Say what you want about Wines' artistic vision, but the sculpture achieves its goal: it enlivens the droll landscape; it lends an adventuresome and comic quality to an otherwise ho-hum shopping center.

The most notorious piece of modern automobile art was created by Los Angeles artist Edward Kienholz in the early 1960s. Using a 1938 Dodge as his vehicle of expression, Kienholz gave form to the car's well-known reputation as a back-seat boudoir, and in the process, caused a furor. Kienholz removed the entire front section of the car, leaving only the back seat, with the windshield, a portion of the hood and the bumper attached, and placed the forms of a man and woman—the former made of

The Ant Farm, a group of New Wave artists, made a controversial and compelling roadside statement by burying these Cadillacs on the ranch of Stanley Marsh 3 near Amarillo.
PHOTO: LANE STEWART/SPORTS ILLUSTRATED

chicken wire and the female cast in plastic—in a sprawling, tangled sexual congress in the back seat. Plus he threw in a couple of Oly empties and left the door open for all to see.

While this portrayal of the automobile's versatility came as news to no one, a politically ambitious county supervisor from Pasadena objected loudly in the media to its inclusion in an exhibition at the L.A. County Museum. "My wife knows art," he said, "I know pornography." The news media milked this petty tempest until it was dry. The museum buckled, and announced the door of the Dodge would be closed to anyone under the age of 18. This scandal, of course, had the effect of dramatically increasing the number of visitors to the exhibit. Kienholz went on to produce a half-dozen more pieces of car-related art, many of which traveled to exhibitions in Europe.

If it seems the automobile is portrayed by modern artists as some comical and queer bedfellow of man's invention, it was not always that way.

The first true hero of the automobile, and the subject of the most spectacular monument to the car, was not Henry Ford, but a Frenchman named Henri Levassor. Like a half-dozen other pioneer automakers in Europe, Levassor had built a car toward the end of the 19th century and in 1895, he entered the world's first endurance test, a non-stop race from Paris to Bordeaux and back, a distance of 732 miles on what amounted to dirt trails. At the time, the infamous Dreyfus case was com-

THE SPACE VEHICLE THAT COULD TRANSPORT YOU INTO THE 21ST CENTURY.

The year 2001 may seem like light years away. But in a Volvo wagon, it's reachable.

You see the Volvos that are here today will be here tomorrow. They're so solidly built that they have an average life expectancy of 15.6 years.* (Of course this is merely an *average* life expectancy. A new Volvo could very well take you to the year 2001 and *beyond*.)

And as you head toward the 21st century in a Volvo wagon, you'll be travelling in space.

The infinitely adjustable front bucket seats can satisfy the dimensional requirements of 97% of the earth's adult population. And with the rear seat down, the cargo bay affords you a full 71 cubic feet of room.

So visit a Volvo dealer and see the space vehicle that can take you to the 21st century.

Then you can select an economical diesel,** dependable gas, or powerful intercooled turbo, depending on how fast you want to get there.

VOLVO

A car you can believe in.

ing to a head, and the Lumiere brothers had astounded all of Paris with the first *cinématographe*, but neither event drew the attention of the newly invented automobile and this race.

Driving a two-cylinder Panhard, Levassor departed Paris at mid-day on June 11, arrived in Ruffec at 3:30 a.m. only to find his relief driver asleep, pressed on and pulled into Bordeaux at 10:30 that morning. He stayed long enough to knock down a few tulips of champagne, jumped back in the Panhard and went roaring—well, 15 miles an hour qualified as "roaring" then— back to Paris. He won the event in two days and 48 minutes. The next year the Automobile Club of France commissioned a monument which today stands like a Roman masterwork cut into an archway at Port Maillot in Paris. The work took ten years to complete; after the commissioned artist, Aimée Jules Dalou, died, his student, Camille Lefebvre, was left to finish it. The marble relief depicts the strange Panhard charging forward out of the archway, with Levassor leaning forward at the wheel (a steering stick) like a cavalry officer, urging on his two-cylinder, surrounded by a crowd of hat-waving spectators.

But because the automobile was a piece of technology, a mechanical invention, "serious" painters ignored it as a possible subject. It was, after all, inhuman.

But one prominent painter broke the ice. Five years before his death in 1901, Henri de Toulouse-Lautrec satirized his cousin, who had purchased one of the original vehicles and apparently became a pioneer car nut. It is a rather ordinary drawing in which the cousin is seen in the foreground at the wheel of his auto, all bundled up in a fur coat, wearing goggles and hat, his face blackened by road dirt, charging headlong past the fine figure of a well-dressed *femme* with parasol who strolls with a small dog in the background. The motorist takes no notice of the fetching woman; perhaps the artist is saying his cousin has discovered a more exciting passion. Still, it is heralded as the first depiction of the automobile by a major modern painter.

In those early years, as the car became more common in Europe where it had been invented, the subject was limited almost exclusively to poster painters, announcing "fetes et concours" and depicting Panhellenic females in *tyre* ads for Michelin.

But it was not long before artists looked beyond iron and glass and exploding engines to find messages for the canvas. European artist Francis Picabia might wish, were he alive, to claim creation of the first "pop" work involving the car. A Cubist and Italian Futurist, Picabia saw the genius of the modern world in terms of the new machinery it could produce. In a lithograph, he simply made a draftsman-quality pen drawing of an upright spark plug with all its precise grooves and castings, and titled the work, *Portrait of a Young American Woman in a State of Nudity*. The message, natch, was that modern woman was hot, able to ignite fires of passion (the

Sixty actual cars are eternally imbedded in this massive 60-foot-high, 20-foot-square sculpture outside Paris. Arman, its creator, aptly named it, *Long Term Parking*.
PHOTO: FRED M.H. GREGORY

While other agencies were making advertising, Kenyon & Eckhardt was making history.

The recovery of Chrysler, under Lee Iacocca, is one of the most significant achievements in the history of American business.

It helped reshape the relationship between government, management, labor and the American people.

And it helped reshape the relationship between an advertising agency and its client.

While other agencies were making advertising, K&E and Chrysler were making history.

From the beginning it was hard to tell who was working for whom.

When the Chrysler management debated whether the company should go to the government for loan guarantees, K&E was there.

We fought for a voice in the debates on whether Chrysler should live or die. We lived with tent sales to unload the sales bank. We put the K on the K-car.

We were part of the marketing group. The P.R. group. The product group. The sales group.

We were part of the company.

We had to invent new ways of doing business or die.

Consumers were running away from the showrooms. Things were bad and the economy made them worse.

The country was facing a deep recession. Inflation and interest rates were rising, and gas prices were going through the roof. The small car revolution had begun.

We knew it would take more than advertising to move 200,000 cars piled up against fences. We ran tent sales in stadiums, baseball fields—even at factories. "Get a car, get a check" became part of the language.

To fight soaring interest rates we launched an Interest Allowance Plan. And to bolster confidence, a 30-day money-back guarantee.

Together with Chrysler, we invented new ways of doing business. We sold cars and Chrysler stayed alive.

The press buried Chrysler a thousand times. And a thousand times it had to be resurrected.

"Why don't they just die with dignity."

That was the overwhelming opinion of America's press.

K&E said, "You can die quietly, or die screaming. Scream. There's a chance someone will hear you."

Lee Iacocca agreed to a series of ads that made marketing history. They asked and answered some hard questions beginning with "Would America be better off without Chrysler?"

We had to convince the Congress, the President, the banks, the business community and the people that Chrysler was worth saving. So we screamed.

And America heard.

The K-car: The beginning of the long road back.

The K-car was probably the most important introduction since the first automobile rolled off the assembly line.

The fate of a whole company hung in the balance.

The stage was set. The world was waiting. And Lee Iacocca introduced the American way to beat the pump.

And America bought it.

Lee Iacocca: An American hero was born.

When Lee Iacocca pointed his finger at the camera and said, "If you can find a better car, buy it," he meant it. And America believed him.

He's made "Made in America mean something again." And he's proved that "In America hard work and commitment still count for something."

On August 12, 1983, Chrysler paid back the loan guarantees. Seven years early.

On February 14, 1985, Chrysler announced the biggest profit in its 60-year history and our "Thank You, America" campaign went on the air and into the press.

History was made again and K&E was part of it. But the reasons for this remarkable turnaround go well beyond the advertising and marketing programs. To the management, the workers, the dealers and to the man himself. He did what he said he'd do. And it paid off. He had a plan . . . a reason for being. To be the best.

And we shared it.

We learned to break the rules and made history!

One thing we learned: the rules don't count. We broke the rules with our agency-client relationship, our marketing and P.R. efforts, our advertising. It worked. Because K&E people make it work. Men and women who met the challenge with hard work, heart and guts. It's not the rules that are important but the problems. And the solutions.

K&E played a unique role in the Chrysler turnaround. We didn't just make advertising.

We made history.

brand name on the plug was "For-Ever"). That may sound frivolous today, but it was strong stuff in 1915, and today it resides in the Art Library at the University of California at Los Angeles and is probably worth a nice waterfront lot in Malibu.

In those years, the Italian Futurists—artists who predicted technology would lead happily to a sort of Buck Rogers world—championed the car and painted all sorts of abstracts depicting motion, speed and the sort of power that technology suggests. In New York, artists of the "Ash Can School" depicted all the wonders and motion of big-city life, including the brash and scattering effects of the car. John Sloan, perhaps the best of the Ashcanners, showed the obese rich, weighted down in their finery, chugging about in their new-found symbols of wealth.

But by and large, the brash and bizarre art we know today that focuses on the car just didn't happen until the second half of the century. Cars were relegated to gangster movies (Howard Hawks' 1930 film, *Scarface*, being a good example) and Keystone Cops flicks and as glittering props for movie stars. The car is suggested in the still lifes of the great American painter Edward Hopper (*Gas*, 1940, and *Western Motel*, 1957) and in Grant Wood's famous *Death on the Ridge Road* (1935), but it is not the *raison d'être* of the paintings. Two very strange paintings by Salvadore Dali in 1925, *Ghosts of Two Automobiles*, almost

defy description; two great black limousines cloaked in funeral garb with root-like growths coming out of the rear sections were as startling then as now.

It seems the car cannot be rendered without offending someone or some institution. Such was the case with the massive murals of Diego Rivera that today fill the walls of a sunlit courtyard at the Detroit Institute of Arts (see page 23).

Although the Depression was two years old when the project was commissioned in 1931, the museum's governing body—which included as a member Henry Ford's son, Edsel—brought Rivera to Detroit to extoll the wonderment of industrial America. He was to depict the marvelous, efficient American assembly line, and the work was to be titled *Detroit Industry*. (In fact, the assembly lines were running throughout the Depression, and though there were fewer buyers, Detroit's automakers did not suffer the economic apocalypse experienced elsewhere.)

Of course, you can't tell an artist what to paint, and Rivera, who would have been only too happy to inform the committee that he was a fervent communist, saw the assembly line differently. On the four walls, he indeed painted the power of the industrial revolution with a multitude of workers bending and straining and lifting amid massive machinery, but he also threw in malignant images: a half-face, half-skull; men packed into tiny spaces; images of the

factory being used to build weapons of war; men dragging themselves to work in an image not unlike *The Prisoners' March*. Above it all, a great Mayan god, powerful arms and fists, is shown protecting the enterprise from the heavens.

Most everyone—the city council and the newspapers and particularly the wealthy art patrons—saw it as their worst dream come true, a blasphemy, perhaps even pornographic. Even the Catholic Church saw some resemblance between the mural of pharmaceutical production and the Nativity Scene. Ironically, Edsel Ford (who appears in one portion of a mural) was one of Rivera's staunchest supporters in the furor. Of course, what could they do—whitewash the walls? Hardly. In time, the controversy just ran out of gas, and today Rivera's work is viewed as one of America's finest examples of mural art.

After World War II, the world—at least as Americans had known it—was never the same, and the car played a principal role in the radical change. The creation of the suburban tract home would have been impossible without the car, and was facilitated by huge state and federal expenditures for vast series of highways. By 1950, there were 50 million cars registered in the U.S., and that number would jump to 75 million at the end of the decade.

From the late '40s into the '50s, America was suddenly bombarded with *new things:* television, tape recorders, stereophonic recording, frozen dinners, Cinemascope!, beer in cans, rock and roll music, the commercial jet airplane, the suburban shopping center and the drive-in movie and restaurant, filtertip cigarettes, hair spray, Brigitte Bardot, power lawnmowers and powerboats, aerosol shaving cream, the hula hoop! Commerce gone mad, flat-tops and crinolines and blue-suede shoes.

And the modern, sleek, aerodynamic, two-tone, chromed-out, fin-crazy automobile was at the forefront. Americans wanted nothing to do with the funeral-car styling of the '30s and '40s—they wanted the future, and it had to be flashy, multi-colored and reeking with chrome.

By 1949, most automakers had come up with some kind of chromed spacemobile. The Studebaker looked like it had come off the cover of a sci-fi pulp magazine; without the grille, it was tough in '49 to tell the front from the back. Cadillac went from boat to bubble baroque, and after designer Harley Earl got a good look at the slick P-38 Lockheed Lightning airplane, he invented the car tail fin. Chevy grew slim, fire-engine red Ford convertibles were everywhere, and Nash built a car in which the seats turned into a bed. The first automatic transmissions arrived, engine performance was increased and the hot-rodder made his first appearance.

The car became the principal driving force of style, fashion and flair. In pop music, Bo Diddley, Chuck Berry, Jan and Dean, and the Beach Boys rhapsodized about cars. Buicks sprouted portholes, Chryslers arrived with unimaginable doodads and gunsights mounted fore and aft, and everywhere, the knife-like tail fins. It seemed during the Eisenhower years that the biggest news story of each year was the first magazine photos of the new models.

Pop art and the car got together about 1956, but let's give credit where it's due: Is not the odd, toy-like Nash Metropolitan a piece of pop art in itself? How about the Henry J? Seen a '55 Buick recently? And certainly the most finned-out of all Cadillacs, the '59, should make the list.

The art world certainly did not turn its head on this explosion of wackiness. Richard Hamilton most likely began the pop school with a collage of the modern family—an update on Jan Van Eyck's 15th century "Arnolfini Wedding"—that cast a body-builder bearing a giant Tootsie Pop as the head of the family and his seductive burleyque wife (wearing a lampshade). All manner of modern invention clutters their front room (including a Ford logo), and the collage is titled, *Just what is it that makes today's homes so different, so appealing?* Another pioneering pop artist, Robert Rauschenberg, inked the tires of his Model A in 1951 and drove it over a 20-foot strip

of heavy paper and voilà! *Automobile Tire Print* was created. Black-and-white photographers like Garry Winogrand and Robert Frank discovered all the surreal possibilities that seem to be everywhere today by simply shooting candid shots of people that inhabit cars on the streets.

Even Picasso couldn't resist; his bronze cast sculpture, *Baboon and Young,* which today stands in the Museum of Modern Art in New York, uses two toy cars to form the head of his subject (the car as baboon?).

Andy Warhol arrived in the early '60s, getting his picture in *Time* and elsewhere for finding profundity in the simple red-and-white label found on a can of Camp-

bell's tomato soup. His most famous car art came in a "car crash series," a group of black and white disasters. Warhol located a frightening photograph of an overturned '55 Ford, a grisly accident in which four passengers are pinned beneath the vehicle. What gives the photo its bizarre quality is the fact that at least two of the victims seem completely unconcerned, and stare blandly into the lens of the camera, as if they couldn't care less. Warhol blew up the

she being Brand

-new;and you
know consequently a
little stiff i was
careful of her and(having

thoroughly oiled the universal
joint tested my gas felt of
her radiator made sure her springs were O.

K.)i went right to it flooded-the-carburetor cranked her

up,slipped the
clutch(and then somehow got into reverse she
kicked what
the hell)next
minute i was back in neutral tried and

again slo-wly;bare,ly nudg.   ing(my

lev-er Right-
oh and her gears being in
A 1 shape passed
from low through
second-in-to-high like
greasedlightning)just as we turned the corner of Divinity

avenue i touched the accelerator and give

her the juice,good

        (it

was the first ride and believe I we was
happy to see how nice she acted right up to
the last minute coming back down by the Public
Gardens i slammed on

the
internalexpanding
&
externalcontracting
brakes Bothatonce and

brought allofher tremB
-ling
to a:dead.

stand-
;Still)

— by e.e. cummings

e.e. cummings' stream-of-imagery captures the anxiety and joy of the first-time driver.

LUXUS
Carvel Affelsmeyer
MERCEDES-BENZ

negative twice, silkscreened it on 50 by 30-inch frames and called it *Five Deaths Twice*. He explained: "When you see a gruesome picture over and over, it really doesn't have any effect."

The boundaries of pop had no limit. Roy Lichtenstein put comic-book characters behind the wheels of cars. John Chamberlain found all the material he would need for his abstract sculptures in auto junkyards. Ed Ruscha painted a modern Standard gas station, tossed in a cocktail olive in the air of one corner and called it, *Cheesemold Standard With Olive*. (Ruscha noted that a lot of his art deals with "highway hypnosis.") Tom Wesselman cut out a Volkswagen Bug from a real billboard, placed it at floor level in front of a bland pastel background and titled it, *Landscape No. 5*.

Sex and the car has been a common theme; one of the first examples recalled Picabia's spark plug—Mel Ramos' 1964 *Kar Kween* has a nude blonde caressing a six-foot AC Delco plug. An artist in L.A., Dustin Shuler, impaled a '59 Cadillac with a 20-foot spike, then cut the car into 59 chunks, each bearing a photo of the original to one side and the artist's signature.

In the '70s, all sorts of expressionists took Tom Wolfe's tribute to the car customizers *(The Kandy Kolored Tangerine-Flake Streamlined Baby)* to heart; cars appeared covered with a bed of moss, covered with sea shells, covered with psychedelic aberrations. The custom van became a national rage, with "van-ins" attracting thousands of owners who displayed their personal art on wheels. Pop art, it seemed, was no longer the bailiwick of artists—it was everywhere.

But where is literature in all this?

When the mavens of culture go poking about in literature for enlightenment concerning the car, they usually come up with themes of worker exploitation on the assembly line (John Dos Passos' *The Big Money*) or kinky corporate-power sex-soaps (Arthur Haley's *Wheels*), which is the same as coming up empty-handed.

But in 1955, ten years after the war and in the midst of America's preoccupation with the glittery new, the Viking Press published a novel that more than any other would embody the spirit and soul of the country's new mobility, the freedom afforded by the automobile and the new highways that criss-crossed the land. The novel was Jack Kerouac's *On the Road*, and for many young people growing up in the '50s, its effect was electrifying. It was a manifesto celebrating wanderlust.

Kerouac became the principal voice of the "beat generation," turning his back squarely on those values epitomized by the

pursuit of a tract home that came with a spouse, two kids and a two-car garage.

Like the poet Walt Whitman a half-century before him, Kerouac looked to the open road as a great source of experience and inspiration. And so he set out "into the holy American night," riding on flat-bed trucks driven by Minnesota farm boys or sitting up front with wild-eyed truck drivers and salesmen heading for the next town; he worked the fields of the Sacramento Valley and felt bliss wandering through railroad yards and slept on floors in San Francisco, Denver and Los Angeles, heading finally into the unknown "inky screaming insect night of Mexico." The car, the road, some new experience.

And what was out there on the road? Just about everything. "As we crossed the Colorado-Utah border I saw God in the sky in the form of a huge gold sunburning cloud above the desert that seemed to point a finger at me and say, 'Pass here and go on, you're on the road to heaven.'"

Years later, after the wide notoriety of *On the Road* and a succession of similar novels, Kerouac would be awakened at all hours of the night by wild-eyed kids pounding on his door, drunk or high, mimicking the voice of Neal Cassady, his road companion, babbling "yass, yass, yass!" and demanding an audience with the "high priest of the Beatniks." They'd point to this battered Pontiac or that panel truck and plead with Kerouac to go on the road with them one more time.

One wonders: Was Kerouac in large part responsible for that common sight in the '60s at freeway on-ramps and on two-lane roads in the middle of nowhere—vast numbers of young longhairs hitch-hiking to no place in particular, carrying back packs

and guitars and clutching girlfriends?

One of his characters in *On the Road* asks, "What is the meaning of this voyage to New York? What kind of sordid business are you on now? I mean, man, whither goest thou? Whither goest thou, America, in thy shiny car in the night?"

Whither indeed? Television producers went quickly to a form of *On the Road*, a weekly series called *Route 66* which followed the less-frantic adventures of Martin Milner, George Maharis and a Corvette. And wasn't *Easy Rider* yet another variation on the idea that the open road could somehow reveal America to itself?

That's what artists are supposed to do, bring revelation. And over the last century, a recurring image in their work has been the automobile and what it means. The kids in *American Graffiti* used their '55 Chevys and Deuce coupes to beat the boredom of small-town Modesto; the Joad family escaped the dustbowl in their decrepit Ford truck in *Grapes of Wrath*. Chuck Berry sang about it in *Maybelline* and George Gershwin put its tooting horn into *An American in Paris*. Artists, writers, composers, movie-makers and poets have glorified, vilified, romanticized and satirized the car. For the last century, it's been a powerful fixture in our store of images. It tugs at our senses and forms our thoughts in more ways than we know.   **MT**

THE ROAD RACES

Taking it to the streets is the time-honored way of settling the question of whose car is the fastest.

By T.C. Browne

☐ It wasn't just *necessary* to have the second car before the first race could happen. It was a requirement that the two of them be at the same place at the same time. Otherwise, the starter wouldn't know when to call "go." This is the way it was in the beginning, and so it has remained.

While the time and place of the first such race is not recorded, there is a wealth of written information available on the events which followed.

The first "organized" motorsports event, a reliability run for *Voitures sans chevaux* was sponsored by the newspaper, *Le Petit Journal*, and it was flagged off at 8 a.m., July 22, 1894, when 21 cars left Paris for Rouen, 79 miles away, with 17 actually arriving. The car that came in first, a De Dion, didn't win, but there was a lot of that sort of thing in the early days. In this case, the driver was a man who would have a major influence on the early history of automobile racing: Le Comte de Dion. He was moved down a slot (for reasons that are sufficiently arcane as to defy explanation here) while the 1st-place honors were shared between the firms of Panhard et Levassor and Peugeot, whose names are also not entirely unknown to the ardent car freak.

The First Real Race

But it is to the next year we must look for the first real motorcar race, which took place June 11, 1895, on the public roads between Paris and Bordeaux, a challenging round-trip run of 732 miles. Organized by the Automobile Club de France, this seminal event saw 22 of the 46 entries actually take the green flag, with 11 of them reaching Bordeaux. The victor, Emile Levassor, took 48 hours and 48 minutes to better the time of the 2nd-place car by 8 hours. All of which sounds fairly impressive when one considers the primitive machinery, poor road surfaces and numerous other hazards the drivers had to face. But the fact that astounds a sophisticated observer is that Emile Levassor never enjoyed the

ly avoided the crowd-control problems of the cities, but drivers greatly feared attracting bandits, should they have the ill fortune to crap out at some remote point on those long, lonely Targa Florio laps.

In 1932, the legendary Tazio Nuvolari set a race record over the 45 miles of sharp turns and steep grades that make up a lap of the "little circuit" (over the years, Sr. Florio changed the course around to suit circumstances like earthquakes, floods and slides) that stood until 1952, when a particularly exciting and competitive running of this peculiar classic took place. With narrow pavement and an altitude variation per lap from 33 to 2000 feet above sea level, it had already been proven that small cars do better than big cars in this grueling test of man and machine. Since the previous year, the paving on many of the 900 curves had been improved, and there was eager anticipation that Nuvolari's ancient record might be broken.

The pre-race favorites were Franco Cortese, the previous year's winner, with the same 2-liter Frazer-Nash he had driven then; Giovanni Bracco, fresh from victory in the Mille Miglia and driving a 4.1-liter Ferrari; three factory-entered Lancia Aurelias, Bonetto, Valenzano, and Anselmi up; and the tiny 1340cc OSCA driven by Cabianca.

On the first lap, Bracco broke his own record, set the previous year, with a turn at 52 minutes. Following came Cabianca, Bonetto, Valenzano, Anselmi. Bonetto retired on lap two, leaving Cabianca and the wee OSCA in the lead. By lap three, Cabianca was so far in front that he changed tires without surrendering a position. Then, he was finally able to put in a record lap of his own, at 51.17,, averaging over 52 mph on a course with 20 curves to the mile. On lap 7, the little OSCA broke its

axle and Cabianca's heart.

Bonetto, in the 2-liter Lancia Aurelia, inherited the lead, with Cortese—driving last year's winning 2-liter Frazer-Nash—rushing him with the idea of repeating his previous year's stellar achievement.

For his next astounding feat, Bonetto ran out of gas on exactly the same corner at which misfortune had struck Cabianca. He snatched a water bottle from the hands of a small boy standing nearby and rushed to the maimed OSCA—which Cabianca was guarding from the ardent souvenir collectors who make up such an important segment of the Sicilian population—emptying the water as he went. With Cabianca lending a hand, he siphoned gasoline, a half-liter at a time, into his own tank. Taking a wild guess at how much he needed to get home, Bonetto set out for the finish line, expecting to feel the hot breath of Cortese on his neck at any moment. There was no way, in that time and place, for Bonetto to have known that Cortese had shed a wheel and taken to the dunes to avoid running down spectators.

Bonetto, rushing onward to avoid being overtaken by the now-retired Cortese, ran out of gas once more, 50 yards short of the finish line and the three million lire. Worse—the man holding the checkered flag so beckoningly was uphill from where the Aurelia had gasped its last. Bonetto, frantic from fear that he would hear the rasp of Cortese's engine at any moment, using one hand on the starter, and shoving with the rest of his body and spirit, arrived at the finish line after seven hours of racing and three minutes of pushing. Exhausted and happy, he had not only won the big purse, but he had broken Nuvolari's 20-year-old record in the process. The fast-lap record still belonged to Cabianca.

The Targa Florio continued into 1973.

What turned out to be the final meeting of this classic was won by Muller van Lennep, driving a Porsche RSR (entirely sufficient justification for ending the series right there). But the petroleum crisis struck in 1974, and the race was canceled, never to be revived. While the long-life record of Sr. Florio's proud challenge to the skills of the world's bravest drivers may one day be broken, the record of their achievements at his weird and wonderful venue never will.

The Tourist Trophy

The other event at one time in contention for longest running race was the Tourist Trophy. But, while the Targa Florio always ran somewhere on the island of Sicily, the TT moved from one venue to another during a history that began in 1905. The motive is involved with that unfriendly reception of the automobile in England. With no place to run off the public roads, and forbidden to run on them, the English enthusiast was obliged to find somewhere more hospitable. And didn't he just! The Isle of Man has been a hotbed of rabid racing enthusiasm ever since, although more associated with motorcycle competitions since the twenties.

Anyway, that first year, the TT ran for 209 miles around a lovely island in the Irish Sea, included some weird miles-per-gallon restrictions, and was won by J.S. Napier, on an Arrol-Johnston, at 34 mph. The following year, the limit was 25 mpg, the average speed of the winner 39.40 mph, the distance was 162 miles on the same circuit, and the winning car a Rolls-Royce, driven by none other than C.S. Rolls, himself. In 1907, E. Courtis, in a Rover, prevailed, at 28.80 mph, over 242 miles with the same mileage restrictions. In 1908, the formula was changed to limit cylinder diameter to four inches, limit the number of cylinders to four, and limit the horsepower rating to 25.6. Winner of this 338-mile contest was W. Watson, on a Hutton, average 50.30 mph. The next race took place in 1914, ran a total of 600 miles over two days (the innkeepers were catching on), had an engine-capacity limit of 3310 cubic centimeters, and was won by K. Lee Guinness, on a Sunbeam, at 56.44 mph.

There was a long pause for a war until 1922, when the distance was 302 miles for race cars up to 3-liters, and the victor was J. Chassagne, at 55.778 mph, driving a Sunbeam.

Another six years went by and the 1928 RAC Ulster TT was planned as some kind of Irish circus. Suddenly, sports cars were all the rage, Le Mans having set a whole new pattern of endurance contests over challenging circuits with demanding bends and undulating surfaces. Everyone wanted to get into the act. Weeks before the August 18 starting date, the advance parties from England and the Continent were arriving to inspect facilities, establish garages, test cars.

The route ran along farm fields, right through town centers, across a level crossing of the Belfast and County Down Rail-

Felice Nazzaro strikes a pose in the Fiat he drove to victory in the 1907 Targa Florio. The race through the barren hills of Sicily has a long and glorious history and ran till 1973 when the cars got too fast for the road and the fuel crisis hit.

It doesn't matter which race, which class, which track. At Bridgestone, we're serious about our performance.

For years, Bridgestone has supplied tires for the European and Japanese Formula Two series, as well as the Porsche 956's in the World Endurance Championship.

Now we're ready to conquer new territory.

So this year, look for Bridgestone tires on Bruce Leven's Bayside Disposal Porsche 962 IMSA GTP team. Bayside's consistent top finishes in 1984 made them a natural for Bridgestone's top performance.

In addition, we'll be supporting several other teams in the GTP and GTU classes this season. All for one reason.

Because what we learn on the racetracks of the world, we put into *every* Bridgestone tire we make.

See you in the winner's circle.

the U.S. Worldwide, Nissan was ranked fourth, about a million cars a year behind arch rival Toyota.

One Mistake at a Time

"Looking back, in my work, I feel that I have made nothing but mistakes, a series of failures, a series of regrets," said Soichiro Honda. "But I also am proud of an accomplishment. Although I made one mistake after another, my mistakes or failures were never due to the same reason. I never made the same mistake twice, and I always tried my hardest and succeeded in improving my efforts."

There is Honda, the advanced motorcycle; Honda, the innovative car; Honda, the industrious company; Honda, the clever advertising campaign—and all of it owes to Honda, the extraordinary man. Mechanic, racing driver, *raconteur*, hell-raising partygoer, philosopher, leader, folk hero, inventor, legend in his own time—all these things and more describe Soichiro Honda.

In 1922, just 16 years old, Honda went to Tokyo to seek his fortune as a mechanic for the then-new automobile. Six years later he set up shop in Hamamatsu and had a patent for making wheel spokes of cast metal instead of wood. By the mid-thirties he was manufacturing piston rings for Toyota and had already survived a pretty serious race-car crash. During the war, he would scrounge drop-tanks that American aircraft discarded over Japan, use the recycled aluminum in manufacturing and save the remaining gasoline that was still in the tanks! In 1948 he established the Honda Motor Company, Ltd., with capital of $3,300, assumed the presidency and started building motorcycles—to succeed the converted bicycles he had been producing. By the early '50s he declared the intention of Honda motorcycles taking on the world's best in international competition; by decade's end Honda was nearly dominant in motorcycle racing. In the early '60s Honda automobile production was begun with a tiny, jewel-like sports car utilizing motorcycle technology. The company entered Formula One racing, and in 1965 a Honda scored its first Grand Prix victory. In 1968 Honda motorcycle production reached a total of 10 million units. By the early '70s the Honda Civic, with its revolutionary CVCC engine that went after automobile emissions problems at their source, was an instant world-wide success. By the early '80s, Honda had established both motorcycle and automobile production in the United States, and the company was on its way to becoming the fourth largest American automaker.

Not, all in all, a bad generation.

There are many reasons for the success of Honda, but one of the more significant is the company's respect for research and development. At Honda, R&D is an entirely separate facility, its people free to try, to experiment, to fail. It's this approach that has resulted in such breakthroughs as the CVCC engine, the oval-piston motorcycle race engine, the original three-wheel

ATC—landmarks of engineering, all. Said Honda, of research: "When we engage in research of any kind, one thing that must not be forgotten is that research means a succession of failures, that more than 99 percent of our research is total failure. A research organization should be structured to enable individuals to make the best of their ability, whereas a manufacturing company should be organized to yield maximum efficiency."

Riding a Rotary

On August 23, 1982, Kenichi Yamamoto, then Senior Managing Director of Toyo Kogyo Company Ltd. (builders of Mazda cars and trucks), and generally accepted as primary developer of the rotary engine, stood before the World Automotive Congress and delivered a speech on the two decades of innovation the rotary represented. He finished that speech with this:

The first "Dat" was made in 1914. But this is the first Dat*sun* (top). It came along in 1932, a modest little ragtop. More than 30 years later, the Datsun Z-cars established the parent company, Nissan, as a high-performance leader. The company is now trying to make everybody forget Datsun and calls its cars Nissans.

"Did I start by saying the rotary is an engine, not a poem? There are many times when I think the similarities are greater than the differences.

"Like a poem, the rotary engine was the child of our dreams.

"Like a poem, it put together elements in a way that was startling in the overall effect.

"And like a poem, the rotary captured a spirit—the pioneering spirit so dear to

Unveiled at the 1985 Frankfurt Auto Show, the Nissan Mid 4 is rumored to be a production prototype. It has a mid-ship, DOHC V-6, 4-WD, and 4-wheel *steering*.

ago, they are incredible.

Three Diamonds

The very first Japanese car to qualify as a standard, production model of reasonable volume was the Mitsubishi Model A, introduced in 1917. It was a dignified and formal-looking automobile, with an open driver's area and a closed compartment for rear-seat passengers. Reportedly, it was based on a Fiat design, and featured a body carved from oak and painted with lacquer. Then, as now, its hood was adorned with the Mitsubishi three-diamond logo, a design based on the family crest of company founder Yataro Iwasaki—three diamonds in a tiered arrangement and that of the Yamanouchi family—three oak leaves arranged radially. In March, 1937, Iwasaki combined the diamonds of one with the radial form of the other, and changed the name of the company from *Tsukumo Shokai* to *Mitsubishi Shokai*; Mitsubishi means three diamonds.

Mitsubishi Motors Corporation is owned primarily by Mitsubishi Heavy Industries, Ltd., with a 15-percent share belonging to Chrysler Corporation. This conglomerate manufactures just about anything and everything: electronics, heavy machinery, shipbuilding, aircraft, chemicals and a whole lot of other things.

While Mitsubishi's presence worldwide is enormous, in the United States its cars are better known for those models sold through Chrysler dealerships. But with the establishment of Mitsubishi Motors Sales of American in 1981, it finally had its own American outlet, competing, ironically, against itself; Chrysler, with its much larger dealer network, still sells many times more Mitsubishi products in this county than Mitsubishi.

Mitsubishi is also a true "full-line" manufacturer—a point many often miss and

Americans and to those of us who admire your country. In turn, that spirit has captured our company.

"We will never be the same."

Toyo Kogyo was renamed Mazda Motors Corporation in 1984. Kenichi Yamamoto, who gave the rotary at least life and breath if not birth, began as an engineer after graduating from Toyko University in 1944, and is now the President. Each of them has come a long way. For Mazda, things indeed are not the same.

Begun as a cork producer—Toyo Cork Kogyo—in 1920, the company was renamed Toyo Kogyo Company, Ltd., in 1927. In 1929 machine tool production was begun, and in 1931 the firm introduced a line of three-wheel trucks were more related to motorcycles than to cars.

For automobiles, the important dates came later. It was not until 1960 that the first Mazda car, a tiny 369-cubic-centimeter coupe, was introduced. But the company was off and running, signing a licensing agreement with NSU/Wankel for rights to the revolutionary rotary engine in 1961. It was a move of the boldest proportions.

In 1967, the 110S Cosmo Sport, an exquisite little car powered by a rotary, was coming down the assembly line. Things looked bright for Mazda, yet less than a decade later the company was nearly out of business. The worldwide energy crunch had hit the rotary hard—it had been developed for performance, not economy—and sales plummeted. How the company saved itself through an aptly named program called the Phoenix Project is a story of determined and innovative management.

For one thing, even in the face of mounting losses, there was a commitment that workers would not be laid off. Instead, many plant and office workers and managers were sent to retail dealerships throughout Japan to help sell cars and keep the assembly lines moving. Meanwhile, a massive program to revamp the entire model lineup was begun, even though cost reduction programs were instituted. Finally, through natural attrition the workforce was reduced by over 6,000 employes in eight years; at the same time productivity was increased from an annual rate of 19 vehicles per employee in 1975 to 48 per employee in 1983. Mazda had saved itself.

As a manufacturer, Madza is known for advanced technology and extremely well-engineered, sophisticated cars; it is the only company in the world building rotary engines, gasoline piston engines, and diesels, and earlier problems of the rotary have been completely eliminated to where the engine is now a model of durability.

For any company, Mazda's achievements are noteworthy. For one teetering on the brink of a corporate grave a decade

This Nissan GTP ZX Turbo was designed to compete in the International Motor Sports Association (IMSA) GTP class of racing. Inspired by the revolutionary Z-car engine, its mission is to prove

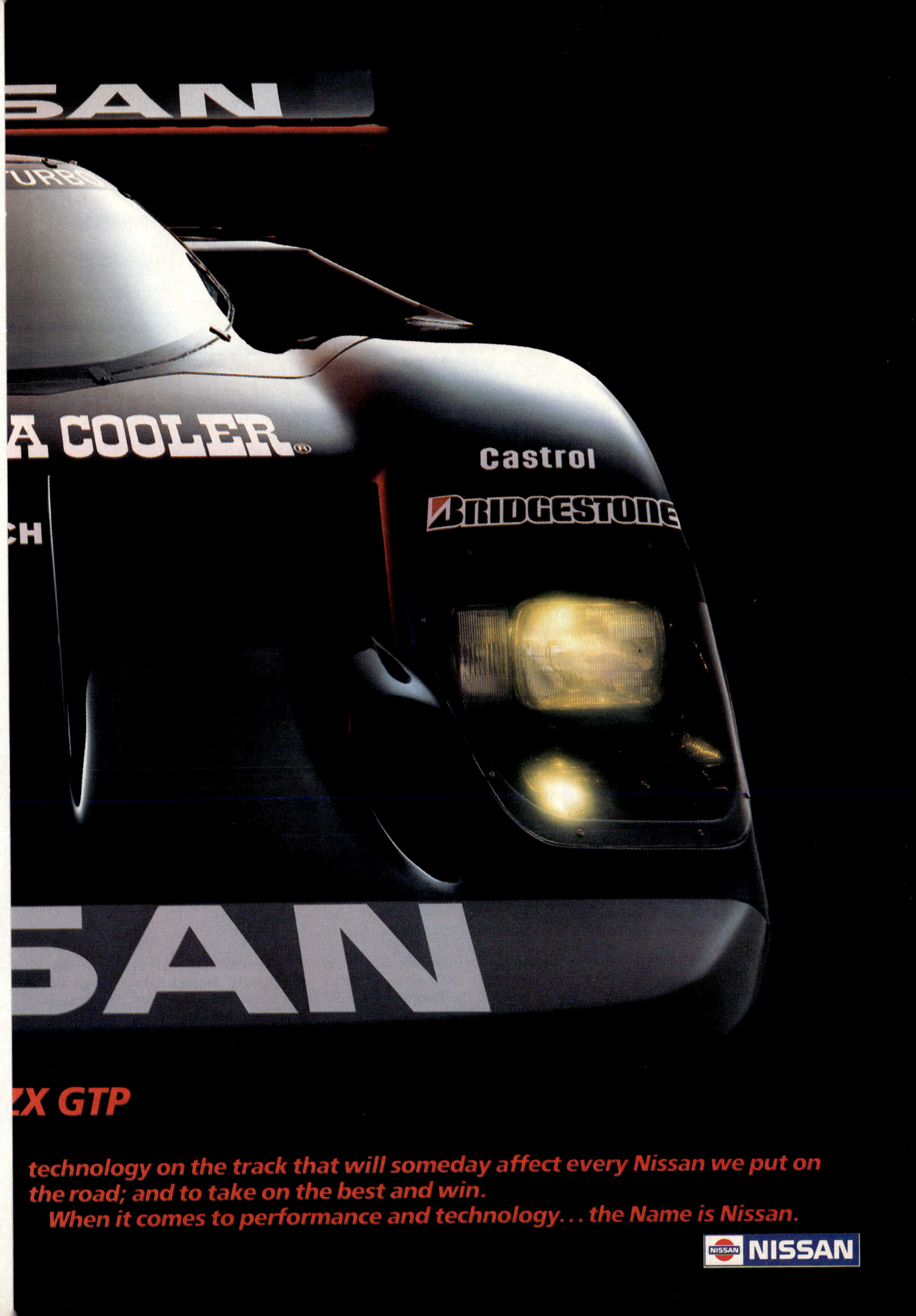
SAN
TURBO
A COOLER®
CH
Castrol
BRIDGESTONE
SAN
ZX GTP
technology on the track that will someday affect every Nissan we put on the road; and to take on the best and win.
When it comes to performance and technology... the Name is Nissan.
NISSAN
NISSAN

Although it never went into anything approaching mass production, the 1967 Toyota 2000GT was one of the first cars from Japan to establish an aesthetic presence. With it, Toyota, and by extension, Japan, demonstrated it could match anything that the world offered.

cans fill the management spots, with Japanese providing technical support and product development.

Lamm, still the president, says Subaru can't reasonably go head-to-head against the big companies, so it exploits whatever niches are left open. It was among the first, for instance, to offer a four-wheel-drive passenger car.

Looming in the Background

Like so many Japanese automotive companies, Suzuki began as something else. Its particular founder, Michio Suzuki, was in the loom business—although history does not record whether he and Sakichi Toyoda knew each other. By the early '50s Suzuki was turning to transportation with a series of small motorbikes; in 1954 the company name was changed to Suzuki Motor Company Ltd., and the next year a tiny car was introduced in the Japanese 360 class.

Now, in addition to the company's motorcycles and cars, there are small trucks and off-road vehicles, outboard motors, small industrial engines, gasoline-powered water pumps and electrical generators.

The largest Suzuki automobile, known as the SA310 in Japan, is a small hatchback coupe with an innovative three-cylinder engine of one-liter displacement. Many lessons learned by the motorcycle division have been incorporated into the SA310, such as a hollow camshaft and crankshaft and other sophisticated weight-reduction measures. In the United States, the car is

The 1917 Mitsubishi Model A (right) was based on a Fiat design and had oak bodywork covered with lacquer. Mitsubishi, one of Japan's industrial giants, was late in the U.S. market. But it's making an impact with cars like the 1986 Starion.

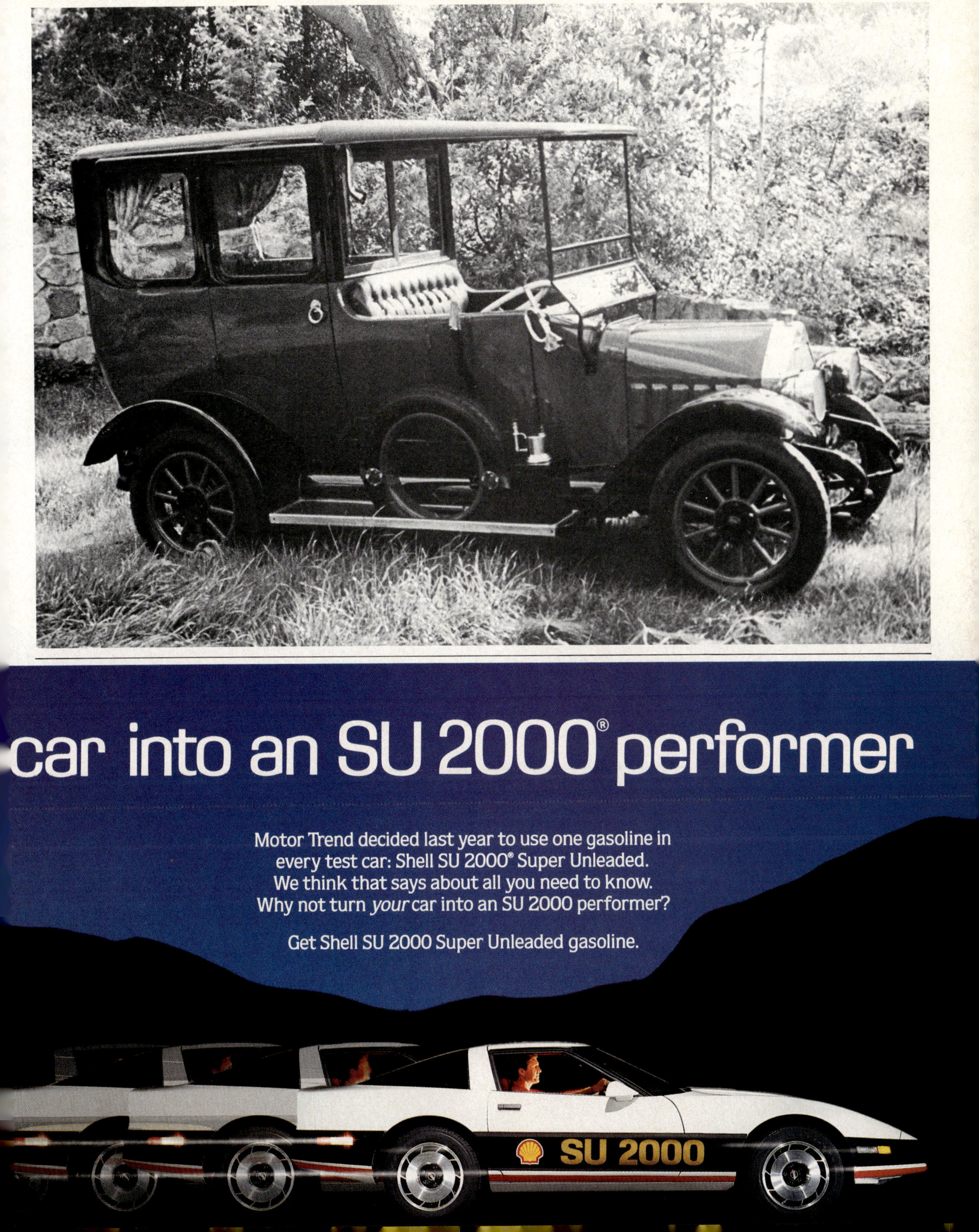

car into an SU 2000® performer

Motor Trend decided last year to use one gasoline in
every test car: Shell SU 2000® Super Unleaded.
We think that says about all you need to know.
Why not turn *your* car into an SU 2000 performer?

Get Shell SU 2000 Super Unleaded gasoline.

4WD TURBO

sold by General Motors as the Chevrolet Sprint. Compared to the big Chevies with which it shares showroom floor space, the Sprint is short on luxury and convenience features. But its low price and fuel economy make it attractive.

Of those Japanese companies not selling cars in the United States, the most important is Daihatsu, which is tied to Toyota and builds a line of small, but technologically advanced sedans geared to suit the special demands of the Japanese domestic market. The old 360 class has long been superseded by a 550 category, which places strict limits on engine displacement and overall size. The advantage of the 550 category is that, unlike for larger cars, a customer living in a large city in Japan needn't show proof of an off-street parking spot before being able to make the purchase.

Daihatsu has always enjoyed a reputation for imaginative small cars. Around 1970, for instance, it was building the Fellow, a 360 mini-car, and from that developed the Fellow SS. At 360 cubic centimeters, its two-stroke twin pumped out a screaming 40 horsepower, a power-per-liter figure that has never been approached by any other production car, even turbos!

Currently, Daihatsu's 550-class cars are the Mira and Cuore, which are for the Japanese market only. But the Charade could be made to work in America if the Suzuki SA310/Chevy Sprint can; the Charade is a highly developed little car, with a one-liter, three-cylinder engine of an overhead camshaft layout—smiliar to the Suzuki.

Any discussion of Japan's automotive industry is incomplete without mention of the concept of Japan, Inc. To westerners, doing business with Japan is often puzzling because it seems not as if you are doing business with one person or firm, but with the whole country. There is some truth to this. The Japanese automotive industry is not without its corporate ties and is more closely knit, certainly, than businesses in America. Then too, in Japan it is not unusual to find banks with more than passing interests in the operations of an automaker. There are the obvious tie-ups, like Yamaha building engines for Toyota. And then, well, "heavies": Mitsubishi Heavy Industries, Fuji Heavy Industries, Kawasaki Heavy Industries. At times it seems like Japan Heavy Industries.

Really, what the westerner is dealing

with is a different form of cooperation. And this close cooperation is probably a necessity of survival. Consider some facts: The country is essentially without natural resources or raw materials, except people of course. Eighty million of them live on a few islands about the size of California, but so ruggedly mountainous and forested that only about 20 percent of that area can be lived on. Japan is crammed full; its only option is to manufacture and export.

And the government played no small part, particularly in the automotive industry through the well-known MITI—the all-powerful Japanese Ministry of International Trade and Industry. Very broadly speaking, MITI is a regulatory agency like America's Interstate Commerce Commission or Department of Commerce; it handles antitrust cases like our Department of Justice and has the promotional functions of the British Board of Trade. If it has to do with cars and Japan, MITI is involved, from setting limits for voluntary restraint agreements to deciding where rear view mirrors should be placed on the fenders.

All this together can often make it seem as if Japan, Inc. is a very real thing. But, perhaps, without Japan, Inc. there would be no Inc. in Japan at all. **MT**

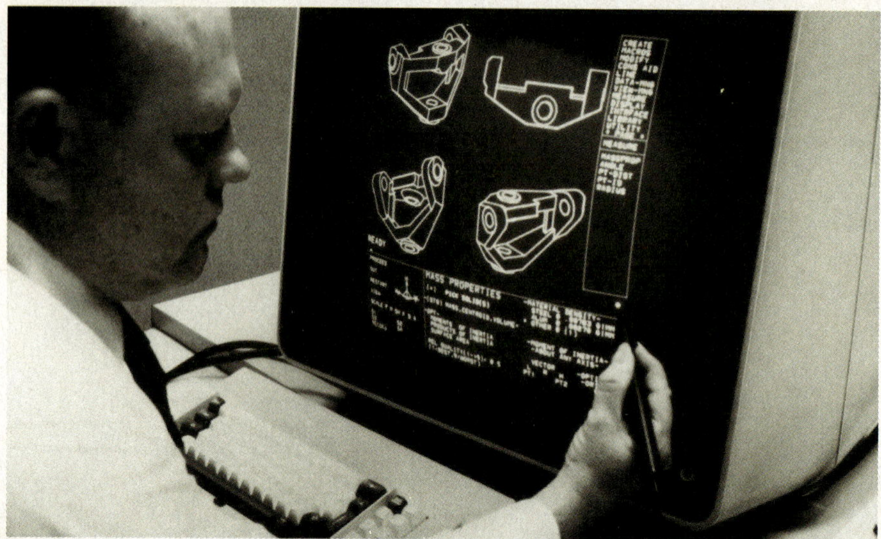

HIGH (AND LOW) TECH

The automobile might still be a clever toy were it not for a series of technological breakthroughs.

By Paul van Valkenburgh

□ What a golden age of discovery we live in. Even scientists, mechanics and engineers are astounded at how quickly the latest technology finds its way into everyday automobiles: engines with overhead cams and four valves per cylinder, air suspension, four-wheel drive. Under development are continuously variable transmissions (CVT), hybrid gas/electric vehicles, wheel-hub motors, and four-wheel steering.

But how many of us know that you could get a four-valve, overhead-cam engine in the 1917 Drexel, air suspension on the 1915 Pneumobile, gas/electric hybrid power on the 1917 Woods, wheel-hub motors on the 1899 Hub electric, CVT on a 1907 ABC—and the 1901 Cotta had four-wheel drive *and* steering.

It's true—the more things change, the more they stay the same. Yet the automobile might still be a novelty if it weren't for many technological breakthroughs over the years. But how do you pin them down? By patent? Some patents preceded working models by decades. By the first running prototype? Some were one-off oddities; others were built and forgotten. Some important developments in auto technology had been common practice in other areas.

Credit has often gone to people or companies that picked up ideas that had been abandoned by others as unworkable at the time. So it's not the fine point of who did it first that's important; it's the technologies themselves. They made the automobile more accessible, acceptable and desirable.

1895—Michelin Brothers Try Pneumatic Tires on Race Car

Actually, the pneumatic tire was invented 50 years earlier, for use on carriages, and even that was predated by Charles Goodyear's 1839 discovery of vulcanization. But neither the technology nor the demand was significant until bicycles became popular in the 1870s. J.B. Dunlop eventually made a practical pneumatic tire for his son's tricycle, and patented it in 1888. The automobile may have seemed like a hopeless market then, due to its rarity and weight, but the Michelin brothers took out a Dunlop license, and tried pneumatic tires in racing

---

OPPOSITE PAGE:
Electronic brains that control every vital function of a car's anatomy are but the latest in a long line of technological advances.

The new Mercury Sable is truly a sweeping automotive advance. One that shows we've kept up with the times as much as you have.

You see it in Sable's wind-slippery shape that moves through the air more efficiently than any other domestic sedan. With flush glass all around to further smooth the passage of air and greatly lessen wind noise.

You see it in Sable's dramatic new "laser" lightbar extending between the flush-mounted aerodynamic headlamps. For efficient engine cooling, air is drawn up from underneath. So Sable's front end can be sculpted smoothly and smartly.

It has front-wheel drive, of course. Driven by a 3.0-liter V-6 that's new right down to the dipstick. Its advanced, electronically controlled fuel injection is of the sequential port variety.

To ensure that this remarkable new Sable rides and handles as good as it looks, there's four-wheel independent rear suspension working in combination with gas pressurized shocks.

Inside, everyone will think of Sable as a driver's car. Except the passengers. Both bucket and split bench seats are available with power lumbar support. Controls are positioned right where your hands and feet would like

1986 Mercury Sable.
You've reshaped your thinking.
Obviously, so have we.

Sophisticated new shape. The 1986 Mercury Sable.

...em to be. Backlighted instruments tell you just about everything you ever wanted to know about a car's condition.

Also, you can order a defrosting windshield that uses a new electronic film to clear your vision —one of the many conveniences offered on Sable.

But perhaps most important of all, Sable is a Mercury. And Mercury's commitment to quality isn't just something written on paper—it's built into the car.

You're ready for a car that suits today. The car you're ready for is ready for you December 26. The 1986 Mercury Sable.

For more information, call 1-800 MERCFAX

LINCOLN-MERCURY DIVISION 

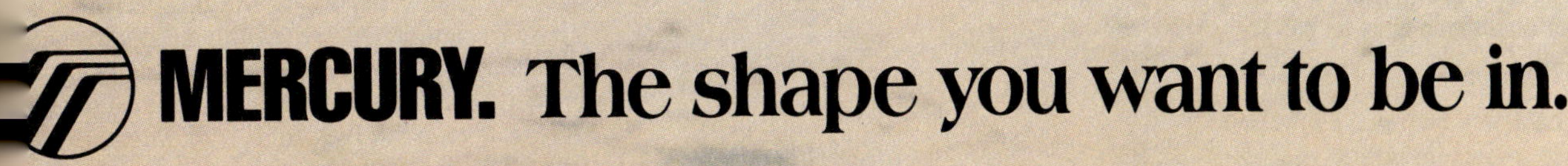

MERCURY. The shape you want to be in.

—unsuccessfully at first. In their first race, which they lost to a solid-rubber tired Panhard, they shredded 22 tubes in less than 732 miles. But within a year, the Lanchester automobile was in production on Dunlop pneumatics.

Development of the pneumatic tire may be second in importance only to the gasoline engine in making the automobile practical. And in spite of the apparent similarity of all tires, the technological advancements have been dramatic. At first, hose-like tires were held on with glue and wrapped with tape. Then in 1890 the idea of wire beads to hold the tire in a wheel flange appeared, reducing tire repair to less than a one-hour task. Surprisingly, it wasn't until the 1900s that manufacturers realized that their smooth tires could get better traction (and product identication) by the use of some sort of "non-skid" tread pattern. At the time, a reasonable tire life, disregarding tube punctures and patches, could be one or two thousand miles.

By the '20s, the conventional tire was refined to the point where it would last 10-15,000 miles, as manufacturers moved away from large diameters and high pressures, to the modern "balloon tire." Then very little happened for 30 years, aside from wartime experiments with rubber substitutes and compounds. Finally, in the postwar decade, the tubeless tire was perfected, and radial, belted and steel-cord bodies were developed. In the most recent three decades, it seems as if auto racing has had the greatest influence by demonstrating the value of larger footprints, wider rims, and lower section heights. It would be an interesting experiment to see if race cars of the '50s wouldn't be faster on production tires of today.

1902—Disc Brake Patented

The earliest automobiles didn't go fast enough to worry about stopping, and at that, their metal-on-metal or leather-on-metal band-wrapped drums were hardly less effective than smooth tires in mud or horseshoes on manure-coated cobblestones. But the stink of burning leather led Herbert Frood (Ferodo) to use asbestos in both brake bands and clutch discs by the 1900s. Still there were considerable problems in finding enough application force. The band-wrapped drum had a sort of self-servo action in the forward direction, but heaven help anyone who had to stop on a hill because in the reverse direction they had only a fraction of the effectiveness.

Advancements came rapidly in the first two decades, and internal-expanding drum brakes came out in 1905. Of course, rear brakes alone were considered adequate until power and speed rose, and the 1919 Hispano-Suiza initiated a four-wheel servo system. Along the way, they and Lozier had also experimented with water-cooled drums to cure the chatter of overheated metal-on-metal brakes. Finally, by 1921, Duesenberg and Bugatti solved the problems of force multiplication and flexible links with hydraulic actuation. Due to their lack of servo action, discs were not commonly used till power boosting became available (although the 1907 Northern did have a compressed-air boost system). It wasn't until 1953 that the C-Jag popularized disc brakes with a victory at Le Mans.

1911—Self-Starter Perfected

The hand-crank was such a vicious weapon that a large number of other starting techniques were tried pre-Kettering. There were mechanical levers and kick-starters operable from the driver's seat, and pneumatic and explosive gas starters, as well as crude electric motor starters going back to 1896. So Kettering didn't invent the starter so much as he developed it. He used his considerable electrical experience to prove that he could drastically overload a small motor (by current engineering standards) for a short period without burning it out. Within a few years, nearly every car in America but the Model T had an electric starter, and the automobile was made accessible to the non-athletic public.

But the starter wouldn't have happened if Kettering hadn't laid the groundwork with his independent research in ignitions, batteries and generators. Magnetos, the first spark igniters, were inefficient at staring speeds and unsuitable for battery charging. By 1909, Kettering and his engineering friends had essentially eliminated the drawbacks of the breaker-arm and coil

TOP:
Edouard Michelin (at the tiller) and brother Andre first used pneumatic tires in 1895.

ABOVE:
This 1924 Flint Six was one of the first cars to use steel disc wheels instead of spokes.

George Chester Mills (first man on left), oversees chassis and body mating on Ford's innovative moving assembly line in 1913.

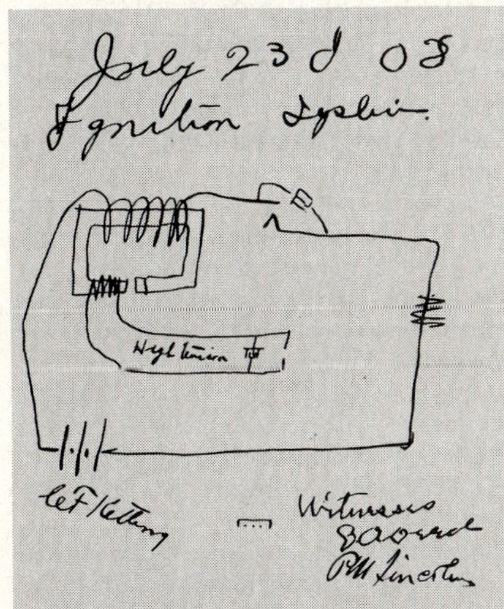

ABOVE LEFT:
C.F. "Boss" Kettering's original drawing for the patent for the automatic starter.

ABOVE RIGHT:
The "Boss" himself tests an early version of the starter while Delco colleagues look on.

LEFT:
The first car to use the starter was the 1912 Cadillac. It earned Cadillac the prestigious Dewar Trophy for the second time.

system, which was to continue almost unchanged for the next half century. His first sale to Cadillac was the beginning of "Delco," and established his credentials for the electric-starter program.

Kettering's first starter was actually a combination motor-generator which was coupled directly to the crank and never disengaged, and therefore was not optimized for either starting or generating. Vincent Bendix, who had tried to manufacture his own automobile as early as 1907, recognized this key deficiency and set out to capitalize on it. By 1913, he had developed a disengaging mechanism, but it required a great deal of hand cutting and fitting—until he discovered it could be easily machined by the makers of bicycle coaster brakes. The first of the famous "Bendix drives"—which are now almost universal—appeared on the 1914 Chevrolet.

1913—Ford Starts Up His First Assembly Line

Henry Ford, significant as he was, didn't *invent* the assembly line, or even mass production. He merely popularized it and exploited it. Ransom Olds produced the first low-priced car in large volumes, selling over 10,000 curved-dash Oldses between 1901 and 1904. In doing so, Olds pioneered the moving automotive assembly line, which required labor specialization and the delivery of parts and materials directly to the workers. Simultaneously, Henry Leland is credited with initiating precision interchangeable parts on his Cadillacs, although the technology was already 50 years old in the firearms industry.

After two business failures, Henry Ford started his third company in 1903, with engines and chassis built by the Dodge brothers. Experimenting with the market, he settled on the absolutely lowest-price segment with his Model T in 1908. With that, he established "mass production" on a level never seen before—or perhaps since. In 1923, Ford produced over two million vehicles of the same model, a record that may be considered unmatched today (depending on the definition of "one model"). He was able to do this by relying heavily on outside suppliers until he had the capital and time to take over their operations. His policy of minimal changes in a simple, basic model—15 million of them over almost two decades—created a familiarity unequaled until the VW *Bug*.

1924—Dodge Produces First All-Steel Body

As usual, the proper credit is slightly misplaced. The first patent for an all-steel body was issued in 1900, and the first running all-steel vehicle was a 1903 Vauxhall. However, to understand Dodge's claim, one must consider the Vauxhall was an open two-seater fabricated from flat sheetmetal panels, and was not a closed, stamped-steel body. The Vauxhall was also the first "unit construction," or monocoque, without separate frame rails. This construction method was occasionally used over the years in such cars as the 1913 Lagonda and 1921 Lancia for weight- or cost-saving reasons.

Although wood was commonly used for reinforcement of body panels, it gradually diminished in popularity, finally being used just as roof support, until it disappeared entirely on the 1924 Dodge. This transition to stamped steel is given credit for burying 90 percent of the smaller manufacturers. The use of stamped-steel compound curve body panels and their inner reinforcements required a considerable tooling investment which only the best capitalized mass-production manufacturers could afford. The number of auto producers in America dropped from a peak of about 500 to less than 50 by 1927. Meanwhile, Budd Co., which supplied bodies to Dodge, built a unit-construction front-wheel-drive prototype to promote the concept. Citroën, however, was the only company with enough foresight to bring the design out as their 1934 Traction Avant.

Along with the enclosed all-steel body, one of the greatest accident-protection advances ever, was the introduction of safety glass. We can take it for granted today, but the incredible hazard of traveling at any speed surrounded by plate glass windows is hard to imagine. In the 1900s, a French chemist named Benedictus discovered laminated glass when a celluloid-lined beaker broke without shattering. His eventual product, a glass-celluloid-glass sandwich called Triplex, was not rapidly accepted, however, because it turned brown as it aged. As an alternative, the 1926 Stutz tried using plate glass reinforced with a fine steel mesh. Although state laws began requiring safety glass in the '30s, it wasn't until 1945 that a stable vinyl interlayer was perfected. Meanwhile, in 1932, tempered glass was introduced. This is a single-layer glass in which the surfaces are toughened by rapidly quenching them into extreme compression. However, due to its tendency to disintegrate into opacity when nicked, it has never been popular for windshields.

1908—First Concrete-Paved Mile: Woodward Ave. in Detroit

Actually, the earliest impetus for better roads came from bicyclists in the 1880s. Long before production automobiles in America, there were millions of bicycles, and the League of American Wheelmen was a strong lobbying force. In 1893, 220 feet of paving was laid in Bellefontaine, Ohio, and the Federal Office of Road Inquiry was organized to promote state highway departments. One can almost imagine small groups of automobile owners pleading for marked-off car paths at the side of new bikeways. The first national survey of roads in America in 1904 showed that out of two million miles, only about two percent were even surfaced with macadam. In 1921 the Federal Highway Act was passed, and by 1927 the first paved transcontinental highway was completed.

Paved roads or no, the ride quality of the first automobiles is hard to imagine. With high-pressure tires, high-friction leaf springs, or totally undamped coil springs, they were seldom much better than a horse carriage. But at twice the speed of a horse, they were lethal. As early as 1900 the value of ride damping was recognized, but only in terms of mechanical friction. A Mors racing car is reported to have used auxiliary friction dampers in 1903. These were usually lever arms with wood or asbestos friction plates at the pivot axis. In the '20s, "rebound snubbers" were common aftermarket items, using a web rebound strap pulling on a one-way friction clutch. Eventually, the Houdaille lever-arm hydraulic damper was developed, which had a double-acting rotary vane in a cylindrical housing. Delco also tried a double piston cam-actuated damper before the industry settled on the familiar double-acting piston design.

1910—DeDion V-8 Into Production

The gasoline engine preceded the automobile, giving it a history of its own. But certain developments were necessary to make it superior to its steam and electric challengers in the automobile. The search for "adequate" power with acceptable weight led to multiple cylinders, first as inline 2's, 4's, 6's, and 8's. Between 1905 and 1909, the V-8 was tried by Rolls, Adams, and Hewitt, but DeDion was the first in series production. It was soon improved upon and popularized in America in the 1914 Cadillac—with Charles Kettering's engineering support.

Kettering can also be credited, along with Dr. Thomas Midgely, with the sensational development of anti-knock gasoline—which has since been realized as a "dubious achievement." Over a period of ten years, Kettering's lab experimented with over 30,000 chemical additives before coming up with tetraethyl lead. In 1923 Ethyl Corp. began marketing the additive in spite of public opposition over its known poisonous characteristics.

As a part of the research, Kettering had also developed the standard single-cylinder variable-compression knock-test engine. Production engines of the period had compression ratios of 4 or 5 to 1, but by the '30s G.M. had an experimental engine running at 10 to 1, and in 1947 had gotten it up to 12.5 to 1 (while 7 to 1 was still common in production). Perhaps more than any other factor, increased compression was responsible for increased power and efficiency—at least until the emission regulations of the '70s. Until then, typical engine power had increased at about one horsepower per liter per year for 80 years.

As combustion chambers were made correspondingly smaller, the valves had to be moved overhead. Although overhead valves (as well as camshafts) are almost as old as the automobile, Detroit's ohv V-8's of the '50s (starting with the '49 Olds Rocket) began the real revolution. Hot-rodders, however, were put off by the increasing use of hydraulic tappets in the valve train. They had been first used in the 1929 Pierce-Arrow, and became more and more popular because they decreased both noise and the frequency of tuneups.

Fuel induction, in the right ratio at the right time, has been a challenge from the first to the present. The earliest drip or wick fuel metering devices were soon replaced by spray nozzles, often powered by a pressure pump instead of venturi vacuum—making fuel injection almost as old as the carburetor. But to eliminate the need for a fuel pump of any kind on less expensive cars, the carb was often mounted at crankcase level and fed by gravity from the fuel tank. Then came the vacuum-powered

fuel pump, and the carb could go back up on top where it belonged.

For years, engine control was a manual nightmare, with throttle controls, chokes, auxiliary air, mixture control, spark control, and occasionally a compression release for starting. And even at that, there was no allowance for acceleration enrichment or high-load metering. Gradually these requirements came under control of a very complex carburetion system, using combinations of electro-hydraulic-pneumatic sensing and operation. Fuel injection was usually just a few steps behind in cost and a few steps ahead in performance. Bosch developed injection for diesels as early as 1912, but it wasn't until 1954 that Mercedes-Benz could justify gasoline injec-

tion on their 300SL.

1937—Olds Offers First Automatic Transmission

The first automatic transmission is almost as hard to pinpoint as the first automobile. The earliest slipping friction drives—belt or clutch—might be considered automatic, and many companies offered variable sheave pulleys or conical friction disc contact to give continuously variable ratios. Even the two-speed planetary gearbox with clutch pedal selection was common in 1900. For more skillful drivers, and for heavier vehicles requiring more than two ratios, the standard spur gear manual was more popular for many decades. Then, in 1929, Cadillac offered a synchromesh 3-

ABOVE:
Though Vauxhall built the first all-steel car in 1903, and Dodge did it in volume in 1924, Budd gets credit for the first all-steel, unit-construction car. Budd couldn't sell the prototype in the U.S. and the '34 Ford look-alike became Citroën's *Traction Avant* 7CV.

LEFT:
Progress in tire development owes a lot to racing. Wide, low-profile tires were first proven in competition, like the Goodyear "Gatorbacks," first used as F1 rain tires.

speed which made it practically impossible for even a novice to clash gears, upshift or downshift.

Through the '30s, a number of companies tried to market a self-shifting transmission, but the Olds semi-automatic gets the credit. This was a 4-speed planetary gearbox with automatic oil pressure actuation—but it still required a conventional clutch to get it rolling. As soon as this unit was released, G.M. immediately began a program to get rid of the clutch entirely, and by 1940 it was replaced by a fluid coupling. The coupling was actually a torque converter, which gave an extra torque multiplication from a dead stop. This was the Hydra-Matic, essentially unchanged in the last 45 years except for the addition of a mechanical lockup device in the torque converter to improve fuel efficiency.

1926—Radio and Heater Available

There is a long list of automotive equipment that we now take for granted which was one considered aftermarket or optional accessories. The windshield wiper, for example, was patented in 1903, but for a couple of decades was available only as a hand-operated mechanism. Eventually vacuum motors were offered as a safety feature to keep both hands free for steering and shifting, and, of course, the electric motor finally eliminated the problem of vacuum loss under acceleration.

The rear view mirror was suggested in a *Popular Mechanics* article in 1907. However, its greatest value is perhaps the justification for "racing improves the breed," when one was used to help win the first *Indy 500* in 1911. Electric headlights were not available until 1911, having been preceded by incredibly ineffective and inconvenient oil and acetylene lamps.

The hot-water heater came into common use in the mid-twenties after the invention of the automatic engine thermostat in 1920. Until then, hot water bottles or hot

air blowing off the engine were considered adequate. And as early as 1938, Nash was offering an air-conditioner.

Car radios had to overcome major ignition interference problems on their way into popular acceptance. At first they had to be operated with the engine off, or with separate batteries, or a motor-generator to provide electrical isolation. By the '30s, vibrators, resistors, and whip antennas were providing unheard-of reception, and it seemed that automotive luxury had "gone about as far as it could go."

1945—Engineers Turned Loose on Consumer Products

The war decade was sort of a transition period for the automobile. It had become an adequate, comfortable means of transportation by more-or-less the blacksmith method of trail-and-error. Now it was time to develop a scientific approach. In this era, it's even harder to give specific credit

Over the years any number of attempts have been made to find an alternative to the internal combustion engine. None has succeeded, including this experimental 1963 turbine-powered car from Chrysler.

or discovery dates for innovation; it was a cumulative science, which overlapped individual or even corporate boundaries. Perhaps partly due to the Selden patent debacle of the early years, automotive engineers tended to interact more freely and pool their knowledge as much as possible.

Serious automotive research was impossible until the '30s due to a lack of basic knowledge about tire characteristics. Only when the tire companies began measuring tire performance on instrumented drum tests could the engineers develop ride and handling theories. A great deal of the

Put a $25 lid on major car repair costs.

With Ford ESP Plus,™ you never pay more than $25—whether it's for a $600 repair or a $60 repair. You pay no parts or labor charges. Just a $25 deductible each repair visit. No matter how many different covered parts need to be fixed.

ESP Plus covers thousands of parts—even high tech components—for up to five years or 60,000 miles, whichever comes first.

ESP Plus is only one of the Ford Extended Service Plans available. There's even a plan that provides scheduled maintenance and no deductible. That's ESP Care.™

If you own (or plan to own soon) a new Ford car or light truck, Mercury, Lincoln or Merkur, find out more about the peace of mind that ESP protection brings. See one of the over 6,100 Ford and Lincoln-Mercury dealers throughout the U.S. and Canada who offer the Ford Extended Service Plan. Or call toll-free 1-800-FORD-ESP. The Ford Extended Service Plan—it's the only plan with the Ford name on it.

Buckle up—together we can save lives.

Ford Extended Service Plan 

groundwork in chassis dynamics was established at the new G.M. Engineering Research Labs and Cornell Aero Labs under the direction of Maurice Olley. Olley's experience at Rolls-Royce and Cadillac led to the elimination of the dreaded "shimmy," with rediscovery of independent front suspensions. Naturally, independent suspension is as old as the automobile, but its dynamic advantages were not fully recognized until G.M. brought it out on the entire line in 1934.

Along the way, automotive engineers developed a whole family of terms which were to become common among the car cult. "Ackerman steering," where the in-side front wheel turns at a greater angle, started with the Ackerman automobile in 1897. Olley is credited with the terms over-steer and understeer although early tiller-steered auto manufacturers such as Lanchester warned drivers that lateral g-forces on the tiller would cause the car to "over-steer" in a corner. G.M. built testing devices to measure the "polar moment" (or inertial resistance to turning), ride rates, and roll rate distribution of entire vehicles. Eventually, Olley produced a multi-volume automotive vehicle dynamics tutorial for new G.M. engineers, and most of the knowledge filtered out in SAE papers.

In the middle of this period, another G.M. engineer made quite a name for himself in vehicle suspensions. Earle MacPherson was chief engineer on a postwar Chevrolet prototype which incorporated an innovative strut-type suspension at all four wheels. When the project was canceled, MacPherson went to work for Ford and brought out his invention on the 1952 British Fords. Since then, the MacPherson strut has almost become the industry standard in front suspensions due to its low cost, simplicity, and space-saving design.

1952—Chrysler Offers Power Steering

Once the automobile became simple

TOP:
A 1982 Chevrolet Celebrity hits the wall at 30 mph without major injury to occupants as part of tests mandated by federal standards.

ABOVE:
General Motors built this Experimental Safety Vehicle (ESV) as part of a government program to develop more crashworthy cars.

enough for novices to operate, the drive was on to make large cars controllable by the "weaker sex." Pneumatic-boosted brakes, of course, originated in 1907, but power steering development had to go through mechanical energy boosters such as recirculating ball gears and rotary friction drivers before Chrysler announced the first hydraulic system. Power steering was actually preceded by power windows which were introduced on the 1946 Daimler and became popular on the 1948 Packard. Whether subsequent accessories such as power seats, mirrors, trunk lids and headlight retractors prove helpful to human development remains to be seen.

1959—Front-Wheel-Drive Rediscovered in Mini

When Alec Issigonis brought out his new transverse engine front-wheel-drive Mini in 1959, it was technically interesting—but hardly innovative. In fact, even the original 1877 Selden patent described a transverse engine front-wheel drive, although with a solid, swiveling front axle. Also, in the 1900s there were some technically sophisticated race cars with FWD transverse V-4s. Inline engines driving the front wheels were not uncommon—the most notable being the Cord and Indy Millers—but the true precursor of the production transverse FWD was the 1931 DKW. Issigonis popu-

larized the concept for truly practical applications, however. He is now recognized as a prophet without enough honor in his own time.

1968—Federal Motor Vehicle Safety Standards

Automakers never intentionally built "unsafe" cars. Common-sense self-preservation led to safety glass and better brakes and tires. But early attempts to market the simplest safety devices, such as seat belts, were failures in the 1949 Nash and 1956 Ford. Anything more elaborate was considered a waste of time—until the Corvair lawsuits redefined the situation. The Feds came up with a mandatory list of crash-avoidance and crash-protection standards which at first appeared impractical to implement and pay for.

Crash-avoidance included such requirements as: windshield and mirror visibility, brake redundancy and warnings, standardized controls, minimums for lights and reflectors, and tire ratings. Crash-protection was more expensive, with standards for roof crush, side intrusion, windshield intrusion, steering wheel displacement, headrests, and seat, seatbelt, and door-latch strength. Perhaps a little less meaningful were requirements for non-reflecting trim, non-projecting hubcaps, speedometer maximums, 5-mph bumpers, interior flamma-

bility, and passing-distance data.

All of the standards were originally developed somewhat intuitively, and some turned out to be not too cost-effective, with demonstrated implementation costs of hundreds of thousands of dollars per statistical life saved—a cost that most customers would not voluntarily incur. But no one will deny that the net result has been the greatest saving in lives and permanent disability in the history of the automobile.

1974—Aerodynamics Re-evaluated for Fuel Economy

The importance of air drag was known to the first owner/builders who raced their vehicles—even at 50 to 60 mph. But a distinction should be made between early attempts at intuitive streamlining and the modern scientific approach to measurable aerodynamics (perhaps also between racing applications and the less dramatic attempts to improve highway performance). Eventually the early racers went beyond the removal of fenders and pointing of the nose and tail, and wind tunnels came into the picture, especially in Germany. As early as 1919, Edmund Rumpler began building automobiles with a patented vertical airfoil shape. His contemporaries, Paul Jaray and Wunibald Kamm, introduced three-dimensional shapes and the familiar Kamm (cutoff) tails which were incorporated into

Advances in manufacturing techniques and materials have spurred auto development. The Pontiac Fiero was designed to use plastics and revolutionary assembly methods.

many other production vehicles.

After the war, an incredible lode of German automotive wind-tunnel data was recovered by Koenig-Fachsenfeld, and published as *Aerodynamik des Kraftfarzeugs.* None of this was to have any lasting effect, however, since aerodynamics was considered no more marketable (in mass production) than safety—as "proven" by failure of the 1934 Chrysler Airflow. In spite of academic and industry engineering research, average production aerodynamic drag continued to be about twice that of Rumpler's first automobiles. Only when the fuel shortages of 1974 made economy a selling point did automakers react. Gradually, low aerodynamic drag coefficients have been pursued and have attained a status previously given to horsepower and mpg.

1963—Transistor Applied to Automobiles

After the self-starter and electric lights, not much happened in automotive electrics for half a century. Then in the mid-'60s, modern electronic developments like the transistor and integrated circuits started to transfer over. The first application was transistorized breaker circuits, soon followed by breakerless distributors. Engineers were rapidly finding ways to make electronic circuits take over control of one system after another. Engine timing and carburetion were first, calling upon new types of electronic sensors and actuators. But early attempts were hampered by the imprecision and unreliability of analog circuit designs.

It wasn't until digital electronics became more durable and commonly available that actual "computers" or microprocessors could be used in the comparatively hostile automotive environment. At that point, engineers got serious about truly sophisticated applications, not only in the engine, but in anti-lock brakes and automatic fault diagnosis. Now it appears that the computer/communications revolution may be superseding transportation as the world's most significant industry. As a clue to the future, automotive industry giants are adapting by investing more heavily in such fields as electronics, computers, and artificial intelligence.   **MT**

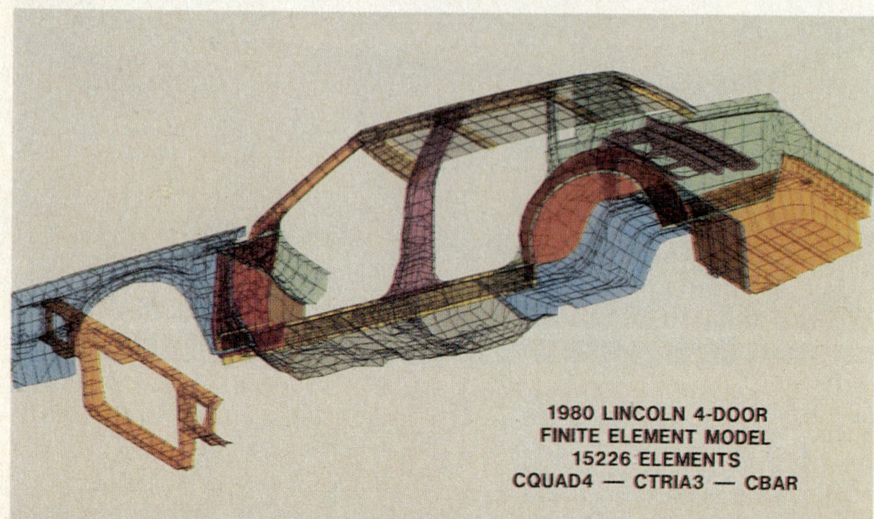

ABOVE:
Aerodynamics is as much an art as a science. Research vehicles like this BMW are used to refine shapes in the wind tunnel.

LEFT:
This mathematical model of a Lincoln lets engineers use computers to simulate a variety of stresses and loads quickly and easily.

THE GOOD OL' BOYS

How America's home-grown brand of racing went from the still-on-the-hill to the super-speedways.

By William Neely

☐ It is difficult to put a handle on where or even when NASCAR got started. If pressed for a date, you would have to say December 14, 1947, because that is when the organizational meeting of NASCAR was held in Daytona Beach, Florida. But the spirit of NASCAR went back a long time before that.

The meeting, which was held appropriately in the lounge of the Streamline Hotel, where all the race drivers gathered daily to drink and live it up, was called to order by Bill France, who also operated the lounge. It was time, they decided, to add some order to the chaos called stock car racing that was taking over the South.

Some racing historians say that it all began on the beach at Daytona in madcap modified races; surely, the spirit of NAS-CAR was there. But, even before that, names like Lee Petty and Buck Baker and Red Byron were well-known in Southern racing circles, some for legendary exploits on back highways at night. The spirit, too, was there as they held their informal drag races. In fact, back roads may well bring us to the real roots of NASCAR because, assuredly, the spirit was there with the boys who ran moonshine.

Names like Junior Johnson, Bob Flock, Buddy Shuman and Curtis Turner were associated with whiskey-running long before they became stock car racing greats. Some of their wildest and certainly bravest deeds were done on dark back roads of the Virginias and the Carolinas, running wide open, often with their headlights off and a Fed hot on their tail.

But how did these men get to NAS-CAR? It wasn't a direct route, but it was a highly predictable one. As more and more dirt tracks sprang up, the lure was too great for many of the whiskey-runners. They had to show the world what they could do with a car. After all, there weren't any grandstands on those old back roads.

still had not brought a lot of order to stock car racing, so France and some of his board decided to hold a race with new cars, and this time, not on sand. It would be something that people could identify with; they could watch cars like the ones they drove to work each day.

They chose a three-quarter-mile dirt track off Wilkinson Boulevard in Charlotte, North Carolina, as the place for the first race between "new" stock cars. It was later to be called *Grand National*.

The purse was $6,000 for the June 19, 1949 race, and if the number of people who turned out for it was an indication, the new racing class was an immediate success. The traffic jam was so bad that many of the race cars themselves were unable to get to the track until just before qualifying. You see, since they were strictly stock, many of the race cars were driven to the track, so they were right in there with the fans.

Once the cars got to the track, they encountered the second problem—dust. Nobody dreamed that the track would become as dusty as it did. One observer said, "It looked like somebody had dropped an atomic bomb. It settled down over everything for blocks around, and they had to get the state police to direct traffic. Nobody could see to drive on Wilkinson Boulevard."

"Easily the most intriguing part of the whole affair was how some of the drivers got their race cars," says Bill Tuthill, who was one of the original NASCAR board members. "For example, Tim Flock spotted a couple watching practice from their brand new 1949 Oldsmobile 88, and, do you know, he actually talked them into letting him race it? He qualified third."

Lee Petty planned things a little more in advance. At least, he arranged to borrow a car *before* he got to the track. He figured that a big, heavy car would work best, so he got a 1948 Buick Roadmaster from a friend, and he started practicing with it, right where he had done most of his racing, on the back roads of North Carolina. He and his brother Julie tuned the car for all it was worth. And then they painted a Number 42 on the side of it "because that's the first number that came to mind."

It was to become one of the most famous numbers in NASCAR history.

Glenn Dunnaway got a ride after he got to the track because Hubert Westmoreland had a '47 Ford and nobody to drive it. So, by the time the qualifying was ready to start, 32 drivers had begged, borrowed or maybe even stolen cars.

Bob Flock, who had started from the pole, took the lead, and war hero Red Byron followed him through the first turn. Right behind them was the rest of the Flock family, Tim and Fonty. The crowd· of 13,000 went wild. New-car racing had been born.

Immediately the Ford owners in the stands picked out their heroes, who were driving Fords, of course, and the Chevy owners did the same thing. On the track, other things were happening. Stock sus-

pensions were causing the cars to bounce all over the track, often into each other. It was mayhem, but the crowd loved it.

One car flipped into a clump of bushes and stirred up a huge nest of yellow jackets. The driver didn't get hurt in the crash, but the yellow jackets brought him out of the car as if it were on fire. And, just as quickly as anyone ran over to see if he could help, the swarm of yellow jackets took after him. In a few minutes, there were people running all over the pits, and the fans couldn't tell what was wrong.

Lee Petty moved up through the pack and just as he was about to take the lead, the radius rod broke on the borrowed Buick, and it flipped three times, totally destroying it.

"Suspension failures took most of the cars out of the race," says Tuthill, "At least, that's what the newspapers said. Actually it was more of a case of most of the guys not knowing what to do."

When it was all over, Dunnaway had won the race in his borrowed car. The man who hadn't had a single lap of practice had won the first new-car race in NASCAR history. Or that's the way it seemed.

A post-race inspection revealed that Westmoreland's car had wedged rear springs, which was an old whiskey-runner's trick. Officials felt that it was the reason Dunnaway had been able to handle the corners better than any of the other cars, so they disqualified him and declared Jim Roper, who had come in behind Dunnaway, the winner.

With all of the accidents and the discord about who won the race, it was still a big step forward. There was no doubt in anyone's mind that NASCAR was on its way.

Whether it would have become the giant

of world race-sanctioning bodies that it is today without Darlington is hard to predict, but certainly that racing facility became the icing on Bill France's cake.

Darlington, South Carolina, was not only the site of the first superspeedway specifically designed for stock cars, but it also became the focal point for street-machine speed lovers all over the United States. It became the Indianapolis of the South.

The first race there ignited the nation's love affair with stock car racing, particularly the champions of the underdog.

The story actually began in Winston-Salem, a few days before the race, when Bill France, Curtis Turner, Alvin Hawkins and Johnny Mantz bought a new Plymouth sedan on their way to Darlington.

They paid $1,700 for the Plymouth, and the only reason they bought it was just so they would have something to run around in once they got there. They figured they would either race it on a short track somewhere later or sell it. They really didn't know what they were going to do with it. But the car came in handy. It was always parked outside the Darlington Motel, and any time anybody needed to go after drinks or food or whatever, they took the little black six-cylinder Plymouth. It was their personal taxi. They took it to the Elks Club in Florence. Everywhere.

Mantz was the hot-shot Indy driver, and he had come down to find a ride for the Southern 500, but by the day before the race, he hadn't found one, so he came back to the motel, looking for the Plymouth.

"Where's the Plymouth?" he asked.

"I think somebody took it to town," France said.

"Well, tell them to leave it here when they get back," Mantz said, " 'cause I'm

Fireball Roberts was 17 when this photo was taken in 1948. He went on to become one of the legends of stock-car racing.

Rickie Smith's Motorcraft
Pro Stock Thunderbird

Willy T. Ribbs
Chris Kneifel
SCCA Trans-Am
Mercury Capri

Wally Dallenbach Jr.
John Jones
IMSA Mustang GTO

Ricky Rudd's NASCAR
Motorcraft Thunderbird

All these winners go with winners: Motorcraft parts.

The Motorcraft Mustang didn't win by just a mile at the 1985 Daytona 24-Hour. It left competition 135 miles behind as Dallenbach, Jones and Bundy took the GTO class. The same car also finished miles ahead of competition in the 12 Hours of Sebring. Mercury Capris flying Motorcraft colors are out to capture the SCCA Trans-Am manufacturer's championship again this year. Motorcraft is on the 1985 NASCAR Winston Cup Circuit with Ricky Rudd in his Thunderbird. Rudd, one of the most promising new-comers, is teamed with veteran car builder Bud Moore. Rickie Smith–first Pro Stock driver to break the 180 mph and 8 second barriers—is driving his Pro Stock Motorcraft Thunderbird in '85 NHRA and IHRA events.

All of these are proof positive of Motorcraft parts' exceptional performance under all types of rugged racing conditions. Get Motorcraft's out-to-win performance going for you out on the street. Motorcraft. Quality parts for all makes of cars and trucks.

Motorcraft
EXCEEDS THE NEED

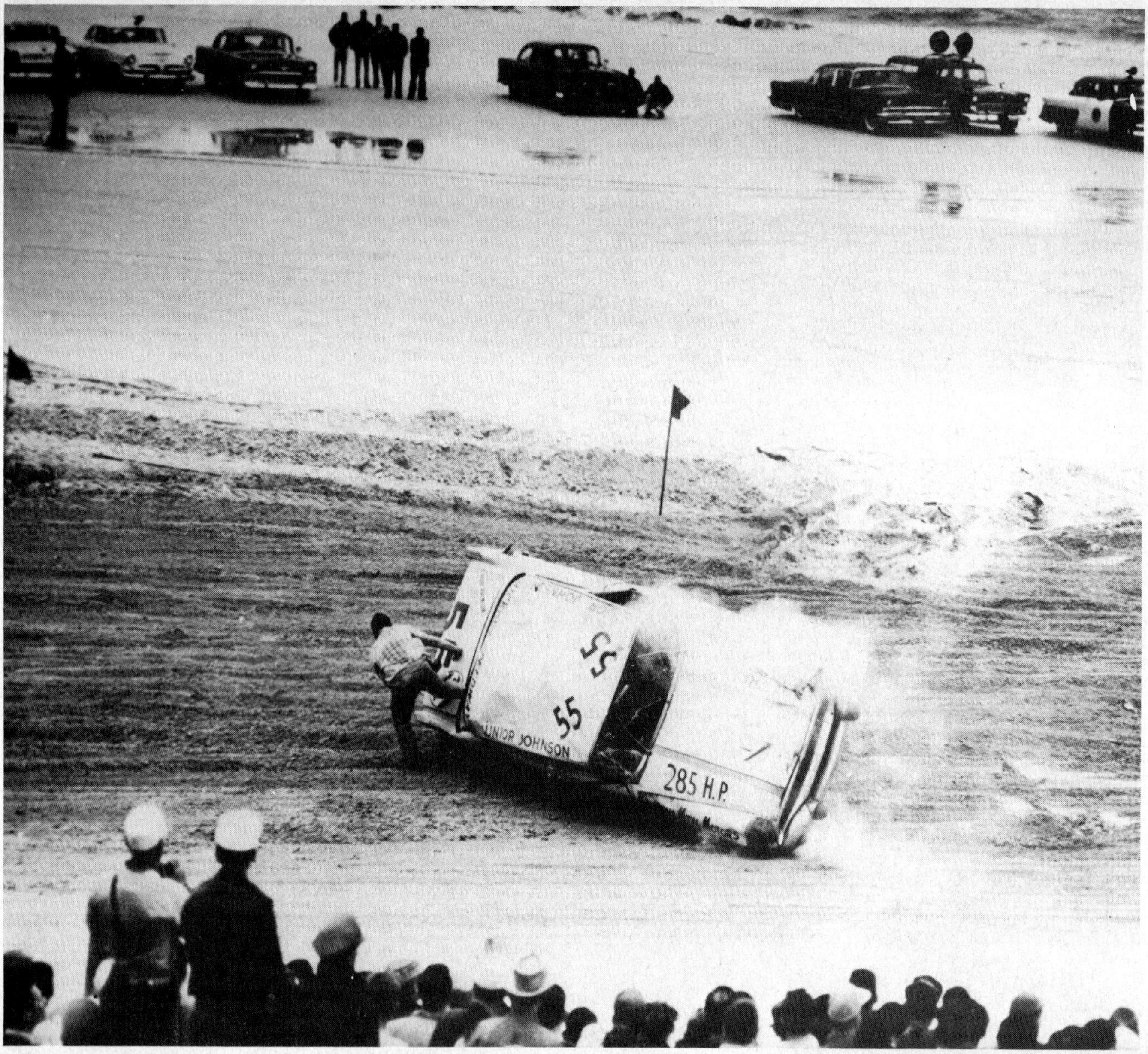

Writer Tom Wolfe called Junior Johnson the last great American hero. Here Junior bails out of one of his racing mishaps.

gonna' race it tomorrow."

To say that everybody thought he had come unglued would be an understatement. But Mantz came up with a set of Firestone Indy tires. He was the only one in the race with anything that even remotely resembled racing tires, although everyone doubted that the tires would make up for the lack of horsepower.

Mantz knew what he had to do, and he put on a show. He drove around the track, way up high, at a steady pace all day—between 70 and 75 miles per hour—and he did everything right. He pitted under caution—which is something he had learned at Indy—and, generally, he made everybody else on the track madder than hell. Particularly after he got the lead.

Red Byron in stock-car expert Red Vogt's Cadillac and Fireball Roberts in an Olds 88 would blow right by him and roar down the back stretch, and then *ker-boom*! a tire would blow and into the pits they would go. And there would be Mantz, tooling along at 72 or 73, right through the turns and down the straightaways, right past the pits where everybody was frantically changing tires.

Curtis Turner said after the race that he knew exactly how many pit stops he had made because he counted the blown-out tires in his pit—27.

When they waved the checkered flag, Mantz had built up a two-lap lead on the field. Everybody was in a state of shock, especially Red Vogt, who kept saying, "There's no way a Plymouth can beat a Cadillac. No way." He demanded that the car be torn down. It was in the rules: "If there is any doubt whether or not a car is in stock configuration, any other car owner or driver may demand an inspection."

The inspection lasted all night. Everything was torn apart—the carburetor, the exhaust, the heads. Everything. The pis-

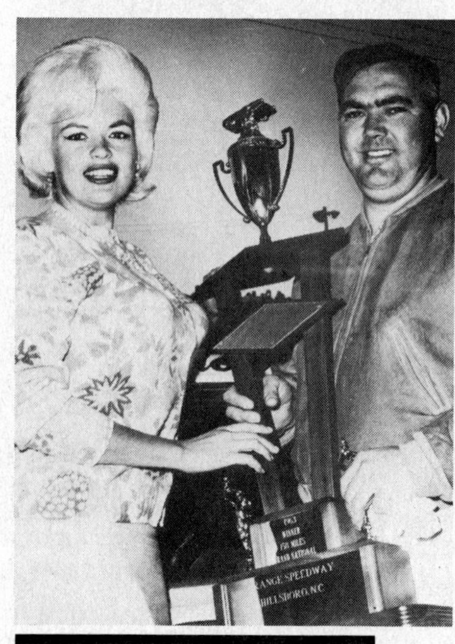

A pair of winners. Jayne Mansfield hands Junior Johnson the victor's loving cup after a 1963 Grand National victory.

TOP:
Just a bunch of country boys? Hardly. In their day the Petty family dominated the sport with a well-drilled team, sophisticated technology, and big sponsor dollars.

ABOVE:
There's never a dull moment in NASCAR racing. The action is sudden, dramatic, and usually ends up with the driver walking away. And the fans love it all.

PHOTO: RON HUSSEY

tons were taken out, the valves, the gas tank, the brakes.

They got the Plymouth dealer out of bed four times to compare valve springs and heads and carbs and suspension parts. They even compared the mill marks on the heads to see if they were turned in the right direction. There was nothing that wasn't stock, so they dumped all the parts in the back seat of the Plymouth and declared Mantz the official winner of the first Southern 500. In the taxi cab. But they never did convince Red Vogt that a Plymouth could outrun a Cadillac.

After Darlington, everything seemed to fall into place. Tracks throughout the Southeast joined the NASCAR ranks. It spread up the East Coast to New England and all up and down the West Coast.

In 1959, the premiere addition to NAS-CAR tracks opened its gates—the Daytona International Speedway. The two-and-one-half-mile track featured the highest banks on the turns of any racing facility in the country, and it didn't take long for the cars to roar past the beach course records. Cotton Owens, in a 1958 Pontiac, turned the fastest *500* qualifying time of 143.198 mph, which was unbelievable considering that this was his average all the way around the tri-oval track. The record for the beach had been set by Paul Goldsmith the year before, also in a 1958 Pontiac. He had been clocked at 140.570, but that had been in a straightaway run down the asphalt section, with no turns.

The stage was set for the inaugural *Daytona 500*.

Had Hollywood written the script for that race, it couldn't have been any more exciting. The lead changed hands almost every other lap until well past the half-way point, when it became a battle between Lee Petty and Johnny Beauchamp. On the last lap, they roared down the tri-oval in front of the grandstands, wheel to wheel. They were still side by side through the first and second turns and down the back straight-away. It was the same through the third and fourth turns. They thundered across the finish line in what appeared to be a dead heat.

At first Beauchamp was thought to be the winner; then they said Petty had won. There was no way the results could become official until they saw the photograph. It took three days of studying the photograph before they gave the race to Lee Petty. His son, Richard, finished a disappointing 57th in the race, but his career in Grand National racing was underway. Twenty-five years later, Richard Petty would win an unprecedented 200th NASCAR race. At Daytona.

In 1976 David Pearson and Richard Petty met violently a few hundred yards from the finish line at the *Daytona 500*. Despite the damage, Pearson limped across first.

A lot has changed since the early days of NASCAR. The purses and the attendance have grown by leaps and bounds; heroes have come and gone, and, for the most part, it has grown up. It is no longer the wild-and-wooly sport it once was.

Some people miss that.

"It used to be a roughneck sport," says Junior Johnson, former NASCAR superstar turned car-owner. "We used to beat on each other out there on the track and then go out and party all night. Now it's a business operation, and if you're not a good businessman, you're not in it long. I mean, a lot of these drivers are *millionaires* today. I made a couple of thousand dollars my first year, and now some of these guys make half a million in a single year. But I still miss the good ol' days," he continued.

"We didn't have what you'd call good handlin' cars—not like today's drivers—but all the drivers I drove against knew how to make them handle good. They just made the adjustments to their driving."

They may have calmed down somewhat, but don't get the impression that today's heroes are soft. They are still tough. Grand National stock car racing is one of the toughest sports in the world. The stress placed upon a driver in a 500-mile race, where the temperature reaches 140 degrees in the cockpit and where they are drafting each other at 200 miles per hour, is one of the most physically and mentally demanding things a man can hold up under.

"It's a full day's work," says Cale Yarborough. "It's a four- or five-hour continuous journey, with no time-outs and no two-platoon system, and things begin to pyramid on you. The wide-open lap is demanding, and the wide-open lap with everybody else trying to beat you is worse. Compared to a lot of other sports, it's a whole season's work in one day."

"Sometimes it gets so hot on the steering wheel that it will burn your hands if you move them, and you have to put them back where they were," says Richard Petty. "Your lips blister, and the floorboard gets so hot that the heels of your shoes melt, and you have to keep lifting them so they won't stick."

A lot of the original heroes are gone now, but there are still links with the past. Names like Richard Petty and Cale Yarborough and Buddy Baker and David Pearson have become household names with racing fans throughout the world. And once more Detroit auto manufacturers are beginning to take an active part in NASCAR, the legendary racing circuit where they showcased their cars for many years. You might say that it is the direct connection between the racing fan and the race track. **MT**

RODS AND CUSTOMS

California's car culture swept the nation with hopped-up mills, Deuce Coupes, and lowered Mercs.

By Bruce Caldwell

□ Cars . . . California. If that isn't the correct answer to some official word-association test, it should be. The American automobile was born in the Midwest, but it came alive in the West. In California, cars are the stars. The right car can give anyone instant "status."

Individuality and the rebel spirit have always been admired in the Golden State. The masses copy the rebels, and soon a fad is launched. Fads that start in California spread eastward and a local phenomenon becomes a national trend. Such was the case with hot rodding.

Hot rods got their start back in the Roaring Twenties. They weren't called hot rods then; the origin of the term is obscure, but they were fast. Speed was the whole essence of these early cars. Remove as much weight as possible, make the engine as powerful as you can, and go like hell. Zero to sixty meant nothing, but going eighty, ninety or that magical century mark was the ultimate. In those days people still remembered when a great horse was measured by how fast it could go and rated cars the same way. A performance car was only as impressive as its top speed. The many dry lakes of Southern California

were the perfect place to run the cut-down Model T's long and hard in search of the upper limits of speed.

A pre-World War II hot rod was typically a stripped-down Model T roadster. Often, only the firewall, cowl and a small windshield were the extent of the creature comforts. The engine was a four-cylinder Ford with power-boosting equipment like a modified cylinder head, bigger carburetor and a hotter ignition. The smallest available wire wheels (19-inch diameter usually) were used, and the fenders were thrown away. Gasoline was kept in the stock Ford oval tank mounted behind the seats. These cars were known as speedsters, jalopies, and jobs. They were primitive, but they were fast, and that was all that mattered.

World War II helped introduce hot rodding to the rest of the country. Uncle Sam scattered Californians around the globe, and they in turn spread the word about hot

Pickwick
THEATRE
Live it up with the Lively Ones from FORD
FORD CUSTOM CAR CARAVAN
NO
UNECESSARY
CONVERSATION
WITH GUARD
TEEN AGE FAIR

rodding. Many of these young men honed their mechanical skills keeping the war machine humming. These talents would serve them well in peacetime.

After the war, the economy was booming. Detroit had trouble meeting the demand for cars, but new models were getting to the public, creating a surplus of cheap used cars: cars of the twenties, thirties, and early forties that were perfect raw material for hot rods. Fords were the rule, and while open cars were preferred in sunny California, coupes were cool, too. Four-doors were like kissing your sister and Chevys were for the mechanically handicapped. The engine of choice was the flathead Ford unless you could get a Mercury (more cubic inches), which was even better.

The quintessential postwar hot rod was the '32 Ford highboy roadster. The highboy look was achieved by trash-canning the stock fenders, running boards, headlights, bumpers, and often the hood. The windshield and windshield posts were lowered, or "chopped," simply by cutting the top few inches off, and the convertible top was usually thrown away. The wheels were cut-down Kelsey-Hayes wires from a '35 or '36 Ford, or steel '40 Ford wheels with small hubcaps. Small "teardrop" taillights were fitted to the rear deck, a pair of headlights were mounted on stalks in the front, and you were off.

The engine was invariably the biggest available flathead Ford V-8 backed by a '39 Ford 3-speed or a '37 Cadillac-La Salle transmission. The rear axle was a late Ford "banjo" unit, or a Columbia 2-speed, or Halibrand quick-change in the cars of more affluent rodders. A close second to the Deuce roadster was a '29 Model A roadster body on a '32 Ford chassis.

Though top speed was still the big thrill, many of the dry lakes were now military installations (Edwards Air Force Base, where Chuck Yeager was going after the sound barrier, among them) and no longer accessible to ground-bound speed seekers. But, closer to home there were long straight roads that bisected the vast orange groves and farm land of still rural Los Angeles and Orange counties. These streets became the hotbed of side-by-side racing. It drew crowds, just like the midnight "chicken run" in *Rebel Without a Cause*; accidents happened, headlines blasted hot rodders, citizens complained, and city hall came down hard on modified cars. The term hot rodder slipped into the language and became almost synonymous with juvenile delinquent.

Hollywood was quick to cash in on the anti-establishment nature of the mobile young. Movies like the aforementioned *Rebel Without a Cause* and *High School Confidential* did little to dispel the link between hot rods and J.D.'s. Naturally, these movies made hot rods, custom cars, rock 'n' roll, and rebellious teenagers even more attractive to young people around the world. Wild cars, wild music, and wild kids were all part of the same revolution.

It was a way of separating yourself from the conformist generation of the Eisenhower fifties and their preoccupation with owning homes, starting families and furthering their careers.

Hot rods were one way of making a statement; customs were another. Each group used their cars, so different from day-to-day rolling stock, to set themselves apart from the boring herd. If there's one car that says "custom" to more people than any other, it's the '49-'51 Mercury. Aficionados call them simply Mercs.

Though the '51 Merc is a facelifted version of the '49 and '50 Merc, the essence of the car is the same for all three years. James Dean did his rebelling in an early edition that was, in the jargon of the time, a "conservative" custom: it was lowered by inserting thick blocks between the leaf springs and rear-end housing, heating the front coil springs until they sagged a bit, and clamping on a pair of skirts over the rear-wheel cutouts. At the other end of the scale, there's Bob Hirohata's classic example of a customized '51 Merc—it was called

A $100,000 '34 Ford three-window coupe (top) is part of today's hot rod revival. But the real thing is the home-built channeled Model "A" roadster (above). "New in town, sailor?" Miss Pedalpusher asks.

"radical" long before the teeny-boppers who say it today were even born.

This definitive Merc was built by the famous Barris brothers, Sam and George. They chopped its top by cutting a section out of the roof pillars; the body seams were filled with lead for a smooth look; all the factory chrome was removed, and a Buick trim spear was grafted to the side. The headlights were "Frenched" by brazing the bezels to the fenders, and Lincoln taillights were fitted to the rear fenders. The grille was handmade; the taillights and antenna were also Frenched. The chassis was modified to get the car as close to the ground as possible. Flared fender skirts were added with long side exhaust pipes known as "lakes pipes." Twin Appleton spotlights,

wide whitewall tires, Oldsmobile Fiesta hubcaps, and a multicoat pearlescent paint job finished off the outside. The interior had yards and yards of rolled and pleated naugahyde, and even the trunk was upholstered. It was low and slow and created a show wherever it went.

The whole idea behind custom cars was to make them look longer, lower and sleeker than anything available from Detroit. Customs were the average man's coachbuilt car. Hollywood stars like Mae West, Clark Gable, Fatty Arbuckle, and Gary Cooper made big impressions on other Californians with their customized Duesenbergs, Pierce-Arrows, Lincolns, Packards, and such. These expensive one-off cars were built by custom coachbuilders whose exotic workmanship inspired young bodymen to modify their humble cars.

Like the coachbuilt cars of the stars, custom cars had a flair and style that was lacking in the slab-sided and boring cars offered by Detroit. Though the automakers often built fascinating "dream cars" they displayed in car shows, their sexy shapes seldom made it to the production line. In fact, the customizers often inspired Detroit's stylists, who freely borrowed such ideas as multi-tone paint schemes and tunneled headlights.

TOP:
It says 1956 on the license plate of this chopped Deuce coupe. The scene? California, of course, way up at the top of the Hollywood Hills. Could a young man want more than a hemi under the hood and a pair of bathing beauties beside the pool?

ABOVE AND LEFT:
A recent replica of Bob Hirohata's Merc is authentic almost to the last detail: chopped top, frenched headlights, custom skirts, Lincoln taillights, and Buick side spear. The original car still exists, out of sight in a California garage.
PHOTO: PAT GANAHL

Most of the well-known customizers
were Californians, from early "stars" like
Henry Westergard and Jimmy Summers to
"second wave" customizers like the Barris
Brothers, Gene Winfield, Joe Bailon, Dean
Jeffries, Bill Cushenberry and Joe Wilhem.
As the trend caught on, customizers from
other parts of the country became well-
known, with people like Darrýl Starbird
and the Alexander Brothers among them.

And, though California was the dominant force in customizing, there was an
"East-coast" look as well. Magazines of
the time ran many "East vs. West" articles
and received tons of mail from provincial
readers. If an east vs. west generalization
could be made, the East-coast cars could
be thought of as extensions of the excess of
Detroit. That is, if dual headlights and 12-
inch fins were stock, then quad headlights
and two-foot fins were even better. Ex-
cesses in chrome, paint and upholstery
were other peculiarities of Eastern cars.
The West-coast look favored smoother
lines and more subtle changes, although
the West had its share of pink upholstery,
chromed kitchen-knob grilles and wildly
canted fins.

The different customizers had their personal styles and specialties. George Barris
was known as the "King of the Kustomiz-
ers" (although his brother Sam played an
important behind-the-scenes role). The
Barris cars were usually quite radical with
chopped tops, slanted windshield posts,
filled seams, rounded corners and a strong
visual presence. George was a master of
promotion, and his cars received much national publicity. Barris was always at the
vanguard of new trends.

Joe Bailon was noted for his excellent
bodywork. Special grille and taillight treat-
ments (often with a type of grille being
formed at the rear of the car, as well) were
found on many of Bailon's wildest cars.
Special flared side exhausts were another
Bailon feature, but the most noteworthy

was his beautiful and revolutionary candy-
apple-red paint.

Gene Winfield was another builder of
radical cars with special emphasis on custom paint jobs. One of Winfield's specialties was the fogged or blended paint job of
the same color. Larry Watson did all his
customizing with paint. He was a master of
the scallop paint job (bold contrasting
bands of color that generally followed the
car's natural styling lines). Watson was also good at pearl paint jobs and intricate
pinstripes. Dean Jeffries was an outstanding pinstriper who also built an occasional
show car, but the undisputed king of the
stripers was the legendary Von Dutch. Von
Dutch was a free spirit of the first order.
When he pinstriped a car, the owner just

sat back and watched. Von Dutch once
striped a car with contrasting themes on
the left and right. When the indignant customer complained, Von shrugged and
asked, "You can't see both sides at once,
can you?" Von Dutch's trademark was a
"flying eyeball" and he is generally credited with the first decorated "weirdo" T-
shirts.

Darryl Starbird did business in Wichita,
Kansas. He started out doing the usual
customizing but really made his mark with

Being on the leading edge of greatness is part of our heritage.

Greatness has clearly been part of the automotive industry's first hundred years. Great names. Great ideas. Great achievements.

Proudly, we've been part of it, too. Way back in 1926, Ross Roy himself championed the notion of comparative selling to the fledgling Dodge Brothers Motor Car Company. Moreover, he developed the tools to do it with.

From that beginning, Ross Roy, the salesman, went on to become Ross Roy, Inc., the advertising agency.

We've been a partner with Chrysler ever since. For over half a century, uninterrupted. A partner. A salesman. A believer. From its inception through its rebirth.

That's why greatness is part of our heritage.

ROSS ROY, INC. Detroit · New York · Chicago · Cleveland · Toronto · Windsor

bubble-topped show cars. His futuristic cars were seldom recognizable as to their origins, but most had his trademark Lucite tops which were very spacey for the late fifties and early sixties. The Alexander Brothers from Detroit were also noted for their forward-thinking cars. Canted headlights, custom grilles made out of expanded metal and plastic rod, flared side pipes, and radical asymmetrical styling were all features of "A-Brothers" cars.

The professional show cars and the "Top Ten Customs" were strictly dream boats what with their expensive bodywork and high dollar touches like a Carson top (a custom-built, chopped and padded, but rigid, convertible top). But a tube grille, Moon discs (spun aluminum wheel covers), simple dechroming, bolt-on lakes pipes, and a fuzzy fur rear-view mirror cover were all relatively cheap and common sights around the country. A whole industry sprang up to cater to the mild custom crowd. The owner of a daily-driver could personalize his car or truck inexpensively using mostly bolt-on parts. Virtually any car of the period lent itself to mild customizing. Besides the cosmetic parts there was also an increasing amount of bolt-on speed equipment becoming available. Much of this hardware was manufactured in California by some of the pioneer hot rodders and racers who turned their hobbies into businesses and became millionaires in the bargain. Vic Edelbrock was typical of these entrepreneurs. He ran a garage and raced flathead Fords on the dry lakes, and when the manifolds he was able to get proved inadequate, he made his own. That was the start of a major company that's still one of

the leaders in an industry that generates billions of dollars worth of business every year.

It wasn't just hardware that came out of the California car scene. The now ubiquitous decorated T-shirt owes its existence to hot rodders. Ed Iskenderian, whose high-performance camshafts were among the first items of speed equipment available, gave some T-shirts to the Lean and Harrison team who raced a hot rod at the Bonneville Salt Flats in the early fifties. They stuck Isky decals on the shirts, and before long every manufacturer in the business was outfitting legions of walking billboards. The idea caught on elsewhere and the rest, as they say, is history.

While the hot rod and custom car crazes may have had their beginnings in California, by the middle fifties the rest of the country had caught the fever. The word was spread by magazines. The first issue of *Hot Rod* appeared in January, 1948 with a print run of 10,000; *Motor Trend* soon followed, and in a very few years their founder, Robert E. Petersen, had become the proprietor of one of the largest publishing empires in the country.

The magazines (Petersen soon had scores of competitors on the stands) also helped spread and promote the sport of drag racing. *Hot Rod* magazine, in particular, was instrumental in legitimizing the sport with its advocacy of safe racing and support of the National Hot Rod Association which was formed in 1951. Organized drag racing was a positive outcome of the notorious street racing of the late forties and early fifties. In an effort to get the kids "off the streets" many communities built

drag strips. Santa Ana, California, is credited with having the first commercial drag strip, the city airport, which ran its first race in June 1950.

The highest possible top speed was the original quest in drag racing. Cars would start from a roll, to keep from breaking axles, and accelerate as quickly as possible for a quarter of a mile, a distance that most local airports could accommodate. Before long, standing starts became the rule and the lowest elapsed time—the number of seconds it took to cover the quarter-mile—the ultimate objective. For a long time, motorcycles were faster than most cars, a dominance which ended when the stripped-down "race only" specials succeeded in topping the power-to-weight ratio of the bikes. These "rail jobs" (they weren't much more than a pair of frame rails and an engine) led to the dragster which soon became, and remains, the fastest accelerating vehicle in motor racing.

At first drag racers were amateurs, weekend warriors who often raced the same cars they drove on the street. But as dragsters became increasingly sophisticated, the sport began to spawn professionals. Among the first, and still the most famous, is Don "Big Daddy" Garlits from Florida. In the late fifties, he found he could make a living traveling from strip to strip challenging the local hot dogs. It was exciting and dangerous racing, the safety equipment of the day being minimal, and drew large crowds. Speeds reached over 200 miles an hour and match races between stars like Garlits and Chris "The Greek" Karamesines were promoted by now classic radio ads that assaulted the brain with:

Even Plymouths got the custom treatment. This jet-age '56 sports louvers, hand-made grille, Moon discs, trick paint, torched front springs, and, natch, lowering blocks.

"Sunday . . . Sunday . . . Big Daddy meets the Greek in a best two out of three . . . BE THERE." In later years, the Funny Car—so called because it originally resembled a stock car, but was, well, funny-looking because of its big tires and slightly altered body—became the chief attraction at the drags. Today, the top racers are all sponsored by major companies and are every bit as professional as their counterparts in other forms of auto racing.

Into the early sixties hot rods, customs, show cars, drag racing, and salt-flats racing were all going strong. But, after many years of a self-imposed high-performance and racing ban, the Detroit car makers were getting much bolder about their "back door" involvement with fast cars. Street versions of high-horsepower two-door hardtops, built with the banked corners of NASCAR speedways in mind, could be found in showrooms and some of these big-engined Fords, Chevys, and Chrysler products appeared with aluminum fenders hoods, and doors which made them terrors on the dragstrip.

In 1964, General Motors did the competition one better when it installed a 389-cubic-inch V-8 in the intermediate-sized Le-Mans and created the Pontiac GTO. The Ford Mustang was a mid-1964 entry which, along with the GTO, signaled the start of the factory musclecar era. Horsepower was the rage, a dollar would buy you three gallons of leaded premium gas, and driving 55 on the freeway would get you a ticket for impeding traffic.

Outstanding performance, good looks, reliability, and comfort were all available for a few bucks down and easy monthly payments, so who needed to build a rod or custom?

Though drag racing continued to flourish, traditional hot rods and custom cars were parked and forgotten, cherished only by a hard core of true loyalists.

But the factory super cars disappeared almost as quickly as they came. High insurance rates and gas shortages turned Hemi Cudas, SS 369 Camaros, and Pontiac Judges into instant dinosaurs. The passing of the powerful pavement pounders helped spark renewed interest in hot rods. This time they were called street rods because the emphasis was on driving rather than racing, although the cars were by no means slugs. The builders tended to be older and more affluent. What was once considered rebellious was now fond nostalgia. Movies like *American Graffiti* and TV shows like *Happy Days* gave a slightly antiseptic view of the fifties and early sixties. People eagerly bought this version as a pleasant diversion from an increasingly complex world.

Traditional customs also staged a comeback. Though not as numerous or well organized as street rodders, custom fans find and restore old chopped-top Mercs and other lead sleds, as they were once called, and meet at nostalgia weekends to talk over old times and listen to Chuck Berry sing *Maybelline*.

Fashions in cars seem to be cyclical, just as in clothes and music. And while the turbo Eurosport coupes and sedans of the eighties may be a far cry from a little Deuce coupe, the thrill is the same. With some period music on the stereo, and a little imagination, it's not hard to settle down behind the wheel, head off into the night, and be California dreamin' again. **MT**

Drag racing is hot rodding's most enduring legacy and Don "Big Daddy" Garlits its ever-reigning King. His first Swamp Rat (above) blew everybody away. And his rear-engined car (left) revolutionized the sport and saved untold numbers of drivers from burns or maybe worse by putting them in front of a 2000-horsepower time bomb.

OVERLEAF:
That's Sam Barris' own chopped Buick (lower left), surrounded by a full-fendered Deuce roadster, chopped '40 convertible with a Carson top, "mild" '40 Coupe, and radical Merc ragtop. The cars were lovingly restored by an Ohio car dealer who couldn't afford them as a teenager and had to wait for 25 years to earn the bucks.

THE CAR AND LIFE

*It gave us mobility, freedom, status and jobs
. . . and in return we became utterly dependent on it.*

By Ted Orme

*It's a lean car . . . a long-legged dog of a
    car . . . a gray-ghost eagle car.
The feet of it eat the dirt of a road . . . the
    wings of it eat the hills
Danny the driver dreams of it when he
    sees women in red skirts and red sox
    in his sleep.
It is in Danny's life and runs in the blood
    of him . . . a lean gray-ghost car.*

"Portrait of a Motor Car"
by Carl Sandburg

☐ Written in 1918, this poem is reported to be one of the first on the automobile. Yet it reveals that Americans—at least some Americans—already had a well-developed passion for the automobile.

In fact, almost from the moment the Duryea brothers unveiled their little one-cylinder horseless carriage in 1893, we were hooked. "More than the flag, the eagle or the Minuteman," notes modern-day writer Stephen White, "the automobile has become our steadfast symbol of freedom and independence." And as auto-industry analyst John Rae adds, "Trying to evaluate the impact of the automobile on American Life seems like an exercise in measuring the immeasurable."

It's a faith-renewing exercise to reflect on just what the car means to this country: how its evolution is irrevocably intertwined with the nation's industrial and social history and how the car has become such a dominant force in our lives today. In the staid terms of the U.S. Department of Transportation:

"There are now over 100 million passenger vehicles in the United States—about one for each two people. Every year automobiles accumulate over a trillion miles of travel over a paved road and street network of nearly four million miles. The automobile influences personal decisions about where to live, work and shop and

OPPOSITE PAGE:
It wasn't long after the advent of the automobile that it became as American as apple pie and mom, influencing virtually every aspect of our culture. Norman Rockwell, whose paintings celebrate the daily lives of everyday Americans, captured the car's impact in a series of studies commissioned by the Ford Motor Company.
COURTESY: DETROIT HISTORICAL MUSEUM

norman rockwell

about hundreds of other activities and pursuits.''

That's putting it mildly. In America today, freedom of mobility is as cherished as freedom of speech. For most people, the car punctuates nearly every notable experience in life. A car was likely used to rush your mother to the hospital for your birth, and one will be used to carry you to your grave. In between, it links you with the basic elements of life—work, play, food, shelter. Multiply that by millions, and we are—by any definition—a car culture.

"Car culture, briefly defined," writes author and scholar Charles L. Sanford, "is the cluster of beliefs, attitudes, symbols, values, behavior and institutions which have grown up around the manufacture and use of automobiles. Its economic base is an enormous, many-faceted industry which leads the business cycle and has profound implications for domestic and foreign policy. It has its own subcultures which specialize in custom vans, sports cars, trailers, professional racing, hot rods and antique cars. As an 'American way of life,' it invests a machine with values transcending in importance that of efficient, economical transportation. . . . It has its own rituals, taboos, folk songs, and legendary heros. The most important puberty rite in the United States occurs when the young man or woman passes the driving examina-

tion, presses down the accelerator, and feels an answering surge of power, as if—some highway poet has written—'wolves howled from extinct caves in the bloodstream.' "

But, there's no free lunch. For all the wonders the automobile holds for us, it exacts a price. It kills people, fouls the air, eats great quantities of energy, and clogs our streets. Right from the start, it has had more than its share of critics.

In the Beginning

Social critics dismissed the early cars, sold then only to the very affluent, as an "appalling manifestation of conspicuous consumption." And in 1906, long before he became President, Woodrow Wilson called the infant car "a picture of the arrogance of wealth." Wilson said the automobile would stimulate socialism by "inciting the poor to envy possessions of the rich."

But America was ripe for the motorcar. More than half the population lived in isolated rural areas, and most of the rest in crowded, congested cities, swollen by huge influxes of immigrants from abroad and migrants from the farm looking for a better life. The primary conveyance was still the horse, which, despite noble service, was doing little to relieve rural isolation and was leaving mountains of manure on city streets. The automobile, you could say, was

literally a breath of fresh air.

As with most innovations, however, there was reluctance. In 1897, the *New York Times* grudgingly announced "the new mechanical wagon with the awful name—automobile—has come to stay, and sooner or later it will displace the fashionable carriage of the present hour." But the *Times* was quick to add, "Sensitive and emotional folk cannot view the impending change without conflicting emotions. Man loves the horse and he is not likely to love the automobile . . . nor will he ever get quite used, in this generation, to speeding along the road behind nothing."

But soon mechanical "contraptions" were seen all over the landscape as Americans took to them like kids to lollipops. It wasn't easy at first. Even though we had more than two million miles of roads at the time, Robert F. Karolevitz points out in his book *Pioneer Motoring*, "most of them were dirt—narrow, winding, shoulderless and ill-tended. When it rained, they were generally impassable; when it didn't, they were dusty and deeply rutted, hardly fit for a cattle drive let alone automobile travel."

It wasn't until Woodrow Wilson, in a dramatic change of heart, signed the Federal Aid Road Act in 1916 that American roads really began to improve. With its emphasis on "dragging the farmer out of the mud," the Good Roads Movement, as it

New York was one of the first cities to experience the massive impact of auto congestion on its streets. The rest of the country soon shared the problem.

TOP:
The horse wasn't the only thing to succumb to the automobile: old ways and old trades had to adjust or perish.

ABOVE:
Garages like this one (circa 1910) soon replaced the village blacksmith.

TOP:
Crude roadside accommodations awaited early motorists. Holiday Inns were yet to come.

ABOVE:
One-stop shopping and parking lots that took up more land than stores spread nationwide.

was called, set the stage for what would become the most magnificent road system in the world.

City planners also liked what they saw in the automobile. It held the promise of decentralizing the city and relieving the intolerable wagon and horse team snarls that slowed commerce and crowded the poor into ghettos. "Street railways" offered only limited mobility, and, like most moguls of their era, trolley-company operators were arrogant and abusive. City planners welcomed the fledgling car as a form of leverage against the mass-transit monopolies.

Unfortunately, it wasn't long before urban policy makers were overwhelmed by sheer numbers. Between 1900 and 1920 motor-vehicle registrations multiplied a thousandfold, from 8,000 to 8 million. During the 1920s, registrations tripled again. The automobile began to dictate to the planners who scrambled to build new streets and highways fast enough to keep up with the exploding numbers. Mass transit became an afterthought, and a pattern developed that would eventually lead to haphazard suburban sprawl and deteriorating inner cities.

"Fordism"

Just after the turn of the century Henry Ford said, "I will build a motorcar for the great multitudes. It will be large enough for the family but small enough for individuals to run and care for it. It will be constructed of the best materials, by the best men to be hired, after the simplest designs that modern engineering can devise. But it will be so low in price that no man making a good salary will be unable to own one—and enjoy with his family the blessings of hours of pleasure in God's great and open spaces."

In 1908, Ford made good his promise, and the Model T was born. Before production was halted in 1927, over 15 million affordable, dependable Tin Lizzies had been sold, American industry had been revolutionized, and American lifestyles would never be the same again.

Commenting on the incredible success of the Model T, Karolevitz says: "The T just happened to come up like a jackpot symbol on a giant industrial slot machine. Somehow it seemed to be the perfect marriage; the Model T entered the language and lives of the American people as no other automobile has, before or since."

But 15 million was just the beginning. As Karolevitz points out, the Model T "was the world's greatest hand-me-down car. Once it finished its original task, it went on to other assignments, often passing from owner to owner until literally hundreds of people were involved in its life history."

Much to the horror of the ruling classes, the automobile had now worked its way into the hands of common folks, and traditional living patterns began to change rapidly and radically. The old boundaries were removed: country people now went to the city and city people began to explore the country. More and more, men *and* women went to work outside the home, and shopped, visited and courted across greater and greater distances. Social life moved from the front porch to the road.

"The weekly trip to town to visit and to sample new ideas became a treat as well as a necessity," commented Bill Moyers on his television series *A Walk Through the 20th Century*. "When a country housewife was asked why her family had a car but not a bathtub, she replied, 'Bathtub? You can't go to town in a bathtub.'"

To build his car and his Fordson Tractor, which revolutionized the farm as the Model T did the roads, Henry Ford perfected the movable-belt assembly line. And, in 1914, to help his workers buy the cars they were building, he instituted the $5-a-day wage, which instantly doubled the wage standard in industrial America.

In combination, these major innovations—car, tractor, assembly line and wage—influenced America in the twentieth century more than the Progressive Era and the New Deal combined, according to James J. Flink's 1975 book *The Car Culture*. Ford, in Flink's view, "set the pace and direction of a new social order based on mass production and mass personal automobility until the early 1920s." But Flink, one of a growing body of authors in the 1970s to take a critical view of those early glory days of the automobile, also pointed out that "mass production meant that neither physical strength nor the long apprenticeship required to become a competent craftsman was any longer a prerequisite for industrial employment." The result was the unskilled son frequently became a more valuable worker than the skilled, but now obsolete, father. Respect for age and parental authority declined, or so it was said, and the car became the target for all manner of social criticism.

Emma Rothchild, who coined the expression "Fordism" in her book *Paradise Lost: The Decline of the Auto-Industrial Age*, also blamed assembly-line work for stifling "the myth of upward mobility" and creating a negative attitude toward work that would continue to modern times and result in chronically poor labor-management relations.

The venerable Model T was finally done in by its competition, which was updating and restyling its cars much more frequently. The passing of the Model T, most agree, marked the end of the first great era of the automobile and the beginning of another—planned obsolescence.

Culture Shock

While the car was turning urban parks into parking lots, it was creating new parks in the countryside as the public hit the road looking for fun and adventure. Tourist cottages set aside by enterprising farmers to take advantage of the new travelers turned into motels. The first drive-in restaurant, Royce Hailey's Pig Stand, appeared in Dallas in 1921, to be followed by literally thousands of copies in the 1920s and 1930s which eventually spawned a whole new sub-culture of their own.

Trucks and cars revolutionized agriculture and commerce. Fewer farmers could grow more crops and get them to distant markets far quicker. Businesses expanded their reach, and salesmen, formerly slaves to trains and horses, could now cover much larger territories. And, of course, everywhere they went with a shiny new auto, there was sure to be a crowd.

"By 1920 the automobile was no longer a pleasurable pastime, it was a practical necessity," writes Folke T. Kihlstedt for the *Michigan Quarterly*. "To serve it, an entirely new architectural infrastructure developed. Gasoline stations, bus terminals, roadside diners, motels, fast-food restaurants, and urban parking garages were designed to meet the demands of automobile and traveler."

At the same time, he points out, "the car began to complement the house as an indicator of social position and prestige." American houses changed, and "such social spaces as the parlor and front porch fell into disuse and atrophied. The garage, hidden at first at the back of the lot, merged into the house itself. The garage, or sometimes a carport, began to dominate the main facade by 1935."

Without the parlor and front porch to do our courting, yet another area of American culture was revolutionized—sex.

It is rumored that Henry Ford allegedly limited the seat length of the Model T to 38 inches in an attempt to inhibit lovemaking. It didn't work. The car was a relatively cozy chamber capable of sweeping young lovers far from prying eyes and ears. In literature, art and advertising the car became a symbol of masculinity and virility, though e. e. cummings compared driving a new car to making love to a virgin. Upright citizens labeled the car "a house of prostitution on wheels." (Had they been able to foresee the custom-van craze of the '60s, it likely would have given them a case of the "vapors.")

Some sociologists of the times went the other way, "One suggested that the reduced birthrate in Kansas was attributable to the inability of young men to support both a wife and an automobile—and the misguided males were too frequently settling for the latter," Karolevitz writes. Another maintained that "the continual jostling and bumping of motor cars over rough, rutted roads was causing an alarming increase in miscarriages—thus affecting population." It was even seriously propounded that the automobile was upgrading the quality of U.S. babies. "By expanding the radius of courtship," the researcher said, "the horseless carriage had a beneficial effect on the problems of inbreeding and intermarriage, especially in the southeastern states."

Books like *The Great Gatsby* and *The Reivers* glorified and romanticized the car, and it rapidly became Hollywood's favorite mobile prop, particularly for the popular new gangster movies. But real life gangsters loved their cars too. Clyde Barrow, of the infamous Bonnie and Clyde fame, wrote Henry Ford a personal note in which he said, "Even if my business hasn't been strictly legal, it don't hurt anyone to

The dream of a car in every driveway became a reality as suburban development changed the face of the country in the fifties. Air pollution, highway fatalities, waste of resources, and the blight of roadside junkyards were all part of the nightmare.

tell you what a fine car you got. I've drove Fords exclusively when I could get away with one."

Depression and War

The dramatic growth of the American automobile industry hit a brick wall in 1929 when the Great Depression caused car sales to plummet. But the car would still play a major role in this sad chapter of American life as countless families again hit the road. This time it was not adventure they were seeking. It was work.

Who can forget John Steinbeck's *Grapes of Wrath*, a poignant account of the great migration to California, in which the automobile played savior to uprooted dust-bowl victims:

"A homeless, hungry man driving the roads with his wife beside him and his thin children in the back seat. And a man driving the trucks, the overloaded cars listened apprehensively. Listened to the motor. Listened to the wheels. Maybe the oil isn't getting someplace. Maybe a bearing starting to go. If it's a bearing, what'll we do?"

But it wasn't only in the vast migration from the parched Midwest that people clung desperately to their cars. In their classic 1935 study of Muncie, Ind., called *Middletown in Transition*, Robert and Helen Lynd discovered that working-class families would go without food and clothes, mortgage their homes or deplete their savings rather than lose their cars. "Car ownership stands to them for a large share of the American dream; they cling to it as they cling to self-respect."

Statistics confirm that, from 1929 to 1932 new-car sales declined 75 percent, from 4.5 to 1.1 million, while car registrations fell by only 10 percent, from 23 to 20.7 million. "Car ownership in Middletown was one of the most Depression-proof elements of the city's life in the years following 1929," said the Lynds, "far less vulnerable, apparently, than marriages, divorces, new babies, clothing, jewelry, and most other measureable things both large and small."

The car really came of age in the '20s, when government expenditures for highway construction exceeded the capital outlay of any single line of private enterprise. But in the '30s, our highway system doubled again as President Roosevelt helped put America back to work again by unleashing an army of unemployed on road and highway projects.

By the mid-'30s the auto industry was once again humming. Gleaming new streamlined models were coming off the assembly line like lemmings off a cliff, and the country appeared to be headed into an unprecedented period of prosperity. But trouble was brewing. Having suffered sweeping layoffs and hard times, auto workers were increasingly discontent over low wages and poor working conditions. In 1937, they went on strike.

Auto towns across the country shut down as workers bedded down in the factories and held open warfare with "goons" sent in by the factories to break the strike. Settlement came 44 days later, and autoworkers would emerge as labor's elite, setting the pace in production, wages and consumption. But they didn't have long to enjoy the fruits of their victory. The country was soon at war.

Production was halted from 1942 to 1945, as the auto industry was converted into a formidable war machine. Before the fighting stopped, the industry had contributed an incredible $29 billion worth of weapons and material to the war effort—one-fifth of the total war production. Meanwhile, the rest of the country learned to live without new cars and on sharply reduced gasoline and tire rations. In the name of victory, we even learned to live with a 35-mph speed limit.

The Halcyon Years

The United States emerged from World War II the richest, most powerful nation in the world. Returning vets quickly found work in a booming postwar economy, and they found affordable housing in the new suburbs. Suburban sprawl assumed massive dimensions as developers rushed to keep pace with the postwar baby boom. The use of the car was planned for because families now had to have a car to get to work or the grocery store. Regional planners had little choice but to lay out new roads and freeways to provide access to the suburbs. And when Eisenhower became president, an interstate highway system—likened to the building of the pyramids—was begun to link every state in the union by superhighway.

Car production doubled to 5.2 million by 1946 and would double again by 1975, as we binged on automobiles—and everything else material. But why not? After many dark years of depression and war, it was time to loosen up a little, kick out the jams, if you will. Automakers were only

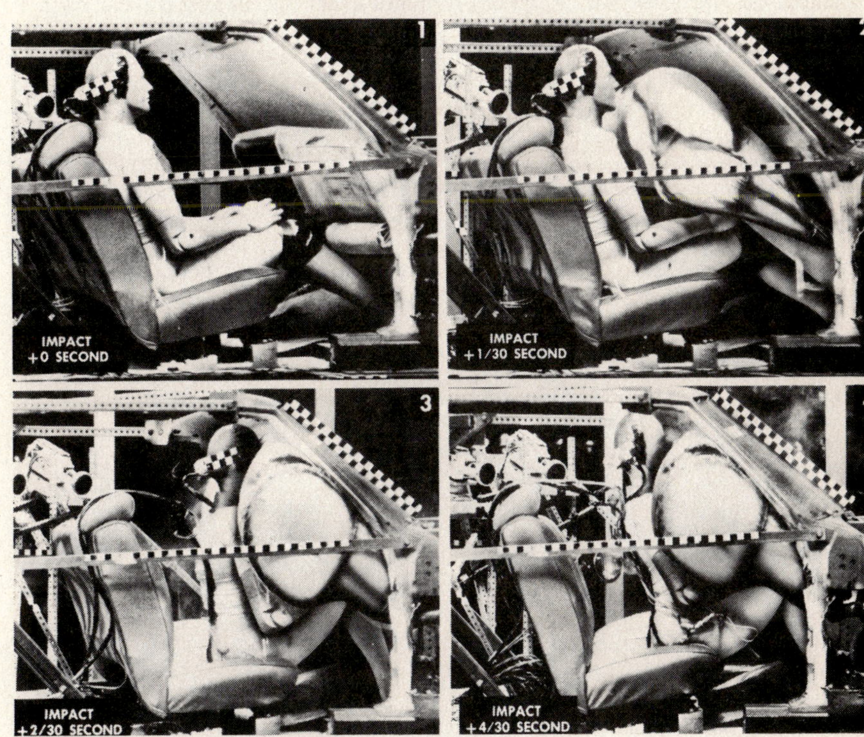

Ralph Nader's indictment of the Corvair (which was later vindicated) and the auto industry in his book, *Unsafe at Any Speed*, helped spur legislation that led to improved auto safety. But controversy still surrounds the air bag and other aspects of regulation.

too happy to oblige. No decade has seen a greater array of overpowered, overweight, chromed and finned and downright garish machinery as that offered in the '50s. And we loved it.

Auto executives grew fat and happy as they watched their business turn into a monstrous money cow. A few critics grumbled about insulated and arrogant fat cats more interested in style and opulence than reliability or innovation. But who cared. We now had jobs, 30-cent gasoline, drive-ins, blue suede shoes, and rock and roll. Everything was papa-ooh-mow-mow.

We became a cruising culture. The first drive-in theater appeared in 1933 in Camden, New Jersey, but by the end of the '50s there were over 4,000. We also had drive-in restaurants, drive-in banks, drive-in churches, even drive-in liquor stores. A new generation of teenagers, with more time and more money, made the car the centerpiece of their culture in a decade-long celebration of freedom and mobility and optimism. Their favorite form of expression was—what else—the custom car. Tom Wolfe called car customizers "America's true folk artists."

In our exuberance, most of us did not notice, or we chose to ignore, the fact that highway fatalities were rising alarmingly; urban and suburban roads approached gridlock, and clouds of smog settled over the cities.

Social Savior or Cultural Villain?

Ford took a stab at safety in 1956 when it introduced the safety belt (as an option), the deep-dish steering wheel and the padded dash. But in Lee Iacocca's words. "It bombed, and GM killed us that year." Snakebit, and convinced safety would not sell, Detroit went back to what it did best—selling luxury, power and status.

The musclecar era of the sixties fed fuel to the fire. "There's a live one under the hood," read a Pontiac GTO ad. "Have you priced a tiger lately? Purrs if you're nice. Snarls when you prod it . . . ."

Ads like these incited a growing army of critics who called the auto industry "sick" and "arrogant" and "not to be trusted in matters of safety." They charged manufacturers had forfeited their right to control how safe their cars should be, and they advocated that the federal government take over the responsibility.

In 1966, championed by a strident young lawyer named Ralph Nader, who skyrocketed to fame with a best-selling condemnation of the GM's Corvair, *Unsafe at Any Speed*, the safety lobby got what it wanted: the National Traffic and Motor Vehicle Safety Act, which created the National Highway Traffic Safety Administration and some 50 auto safety regulations in the next decade. Four years later, the Clean Air Act would require car exhaust to become chemically cleaner than the air we breathe. The federal government was now a full-fledged partner in the design of automobiles sold in America.

Worse, the car had overnight become a cultural villain. Bookstands filled with ghastly accounts of the evils of the automobile. In addition to Rothchild and Flink, Kenneth R. Schnieder charged in his *Autokind Versus Mankind* that "rarely in history is there a tyrant who creates intolerable social problems and then presents himself as the Savior." He claimed that dependence on the automobile was a social malignancy that "gradually permeates the daily behavior of people, the purpose of institutions, and the structure of the cities and countryside. This tyranny has been promoted under the cunning popular myth of expanding freedom and affluence."

John Jerome, a former editor of *Car and Driver* magazine, no less, published *The Death of the Automobile* in 1972, in which he called the car "a bad machine" that murdered people, wasted natural resources, polluted the air, added to problems of race and poverty, altered sexual customs, loosened family ties and held the economy hostage to unreliable engineering. He condemned Detroit's practice of

concentrating on styling and status instead of engineering and reliability, and he called the Chevy Impala of the early '70s "a stagnant monstrosity."

The consumer revolt was on, and Detroit reacted poorly. Clinging desperately to the "nut behind the wheel" philosophy of auto safety, auto executives became a regular presence in Washinton, D.C. as they vehemently resisted any and all regulation. This only served to further erode their image and credibility before a public that now had little sympathy for them.

So it was, that when OPEC shut off our oil in 1973-74, gas lines formed and prices shot up, Detroit somehow got all the blame. Congress reacted with corporate average fuel economy (CAFE) standards that required Detroit to "reinvent" the car, in the words of former Transportation Secretary Brock Adams, and car buyers responded by flocking to buy fuel-thrifty imports, leaving the Great American Large Car to gather dust in storage lots like beached whales.

Like a fat man who, after having a heart attack, is forced to train for a marathon, the domestic auto industry staggered through the 1970s, offering the buying public probably the worst assortment of products in history. Performance and pizzazz were forgotten in favor of anything to clean up, shore up and shave down cars to meet, not only myriad federal standards, but the new competition from abroad as well.

American consumers are a fickle lot, however. As soon as the gas lines disappeared and they adjusted to 60-cent gasoline, they went right back to buying big cars. In 1978, Detroit would have its best year ever, selling over 10 million models, while inventories of small Japanese cars swelled and gathered dust.

But the second gas crisis in 1979 would be followed by the worst recession in 50 years—a double whammy that literally brought Chrysler and American motors to their knees and jolted the domestic auto industry. Prophets of doom, now a sizable contingent, were quick to sound the death knell for U.S.-built cars, and there was much clamor about alternative fuels, vehicles and transit in general. But Detroit persevered, and poured billions of dollars into new engineering, production and marketing techniques. The result has been an almost miraculous improvement in the industry and its products. Whether it has been enough must await future analysis.

Throughout it all, however, and in spite of the high social price, America has not lost its love for the automobile. As Bill Moyers asks, "Can you imagine this century without it? We may curse it when it stalls, kick it when it's flat. We may even want to 'shoot the beast' as one social critic recommended. But live without it? Not likely, not in this century. We've struck a bargain with this thing. It gave us mobility, romance, freedom, status and jobs, and required in return only that we come utterly to depend on it. That we did." **MT**

The automobile transcends even the most diverse ideologies. In 1985 Cadillac sold 20 Fleetwood Seventy-Five limousines to the People's Republic of China.

CIRCLE TRACK puts you in the driver's seat !

The accelerator thrusts forward, sparks fly, you smell the wheels smoking, and the course becomes a blue blur, as CIRCLE TRACK puts YOU in the driver's seat!

Every month America's fastest growing magazine for oval track enthusiasts celebrates the sport you love best with exhilarating editorial and colorful action photos you'll want to frame!

Regular features include personality profiles of today's top racers; how-to tips; analysis of the latest equipment; nostalgia highlights; and insightful guides to race tracks across the country— from Daytona to Indy to Eldora! CIRCLE TRACK's experts also provide invaluable dollar-saving advice on engine technology, suspension and chassis setups for all kinds of cars and a special tech section written monthly by the legendary master Smokey Yunick. Whether you're into stock cars, sprint cars, midgets, or Indy cars, CIRCLE TRACK covers the entire spectrum of racing to put you in the driver's seat!

Now On Sale At Your Local Newsstand 

THE NEXT CENTURY

Better cars, more models, and a revolution in materials and manufacturing lie in the future.

By David E. Cole and Lawrence T. Harbeck

☐ Imagine a 2085 model-year car that weighs 1400 pounds, is rustproof, has a sealed hood that never needs to be opened, carries six passengers and all their luggage, accelerates from 0–60 mph in under 5.0 seconds, gets 75 miles per gallon at 100 miles per hour, and costs about $4,000. Sound too good to be true? Correct. But now that you have imagined it out of your system, you can consider the future of the real-world car, although perhaps sooner than 2085.

It is impossible to predict the future with any accuracy, let alone the car of the future or the automotive industry of the future. To paraphrase the Frenchmen's saying though, it is clear that the future is not going to be what it used to be. Broadly speaking, the car of tomorrow will be the product of an international industry in which quality, productivity, risk, and innovation will dominate. That high-tech world industry, populated by both large and small companies, will be producing a broad spectrum of vehicles for an increasingly demanding and fragmented customer base.

We should think of the car not merely as a machine for moving from place to place but as the embodiment of radical changes now occurring in the planning, design, production, sales, service, and ultimate disposal of motor vehicles. Moreover, changes in the fundamental nature of the industry, including the forms of enterprise, management style, location of production, and cast of industrial characters, are all important ingredients in the equation of the future.

Changes in the car will be dwarfed by changes in production. Today about 200 man-hours (labor and management) are required to transform the car from raw material to end product. This will be reduced to perhaps 20–30 total hours in the next 10–30 years, with almost complete automation of production and management.

Competitive pressures and technological advances are changing the industry. It will be flexible as it adapts to a fast-paced and changing times. Management has undergone a basic philosophical change, which, in effect, has "set the table" or created the

design giugiaro illustration:

Two views of the future. At the 1939
World's Fair in New York, General Motor's
Highways and Horizons exhibit forecast huge
superhighways (top). In 1956, GM saw roads
with electronic "beams" controlled from tow-
ers. "The driver could sit back and relax and
let the operator take over his driving in
absolute safety."

environment for change throughout the industry—in labor-management relations, inventory management, worldwide sourcing, integration of design and manufacturing, and relations between manufacturers and their suppliers. But now let's look at the future automobile, beginning with energy sources and future fuels.

Energy will remain an important issue, both for car owners and manufacturers. We do not foresee a long-term energy problem, particularly for vehicle fuel. Similarly, in the short term, there are adequate petroleum supplies, barring a major world political crisis. There is a growing consensus that the long-term fuels are methanol, or liquid hydrocarbons derived from our enormous coal resources. In fact, one of the most attractive feedstocks for methanol production is high-sulfur eastern U.S. coal that has relatively little value for other purposes today. The major problem likely to be encountered with fuel is in the transition period between petroleum and coal-based fuel, which will occur in the next century. However, even in this period the present growing availability of methanol, from remote or waste natural gas, should smooth the transition. The fuel of tomorrow probably will have high energy density, be adaptable to a variety of powerplants, and have an attractive price. Past events have led some analysts to be overly concerned about fuel cost and fuel economy, to the point where many see $3.00 per gallon fuel prices and 50+ miles-per-gallon cars as inevitable. Such a forecast is pessimistic. Our recent Delphi Forecast predicts 1990 fuel prices at about $1.50 per gallon. Furthermore, when one examines yearly fuel cost for an average car owner, it is clear that one can cut that in half through a change from 10 to 20 miles per gallon. But an improvement from 30 to 40 miles per gallon offers an additional savings of only 25 percent. Customers may not be eager to sacrifice such features as size, comfort, and safety for modest fuel savings.

The car is undergoing a macro-evolution propelled by a host of micro-revolutions. Said another way, cars of today and tomorrow can be expected to change gradually. They will remain essentially a people-housing box with an engine, four wheels, and seats. Vehicle passengers and their luggage, grocery bags, boxes, bales, and pets are a powerful limiting factor on automotive design. The size of human beings cannot be predicted to change significantly in the next 100 years. In fact, based on past experience, people may indeed become larger. Nor can we design just for athletic astronauts—we have to allow for feeble grandparents and boisterous kids, too. There must be comfortable accommodations for all. So the "box" cannot be too small, or oddly shaped. However, as we look at details of the vehicle, an accelerating revolution is evident in materials, electronics, the engineering and manufacturing processes, and aerodynamics, to mention several key areas.

It is becoming clear that the most important mass transportation mode of the future is likely to remain the personal automobile, augmented by other forms such as subways, trains and buses. In our wildest imagination, we do not envision a three-dimensional transportation system—that is, a levicar—for handling people's short-trip needs. Of course we cannot discount the possibility of a scientific breakthrough that will make even this technology "state of the art."

Future customers will have an incredible choice of products, from the relatively low-cost econobox with a mini collection of features, to the mid-sized car aimed at the center of the market, to a plethora of low-volume, upper-scale specialty vehicles. Product diversification is in step with the increasing individualism of the customer. In the past, one sought to keep up with the Joneses by buying an automobile like the Joneses'. Tomorrow the trend is not only to maintain the pace of the Joneses, but to do so with a more personal or unique product. But, model proliferation is creating a problem for manufacturers seeking to develop a comprehensive long-term product and production strategy.

Over the next few decades it will undoubtedly be possible to provide an electronically-guided vehicle. Yet this probably will not occur, mainly because most drivers will continue to want to control their car. Of course, some superhighways or guideways will likely offer the opportunity to turn the driving over to the computer for the long trip. But, for much of the short-trip driving, drivers will not want to relinquish rather intimate control.

The basic design of the overall vehicle, in addition to satisfying the demands of the customer, will be heavily oriented to manufacturing. That is, design and manufacturing will be highly integrated. This will be particularly important in the higher-volume products, but it will also be true of the specialty products. Flexible automated facilities will be standard; the old rigid automation will be part of history.

Future cars and trucks will be much more aerodynamic, particularly in design to minimize disturbance of an orderly pattern of air flow over the body. One important recent finding is that a variety of shapes can be equally highly aerodynamic. This will preserve the integrity of individual styling that is so important to the customer. The size, in all likelihood, will resemble the spectrum of sizes available today. Cars will be lighter, with increasing use of lightweight and more efficiently designed materials.

Powertrain

The engine of 2085 is difficult to forecast because of technology yet to be developed. However, we can look at history to gain some insight. Thirty years ago the gas turbine was viewed as being ten years in the future. Today, the gas turbine is viewed as more than 30 years away. And electric

powerplants are still waiting for that critical breakthrough in battery technology. For the next 30 or 40 years, spark-ignition and diesel engines will dominate. The best features of both engines will also be used in a so-called hybrid internal-combustion engine—a kind of spark-ignited diesel. This engine will be small, powerful, and high-revving. It will be very precisely and economically made, and will have low friction. All of its elements will be under electronic control, including fuel management, combustion timing, and valve operation.

It is entirely possible that a different engine will come into common use, although the basic operating cycle of current engines is likely to remain intact. There is already an important rival for the reciprocating engine in the Wankel, or rotary engine, such as Mazda uses in its RX-7 sports car. But many other mechanisms are being considered and may appear in the years ahead.

We must keep in mind that the basic fundamentals of engine operation—the conversion of fuel energy to another form—are governed by the laws of thermodynamics. Those place rather specific limitations on efficiency for a given engine. Even fuel cells, a direct means of energy conversion and a possible power system of the future, must face the laws of thermodynamics and their irrefutable limits.

On the horizon, we foresee elimination of the cooling system, including the radiator, with the advent of a low-heat-rejection or so-called adiabatic spark-ignited/diesel hybrid if fuel costs become excessive or supply is limited. This engine could easily be 30–40 percent more efficient than current ones. The low-heat-rejection diesel is indeed a likely candidate for trucks and buses because of its efficiency, but it will be more expensive and hard to manufacture and may not offer sufficient economic incentives in light-duty hybrid versions for the automotive customer. The arrival of relatively inexpensive and manufacturable ceramic materials and advanced lubricants increases the likelihood of this engine and the gas turbine as well.

One important feature of both the hybrid and the gas turbine engine is reduced sensitivity to fuel quality. Present diesels require a fuel that self-ignites easily, while gasoline engines need just the opposite—resistance to auto-ignition.

Multipoint electronic fuel injection will be standard, either in the cylinder for the hybrid or at the inlet port for a conventional spark-ignited engine.

Ignition will probably be some form of electronically controlled plasma or advanced spark-ignition system, which will assure reliable starting and smooth operation and will probably entail use of an ignition module in each cylinder, eliminating the need for a conventional high-voltage distributor. This sytem is, in fact, here today. Electronics will be in control of everything, and we will indeed be "driving by wire." Valves, which are the doors in and out of the engine's cylinders, will employ

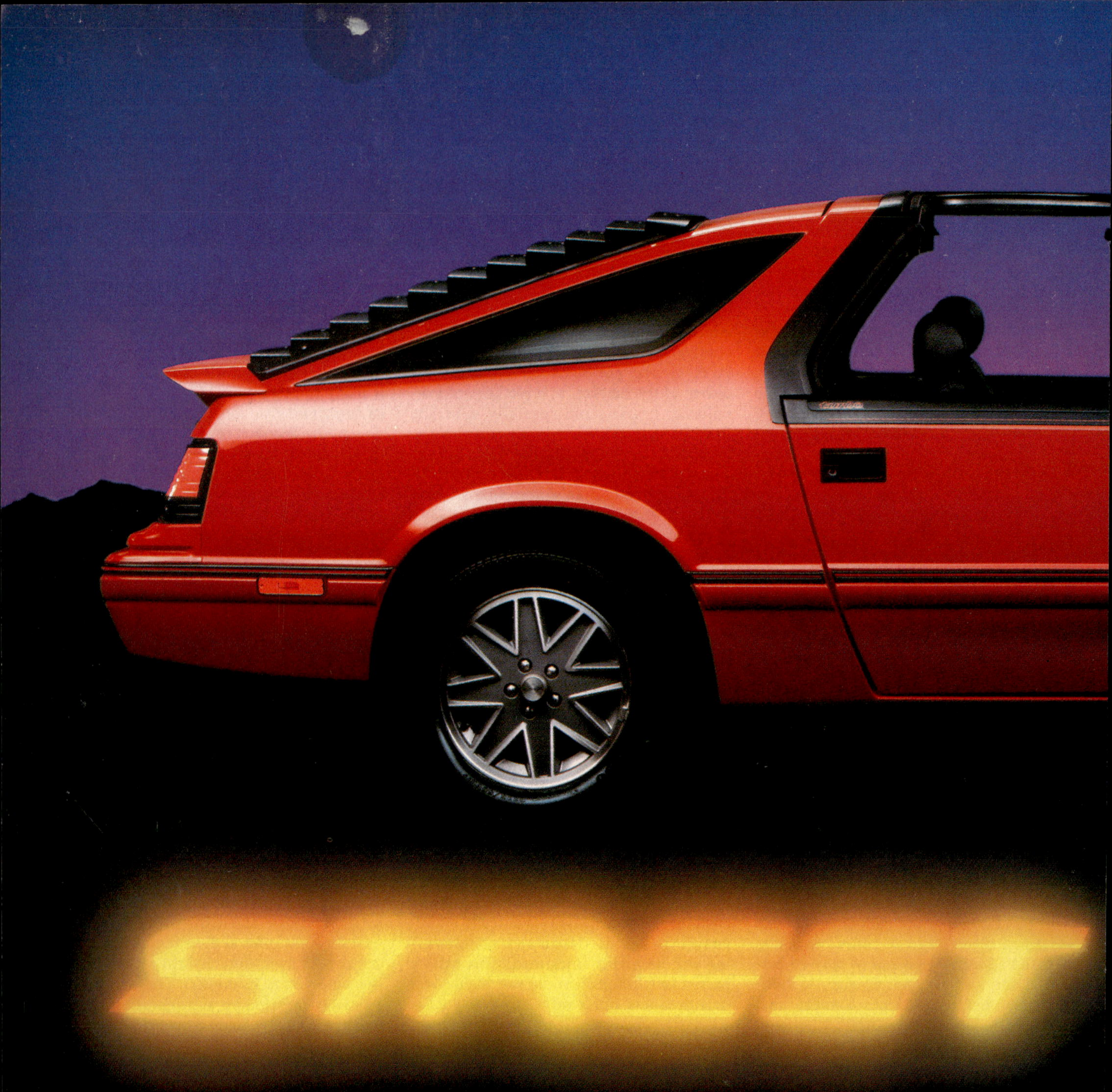

Chrysler creates the new Laser XT.

The competition is hot. So we turned on the heat and made Laser hotter. We gave it a sleek skin and new low ground effects. So air will get out of its way. We made it flash red. So traffic will stop. We gave it a turbocharged heart,

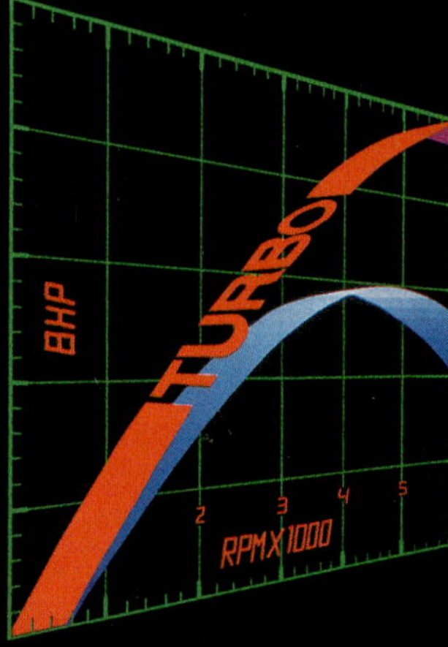

front-wheel drive, Euro handling suspension, 5-speed, 15″ alloy wheels and bigger Eagle GT Gatorback radials—all standard.

In 1,800 runs during U.S. Auto Club tests Laser XT dominates the competition.* Laser is first on the slalom course. Has the shortest distance in braking. And with a surge of turbopower, Laser leaps from 0 to 50 in 5.5 seconds. Faster than Camaro Z28, Trans Am, Toyota Supra, Nissan 300 ZX. Inside Laser's fitted cockpit, the

BUCKLE UP FOR SAFETY.

*Results of USAC tests for 1985 cars with standard engine/transmission. **Whichever comes first.

performance continues. Your driver's seat responds with pneumatic thigh and lumbar supports. And you control 6-speaker AM/FM stereo, tilt steering wheel, power mirrors and over 40 other standard features.
Want even more? Equip your Laser XT with T-Top, rear lift-gate louvers and premium leathers.

Chrysler believes: To be first, a sports car must last. So Laser's engine, its 5-speed and even its turbo are backed by a 5-year or 50,000-mile Protection Plan.** Not even Porsche gives you that.

"THE COMPETITION IS GOOD. WE HAD TO BE BETTER."

variable lift and timing. Rotary valves are a possibility and have been envisioned for years, but with future materials they are a possibility.

Of course, in the long term, electrics, fuel cells, or turbines are candidate engines. However, the economic and technical barriers at this point are rather formidable. And, even if those problems are resolved, the current engines are not standing still; they are improving at a fast pace and are a moving target.

Future engines will be made from lightweight materials, perhaps even plastics in various parts. Aluminum will, in the midterm, probably be the basic material in the head and block. But cast iron and steel in more efficient structural configurations may also be used. Precise and highly productive manufacturing operations will be critical. Essentially every U.S. passenger car engine will be redesigned in the next decade. Precise manufacturing is particularly important to ensure low friction. Some parts may be integrated, such as a combination of the head and block, or block and transmission case. Engines will continue to have multiple cylinders. One of the inherent advantages of the many-chambered engine is its basic smoothness, in contrast to those with three or fewer cylinders. Future engines will probably be so reliable that we may dispense with the conventional hood and only provide a small access door for service.

All in all, as we look at the engine of the future, we must remember that selection is governed by multiple criteria. Any competitor must not only be just as good in every category (cost, emissions, performance, package size, weight, smoothness, etc.) but must be better in some way, or there will be little incentive for change.

If the internal-combustion engine survives, a transmission will be needed to match the engine output to the vehicle. An important new technology is on the horizon because of advances in manufacturing and design. The most interesting future prospect is the continuously variable transmission (CVT), which provides an almost infinite selection of speed ratios between the engine and the axles and, with electronic control, permits optimization of the engine under all conditions. However, even with the advent of continuously variable automatic transmissions, the love affair with the automobile and desire for manual control still ensures a future for the conventional manual transmission. Some of us do enjoy the thrill of shifting.

Front-wheel drive with front engine location will dominate, although a significant fraction of vehicles will remain rear-drive, particularly those intended for high power-to-weight ratio application and those, such as station wagons, intended for carrying a wide range of loads. Also, the mid-engine vehicle, like the Pontiac Fiero or Toyota MR2, will have a role.

Chassis and Basic Structure

Important adjustment, even a revolution, is in progress in the basic chassis of the vehicle. One glimpse of a possible future technology is offered by the Fiero, which in effect uses a drivable chassis to which the exterior plastic body panels are attached. The chassis, or basic body and chassis structure, must ensure that the occupants are packaged in safe, energy-absorbing housing. The trend is to more efficient designs using low-cost, non-corrosive materials. Body panels themselves can be used as a part of the structure, in contrast to the Fiero approach. There are multiple ways to solve the same problem. In the future we will see structures ranging from the Fiero concept, which relies on a basic frame, to variations on the body-frame design of today, to a true monocoque, where the body elements are used as structural members. New materials (plastics and metals, or innovative combinations of both) together with advanced processing techniques will heavily influence future decisions.

Looking at this historically, just in the last ten years we have witnessed a major transition from a separate body/frame de-

ABOVE:
General Motors' 1983 Aero 2000 relfects the current thinking of how future cars will look with its obvious emphasis on aerodynamic design as a functional and aesthetic element.

RIGHT:
In 1967, Chevrolet's Astro I also had an aerodynamic look, but it was more a result of the stylists' imagination than today's scientifically calculated, wind-tunnel-tested shapes.

sign to an integral or unibody design. The main reason for this change is that the unibody is a much more efficient lightweight structure. Perhaps one can think in terms of the market as the key factor influencing design, where the specialty vehicle may dictate the use of a space frame, which permits a variety of different styles at low cost and low volume. High-volume models, in all probability, will use variations on the integral body frame, but made from different materials with different processing technology. The most imponderable part of the materials future is reinforced plastics because the technology is in its infancy, and the future may yield products that we cannot even envision today. In any case, whatever material is selected for various applications, cost and materials properties themselves are not the only factors of import; manufacturability is critical.

Some rather exotic fiber-reinforced plastic and aluminum structural vehicles are being evaluated for high-production uses. Long-range speculation is difficult because the specific properties of the materials that will be available are not yet known.

Brakes, suspension members and other components will evolve, with possible breakthroughs expected in various details. Again, electronics will play a role leading to anti-lock braking and true active suspensions, which will provide unheard-of control, handling, and ride. Regenerative braking (where the energy is stored for reuse) is likely.

Tires, which might be considered a part of the chassis group, have changed dramatically in the past few years with the transition from bias to belted bias to today's radial ply tires. Further changes with new technology will lead to improvement of all properties, including traction, rolling resistance, wear, penetration resistance, and other factors. Cast, run-flat designs are even on the horizon. The spare will probably become an item of history.

Body

From a functional view, the aerodynamics of the car will be improved dramatically. Sedans today generally have drag coefficients (Cd) in the area of .4 to .5, but it seems entirely likely that .2 or even less is achievable.

For exteriors, we expect the use of polymer-based materials (flexible, durable, lightweight plastic), although steel in new and hybrid forms may still be used. Attractive features of the non-metallics include ease of redesign and resilient surfaces that will resist stone damage, parking lot dings, and other minor impacts. Advanced paint systems are ensuring richness of color and resistance to fade and wear. All coating applications in future will be done automatically with a minimal labor content. Color molded into body materials is likely.

Composite or "hybrid" materials will offer exciting opportunities. When one considers the properties of aluminum, steel, and various plastics, the tendency is to look at each material uniquely to try to achieve a given set of goals with a single material. The future may more properly belong to hybrid materials, where one can take advantage of special features of a material and develop combinations with other materials for an optimum composite.

Another important element of the exterior surface of the vehicle is the glass. We look for scratch-resistant, flexible, transparent materials that are much lighter than present glass materials. Windows will still be movable but will be flush with the exterior surface to enhance aerodynamics and reduce wind noise. Photochromic materials are possible, using an electrical charge applied to the transparent surfaces to change light transmission.

Corrosion protection will be tremendously improved. In fact, by 1992 we envision that there will be no externally visible corrosion in a salty environment for more than ten years. The average 1992 car is expected to last more than two years longer than today's car. This is certainly a dramatic improvement.

We live in a culture that values youth. As wrinkles gather with age, we may choose to visit the local plastic surgeon for an adjustment. We think we can extend this fashionable trend to the vehicle, which will last longer but will need a refreshing update. Thus the "automotive facelift" may become a standard feature of the vehicle of tomorrow.

Bumpers will be able to resist minor impacts without damage. The watchword of crashworthiness will be total management, ranging from the small accident in a parking lot through high-speed crashes, with the goal of minimizing damage to the vehicle and most importantly to the occupants.

Interior

The interior will continue to be designed around the driver and passengers. Improvements in comfort will be dramatic. Seats will be thin, easily manufactured shells individually adjustable to one's shape.

Controls will be highly functional. The steering wheel will remain, although a "joy stick" incorporating all driver-operated functions is possible. This decision rests with the customer and of course with the eternally present regulator. The future vehicle will feature a "friendly" interior much more conducive to impact protection of driver and passengers. The future restraint system may be a hybrid of the airbag and seat belt.

Ergonomics, the science of adapting working conditions to workers, will dominate the design of the interior and will become the major factor in optimizing the relationship between the driver, passengers and the vehicle. All controls will be accessible, and voice-actuated components will be common. Features such as entertainment, communication, and diagnostic systems will incorporate advanced electronics that will offer satisfaction beyond what we can imagine today. The concert hall will truly move into the car.

Electronics

Of all of the changes sweeping the automobile, none is more profound than the electronic revolution. Advanced electronic components are now performing important functions, sush as providing optimum control of the engine for good drivability, performance, fuel economy, and low emissions. In fact, without electronic systems, it would be impossible to meet regulatory and consumer criteria.

Most electronic components are almost invisible to the driver/passenger. This will continue, but consumer-related electronic componentry will increase. Within the next ten years, more than 12 percent of the vehicle cost will be in electronic components and this does not include basic electrical devices such as motors and wiring. Total system diagnostics will provide a detailed measure of the state of the vehicle and will forecast failures based on trends in vehicle characteristics. Maintenance will be based on need rather than a fixed schedule. Anti-lock braking systems will be standard in a few years and will be followed by radar braking systems, which will provide an unheard-of margin of safety. High-speed guideways for "hands off" travel will also be made feasible by electronics.

Power steering is moving toward electric power rather than fluid power, but electronic control is a key ingredient. In fact, accessories and peripherals such as the alternator or power brakes will undergo fundamental changes to consume less power and be more compact.

On a trip, we will be in constant contact with a base and our exact position known. The driver will be prompted as to the optimum route from Point A to Point B.

Anti-theft systems will be effective beyond our present imaginations and be keyed to the unique qualities of the owner or specified operator. Another feature of considerable social merit will be systems preventing the impaired driver from operating the car. In fact, the driver may just be able to go to sleep and be driven automatically home.

All in all, the massive application of electronics will be an important part of making the future vehicle far more effective, reliable, inexpensive, and comfortable.

Engineering Process

Tremendous changes are occurring in the entire engineering process. Already CAD/CAM (Computer-Aided Design/Computer-Aided Manufacturing) is almost history as we look at complete penetration of the computer into research, design, development, and testing. One special element of this is the merging of product and manufacturing technology. A major criterion for future product design is that the vehicle must be produceable in the flexible automated facility.

As an example of the new technology,

once an exterior design is created in the styling studio with the aid of computer techniques, that shape will be measured and stored (without significant human involvement) in a computer. The computer will then direct machines to produce the dies from which the finished parts can be made in an automated factory. This will all be done in a relatively short time and at a far lower cost than today. Research and development, augmented by the computer, will greatly improve engineering productivity and generate creative solutions to the international automotive challenges ahead.

Production

While the car of the future is the focus of this story, the revolution in production processes (which has just begun) deserves mention. Change abounds, from hardware on the shop floor, to new management practices, to restructured labor-management relationships. We are seeing evidence of this change in the auto industry with startling new projects, such as Saturn at General Motors, where primary emphasis is on the process rather than the product. The product and process are viewed as integral components of an interrelated and complex system. Clearly, international pressures are forcing the industry to make giant strides, and the auto industry is perhaps the leader in applying advanced technology to the challenges of manufacturing.

We foresee the day where cars will be produced in an almost totally automated environment. Roughly speaking, today's U.S. vehicle requires perhaps 200 manhours to produce from the "ore pile" to the showroom. In 10–15 years this will be reduced to 30–40 hours, with even greater reductions beyond that level. Of course, labor content will not be reduced to zero, but labor contribution to car production, both blue and white collar, will be far less than today. Robots are only one part of the equation. The factory of the future will become a center of computer-integrated manufacturing (CIM). The single most important technology leading us into the future is the microprocessor and other electronic technology. Without electronic control, discussion of the factory of the future or a revolutionary new production system is but an academic exercise.

Another dimension of change is in the flexibility of automation. We now talk of Flexible Manufacturing Systems (FMS). Historically, the automotive plant has been characterized by rigid automation designed for high-volume production of a limited variety of parts. The watchword of tomorrow is flexibility, which means several things, one of which is the ability to shift quickly from one component or system to another. Another is to dramatically reduce the economies of scale for components or systems. This latter point is one key to the proliferation of the low-volume products we expect in the future. All in all, the manufacturing revolution is profound.

Marketing

One element of change often overlooked in a view of the car's future is the selling or leasing process. We envision that the dealership experience may involve a visit to the "viewing" center, where the customer will be able to observe a three-dimensional hologram of the vehicle, simply change features, trim, and colors of the vehicle, and see it just as if he were looking at the real thing. One intriguing and likely trend is that with electronic dashboard displays, customers will be able to custom-design the dash from a menu to suit their whims. This will all be done electronically. For example, the customer could choose a digital speedometer, analog fuel gauge, and so forth. Later this could be altered by a simple electronic manipulation if one desires.

The customer will sit at a terminal after selection and be able to perform a competitive analysis with other products and if satisfied, place the order, learn exactly when the car will be made, arrange for payment or financing, and be told the exact time of delivery—which should be within 10 days.

The availability of personal computers may give prospective buyers access to an incredible database of comparative information on cars, including service and warranty costs, prices, etc. This will greatly add to the objectivity of the entire process of product selection.

Of course, with "high-teching" of the car and the entire sales process, it will be necessary to provide some human contacts. Customers will demand this. Therefore, the human element—the salesperson and the mechanic—will still be needed, but in far fewer numbers.

Servicing

An important and standard feature on all future vehicles will be an on-board diagnostic system with the ability to forecast developing problems. When a car is produced, a signature, like a fingerprint, of the various operating mechanisms will be created and carried onboard. This signature will be continually updated with use. When key variables begin to drift beyond specifications, the driver will be alerted to the proper service needed. Of course, a standard feature of tomorrow's vehicle will be a major reduction in maintenance. Even today we forecast that by 1992, the scheduled maintenance interval will be extended to over 12,000 miles from the 7,000–8,000 miles currently. Furthermore, with diagnostic capability, service will not be based on mileage or time but "as-needed," which may extend the interval. Service centers, separate from selling centers, will be sophisticated organizations capable of fixing the right problem—the first time.

An exciting future lies ahead as we look at tomorrow's automobile. Every dimension of the industry is changing and will continue to experience dramatic change in the future. Clearly, cars will meet the needs of an increasingly diverse set of customers. All of their functions will be improved, from durability and fuel efficiency to safety and general value.   **MT**

The most futuristic vehicle ever built, the Lunar Rover, had more in common with the basic Model T than any other cars.

THE PUBLICATION OF THE CENTURY!

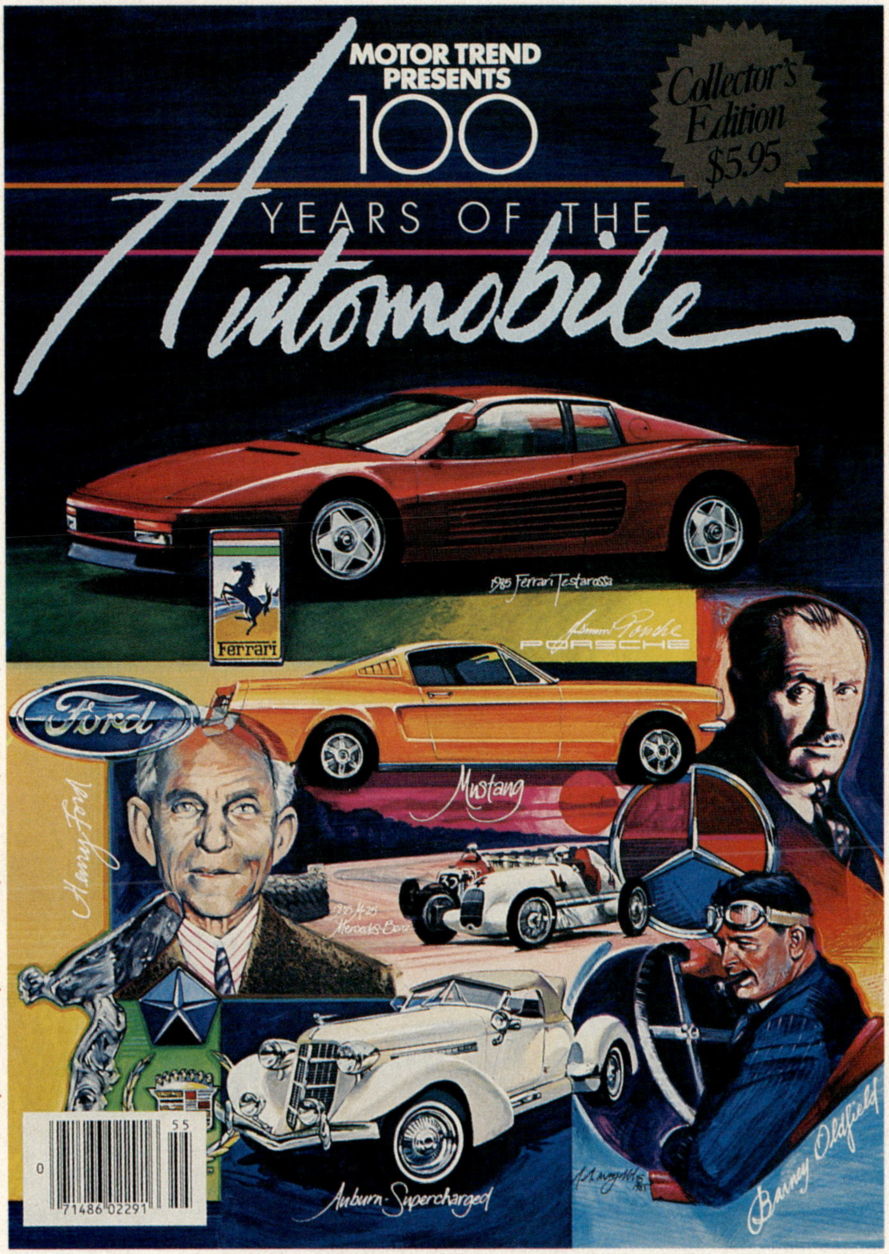

ONLY $5.95

NOW ON SALE AT YOUR LOCAL NEWSSTAND OR WRITE FOR YOUR COPIES TO:

Petersen Retail Sales Services
6725 Sunset Blvd.
Los Angeles, CA 90028

Send $5.95 in check or money order plus 65¢ handling charge per copy ordered. U.S. funds only. Allow 4-6 weeks for delivery. Residents of L.A. County add 6½% sales tax; all other CA residents add 6%. Please print clearly and be sure to include your return address.

FACTS AND FIGURES

Indianapolis 500-Mile Race Winners

Year	Winner	Car	Time	MPH
1911	Ray Harroun	Marmon Wasp	6:42:08.00	74.602
1912	Joe Dawson	National	6:21:06.00	78.719
1913	Jules Goux	Peugeot	6:35:05.00	75.933
1914	Rene Thomas	Delage	6:03:45.00	82.474
1915	Ralph DePalma	Mercedes	5:33:55.51	89.840
1916	Dario Resta	Peugeot	3:34:17.00	84.001
1919	Howard Wilcox	Peugeot	5:40:42.87	88.050
1920	Gaston Chevrolet	Monroe	5:38:32.00	88.618
1921	Tommy Milton	Frontenac	5:34:44.65	89.621
1922	Jimmy Murphy	Murphy Special	5:17:30.79	94.484
1923	Tommy Milton	H.C.S. Special	5:29:50.17	90.954
1924	L. L. Corum & Joe Boyer	Duesenberg Special	5:05:23.51	98.234
1925	Peter DePaolo	Duesenberg Special	4:56:39.46	101.127
1926	Frank Lockhart	Miller Special	4:10:14.95	95.904
1927	George Souders	Duesenberg	5:07:33.08	97.545
1928	Louis Meyer	Miller Special	5:01:33.75	99.482
1929	Ray Keech	Simplex Piston Ring Spl.	5:07:25.42	97.585
1930	Billy Arnold	Miller-Hartz Special	4:58:39.72	100.448
1931	Louis Schneider	Bowes Seal Fast Special	5:10:27.93	96.629
1932	Fred Frame	Miller-Hartz Special	4:48:03.79	104.144
1933	Louis Meyer	Tydol Special	4:48:00.75	104.162
1934	William Cummings	Boyle Products Special	4:46:05.20	104.863
1935	Kelly Petillo	Gilmore Speedway Spl.	4:42:22.71	106.240
1936	Louis Meyer	Ring-Free Special	4:35:03.39	109.069
1937	Wilbur Shaw	Shaw-Gilmore Special	4:24:07.80	113.580
1938	Floyd Roberts	Burd Piston Ring Spl.	4:15:58.40	117.200
1939	Wilbur Shaw	Boyle Special	4:20:47.39	115.035
1940	Wilbur Shaw	Boyle Special	4:22:31.17	114.277
1941	Floyd Davis & Mauri Rose	Noc-Out Hose Clamp Spl.	4:20:36.24	115.117
1946	George Robson	Thorne Engineering Spl.	4:21:16.70	114.820
1947	Mauri Rose	Blue Crown Spark Plug Spl.	4:17:52.17	116.338
1948	Mauri Rose	Blue Crown Spark Plug Spl.	4:10:23.33	119.814
1949	Bill Holland	Blue Crown Spark Plug Spl.	4:07:15.97	121.327
1950	Johnnie Parsons	Wynn's Friction Proofing Spl.	2:46:55.97	124.002
1951	Lee Wallard	Belanger Special	3:57:38.05	126.244
1952	Troy Ruttman	Agajanian Special	3:52:41.88	128.922
1953	Bill Vukovich	Fuel Injection Special	3:53:01.69	128.740
1954	Bill Vukovich	Fuel Injection Special	3:49:17.27	130.840
1955	Bob Sweikert	John Zink Special	3:53:59.53	128.209
1956	Pat Flaherty	John Zink Special	3:53:28.84	128.490
1957	Sam Hanks	Belond Exhaust Special	3:41:14.25	135.601
1958	Jim Bryan	Belond AP Special	3:44:13.80	133.791
1959	Rodger Ward	Leader Card 500 Roadster	3:40:49.20	135.857
1960	Jim Rathmann	Ken-Paul Special	3:36:11.36	138.767
1961	A. J. Foyt, Jr.	Bowes Seal-Fast Special	3:35:37.49	139.131
1962	Rodger Ward	Leader Card 500 Roadster	3:33:50.33	140.293
1963	Parnelli Jones	Agajanian-Willard Battery Spl.	3:29:35.40	143.137
1964	A. J. Foyt, Jr.	Sheraton-Thompson Special	3:23:35.83	147.350
1965	Jim Clark	Lotus powered by Ford	3:19:05.34	150.686
1966	Graham Hill	American Red Ball Special	3:27:52.53	144.317
1967	A. J. Foyt, Jr.	Sheraton-Thompson Special	3:18:24.22	151.207
1968	Bobby Unser	Rislone Special	3:16:13.76	152.882
1969	Mario Andretti	STP Oil Treatment Special	3:11:14.71	156.867
1970	Al Unser	Johnny Lightning 500 Special	3:12:37.04	155.749
1971	Al Unser	Johnny Lightning Special	3:10:11.56	157.735
1972	Mark Donohue	Sunoco McLaren	3:04:05.54	162.962
1973	Gordon Johncock	STP Double Oil Filters	2:05:26.59	159.036
1974	Johnny Rutherford	McLaren	3:09:10.06	158.589
1975	Bobby Unser	Jorgensen Eagle	2:54:55.08	149.213
1976	Johnny Rutherford	Hy-Gain McLaren	1:42:52.48	148.725
1977	A. J. Foyt, Jr.	Gilmore Racing Team	3:05:57.16	161.331
1978	Al Unser	F.N.C.T.C. Chaparral Lola	3:05:54.99	161.363
1979	Rick Mears	The Gould Charge	3:08:47.97	158.899
1980	Johnny Rutherford	Pennzoil Chaparral	3:29:59.56	142.862
1981	Bobby Unser	Norton Spirit Penske PC-9B	3:35:41.78	139.084
1982	Gordon Johncock	STP Oil Treatment	3:05:09.14	162.029
1983	Tom Sneva	Texaco Star	3:05:03.066	162.117
1984	Rick Mears	Pennzoil Z-7	3:03:21.660	163.612
1985	Danny Sullivan	Miller American	3:16:06.069	152.982

1916, 1926, 1950, 1973, 1975 and 1976 races less than 500 miles.

Indianapolis 500 Pace Cars

Year	Pace Car	Driver
1911	Stoddard Dayton	Carl G. Fisher
1912	Stutz	Carl G. Fisher
1913	Stoddard Dayton	Carl G. Fisher
1914	Stoddard Dayton	Carl G. Fisher
1915	Packard "6"	Carl G. Fisher
1916	Premier "6"	Frank E. Smith
1919	Packard V-12	Frank E. Smith
1920	Marmon V-16	Barney Oldfield
1921	H.C.S. "6"	Harry C. Stutz
1922	National "8"	Barney Oldfield
1923	Duesenberg	Fred S. Duesenberg
1924	Cole V-8	Lew Pettijohn
1925	Rickenbacker "8"	Capt. E.V. Rickenbacker
1926	Chrysler "8"	Louis Chevrolet
1927	LaSalle V-8	"Big Boy" Raeder
1928	Marmon	Joe Dawson
1929	Studebaker	George Hunt
1930	Cord V-8	E.L. Cord
1931	Cadillac	"Big Boy" Raeder
1932	Lincoln	Edsel Ford
1933	Chrysler	Byron Foy
1934	LaSalle	"Big Boy" Raeder
1935	Ford V-8	Harry Mack
1936	Packard	Tommy Milton
1937	LaSalle	Ralph DePalma
1938	Hudson	Stuart Baits
1939	Buick	Charles Chayne
1940	Studebaker	Harry Hartz
1941	Chrysler	A.B. Couture
1946	Lincoln V-12	Henry Ford II
1947	Nash	George W. Mason
1948	Chevrolet	Wilbur Shaw
1949	Oldsmobile	Wilbur Shaw
1950	Mercury	Benson Ford
1951	Chrysler	Dave Wallace
1952	Studebaker	P.O. Peterson
1953	Ford	William C. Ford
1954	Dodge	William C. Newburg
1955	Chevrolet	T.H. Keating
1956	DeSoto	L.I. Woolson
1957	Mercury	F.C. Reith
1958	Pontiac	Sam Hanks
1959	Buick	Sam Hanks
1960	Oldsmobile	Sam Hanks
1961	Ford Thunderbird	Sam Hanks
1962	Studebaker	Sam Hanks
1963	Chrysler	Sam Hanks
1964	Ford Mustang	Benson Ford
1965	Plymouth Sports Fury	P.N. Buckminster
1966	Mercury Comet Cyclone GT	Benson Ford
1967	Chevrolet Camaro	Mauri Rose
1968	Ford Fairlane Torino	William C. Ford
1969	Chevrolet Camaro	Jim Rathmann
1970	Oldsmobile 4-4-2	Rodger Ward
1971	Dodge Challenger	Eldon Palmer
1972	Hurst/Olds	Jim Rathmann
1973	Cadillac Eldorado	Jim Rathmann
1974	Hurst/Olds	Jim Rathmann
1975	Buick V-8	James Garner
1976	Turbocharged Buick V-6	Marty Robbins
1977	Oldsmobile Delta 88	James Garner
1978	Chevrolet Corvette	Jim Rathmann
1979	Ford Mustang	Jackie Stewart
1980	Pontiac Turbo-Trans Am	Johnnie Parsons
1981	Buick Regal V-6	Duke Nalon
1982	Camaro Z28	Jim Rathmann
1983	Buick Riviera	Duke Nalon
1984	Pontiac Fiero	John Callies
1985	Oldsmobile Calais	James Garner

A. J. Foyt, Jr. Indianapolis Record

Year	Car	Laps Led	Qual.	S	F	Laps	Speed or Reason Out
1958	Dean Van Lines		143.130	12	16	148	Spun Out
1959	Dean Van Lines		142.648	17	10	200	133.297
1960	Bowes Seal Fast		143.466	16	25	90	Clutch Failure
1961	Bowes Seal Fast	71	145.907	7	1	200	139.130
1962	Bowes Seal Fast	2	149.074	5	23	69	Wrecked
1962R	Sarkes Tarzian	(Relieved E. George 127-146)			17	20	Starter Failure
1963	Sheraton-Thompson		150.615	8	3	200	142.210
1964	Sheraton-Thompson	146	154.672	5	1	200	147.350
1965	Sheraton-Thompson	10	161.233	1	15	115	Broken Gearbox
1966	Sheraton-Thompson		161.355	18	26	0	Wrecked
1967	Sheraton-Thompson	27	166.289	4	1	200	151.207
1968	Sheraton-Thompson		166.821	8	20	86	Blown Engine
1969	Sheraton-Thompson	66	170.568	1	8	181	Flagged
1970	Sheraton-Thompson	2	170.004	3	10	195	Transmission
1971	ITT-Thompson		174.317	6	3	200	156.069
1972	ITT-Thompson		188.996	17	25	60	Turbocharger
1973	Gilmore Rac. Team		188.927	23	25	37	Connecting Rod
1973R	Gilmore Rac. Team	(Relieved George Snider 58-101)				44	Gear Box
1974	Gilmore Rac. Team	70	191.632	1	15	142	Oil Line
1975	Gilmore Rac. Team	53	193.976	1	3	174	147.684
1976	Gilmore Rac. Team	29	185.261	5	2	102	148.355
1977	Gilmore Rac. Team	46	194.563	4	1	200	161.331
1978	Gilmore Rac. & Citicorp		200.122	20	7	191	Flagged
1979	Gilmore Rac. Team	1	189.613	6	2	200	158.260
1980	Gilmore Rac. Team		185.500	12	14	173	Stalled Turn #3
1981	Valvoline-Gilmore		196.078	3	13	191	Flagged
1982	Valvoline-Gilmore	32	203.332	3	19	95	Shift Linkage
1983	Valvoline-Gilmore		199.557	24	31	24	U-Joint
1984	Gilmore-Foyt		203.860	12	6	197	Flagged
1985	Copenhagen-Gilmore	27	205.782	21	28	62	Front Wing
28 Races						3,996	(9990 miles)

USAC National Champions

Year	Driver
1956	Jimmy Bryan
1957	Jimmy Bryan
1958	Tony Bettenhausen
1959	Rodger Ward
1960	A. J. Foyt
1961	A. J. Foyt
1962	Rodger Ward
1963	A. J. Foyt
1964	A. J. Foyt
1965	Mario Andretti
1966	Mario Andretti
1967	A. J. Foyt
1968	Bobby Unser
1969	Mario Andretti
1970	Al Unser
1971	Joe Leonard
1972	Joe Leonard
1973	Roger McCluskey
1974	Bobby Unser
1975	A. J. Foyt
1976	Gordon Johncock
1977	Tom Sneva
1978	Tom Sneva
1979	A. J. Foyt
1980	Johnny Rutherford
1981/82	George Snider
1982/83	Tom Sneva
1983/84	Rick Mears
1984/85	Mario Andretti

National Champions Prior to 1956

Year	Driver	Year	Driver
1902	Harry Harkness	1927	Peter DePaolo
1903	Barney Oldfield	1928	Louis Meyer
1904	George Heath	1929	Louis Meyer
1905	Victor Héméry	1930	Billy Arnold
1906	Joe Tracy	1931	Louis Schneider
1907	Eddie Bald	1932	Bob Carey
1908	Louis Strang	1933	Louis Meyer
1909	George Robertson	1934	Bill Cummings
1910	Ray Harroun	1935	Kelly Petillo
1911	Ralph Mulford	1936	Mauri Rose
1912	Ralph DePalma	1937	Wilbur Shaw
1913	Earl Cooper	1938	Floyd Roberts
1914	Ralph DePalma	1939	Wilbur Shaw
1915	Earl Cooper	1940	Rex Mays
1916	Dario Resta	1941	Rex Mays
1917	Earl Cooper	1946	Ted Horn
1918	Ralph Mulford	1947	Ted Horn
1919	Howard Wilcox	1948	Ted Horn
1920	Gaston Chevrolet	1949	Johnnie Parsons
1921	Thomas Milton	1950	Henry Banks
1922	James Murphy	1951	Tony Bettenhausen
1923	Eddie Hearne	1952	Chuck Stevenson
1924	James Murphy	1953	Sam Hanks
1925	Peter DePaolo	1954	Jimmy Bryan
1926	Harry Hartz	1955	Bob Sweikert

USAC Top-Ten Prize Money Leaders (through 1984)

Driver	
A.J. FOYT	$3,719,686
AL UNSER	$3,048,554
BOBBY UNSER	$2,379,296
JOHNNY RUTHERFORD	$2,348,720
GORDON JOHNCOCK	$2,050,806
MARIO ANDRETTI	$1,716,091
TOM SNEVA	$1,674,428
ROGER McCLUSKEY	$1,373,529
RICK MEARS	$1,317,157
GARY BETTENHAUSEN	$1,273,819

Michigan accounts for 32% of U.S. car production, Missouri is second with 9.3%.

Motor vehicles are produced in 26 states, including Utah, Maryland and Delaware.

The place with the highest ratio of cars to people is the Falkland Islands with one car for each inhabitant; Monaco and the U.S. are next with 1.8 persons per car. There are 27 people for each car in the U.S.S.R.; 785 in India; and 14,402 in China.

World's Land Speed Record Holders

Date	Car	Driver	Place	Speed-MPH
12-18-98	Jeantaud Electric	Comte Gaston de Chasseloup-Laubat	Achères, France	39.24
1-17-99	Jenatzy (La Jamais Contente)	Camille Jenatzy	Achères, France	41.42
1-17-99	Jeantaud Electric	Comte Gaston de Chasseloup-Laubat	Achères, France	43.69
1-27-99	Jenatzy Electric	Camille Jenatzy	Achères, France	49.92
3-4-99	Jeantaud Electric	Comte Gaston de Chasseloup-Laubat	Achères, France	57.60
3-29-99	Jenatzy Electric	Camille Jenatzy	Achères, France	65.79
4-13-02	Serpollet Steam	Leon Serpollet	Nice, France	75.06
8-5-02	Mors 4 cylinder	William K. Vanderbilt, Jr.	Ablis, France	76.08
11-5-02	Mors 4 cylinder	Henri Fournier	Dourdan, France	76.60
11-17-02	Mors 4 cylinder	Augières	Dourdan, France	77.13
7-17-03	Gobron-Brillié 4 cylinder	Arthur Duray	Ostend, Belgium	83.47
11-5-03	Gobron-Brillé 4 cylinder	Arthur Duray	Dourdan, France	84.73
1-12-04	Ford 4 cylinder "Arrow"	Henry Ford I	Lake St. Claire, MI	91.37 (1)
1-27-04	Mercedes 4 cylinder	William K. Vanderbilt, Jr.	Daytona, Florida	92.30
3-31-04	Gobron-Brillié 4 cylinder	Louis Rigolly	Nice, France	94.78
5-25-04	Mercedes 4 cylinder	Baron Pierre de Caters	Ostend, Belgium	97.25
7-21-04	Gobron-Brillié	Louis Rigolly	Ostend, Belgium	103.55
11-13-04	Darracq 4 cylinder	Paul Baras	Ostend, Belgium	104.52
1-25-05	Napier 6 cylinder	Arthur E. MacDonald	Daytona, Florida	104.65 (1)
12-30-05	Darracq V-8	Victor Héméry	Arles-Salon, France	109.65
1-23-06	Stanley Steam "Rocket"	Fred Marriott	Daytona, Florida	121.57 (4)
11-9-09	Bens 4 cylinder "Blitzen Benz"	Victor Héméry	Brooklands, England	125.95
3-16-10	Benz 4 cylinder "Blitzen Benz"	Barney Oldfield	Daytona, Florida	131.275 (1)
4-23-11	Benz 4 cylinder "Blitzen Benz"	Bob Burman	Daytona, Florida	141.37 (1)
6-24-14	Benz 4 cylinder	L.G. Hornsted	Brooklands, England	124.10 (3)
2-17-19	Packard V-12	Ralph DePalma	Daytona, Florida	149.875 (1)
4-27-20	Duesenberg 16 (two eights)	Tommy Milton	Daytona, Florida	156.03 (1)
5-17-22	Sunbeam V-12	Kenelm Lee Guinness	Brooklands, England	133.75 (1)
7-6-24	Delage V-12	Rene Thomas	Arpajon	143.31
7-12-24	Fiat 6 cylinder	Ernest Eldridge	Arpajon	146.01
9-25-24	Sunbeam V-12	Malcolm Campbell	Pendine, Wales	146.16
7-21-25	Sunbeam V-12	Malcolm Campbell	Pendine, Wales	150.76
3-16-26	Sunbeam V-12	Major Henry O.D. Segrave	Southport, England	152.33
4-27-26	Babs V-12	J.G. Parry Thomas	Pendine, Wales	169.30
4-28-26	Babs V-12	J.G. Parry Thomas	Pendine, Wales	171.02
2-4-27	Napier V-12 "Bluebird"	Malcolm Campbell	Pendine, Wales	174.883
3-29-27	Sunbeam V-12 (2)	Major Henry O.D. Segrave	Daytona, Florida	203.792
2-19-28	Napier-Campbell "Bluebird"	Malcolm Campbell	Daytona, Florida	206.956
4-22-28	White Triplex V-12 (3)	Ray Keech	Daytona, Florida	207.552 (5)
3-11-29	Irving-Napier "Golden Arrow"	Major Henry O.D. Segrave	Daytona, Florida	231.446
2-5-31	Bluebird V-12	Malcolm Campbell	Daytona, Florida	246.09
2-24-32	Bluebird V-12	Malcolm Campbell	Daytona, Florida	253.97
2-22-33	Bluebird V-12	Sir Malcolm Campbell	Daytona, Florida	272.46
3-7-35	Bluebird V-12	Sir Malcolm Campbell	Daytona, Florida	276.82
9-3-35	Bluebird V-12	Sir Malcolm Campbell	Bonneville, Utah	301.129
11-19-37	Thunderbolt V-12 (2)	Capt. George Eyston	Bonneville, Utah	312.00
8-27-38	Thunderbolt V-12 (2)	Capt. George Eyston	Bonneville, Utah	345.50
9-15-38	Railton W-12 (2) "Mobil Spl"	John Cobb	Bonneville, Utah	350.20
9-18-38	Thunderbolt V-12 (2)	Capt. George Eyston	Bonneville, Utah	357.50
8-23-39	Railton W-12 (2) "Mobil Spl"	John Cobb	Bonneville, Utah	369.70
9-16-47	Railton W-12 (2) "Mobil Spl"	John Cobb	Bonneville, Utah	394.20
8-15-63	Spirit of America GE J-47 Jet	Craig Breedlove	Bonneville, Utah	407.45 (2)
7-17-64	Bluebird Gas Turbine	Donald Campbell	Lake Eyre, Aust.	403.10
10-2-64	Wingfoot Express J-46 Jet	Tom Green	Bonneville, Utah	413.20
10-5-64	Green Monster J-79 Jet	Art Arfons	Bonneville, Utah	434.02
10-13-64	Spirit of America J-47 Jet	Craig Breedlove	Bonneville, Utah	468.72
10-15-64	Spirit of America J-47 Jet	Craig Breedlove	Bonneville, Utah	526.28
10-27-64	Green Monster J-79 Jet	Art Arfons	Bonneville, Utah	536.71
11-2-65	Spirit of America Sonic I	Craig Breedlove	Bonneville, Utah	555.483
11-7-65	Green Monster J-79 Jet	Art Arfons	Bonneville, Utah	576.553
11-13-65	Golden Rod V-8 (4)	Bob Summers	Bonneville, Utah	409.277
11-15-65	Spirit of America Sonic I	Craig Breedlove	Bonneville, Utah	600.601
10-23-70	The Blue Flame liq. fuel rocket	Gary Gabelich	Bonneville, Utah	630.338
10-4-83	Thrust 2, jet car	Richard Noble	Blackrock, Nevada	633.468

(1) One-way records set in America and not recognized by the International governing body. (2) Three-wheeled car, not recognized by the F.I.A. Runs timed by Federation Internationale Motorcycliste. (3) First record set under two-way run ruling. (4) Marriott had achieved 127.6 mph on the measured mile, but only the kilometer record at 121.57 was recognized by the world governing body. (5) First American to hold World Speed Record after two-way runs were required.

Countries in Which World Land Speed Records Have Been Set

France
Ablis, Achères, Arles-Salon, Arpajon, Dourdan, Nice

Belgium
Ostend

United States
Blackrock Desert, Bonneville Salt Flats, Daytona/Ormond Beach, Lake St. Clair

England
Brooklands, Southport

Wales
Pendine Sands

Australia
Lake Eyre

Countries of World Land Speed Record Drivers

France
Augières, Baras, Chasseloup-Laubat, Duray, Fournier, Héméry, Rigolly, Serpollet, Thomas

Belgium
de Caters, Jenatzy

United States
Arfons, Breedlove, Burman, DePalma, Ford, Gabelich, Green, Keech, Marriott, Milton, Oldfield, Summers, Vanderbilt

England
Campbell, Campbell, Cobb, Eldridge, Eyston, Guinness, Hornsted, MacDonald, Noble, Segrave, Thomas

Countries in Which World Land Speed Record Cars Have Been Built

France
Darracq, Delage, Gobron-Brillié, Jeantaud, Mors, Serpollet

Belgium
Jenatzy

United States
Blue Flame, Duesenberg, Ford, Golden Rod, Green Monster, Packard, Spirit of America, Spirit of America Sonic I, Stanley, White, Wingfoot Express

England
Babs, Bluebird (Napier-Campbell), Bluebird, Bluebird-Proteus, Irving-Napier, Napier, Railton, Sunbeam, Thunderbolt

Italy
Fiat

Germany
Benz, Blitzen Benz, Mercedes

Vehicle registrations in 1983 in the U.S. neared 162 million, 125 million of these being passenger cars.

The day everything changed.

The horse was more than sleek flanks , flaring nostrils and sinewy beauty. It represented a way of life. It was the status quo.

Ah, but the car. It was rawboned and rudimentary, it ran like prairie wind and it was determined to shoulder its way into a world still not completely at ease with machines.

There had to be a confrontation.

The machine had to be put in its place.

And so, in some unremembered pasture, on some unremembered day, the people lined up to watch some unremembered horse defend their way of life.

What they saw was history.

It didn't matter that the car had won. The mere fact that it was there was a victory.

The automobile had arrived. And the technology and tempo of an entire country — indeed, the entire world — had changed forever.

Now the automobile has been here for a full hundred years. And Buick takes pride in having been part of the adventure for more than three quarters of that century. Making cars. Making changes. Making history.

Wouldn't you really rather have a Buick?

The GP Championship was initiated in 1950, and 413 races have taken place (through August, 1985) within the series. This total includes 11 Indianapolis 500 races, which between 1950 and 1960, were considered Grand Prix events.

Grand Prix Driver's Victories
(through the Grand Prix of Austria, August 18, 1985)
*Drivers still competing

Driver	Wins	Driver	Wins
Jackie Stewart	27	Gunnar Nillson	2
Jim Clark	25	Patrick Depailler	2
Niki Lauda*	25	J-P. Jabouille	2
Juan Manuel Fangio	24	Peter Revson	2
Alain Prost*	19	Wolfgang von Trips	2
Stirling Moss	16	Peter Collins	2
Jack Brabham	14	Froilan Gonzales	2
Graham Hill	14	Bill Vukovich	2
Emerson Fittipaldi	14	Mike Hawthorn	2
Alberto Ascari	13	Maurice Trintignant	2
Nelson Piquet*	13	Pedro Rodriguez	2
Mario Andretti	12	Jo Siffert	2
Carlos Reutemann	12	Johnny Parsons	1
Alan Jones*	12	Lee Wallard	1
Jody Scheckter	10	Luigi Fagioli	1
Ronnie Peterson	10	Piero Taruffi	1
James Hunt	10	Troy Ruttman	1
Denny Hulme	8	Bob Sweikert	1
Jacky Ickx	8	Louigi Musso	1
Rene Arnoux	7	Pat Flaherty	1
Jochen Rindt	6	Sam Hanks	1
Tony Brooks	6	Jimmy Bryan	1
John Surtees	6	Rodger Ward	1
Jacques Laffite*	6	Jo Bonnier	1
Gilles Villeneuve	6	Jim Rathman	1
Clay Regazzoni	5	Giancarlo Baghetti	1
Giuseppe Farina	5	Innes Ireland	1
John Watson	5	Lorenzo Bandini	1
Michele Alboreto*	5	Richie Ginther	1
Keke Rosberg*	4	Ludovico Scarfiotti	1
Bruce McLaren	4	Peter Gethin	1
Dan Gurney	4	Francois Cevert	1
Phil Hill	3	J-P. Beltoise	1
Didier Pironi	3	Carlos Pace	1
Riccardo Patrese*	2	Jochen Mass	1
Patrick Tambay*	2	Vittorio Brambilla	1
Elio de Angelis*	2	Ayrton Senna*	1

Each year more than 6 million cars are retired from use in America.

Nearly $25 billion worth of new cars are imported into the U.S. every year.

Grand Prix World Champions

Year	No. Races	Driver	Car	Wins	Pole Pos.	Fast Lap
1950	7	Giuseppe Farina	Alfa Romeo	3	2	3
1951	8	Juan Fangio	Alfa Romeo	3	4	5
1952	8	Alberto Ascari	Ferrari	6	5	5
1953	9	Alberto Ascari	Ferrari	5	6	4
1954	9	Juan Fangio	Mercedes-Maserati	6	5	3
1955	7	Juan Fangio	Mercedes	4	3	3
1956	8	Juan Fangio	Ferrari	3	5	4
1957	8	Juan Fangio	Maserati	4	4	2
1958	11	Mike Hawthorn	Ferrari	1	4	5
1959	9	Jack Brabham	Cooper-Climax	2	1	1
1960	10	Jack Brabham	Cooper-Climax	5	3	3
1961	8	Phil Hill	Ferrari	2	5	2
1962	9	Graham Hill	BRM	4	1	3
1963	10	Jim Clark	Lotus-Climax	7	7	6
1964	10	John Surtees	Ferrari	2	2	2
1965	10	Jim Clark	Lotus-Climax	6	6	6
1966	9	Jack Brabham	Brabham-Repco	4	3	1
1967	11	Denny Hulme	Brabham-Repco	2	—	2
1968	12	Graham Hill	Lotus-Ford	3	2	—
1969	11	Jackie Stewart	Matra-Ford	6	2	5
1970	13	Jochen Rindt	Lotus-Ford	5	3	1
1971	11	Jackie Stewart	Tyrrell-Ford	6	6	3
1972	12	Emerson Fittipaldi	Lotus-Ford	5	3	—
1973	15	Jackie Stewart	Tyrrell-Ford	5	3	1
1974	15	Emerson Fittipaldi	McLaren-Ford	3	2	—
1975	14	Niki Lauda	Ferrari	5	9	2
1976	16	James Hunt	McLaren-Ford	6	8	2
1977	17	Niki Lauda	Ferrari	3	2	3
1978	16	Mario Andretti	Lotus-Ford	6	8	3
1979	15	Jody Scheckter	Ferrari	3	1	1
1980	14	Alan Jones	Williams-Ford	5	3	5
1981	15	Nelson Piquet	Brabham-Ford	3	4	1
1982	16	Keke Rosberg	Williams-Ford	1	1	—
1983	15	Nelson Piquet	Brabham-BMW	3	1	4
1984	16	Niki Lauda	McLaren-Porsche	5	—	5
	404					

Grand Prix Constructor Victories

	Grand Prix Contested	Victories
Ferrari	385	91
Lotus	341	74
McLaren	259	45
Brabham	304	35
Tyrrell	202	23
Williams	178	19
BRM	197	17
Cooper	129	16
Renault	117	15
Alfa Romeo	105	10
Mercedes	12	9
Vanwall	28	9
Matra	61	9
Maserati	63	9
Ligier	148	8
Wolf	48	3
March	137	3
Honda	35	2
Eagle	25	1
Penske	30	1
Porsche	33	1
Hesketh	52	1
Shadow	104	1

World motor vehicle registrations in 1983 were 437 million.

1982 was the worst year for sales of U.S. cars since 1961.

Sales of Japanese cars in the U.S. went from 5.7% of the total in 1971 to 22.6% in 1982.

Grand Prix Starts*

Driver	Starts	Driver	Starts
Graham Hill	176	Patrick Depailler	93
Niki Lauda	157	James Hunt	92
Jacques Laffite	152	Elio deAngelis	88
John Watson	151	Dan Gurney	86
Carlos Reutemann	146	Patrick Tambay	85
Emerson Fittipaldi	144	Jean-Pierre Beltoise	85
*Jean-Pierre Jarier	136	Keke Rosberg	82
Clay Regazzoni	132	Maurice Trintignant	82
Mario Andretti	128	Vittorio Brambilla	74
Jack Brabham	126	*Hans Stuck	74
Ronnie Peterson	123	Alan Prost	73
Jacky Ickx	116	Jim Clark	72
Riccardo Patrese	112	Carlos Pace	72
Jody Scheckter	112	Didier Pironi	70
John Surtees	111	*Eddie Cheever	69
Jochen Mass	105	*Bruno Giacomelli	69
Jo Bonnier	102	Gilles Villeneuve	67
Denny Hulme	102	Stirling Moss	66
Bruce McLaren	101	*Marc Surer	65
Jackie Stewart	99	*Andrea deCesaris	62
Alan Jones	97	Jochen Rindt	60
Jo Siffert	97	*Nigel Mansell	59
*Chris Amon	96	Michele Alboreto	57
Rene Arnoux	95	*Arturo Merzario	56
Nelson Piquet	94	*Henri Pescarolo	56

* Never won a Formula One race

Grand Prix Point Leaders*

Driver	Points	Driver	Points
Niki Lauda	423.5	Bruce McLaren	198½
Jackie Stewart	360	Jacques Laffite	198
Carlos Reutemann	310	Stirling Moss	186½
Graham Hill	289	Jacky Ickx	181
Emerson Fittipaldi	281	Mario Andretti	180
Juan Fangio	277½	John Surtees	180
Jim Clark	274	James Hunt	170
Jack Brabham	261	John Watson	169
Jody Scheckter	255	Rene Arnoux	161
Denny Hulme	248	Patrick Depailler	141
Nelson Piquet	215	Alberto Ascari	139
Clay Regazzoni	212	Dan Gurney	133
Alan Prost	210½	Giuseppe Farina	128½
Ronnie Peterson	206	Mike Hawthorn	127½
Alan Jones	202		

*Through 1984 season.

Grand Prix Records

Most races contested: 176, Graham Hill
Most pole positions: 33, Jim Clark
Most consecutive pole positions: 6, Niki Lauda (1974)
Most pole positions in one season: 9, Niki Lauda (1974), Ronnie Peterson (1973), Nelson Piquet (1984)
Most wins: 27, Jackie Stewart
Highest winning percentage: 47.06, Juan Manuel Fangio
Most consecutive wins: 6, Alberto Ascari (1952)
Most wins in a season: 7, Jim Clark (1963), Alain Prost (1984)
Youngest Grand Prix winner: 22, Bruce McLaren (1959 U.S. GP)
Oldest Grand Prix winner: 53, Luigi Faioli (French GP, 1951)
Most GP points accumulated: 423.5, Niki Lauda
Most laps in the lead: 2093, Jim Clark
Most fastest laps of the race: 27, Jim Clark
Most World Championship titles: 5, Juan Manuel Fangio (1951-54-55-56-57)
Most wins by nationality: 117, Great Britain

NASCAR Grand National Champions

Year	Champion	Year	Champion
1949	Red Byron	1967	Richard Petty
1950	Bill Rexford	1968	David Pearson
1951	Herb Thomas	1969	David Pearson
1952	Tim Flock	1970	Bobby Isaac
1953	Herb Thomas	1971	Richard Petty
1954	Lee Petty	1972	Richard Petty
1955	Tim Flock	1973	Benny Parsons
1956	Buck Baker	1974	Richard Petty
1957	Buck Baker	1975	Richard Petty
1958	Lee Petty	1976	Cale Yarborough
1959	Lee Petty	1977	Cale Yarborough
1960	Rex White	1978	Cale Yarborough
1961	Ned Jarrett	1979	Richard Petty
1962	Joe Weatherly	1980	Dale Earnhardt
1963	Joe Weatherly	1981	Darrell Waltrip
1964	Richard Petty	1982	Darrell Waltrip
1965	Ned Jarrett	1983	Bobby Allison
1966	David Pearson	1984	Terry Labonte

Most NASCAR Wins by Car Make 1949-1984

Make	Wins
Ford	316
Chevrolet	276
Plymouth	190
Dodge	116
Oldsmobile	104
Mercury	96
Hudson	84
Pontiac	73
Chrysler	65
Buick	61
AMC	5
Lincoln	4
Studebaker	3
Nash	1

More than half of American households have two or more automobiles.

The average auto production worker in the U.S. earns a total of $19 per hour; in Germany it's about $13; in Japan it's about $8; in Korea it's $1.68.

NASCAR Victories by Driver

Driver	Victories	Driver	Victories
Richard Petty*	200	Red Byron	2
David Pearson*	105	Gober Sosebee	2
Bobby Allison*	81	Danny Letner	2
Cale Yarborough*	81	Bill Myers	2
Darrell Waltrip*	64	Marvin Porter	2
Lee Petty	54	Johnny Beauchamp	2
Ned Jarrett	50	Tom Pistone	2
Junior Johnson	50	Bobby Johns	2
Herb Thomas	49	Emanuel Zervakis	2
Buck Baker	46	Jim Pardue	2
Tim Flock	40	Elmo Langley	2
Bobby Isaac	37	James Hylton	2
Fireball Roberts	32	Ray Elder	2
Rex White	26	Joe Lee Johnson	2
Fred Lorenzen	26	Tommy Thompson	1
Jim Paschal	25	Bob Burdick	1
Joe Weatherly	24	Neil Cole	1
Jack Smith	21	Marvin Burke	1
Benny Parsons*	21	Denny Weinberg	1
Fonty Flock	19	Bill Norton	1
Speedy Thompson	19	Buddy Shuman	1
Buddy Baker*	19	Dick Passwater	1
Curtis Turner	17	Al Keller	1
Marvin Panch	17	John Soares Sr.	1
Dick Hutcherson	14	Chuck Stevenson	1
LeeRoy Yarbrough	14	Johnny Kieper	1
Dick Rathman	13	Royce Hagerty	1
Donnie Allison*	13	Art Watts	1
Neil Bonnett*	13	Bill Amick	1
Dale Earnhardt*	11	Danny Graves	1
Paul Goldsmith	9	Frankie Schneider	1
Cotton Owens	9	Shorty Rollins	1
Marshall Teague	7	Jim Cook	1
Bob Welborn	7	Morgan Shepherd*	1
Jim Reed	7	Jody Ridley*	1
Darel Dieringer	7	Jim Roper	1
A.J. Foyt*	6	June Cleveland	1
Harry Gant*	6	Jack White	1
Ralph Moody	5	Harold Kite	1
Dan Gurney	5	Bill Rexford	1
Dave Marcis*	5	Johnny Mantz	1
Pete Hamilton	4	Leon Sales	1
Bob Flock	4	Lloyd Moore	1
Hershel McGriff*	4	Joe Eubanks	1
Lloyd Dane	4	John Rostek	1
Ed Pagan	4	Johnny Allen	1
Eddie Gray	4	Larry Frank	1
Glen Wood	4	John Rutherford*	1
Nelson Stacy	4	Wendell Scott	1
Billy Wade	4	Sam McQuagg	1
Charlie Glotzbach	4	Paul Lewis	1
Parnelli Jones	4	Earl Balmer	1
Bill Elliott*	4	Jim Hurtubise	1
Tim Richmond*	4	Mario Andretti*	1
Terry Labonte*	4	Richard Brickhouse	1
Dick Linder	3	Mark Donohue	1
Frank Mundy	3	Dick Brooks*	1
Bill Blair	3	Earl Ross	1
Gwyn Staley	3	Lou Figaro	1
Tiny Lund	3	Jimmy Florian	1
Ricky Rudd*	3	Lennie Pond*	1
Geoff Bodine*	3	Ron Bouchard*	1

*Indicates currently active drivers.

Daytona 500 Winners

Year	Driver	Car	Average Speed
1959	Lee Petty	59 Oldsmobile	135.521
1960	Junior Johnson	59 Chevrolet	124.740
1961	Marvin Panch	60 Pontiac	149.601
1962	Fireball Roberts	62 Pontiac	152.529
1963	Tiny Lund	63 Ford	151.566
1964	Richard Petty	64 Plymouth	154.334
1965	Fred Lorenzen	65 Ford	141.539
1966	Richard Petty	66 Plymouth	160.627
1967	Mario Andretti	67 Ford	146.926
1968	Cale Yarborough	68 Mercury	143.251
1969	LeeRoy Yarbrough	69 Ford	157.950
1970	Pete Hamilton	70 Plymouth	149.601
1971	Richard Petty	71 Plymouth	144.462
1972	A.J. Foyt	71 Mercury	161.550
1973	Richard Petty	73 Dodge	157.205
1974	Richard Petty	74 Dodge	140.894
1975	Benny Parsons	Chevrolet	153.649
1976	David Pearson	Mercury	152.181
1977	Cale Yarborough	Chevrolet	153.218
1978	Bobby Allison	Ford	159.730
1979	Richard Petty	Oldsmobile	143.977
1980	Buddy Baker	Oldsmobile	177.602
1981	Richard Petty	Buick	169.651
1982	Bobby Allison	Buick	153.991
1983	Cale Yarborough	Pontiac	155.979
1984	Cale Yarborough	Chevrolet	150.994
1985	Bill Elliott	Ford	172.265

NASCAR All-Time Records

Most Races Started ....958, Richard Petty
Most Races Won ....200, Richard Petty
Most Victories In Single Season ....27, Richard Petty, 1967
Most Superspeedway Victories In Single Season.................10, David Pearson, 1973 and 1976
Most Consecutive Victories......................10, Richard Petty, 1967
Most Money Won In Single Season...................$873,118 Darrell Waltrip in 1982
Fastest Qualifying Speed...........202.692 mph, Cale Yarborough, Alabama International Motor Speedway, May 3, 1984
Fastest Winston Cup Race...............177.602 mph, Buddy Baker, 1980 Daytona 500 Daytona International Speedway
Largest Winner's Purse.............$160,300, Cale Yarborough, 1984 Daytona 500, Daytona International Speedway
Most Lead Changes In Single Race.........75 among 13 drivers 1984 Winston 500 Alabama International Motor Speedway

The U.S. Bureau of Labor Statistics figures the cost of safety and emission equipment on the average 1984 car at $1699.20.

U.S. Imports of New Assembled Passenger Cars

Year	Belgium	Canada	France	West Germany	Italy	Japan	Sweden	United Kingdom	Others	Total Imports
1983	5,230	836,756	212,858	330,263	5,347	2,112,011	109,494	53,284	1,780	3,667,023
1982	825	702,530	90,142	337,628	9,307	1,823,111	89,231	13,023	1,195	3,066,992
1981	66	563,943	42,477	376,327	21,635	1,911,525	68,042	12,728	1,818	2,998,561
1980	40	594,771	47,386	470,528	46,899	1,991,502	61,496	32,517	3,127	3,248,266
1979	85	677,008	27,887	495,565	72,456	1,617,328	65,907	46,911	2,376	3,005,523
1978	1,530	833,061	28,502	416,231	69,689	1,563,048	56,140	54,478	2,303	3,024,982
1975	38,176	733,766	15,647	370,012	102,344	695,573	51,993	67,106	36	2,074,653
1970	50,602	692,783	37,114	674,945	42,523	381,338	57,844	76,257	14	2,013,420
1965	332	29,135	24,941	376,950	9,509	25,538	26,010	66,565	450	559,430

Privately Owned Vehicles in U.S.

1983	124,435,000
1982	122,763,369
1981	122,604,584
1980	120,865,799
1979	117,645,166
1978	115,826,496
1977	112,968,806
1976	109,513,168
1975	106,077,384
1974	104,228,855
1973	101,412,229
1972	96,553,073
1971	92,221,291
1970	88,775,294
1969	86,414,179
1965	74,909,365
1960	61,419,948
1955	51,960,532
1950	40,190,632
1945	25,694,926
1940	27,372,397
1935	22,494,884
1930	22,972,745
1925	17,439,701
1920	8,131,522
1915	2,332,426
1910	458,377
1905	77,400
1900	8,000

Highest Annual U.S. Production Years

Passenger Cars

Year	Units
1973	9,667,152
1965	9,335,227
1977	9,213,654
1978	9,176,635
1968	8,848,620
1972	8,828,205
1966	8,604,712

Females account for 48% of licensed drivers.

Highest Annual U.S. Retail Sales Year (domestic cars)

Passenger Cars

1973	9,675,789
1972	9,326,776
1978	9,311,666
1977	9,109,022
1965	8,763,197
1971	8,681,409
1968	8,624,819

U.S. Production Milestones*

Year	Units
	Passenger Cars
1912	1 millionth
1920	10 millionth
1935	50 millionth
1952	100 millionth
1960	150 millionth
1967	200 millionth
1972	250 millionth
1979	300 millionth

Year	Units
	Total Motor Vehicles
1906	100,000th
1912	1 millionth
1920	10 millionth
1931	50 millionth
1948	100 millionth
1955	150 millionth
1962	200 millionth
1968	250 millionth
1972	300 millionth
1982	400 millionth

*Based upon U.S. total factory sales data.

SOURCE: Motor Vehicle Manufacturers Association of the U.S., Inc.

The average age of the cars on the road has climbed from 5.7 years in 1973 to 7.4 years in 1983.

World's Top 40 Auto Manufacturers*

		Total	Passenger Cars	Commercial Vehicles
1.	General Motors-U.S.A.	7,637,965	6,098,880	1,539,085
2.	Ford Motor-U.S.A.	4,727,592	3,416,008	1,311,584
3.	Toyota-Japan	3,274,835	2,380,753	894,082
4.	Nissan-Japan	2,586,295	1,899,323	686,972
5.	Renault-France	2,255,524	1,983,237	272,287
6.	Volkswagen-W. Germany	2,087,801	1,936,350	151,451
7.	Peugeot-France	1,813,416	1,608,191	205,225
8.	Fiat-Italy	1,718,283	1,442,356	275,927
9.	Mazda-Japan	1,171,350	861,580	309,770
10.	Chrysler-U.S.A.	1,339,127	1,036,342	302,785
11.	Honda-Japan	1,087,775	913,021	174,754
12.	Mitsubishi-Japan	974,705	523,754	450,951
13.	Lada-U.S.S.R.	780,000	780,000	—
14.	Daimler-Benz-W. Germany	679,313	483,359	195,954
15.	Suzuki-Japan	631,310	137,528	493,782
16.	Leyland-U.K.	578,847	473,341	105,506
17.	Fuji-Japan	540,680	230,462	310,218
18.	Daihatsu-Japan	530,296	185,159	345,137
19.	B.M.W.-W. Germany	407,507	407,507	—
20.	Volvo-Sweden	400,158	364,665	35,493
21.	Isuzu-Japan	390,701	116,184	274,517
22.	American Motors-U.S.A.	343,096	229,833	113,263
23.	Polski Fiat-Poland	250,000	250,000	—
24.	Skoda-Czechoslovakia	233,000	178,000	55,000
25.	Alfa Romeo-Italy	208,116	206,926	1,190
26.	Moskvitch-U.S.S.R.	200,000	200,000	—
27.	Zastava-Yugoslavia	154,122	145,448	8,674
28.	Zaz Zaporojetz-U.S.S.R.	145,000	145,000	—
29.	G.A.Z. Volga-U.S.S.R.	125,000	125,000	—
30.	Saab-Scania-Sweden	116,783	96,012	20,771
31.	Hyundai-South Korea	108,117	93,015	15,102
32.	Kia-South Korea	63,638	136	63,502
33.	International Harvester-U.S.A.	58,629	—	58,629
34.	Hino-Japan	52,129	—	52,129
35.	Porsche-W. Germany	48,288	48,288	—
36.	I.M.V.-Yugoslavia	43,688	42,059	1,629
37.	Daewoo-S. Korea	36,312	27,406	8,906
38.	U.N.I.S.-Yugoslavia	26,204	15,957	10,247
39.	Motor Iberica-Spain	20,297	—	20,297
40.	M.A.N.-W. Germany	15,848	—	15,848
	TOTAL 40 MANUFACTURERS	37,861,747	29,081,080	8,780,667
	OTHERS	1,872,972	599,113	1,273,859
	TOTAL PRODUCTION	39,734,719	29,680,193	10,054,526
	North American Companies	14,106,409	10,781,063	3,325,346
	Japanese Companies	11,240,076	7,247,764	3,992,312
	Western European Companies	10,350,181	9,050,232	1,299,949
	Eastern European Companies	1,957,014	1,881,464	75,550

Data compiled by **MVMA** from various overseas sources.

*Based on 1983 sales.

Motor Vehicle Production (1900-1983)

	United States	World Total		United States	World Total
1900	4,192	9,504	1946	3,100,820	3,913,410
1901	7,000	15,509	1947	4,795,587	5,853,636
1902	9,000	23,088	1948	5,220,755	6,564,946
1903	11,235	32,447	1949	6,243,834	8,044,400
1904	22,830	54,280	1950	8,005,859	10,579,168
1905	25,000	62,799	1951	6,757,014	9,453,285
1906	34,000	82,099	1952	5,561,796	8,320,091
1907	44,000	76,327	1953	7,349,123	10,500,267
1908	65,000	106,024	1954	6,536,729	10,226,561
1909	127,287	184,916	1955	9,204,049	13,221,695
1910	187,000	254,756	1956	6,918,758	11,654,526
1911	210,000	295,620	1957	7,220,431	12,530,056
1912	378,000	480,774	1958	5,121,269	11,355,197
1913	485,000	606,124	1959	6,723,588	13,870,355
1914	573,039	600,217	1960	7,905,119	16,376,865
1915	969,930	1,014,904	1961	6,652,938	15,209,431
1916	1,617,708	1,676,367	1962	8,197,311	18,202,770
1917	1,873,949	1,993,039	1963	9,108,776	20,720,346
1918	1,170,686	1,275,324	1964	9,307,860	22,020,434
1919	1,876,356	2,000,091	1965	11,137,830	24,567,935
1920	2,227,349	2,382,573	1966	10,396,298	24,980,719
1921	1,616,119	1,752,595	1967	9,023,736	24,183,786
1922	2,544,176	2,809,573	1968	10,820,410	28,610,475
1923	4,034,012	4,409,034	1969	10,205,911	30,079,490
1924	3,602,540	4,094,522	1970	8,283,949	29,707,665
1925	4,265,830	4,900,730	1971	10,671,654	33,727,142
1926	4,300,934	5,029,230	1972	11,310,708	35,832,772
1927	3,401,326	4,188,380	1973	12,681,513	39,214,881
1928	4,358,759	5,278,044	1974	10,071,042	35,060,915
1929	5,337,087	6,344,999	1975	8,986,513	33,321,955
1930	3,362,820	4,133,437	1976	11,497,596	38,618,368
1931	2,380,426	3,015,818	1977	12,702,782	41,227,398
1932	1,331,860	1,915,656	1978	12,899,202	42,689,091
1933	1,899,817	2,635,227	1979	11,479,993	41,954,523
1934	2,737,070	3,686,985	1980	8,009,841	38,805,473
1935	3,971,241	5,134,340	1981	7,942,916	37,551,847
1936	4,461,462	5,793,652	1982	6,985,595	36,399,505
1937	4,820,219	6,362,762	1983	9,205,375	39,966,429
1938	2,508,407	3,996,243			
1939	3,588,889	4,779,049			
1940	4,512,895	4,941,867			

Americans use private motor vehicles for 83% of their travel.

Automatic transmissions and air conditioning are installed in eight out of ten new cars in the U.S.

The price of an average new car is around $11,000 in the U.S. In 1950 it was $2210 and in 1970 it was $3542.

One out of every 160 registered motor vehicles in the U.S. is stolen. In 1983, thieves made off with more than a million automobiles.

ACKNOWLEDGEMENTS

Putting together a project like this book takes the cooperation, encouragement and help of many people. It's impossible to thank them all, but the editors would especially like to extend their gratitude to Jane Barrett, curator of the Petersen Publishing Co. Photo and Research Library; Bill Claxton, Art Director of *Motor Trend*; Susan E. Teubert of the Motor Vehicle Manufacturers Association; and Jim McCraw of the Ford Motor Co. Without their enthusiastic assistance, this book would not have been possible. The editors would also like to express their thanks to the following people and companies for sharing their resources and providing an invaluable contribution to making *100 Years of the Automobile* possible:

American Automobile Association
American Motors Division—Steve Harris, Lloyd Northard
Cadillac Motor Division, General Motors Corp.
Chrysler Corporation—Moon Mullins, Carla Rosenbush
The Detroit Institute of the Arts
The Detroit Library, National Automotive Historical Collection
Ford Motor Co.
General Motors Corporation—Harold Jackson
General Motors Design Center—Floyd Joliet
The Henry Ford Museum—Randy Mason and Cynthia Reed Miller
Indianapolis Motor Speedway
The Nicholas Lazarnick Picture Collection
Liveright Publishing Corporation
Mercedes Benz of North America—Leo Levine and A.B. Shuman
Motor Vehicle Manufacturers Association—James Wren
Peugeot Motors of America—Robert Beaver
Posters Please, New York—Jack Rennert
Quadrant Picture Library, London
Renault USA, Inc.—Leon Forth
Williams College Museum of Art